Enacting the Corporation

The University of California Press gratefully acknowledges the support of the Hull Memorial Publication Fund of Cornell University, which provided funds toward the publication of this book.

Enacting the Corporation

*An American Mining Firm in
Post-Authoritarian Indonesia*

Marina Welker

UNIVERSITY OF CALIFORNIA PRESS
Berkeley · Los Angeles · London

University of California Press, one of the most
distinguished university presses in the United States,
enriches lives around the world by advancing scholarship
in the humanities, social sciences, and natural sciences. Its
activities are supported by the UC Press Foundation and
by philanthropic contributions from individuals and
institutions. For more information, visit www.ucpress.edu.

University of California Press
Berkeley and Los Angeles, California

University of California Press, Ltd.
London, England

Library of Congress Cataloging-in-Publication Data

Welker, Marina, 1973–, author.
    Enacting the corporation : an American mining firm in
post-authoritarian Indonesia / Marina Welker.
        pages   cm
    Includes bibliographical references and index.
    ISBN 978-0-520-28230-8 (cloth : alk. paper)
    ISBN 978-0-520-28231-5 (pbk. : alk. paper)
    ISBN 978-0-520-95795-4 (ebook)
    1. Newmont Mining Corporation.   2. Newmont
Nusa Tenggara, PT.   3. Mineral industries—Social
aspects—Indonesia—Sumbawa Island.   4. Social
responsibility of business—Indonesia—Sumbawa
Island.   5. Social responsibility of business—Colorado—
Greenwood Village.   6. Capitalism—Indonesia—
Sumbawa Island.   7. Ethnology—Indonesia—Sumbawa
Island.   I. Title.
    HD9506.I54N49   2014
    338.8′872209598—dc23   2013041573

Manufactured in the United States of America
23 22 21 20 19 18 17 16 15 14
10 9 8 7 6 5 4 3 2 1

In keeping with a commitment to support
environmentally responsible and sustainable printing
practices, UC Press has printed this book on Natures
Natural, a fiber that contains 30% post-consumer waste
and meets the minimum requirements of ANSI/NISO
Z39.48–1992 (R 1997) (Permanence of Paper).

Contents

Illustrations

TABLE

Abbreviations

BSR   Business for Social Responsibility

CSR   Corporate Social Responsibility

DPR   Dewan Perwakilan Rakyat (People's Representative Council, or House of Representatives)

IFC   International Finance Corporation (part of the World Bank)

IMS   Integrated Management System

IPM   Integrated Pest Management

LBI   Local Business Initiative

LOH   Lembaga Olah Hidup, an environmental and social justice NGO based in Sumbawa Besar

NGO   Nongovernmental Organization

NNT   Newmont Nusa Tenggara

NTB   Nusa Tenggara Barat, a province that encompasses Lombok and Sumbawa island, with provincial headquarters in Mataram, Lombok

PBU   PT Prasmanindo Boga Utama, a catering firm that supplies mining companies

PRA   Participatory Rural Appraisal

PT   Perseroan Terbatas, limited liability company

Acknowledgments

It has taken me a long time to research and write this book, and I have accrued many debts along the way. I can name only some of those who have helped me here.

Over the course of my research in southwest Sumbawa, many people allowed me to take part in their lives, sometimes for extended periods of time, and they patiently answered my questions. I am deeply grateful to them, and to the Newmont employees, some of whom were also village residents, who kept me apprised of and included in their activities. Among those living in the villages of Sekongkang Bawah, Sekongkang Atas, Tongo-Sejorong, SP1, SP2, Maluk, Benete, Goa, Beru, and Belo, I am especially indebted to Fadila Marleni, Pak Rahmat Hidayat, Bu Madiana, Pak Puakang, Bu Mari, Pak Samrah, Pak Teten, Mama Esi, Bu Subaedah, Mbak Endang, Bu H. Ipa, Pak H. Mukhlis, Bu H. Asia, Pak H. Nasaruddin, Pak H. Ali, Bu Palisa, Pak H. Sarugyi, Bu Nani, Pak Yasin, Bu Badariah, Pak Dahlan, Pak Adam Master, Pak Muhid, Bu Suriya, Bibi Ibok, Wildan, Bu Boya, Pak Mahdar, Bu Gira, Pak Saluddin, Bu Norma, Bu Ratmina, Pak Zak, Bu Mirna, Pak M. Ali, Pak Sirajuddin, Pak Sanawi, Bu Martini, Pak Abdul Kadir, Bu Mindawati, Pak Abdul Manaf, Pak Syafruddin, Pak Syafi'i, Pak M. Saleh, Pak Zulkifli, Pak Hamim, Bu Erni, Pak Wahab, Pak Ahmad, Pak Isafie, Bu Nurol, Bu Titin, Pak Pare, Pak Sanusi, Pak H. Najamuddin, Pak Wahid, Pak Abdul Majid R., Bu Halimah and Pak Hamzah, Pak Agus, Bu Sri Nurnani, Pak H. Ismail, Pak Sanang, Pak Eiho, Bu Saridia, Pak H.

Sidik, Pak Suleiman, Bu Hatma, Bu Sarinah, Pak Budi, Pak M. Saleh, Pak Farhan, Pak Jarwo, Pak H. Riu, Pak Ibrahim, Pak Rahmat, Bu Masriana, Bu Lindawati, Pak Hassanuddin, Pak Jabir, Pak Baharuddin Bayuk, Pak Baron/Abdul Azis, Pak Tahir, Pak Hamzah, Pak H.M. Fitra, Pak Darmansa, Pak Lalu Murdan, Pak Adnan, Muhammad Rizal, Pak Muchtasil/Acing, Dr. Adib, Dr. Abdullah, Pak Paiman, Pak Sukrie, Pak Arman, Pak M. Zambani, Pak Amril, Pak Syamsul, Pak Basuki, Pak Ramli, Pak Panidi, Pak Ivan Faturachman, Abdul Wahid, Bu Anisah, Lalu Mahfid, Pak Wagimin, Pak Iqbal, Lalu Yusuf, Agus Salim, Pak Basar, Pak Yuyud, and Pak Ismed.

I am grateful to Pusat Penelitian Bahasa dan Kebudayaan (P2BK, the Center for the Study of Language and Culture) at the University of Mataram for kindly supporting my research and providing swift help with all bureaucratic hurdles. The center's director, Dr. Husni Muadz, always provided a warm reception and stimulating conversation. Lembaga Ilmu Pengetahuan Indonesia (LIPI) in Jakarta sponsored my research.

I am also indebted to Helen Macdonald and Chris Anderson, and to their colleagues, consultants, and visitors at Newmont Mining Corporation's headquarters in Denver, for allowing me to join meetings and conduct interviews and for providing requested materials. Sandi Yokooji was a great help as well. I also had meetings with government officials, activists, CSR professionals, and corporate employees in Sumbawa Besar, Mataram, Bali, Jakarta, and elsewhere in Indonesia, as well as in London, Brisbane, Berkeley, San Francisco, and Los Angeles. I am grateful to them all.

At a time when I was casting about for a feasible project on transnational extractive industries in Indonesia, I was fortunate to have help from a generous colleague, Brigham Golden. Brigham suggested I consider Newmont in Sumbawa and helped me get my research off to an auspicious start.

For various research phases I had material support from the Fulbright-Hays Program for Doctoral Dissertation Research, the Wenner-Gren Foundation for Anthropological Research, the National Science Foundation, the University of Michigan's Center for International Business Education, and the Social Science Research Council's Program on the Corporation as a Social Institution. I also benefited profoundly from meetings held as part of the SSRC Program on the Corporation, ably led by Doug Guthrie. I am also grateful for a Weatherhead Fellowship at the School for Advanced Research and a Harry Frank Guggenheim

Fellowship that supported the first incarnation of this project as a dissertation. An American Council of Learned Societies Fellowship, a Faculty Fellowship at Cornell's Society for the Humanities, and Cornell's Institute for the Social Sciences helped me turn the project into a book.

Over time, my appreciation has grown for how we become anthropologists not just through fieldwork but also through the extended process of writing. I owe thanks to many for accompanying me during various phases of that journey, beginning with my remarkable dissertation committee at the University of Michigan, including Sharad Chari, Nancy Florida, Gabrielle Hecht, and Stuart Kirsch, and chaired by Webb Keane. At Michigan, Rudolf Mrázek and Andrew Shryock, too, shaped my thinking. At the School for Advanced Research, I was fortunate to have the excellent social company and intellectual input of Rebecca Allahyari, James Brooks, Cam Cocks, Jeanne Fitzsimmons, Laura Gómez, Cory Kratz, Joe Masco, Sean Teuton, Jessica Winegar, Kay Yandell, and the much-missed Ivan Karp. Writing at a distance from Ann Arbor unfortunately meant I got to spend less time than I would have liked with friends I met there, including Michael Baran, Frank Cody, Jill Constantino, Naisargi Dave, Jesse Grayman, Karen Hebert, and Ronit Ricci.

At Cornell, I have found many supportive and inspiring colleagues both in my home department of anthropology and in the Southeast Asia Program. Jane Fajans, David Holmberg, Kath March, Hirokazu Miyazaki, Viranjini Munasinghe, Lorraine Paterson, Eric Tagliacozzo, and Andrew Willford have provided advice and support at key junctures. Fellow faculty in my writing group—which has included, at various times, María Fernández, Durba Ghosh, TJ Hinrichs, Stacey Langwick, Sherry Martin, Rachel Prentice, Sara Pritchard, Kathleen Vogel, and Wendy Wolford—have provided generous feedback at numerous stages of this project, and I cherish their friendship as well. Our writing group has been nourished in turn by a Brett de Bary Interdisciplinary Writing Group grant through Cornell's Society for the Humanities and multiple CU-ADVANCE Small Group Mentoring Grants. Peter Wissoker provided immensely helpful feedback on the entire manuscript, and Curtis Brown helped unclutter my prose. I am also grateful to the undergraduate and graduate students who have participated in my courses at Cornell (especially Anthropology of Development, Anthropology of Corporations, and Risk Work) and have contributed to my thinking on these themes. During my year at the Society for the Humanities, the ideas of Paulina Aroch, Ingrid Diran, Lorenzo Fabbri, Bishnupriya Ghosh, Patty Keller, Bill Leiss, Gaspar Mairal, Annie McClanahan, Tim Murray, Emily Nacol, Erin Obodiac, Annelise Riles, Bhaskar Sarkar, Matthew Smith, Clauida Verhoeven, Vivian Choi, Miloje Despic, Anna Fisher, and Brían Hanrahan all left their imprints on my approach. Further afield, Bob Foster, Ken George, and Jane Guyer have provided support and inspiration at various times.

I have presented portions of this book at meetings of the American Anthropological Association, the American Ethnological Society, the Society for Cultural Anthropology, and the Association for Asian Studies, as well as at the University of Texas, San Antonio, Department of Anthropology; the Third Annual Symposium of the Adolf A. Berle Jr. Center on Corporations, Law & Society at the Seattle University School of Law; the Department of Anthropology and the Department of Science and Technology Studies at Cornell University; the Department of Anthropology at the University of Toronto; the Culture, History, and Society in Southeast Asia series at Harvard University; and the Anthropology Department at Lehigh University. I am grateful to the organizers of these events and to participants for their questions and comments. Earlier versions of chapters 4 and 5 appeared in *American Ethnologist* (Welker 2012) and *Cultural Anthropology* (Welker 2009), respectively. Both chapters benefited from the feedback of anonymous reviewers and the oversight and suggestions of the journal editors.

I am grateful to Reed Malcolm at the University of California Press for his interest in this project and alacrity in shepherding it through the early stages, and to Stacy Eisenstark and Chalon Emmons for seeing it through the later stages. Three reviewers—Elizabeth Dunn, Elizabeth Ferry, and Matthew Hull—provided excellent suggestions; I know I have done them only partial justice. I am also very thankful to Ken Wisoker and Jade Brooks at Duke University Press, as well as to two anonymous reviewers for their thoughtful feedback on the manuscript. I received attentive and patient copyediting support from Bonita Hurd, and Do Mi Stauber prepared the index. Nij Tontisirin and Bill Nelson drew the maps.

I owe thanks to many family members for their steadfast support, especially my mother and father, Ann and Eberhard Welker, and my sisters, Carla and Renata. For most of his working life, my father was a mechanical engineer who worked on oil and natural gas pipeline projects for Bechtel, a privately owned firm whose clients have included Newmont and, infamously, the U.S. government in Iraq. My father traveled the world for various pipeline projects, sometimes taking me, my mother, and sisters along, including for a seven-year stay in Australia. I trace my academic interest in how U.S. capital affects people in far-flung places to this period of my life. I attribute my interest in how people develop moral expectations of corporations to my mother. The birth of my wonderful and energetic sons, Andor and Zoltan, in 2008, and my father's battle with cancer and his death in 2010, both slowed down the writing of this book. In different ways, they also deepened my desire to reflect on how people reproduce capitalism. Paul Nadasdy has been my best critic, supporter, and companion in writing this book, and he, Zoli, and Andor have also been my favorite escape from it.

Note on Pseudonyms and Quoted Sources

I decided from the beginning of this project that I would not anonymize the island on which most of my research would take place. This also meant naming the mine I studied and the chief companies involved. I have adopted a mixed strategy with regard to naming people. In many cases, I have left identities vague by specifying only an individual's status (e.g., a village resident, contractor, village head, senior executive). In other cases I have applied pseudonyms for clarity and consistency, often using first names only. I have also followed a common practice in southwest Sumbawan villages of naming people by their position titles (e.g., Ibu Comdev, Pak Camat). Some of the individuals for whom I use pseudonyms or position titles are no doubt identifiable to people familiar with the company and region, but for those people I anticipate that the perspectives and conflicts I depict will be similarly familiar. I use real names for public figures involved in public events, and I also use real names in chapter 5, where I deal with an incident that was thoroughly covered by local media. With their permission, I use the names of Helen Macdonald and Chris Anderson in chapter 1 and Richard Boele in chapter 6. This allowed me to reference more of their biographical background and publications and to include photos of Boele conducting a social assessment.

I occasionally made audio recordings of public events and interviews, but for the most part I jotted notes in a small notebook (on rare occasions I took notes directly on my laptop during office meetings where others were using laptops) and later expanded these into my field notes. As a result, outside of a few exceptions, my quotations generally represent my best effort to capture the actual words of individuals and are not necessarily fully accurate reproductions of recorded speech. All translations are my own. Most are from Indonesian, although some are from the Sekongkang dialect of the Sumbawan language (Basa Samawa).

Introduction

What is a corporation? What does it do? To whom is it responsible? This book, a study of the Denver-based Newmont Mining Corporation and its Batu Hijau Copper and Gold Mine in Sumbawa, Indonesia, shows that each of these questions can be answered in multiple ways. Newmont does many things. These include mining ore; employing workers; expelling waste; building mosques, schools, and clinics; and gathering intelligence on environmental activists and Muslims. In popular, activist, and scholarly accounts, publicly traded corporations like Newmont often figure as actors single-mindedly seeking to maximize profits for shareholders, which is seen as their overarching, legally determined responsibility (Achbar and Abbott 2003; Fortun 2001:104). Without denying profit as a motivation, in this book I show that people enact corporations in multiple ways, and that these enactments involve struggles over the boundaries, interests, and responsibilities of the corporation.

The figure of the corporation as an actor with prior interests that govern and explain its actions is an important orienting device,[1] but it rests on a model of the human subject—the natural, fully realized, discrete, unfettered, self-present, and self-knowing liberal individual—that anthropologists largely reject. Close cousin to this "abstract, rather contentless, entity in social space" (Meyer and Jepperson 2000:109) is the *Homo economicus* of rational choice theory. Both lack the complexity and contradiction constitutive of human subjectivity within our discipline.

The *Homo economicus* model of the corporation persists because it has a couple of important functions. For those who believe that corporations should be maximizing profits for shareholders, it offers a prescriptive account of what corporations ought to do. In addition to its prescriptive role, the model also has a forensic one. A crucial question of our time is: "How to identify a unit of responsibility, in a fiendishly complex, multiply-layered and decidedly trans-national apparatus of harm-production?" (Ferguson 2012:560). By construing corporations as not simply responsible for harm but as actors who cause harm as a result of their intentional actions, the model allows us to imagine them in ways that conform to a convention of Euro-American thought: culpable subjects are ideally intentional subjects. As John Locke ([1690] 2001:278) himself argued, *person* is fundamentally a forensic term, useful for assigning blame. In our blaming practices, as political theorist Iris Marion Young (2006:42) noted, "we tend to see those blamed as guilty of willful harm." Similarly, experimental philosopher Joshua Knobe (2005) found that when people are confronted with a hypothetical case in which business activities have produced side effects that are by turns beneficial or harmful to the environment, they are more likely to classify benefits as unintentional and harms as the product of deliberate intention.

Both the prescriptive and forensic roles of the *Homo economicus* model of the corporation need to be taken seriously. At the same time, if the model provides an impoverished basis for understanding individual humans from an anthropological perspective (Douglas and Ney 1998; Godelier 1999; Mauss 1990; Polanyi 2001; Sahlins 1972), then it follows that it will do the same for complex collectives.

Problems with *Homo economicus* and the more generic liberal actor model become apparent when we try to figure out where a corporation begins and ends, where exactly its boundaries lie (see also Golub 2014).[2] Is it coterminous with those it employs? Or does it also include creditors, subcontractors, and suppliers? And what of those who own it? In the case of large, publicly traded companies in the United States, the category of owners is often presumed to encompass the millions of people who own shares indirectly through pensions and mutual-fund-based retirement plans, who often experience themselves as passive or even reluctant investors at the mercy of the financial services industry (*Frontline* 2013).[3] What about corporate property, tangible (e.g., buildings, computers, documents) and intangible (ideas, reputation)? And what of material waste? Can striking workers, passive investors, built infrastructure, equipment, documents, and waste all be satisfactorily reconciled with an understanding of the corporation as an actor with interests? Under what circumstances does all of this diversity belong inside the container of the corporation?

We sidestep these thorny questions when we imagine corporations as metaphysical subjects. In the later Middle Ages, Ernst Kantorowicz tells us, political and legal thought construed corporations in theological terms. The world "began to be populated by immaterial angelic bodies, large and small: they were invisible, ageless, sempiternal, immortal, and sometimes even ubiquitous; and they were endowed with a *corpus intellectuale* or *mysticum* which could stand any comparison with the 'spiritual bodies' of the celestial beings" (Kantorowicz 1997:283). Thinkers today continue to conceive of corporations in abstract and dematerialized terms. Analytic philosophers have argued for the existence of corporate agents—variously called joint, collective, or plural subjects—by exploring the pooling of will and intention in pursuit of particular goals. Such work often deploys hypothetical examples and imaginary conversations between disembodied human subjects (Gilbert 1989; List and Pettit 2011). Some organizational theorists have also argued that organizations merit the ontological status of actors because they possess the requisite traits: intentionality, responsibility, sovereignty, goals, values, self-reflexivity, and self-identity (King, Felin, and Whetten 2010). In such renderings the corporation requires, and has, no corpus, no body.

As an anthropologist I am not interested in setting forth the metaphysical conditions of possibility for the existence of corporations. My analytic approach is resolutely materialist (see also Rogers 2012). Literature on the state makes for a useful analogy (Shever 2012, Subramanian 2010). By historicizing, localizing, and disaggregating state practices, scholars have called into question the integrity of "the state" as a coherent, unified, bounded, and autonomous agent (Aretxaga 2003; Corrigan and Sayer 1985; Das and Poole 2004; Hansen and Stepputat 2001; Migdal 2001; Sharma and Gupta 2006; Steedly 1999; van Klinken and Barker 2009). The challenge, however, is not simply to take such entities apart but to understand how in everyday life ordinary actors put them together (Weber 1947:102), enacting them as collective subjects that actually exist and have interests, rights, and obligations.

Political theorist Timothy Mitchell (1999:90) points out that we derive the seemingly metaphysical effect of the state as an actor—along with abstract traits such as sovereignty—from material relations and practices. "Setting up and policing a frontier," for example, "involves a variety of fairly modern social practices—continuous barbed-wire fencing, passports, immigration laws, inspections, currency control, and so on" (see also Callon and Latour 1981:283–84; Hull 2012).[4] Philip Abrams (1988:58) distinguishes between the "state-idea"—the reified notion that the state exists as a separate, autonomous, unified, intentional, and powerful actor—and the "state-system," the "palpable nexus of practice and institutional structure centred in government and more or less extensive, unified and dominant in any given society." Abrams argues that the idea of the state has to be taken very seriously because of its effects in the world, but that it should not be granted the status of a unified actor. By approaching the corporation as enacted, I aim to bring together the "idea" of the corporation as an actor endowed with particular goals and rationalities with the corresponding "system" of material relations and practices. Multiple, but connected, ideas and systems "hang together" despite tensions and inconsistencies (Mol 2002).

This book approaches corporations as inherently unstable and indeterminate, multiply authored, always in flux, and comprising both material and immaterial parts. My objective is to train anthropological attention on the everyday work that people perform as they struggle to deploy corporations as actors with particular components, relations, interests, and boundaries. Different corporate enactments involve descriptive and prescriptive dimensions, offering accounts of what is and what ought to be. How we construct corporations as actors has crucial entailments for how we assign responsibilities to them, and vice versa. Corporations can be constituted to extend and embrace, or to retract and disavow, responsibility for actions, objects, and persons (Laidlaw 2010). What appears as ontological flux, or changes in the nature of the corporation, is closely tied to fluctuating corporate responsibilities.

In positing how corporate agency and responsibility are constructed, relational models of personhood developed by anthropologists working in South Asia and Melanesia (e.g., Marriott 1976; Strathern 1988) hold more promise than the more pervasive liberal-person model. In a comparative, historical excavation of the concept of the person, Marcel Mauss (1985) discusses the Latin and Greek roots of the word in *mask*, emphasizing how the donning of masks marks out mutable and contextually defined social roles. His example of Tlingit shutter masks, "which open up to reveal two or three different creatures (totems placed one upon the other) personified by the wearer of the mask," is particularly suggestive of the multiplicity of the person (9). Applied to corporations (Foster 2011), a relational model that treats persons as partible (subject to external claims and extractions), composite (made up of heterogeneous parts), and permeable (assimilating ideas and substances from the outside) allows us to explore how corporate identity and interests are distributed and contextual, produced through interactions and temporary associations between humans, animals, and objects in particular places (Latour 2005). Always in the process of being enacted, corporations incorporate parts that originate elsewhere without fully assimilating them (Mol 2002:148). Rather than posing a problem, complexity and contradiction are regular features of the relational model. Anthropology's relational model of personhood is also consonant with an antiessentialist view of the firm, which economic geographers and some economists have argued is crucial for an antiessentialist analysis of capitalism (O'Neill and Gibson-Graham 1999; Resnick and Wolff 1987).

In approaching the corporation as multiple and enacted, I draw inspiration from Annemarie Mol's 2002 ethnography of atherosclerosis. Studying how various hospital personnel use instruments, forms, and questions to diagnose and treat it, Mol argues that the disease is multiply enacted, it has a "manyfoldedness" but "hangs together" or is "coordinated" into a "patchwork singularity," a "composite reality," or a "coherence-in-tension" (72, 83, 84).[5] Mol notes that different enactments of the body have different moral and political entailments, but she deliberately brackets these and excludes them from her inquiry. This is appropriate for her object, a disease that her interlocutors all agree has deleterious effects on human health. By contrast, among those enacting mining corporations there is no consensus about whether their very existence should be regarded, on balance, as positive or negative.

Publicly traded mining corporations like Newmont employ workers, produce commodities, consume natural resources, expel waste, borrow and lend money, pay taxes, lobby governments, disburse returns to investors, engage in lawsuits, establish subsidiaries, and subcontract, partner, invest, and compete with other corporations. All these transactional activities—and the social relations they constitute—are latently available for identifying, evaluating, and transforming the corporation. David Graeber's gloss of Marilyn Strathern's notion of the partible person is useful for exploring how this happens:

> People have all sorts of potential identities, which most of the time exist only as a set of hidden possibilities. What happens in any given social situation is that another person fixes on one of these and thus "makes it visible." One looks at a man, say, as a representative of his clan, or as one's sister's husband, or as the owner of a pig. Other possibilities, for the moment, remain invisible. It is at this point that a theory of value comes in: because Strathern

uses the phrases "making visible" and "giving value" more or less inter-changeably. (Graeber 2001:39–40)

Similarly, we might fix on Newmont's waste disposal practices, freshwater consumption, destruction of mountains and forests, and release of airborne pollutants to enact Newmont as an environmental threat that people should oppose and governments should restrain. But another shutter may open to reveal the company's employment of local people and construction of schools and clinics in remote regions, enacting it as an important source of income and development, deserving of local and government support. Such enactments are provisional, context-specific, and variously successful and resonant: sometimes they hold together, at other times they fall apart, exposing the constitutive pieces with material consequences for the people involved and for the corporation itself.

MOBILE CORPORATE BOUNDARIES AND THE EMBEDDED ANTHROPOLOGIST

The socially constructed, materially mobile character of corporate boundaries was apparent in both of my primary fieldwork sites: the headquarters of Newmont Mining Corporation in Denver, and villages near Newmont's Batu Hijau Copper and Gold Mine on the eastern Indonesian island of Sumbawa. Newmont Mining Corporation was the world's largest gold producer in 2003 when I spent a summer doing fieldwork in the company's Denver headquarters. Occupying a cubicle on the same floor as the corner offices of the CEO and president, given access to Newmont's intranet, and sitting among senior executives in meetings where corporate strategies and projects were produced and debated, I felt as if I were in the very heart of the corporation. In southwest Sumbawa, which was my primary residence from November 2001 to May 2003 (with preliminary fieldwork in 2000 and follow-up trips in 2004 and 2007), I found Newmont's Batu Hijau mine and its administrative offices, recreation facilities, commissary, and living quarters cordoned off with fences from the villages where I lived. The mine, which began operating in late 1999, cost $1.9 billion to build and was at that time the world's largest start-up mine operation. When visiting mine facilities, I had to park my motorbike at the gates, but after scanning my Newmont student badge I could proceed on foot from there. I met frequently with mine staff in Newmont's offices, but spent the vast majority of my time "outside," in the villages and in the orchards, gardens, paddy fields, and beaches that surrounded them. In many ways, however, my life was more palpably intertwined with Newmont at the corporate periphery than it was in the center.

Every time I left the Wells Fargo Center, which housed Newmont's corporate headquarters, I had the sensation of leaving Newmont behind. The company had barely a role in (much less a monopoly over) Denver's infrastructure, options for safe transportation, mobile phone towers, Internet access, medical facilities and pharmaceuticals, drinking water, electricity, or garbage disposal. In the villages of Sumbawa, by contrast, the idea of Newmont was omnipresent. It was there in what we had and what we lacked: in our drinking water; in the spotty mobile phone reception (which improved as one approached mine facilities); in the paved roads and potholes; in the markets, schools, public toilets, and drainage ditches; and in the apples workers brought home from the mine. Newmont was also in the cast-off and stained—but still coveted—mattresses we slept on; in the fish we ate from the ocean waters (into which the mine pumped up to 160,000 tons of tailings each day); and in the air we breathed, located as we were next to Newmont's coal-fired power plant and in the target zone of Newmont's antimalaria program, subject to routine nighttime fogging.[6] Our bodies literally absorbed the externalities of the mine production process (Guthman 2011:181).

Critiquing academic anthropologists who carry out paid consulting work for mining companies, activist and anthropologist Catherine Coumans (2011:S33) writes that while such "embedded anthropologists" may "gain unique insider perspectives and information[,] . . . their ability to publicize those insights or perspectives may be restricted, and their reporting may be biased by their operating environment."[7] With independent funding for my research and no contractual restrictions on what I might publish, I fell into a "fuzzier" form of embeddedness that Coumans (S33) identifies but does not elaborate on. I requested and received logistical support of various kinds from Newmont—for example, the badge, company transportation, and even health care when I developed tonsillitis. The negative connotations of the "embedded anthropologist" label are worth exploring here insofar as they sit contrary to anthropological conceptions of "embeddedness" in more routine field sites.[8]

Although anthropologists have questioned whether the staple long-term, single-sited research approach is adequate for tackling pressing

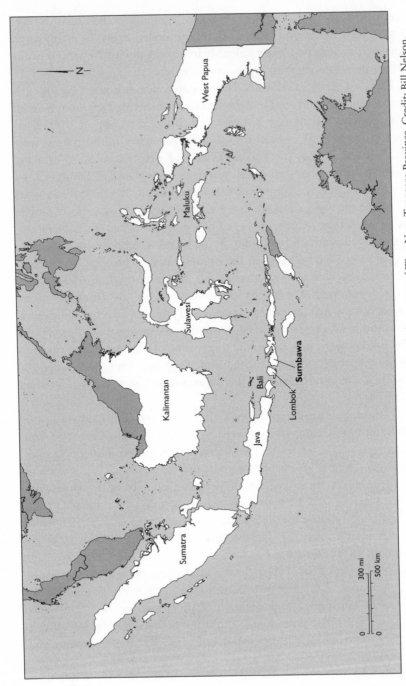

MAP 1. In the Indonesian archipelago, the islands of Sumbawa and Lombok are part of West Nusa Tenggara Province. Credit: Bill Nelson.

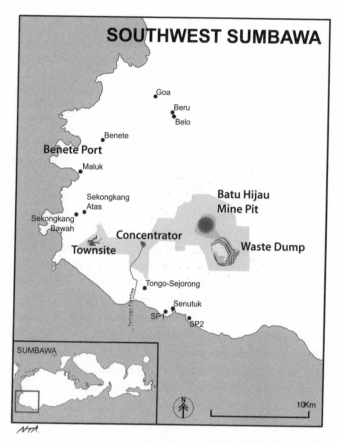

MAP 2. The Batu Hijau Copper and Gold Mine's main infrastructure and surrounding villages. Benete Port is the site of Newmont's coal-fired generator, copper concentrate storage, and administrative offices. Additional administrative offices, a clinic, international school, commissary, and housing ranging from crowded dorm-style barracks for workers to condominiums and luxurious homes for more senior staff are situated in Townsite. I lived in the villages of Tongo-Sejorong, Sekongkang Bawah, Sekongkang Atas, Maluk, and Benete. Credit: Nij Tontisirin.

social questions today (Faubion, Marcus, and Fischer 2009; Marcus 1995), embedding oneself in social life among particular people in particular places remains a methodological hallmark of the discipline (Borneman and Hammoudi 2009). Sherry Ortner (1995:173) suggests that in its minimal conventional sense, *ethnography* refers to "the attempt to understand another life world using the self—as much of it as possible—as the instrument of knowing. . . . Classically, this kind of understanding has been closely linked with field work, in which the whole self physically and in every other way enters the space of the world the researcher seeks to understand."[9]

Living in Sumbawan villages, I was always set apart from local residents by my appearance, my relatively privileged background, and my incompetent or peculiar approach to various basic routines of everyday life (from transplanting paddy to washing my clothes in the river). Over the course of my stay, I nonetheless became part of local social relations and circuits of exchange, breathing the same air (the original meaning of the word *conspire*) and becoming involved and entangled (a synonym for *complicit*) in everyday life (Marcus 1997).[10] I became renowned in villages and among Sumbawan mine workers for speaking a local Sumbawan dialect, although in practice I mostly relied on Indonesian, my Sumbawan flowing freely only between the narrow banks of familiar small talk. Sumbawans commented with delight on my consumption of local dishes and foods harvested from the sea, including sea urchins, sea worms, seaweed, and sea turtle eggs. But I also ate a number of meals with Newmont staff and managers in the mine mess halls and accepted occasional invitations to social dinners. And when an Environment Department manager urged me to handle and lick mine tailings during a tour of the mine's environmental programs (a practice I return to in chapter 5), I ingested those too.

For scholars and cosmopolitan activists alike, embeddedness can take on a different valence as soon as "the community" is a corporation. When an environmental activist and Newmont critic from the northern town of Sumbawa Besar took a tour of the mine, concluding at the mess hall, he described the meal they were about to eat as *haram* (sinful or forbidden by Islamic law). At that point, the mess hall did in fact still serve pork, but his use of the term suggested the meal's sinfulness in light of social and environmental—not only religious—principles. This view resonates with the negative connotations of the "embedded anthropologist" label. Other academics studying extractive industry corporations have hastened to assure me that they "kept their distance" from the company they studied and held it "at arm's length," emphasizing their solidarity with those who stood outside company fences. In this view (shared by many progressive social and environmental activists), even a mess hall meal is potentially dangerous and polluting (Douglas 1966). I too wrestled with this problem, having sufficiently internalized journalistic and scientific ideals of independence and objectivity—especially in light of compelling evidence of the problematic nature of industry-funded and -influenced research in domains from mining to tobacco, gambling, climate change, and pharmaceuticals (Applbaum 2010; Brandt 2007; Coll 2012; Kirsch 2010a; Proctor and Schiebinger 2008; Schüll 2012, chap. 10).[11] Ideally, from this perspective, the researcher should remain immune from the responsibilities and obligations of reciprocal gift-giving that bind members into community, jeopardizing individual identity (Esposito 2006:27). The idea of living in southwest Sumbawa villages and studying Newmont while somehow remaining apart from my subject of inquiry, however, seemed to involve an ideal of purity that stood in contrast to the practices and desires of most village residents. It also hinged on a specious view of "mine" and "village," or "corporation" and "community," as distinctly demarcated pairs.

In southwest Sumbawan villages, hundreds of people who work for the mine and its contractors pass through the mine gates every day and eat meals prepared by Newmont's caterer, often returning home with fruit (mess-hall goers were allowed to leave each meal with two pieces of fruit). Newmont frequently donated money for snacks distributed at various village festivities, subsidized meals in village mosques for breaking the fast during Ramadan, and donated animals for the Day of Sacrifice. As I describe in chapters 2 through 4, Newmont also distributed tree seedlings, chickens, goats, cows, and rice seeds to villages, and built and repaired the infrastructure supporting agricultural production. If Newmont's touch rendered food haram, there was not much halal (permissible) food to be had in villages around the mine.

One might array food consumption along a spectrum from more to less polluted: meals in the staff mess halls or the elitist Batu Hijau "Ladies Lunches," which would be the most polluted, followed by meals in nonstaff mess halls, boxed snacks and lunches served during community development trainings in villages, meals at village mosques for breaking the fast, meals in village homes prepared with Newmont-subsidized rice, and finally, Newmont-free food. The greater the purported distance between the food and Newmont, and the more closely it was associated with subaltern consumers (e.g., nonstaff workers, village farmers), the purer it would be.

The implicit moral yardstick here, however, is borrowed from a modernist ideal of the virtuous subject whose political ideals are reflected in her consumption choices. If we apply this same moral yardstick to Sumbawan village residents who want to work for Newmont and eat in company mess halls, then we must either condemn their desire (as an expression of false consciousness: they have fallen for ideologies of development and modernization) or excuse it (capitalism has left them with no alternative but to jettison their ethics and offer themselves up for exploitation). In either view, ethics becomes a privilege reserved for those with sufficient political consciousness and economic means to make informed choices about what they will produce and consume.

While some village residents did find the idea of development seductive, and the loss of land had "freed" others to be laborers, this is not the whole story. Village residents were typically more concerned with increasing the flow and broadening the distribution of goods from Newmont than with the purity of their origins. Local distributional concerns served in various cases to obscure broader relations of exploitation, but they were rooted in moral views and practices that could also reconfigure Newmont as a subject that bore responsibility for ameliorating the inequalities it had created. I return to this idea in chapters 2 through 5, where I examine how local residents insisted upon the interdependence of mine and village and the reciprocal obligations of the company and local residents. Village ideas and practices for moralizing Newmont interacted and conflicted with Newmont officials' efforts to implement the insights of the Corporate Social Responsibility movement.

MAKING CORPORATIONS, MAKING CORPORATE RESPONSIBILITIES

The Corporate Social Responsibility (CSR) movement, which provides an important lens through which to view corporate enactment, came to prominence in the late 1990s and the first decade of the new millennium with the growth of new business school curricula, consulting and non-profit organizations, books, dedicated journals, awards, voluntary codes of conduct, and certification mechanisms. Transnational advocacy and direct action networks opposed to powerful multinationals and the World Bank, International Monetary Fund, and the World Trade Organization (Graeber 2009; Juris 2008; Keck and Sikkink 1998; Soule 2009) paved the way for the CSR industry, which advanced in part by adopting and depoliticizing the discourse of corporate opponents.[12]

Efforts to theorize corporations and their responsibilities are as old as the corporate form itself. Since its invention under Roman law, legal scholars have debated whether corporations (be they charities, religious organizations, universities, municipalities, or businesses) are best approached as aggregate collections of individual persons (e.g., members or shareholders), artificial creatures of the state, or real and natural entities. And they have argued over what entitlements and responsibilities flow from the theory adopted (Allen 1992–93; Avi-Yonah 2005; Horwitz 1985; Mark 1987; Millon 1990; Ripken 2009; Sawyer 2006).[13]

The contemporary CSR industry, heterogeneous as it is, has two fairly striking and consistent features. First, its proponents are generally invested in developing voluntary regulatory principles and practices that tend to serve as surrogates for state regulations.[14] Second, they justify CSR interventions as being in the interest of the corporate bottom line. According to the "business case" for CSR, the costs of behaving responsibly toward workers, downstream communities, consumers, and the environment will pay in the end by enhancing the corporation's reputation, providing new opportunities, and mitigating risk and its associated costs.

Newmont managers formulated the business case for CSR, along with those for the allied "disciplines" of safety and environment (see chapter 1), around a corporate goal of becoming the "miner of choice" for governments and communities, lenders, potential and current employees, institutional investors, and ordinary shareholders. Whereas labor issues form the central focus of CSR in some companies and industries (e.g., apparel manufacturing), in Newmont social responsibility questions related to workers were generally addressed by long-standing Departments of Human Resources and Health and Safety.[15] Newmont's CSR focused instead on developing "socially responsible" relations with communities living near large-scale and capital-intensive mines that consume massive quantities of resources and generate massive quantities of waste while offering only limited employment opportunities (Ballard and Banks 2003).[16] An explicit CSR concern in this context was how to ward off the threat of local communities shutting down mining projects, either by themselves or in alliance with more metropolitan activists, journalists, and lawyers.

The business case for CSR renders the industry consistent with Milton Friedman's 1970 doctrine that "the social responsibility of business is to increase its profits." Although corporate critics often invoke Friedman's doctrine, along with the Michigan Supreme Court ruling in *Dodge v. Ford* (Bakan 2004),[17] to reinforce a vision of corporations as amoral actors single-mindedly maximizing profit, Friedman's formulation is more flexible than it at first appears. He allows, for example, that businesses must conform to both laws and ethical custom. He does not argue that corporations should calculate the cost-effectiveness of abiding by the law or breaking it and risking a fine; rather, he maintains simply that they should abide by the law. Those who argue that the profit maximization imperative should or does override the law are assuming a more extremist position than even Friedman publicly took.[18] (The problem of how businesses actively *shape* the law meanwhile remains thorny.) Friedman's belief that business should conform to "ethical custom" can support a range of ethical positions, moreover, depending on the social norms seen to hold sway in a particular context; ethical custom might be invoked to support racial segregation in one setting, for example, and the granting of gay partner benefits in another.

Friedman acknowledges that cases arise in which it is in the long-term interests of a business to generate goodwill through charitable contributions and the provision of community amenities, and to cloak what is in fact "self-interest" in a mantle of "social responsibility." Interestingly, those who make the business case for CSR may simply reverse Friedman's argument by starting with ethical beliefs about corporate responsibility and then cloaking these in a mantle of "self-interest." As sociologist Ronen Shamir (2008:3) puts it, CSR works to economize morality, to "ground and reframe socio-moral concerns from *within* the instrumental rationality of capitalist markets."

Many progressive scholars and activists have critiqued CSR precisely because of this economic instrumentalism. One perspective dismisses CSR outright as a smoke-and-mirrors public relations exercise that is meant to cleanse the public image of corporations through "greenwashing," "pinkwashing," and "bluewashing,"[19] with business going on as usual. When I asked a noted sociologist whether he saw precursors to the contemporary CSR industry in his earlier research on mine labor politics, he dismissed my question, admonishing me for treating CSR as real and failing to "strip away" the veneer to get at "what is really going on."

A second form of progressive critique goes beyond skepticism of CSR claims and criticism of its PR component to uncover its more profound role in advancing various corporate interests and rolling back the welfare and regulatory state. Shamir (2008; 2010:534), for example, depicts CSR as partnered with neoliberalism in replacing government and its traditional instruments ("formal rules and stipulations, adversarial methods, enforceable means of dispute resolution, and command-and-control regulatory mechanisms") with governance. Governance works through a new set of tools ("nonadversarial dialogue and organizational learning, presumably leading to the development of principles, guidelines, best-performance standards, and various soft law instruments") that are treated as commodities, produced by multiple and competing "stakeholders" and marketed to corporations that voluntarily adopt them for the purpose of self-regulation. The UN Global Compact, launched in 2000 under Kofi Annan's leadership to promote, for business, universal principles of human rights, labor and environmental protection, and anticorruption, is emblematic of a neoliberal approach to CSR that puts faith in voluntary forms of corporate self-regulation with no significant policing mechanisms or punitive sanctions for violating principles.

In addition to linking the CSR movement to neoliberalism, critics have argued that it enables corporations to co-opt the discourse of their opponents while cutting costs, increasing profits, eliminating competitors, opening new markets, fragmenting activist opposition, exercising control over various social groups (e.g., workers, suppliers, contractors, consumers, downstream communities), and dodging state regulations. In tying CSR closely to corporate power and interests, however, those making the ethical case against CSR strikingly echo those making the business case for it. While critics tend to look backward, focusing on harm and assigning blame to corporations, proponents tend to look forward in developing marketing pitches for new programs, which they cast in terms of corporate benefits or win-win solutions that simultaneously support people, the planet, and profits.

CSR is undoubtedly useful in many cases for overcoming social and political challenges, shoring up profits, mitigating risks, and so on. It is also clearly linked to various modes of social and environmental violence and harm—including, broadly speaking, the perpetuation of capitalism itself. My aim, however, is to question a *Homo economicus* version of the corporate person where it structures accounts of CSR such that the bottom line of corporate profits is also the bottom line of critical analysis. In his richly ethnographic and historical analysis of structural violence and subjective experience in tobacco capitalism, for example, Peter Benson (2011:57) writes, "However well intentioned corporate actors may be or claim to be, their social responsibility agendas are beholden to their fiduciary responsibility to shareholders requiring them to constantly maximize profits." This line reproduces assumptions about corporations (they are actors, have intentions, and constantly and consistently act on the profit-maximizing imperative) that implicitly or explicitly underwrite much academic and activist critique of CSR, including at times my own.

To counter an a priori dismissal of CSR, I have often relied on a shorthand description of my own research: *I am examining CSR as an extension of corporate knowledge and power.* Yet when CSR practices are analyzed primarily in terms of how they promote the accumulation and exercise of corporate power, transform "social relations and projects according to a particular set of corporate interests and values," and provide corporations with "a moral mechanism through which their authority is extended over the social order" (Rajak 2011a:2, 12, 13), the profit-maximizing corporation becomes the central protagonist, emerging stronger than ever from each bout of combat with social, political, or environmental opponents (Boltanski and Chiapello 2005; Frank 1997). We emphasize the ability of corporations to convert seeming capitulations into victories (Benson 2011:60), as if each concession were part of a master plan scripted in advance. Part of the appeal of such analyses is their affirmation of a prior, half-latent politically progressive cosmology in which corporations figure as harmful profit-maximizing actors. However, by affirming negative beliefs about corporations that many of us hold in advance, they sacrifice anthropology's characteristic "unruliness and surprise, especially the surprise that comes with ethnographic research" (George 2014:34).

By making the profit-maximizing corporation the central protagonist, we perform our criticality in opposition to a corporate actor while disengaging "it" from the human and nonhuman agents involved in enacting and contesting corporations and their responsibilities.[20] The corporation is left, to use Mol's terms, "intangibly strong" (2002:12). The political satisfaction afforded by the performance comes at an ethnographic and epistemological cost, severing corporations from the ordinary materials, human practices, ethics, and sentiments (such as desire, fear, shame, pride, jealousy, and hope) that sustain them.

The perspective that corporations are enacted enables a different approach to the CSR industry, one that attends to the specific cultural actors and scenes of struggle involved in introducing particular CSR initiatives; to the resistance CSR provokes from various quarters; to the contingent ways in which CSR programs are rolled out and rolled back; and to the unexpected consequences and failures CSR may yield. It leaves open the possibility that CSR may at times constrain profit accumulation rather than solely enabling it.

Although the CSR industry is itself heterogeneous, it offers a mainstream model of sustainable development for extractive industries. By reducing expenses associated with local "dependency," deflating irrational and unrealistic hopes and "expectations of modernity" (Ferguson 1999; Weszkalnys 2011), and encouraging local people to be responsible for their own welfare, the mainstream model fits with understand-ings of CSR as a neoliberal endeavor. This neoliberal model is a recur-ring theme in the chapters that follow. But this is not a story of neoliberal triumph. Instead, I show that the neoliberal model competes with, and often loses out to, alternative conceptions of the corporation and its responsibilities. In exploring struggles over how corporations and their responsibilities are enacted, I demote neoliberalism from its accustomed position as the best device for explaining contemporary capitalism. Many critics use the concept deftly, and I appreciate the advantages it holds over the related notion of "globalization" in pointing to specific actors and policies, a particular geographic and historical genesis, and a clear political valence. Nonetheless, I have found that it too frequently pulverizes granularity, causing us to lose sight of the very unevenness stressed by economic geographers who played an important role in pro-moting the concept.[21]

The power of neoliberalism, like other epochal or stage theory con-cepts, is that it labels, unifies, and critiques a set of institutional actors and processes unfolding in the world. This is also its weakness: it does too much, becoming a one-size-fits-all critique. If the familiar critical account of neoliberalism predisposes us to attribute the rise of CSR to capitalism's capacity to alert itself to new threats, neutralize opposition, and develop new moral justifications for increasing profitability (Shamir 2010:537), and if this account meanwhile forecloses more agnostic and nonteleological examinations of CSR as part of a contemporary mani-festation of capitalism (Callon 2009), then it has become too blunt a tool for my purpose, which is to dissect the uneven and contingent ways in which capitalism is promoted and contested in particular places and among particular people (Striffler 2002).[22]

More promisingly, Ronen Shamir describes CSR as part of a "capital-ist project of constructing the moral corporation," which "does not mean a naive belief in the morality of corporations, but rather a norma-tive vision and a theoretical effort to identify the conditions that may lead to the moralization of the corporation" (2010:535). If we go beyond the confines of mainstream CSR to examine efforts at moralizing corpo-rations, we find a wider spectrum of beliefs about what the corporation is, where its boundaries lie, what its responsibilities are, and what mech-anisms can be used to lead corporations to assume their purported responsibilities.

Anthropologists have attended closely to the fashioning of person-hood and subjectivity among individual humans, from the neoliberal constitution of enterprising, risk-taking, and "responsibilized" subjects (Rose 1999) to the ethical self-cultivation of nonliberal, pious religious subjects (Mahmood 2005). I advocate here an exploration of how such individual subject-making projects are embedded within a larger struggle over how to constitute, extend, and render responsible a collective subject: the corporation.[23] Neoliberal ideas support certain models of what the corporation is and what its responsibilities should be, but other models exist, rooted in alternative political, national, kinship, and religious commitments. Studying how various actors in southwest Sumbawa accommodate and contest religious expression in and around Newmont's mine affords a window into the localizing processes that transnational corporations necessarily undergo.

ISLAMIZING NEWMONT IN POST-AUTHORITARIAN AND POST-9/11 INDONESIA

In her study of the mining company Anglo American, Dinah Rajak claims that anthropologists have studied CSR "primarily from the perspective of the intended targets, rather than the architects, of these ethical regimes" (2011a:16; see also 2011b:10). Concerned with the agency of "powerful corporate actors," she proposes instead to study "not the targets of the CSR agenda, but its purveyors, and the apparatus through which it is deployed and dispensed" (2011a:17). A dynamic and relational model of the corporation, however, presumes no clear separation between the "architects" or "purveyors" of ethical regimes who act (and faithfully channel self-evident corporate interests) and the "intended targets" acted upon. The character and identity of Newmont in Sumbawa was shaped by struggles over how the company should respond to the religious beliefs of local village residents and workers, the majority of whom identified as Muslim. The Islamization of PT Newmont Nusa Tenggara (*PT* stands for *perseroan terbatas,* or "limited liability company"), the subsidiary of Newmont Mining Corporation that owns the Batu Hijau mine, illuminates the partible, permeable, and composite dynamic of corporations. Adopting a relational approach to Newmont's Islamization means not assuming in advance a fixed corporate actor and its interests but instead exploring the processes and relations through which the corporation, "conceived to exist in change," is enacted (Resnick and Wolff 1987:165). It also involves exploring practices, beliefs, and sentiments—from the material infrastructure of worship and expectations of reciprocity to fears of Christian proselytizing, capitalist moral corrosion, and Muslim militancy—that are neither governed by nor subordinated to neoliberal commitments in any straightforward fashion.

Some basic background on religion in Indonesia and Sumbawa will be helpful here. Indonesia is the largest Muslim country in the world, with around 88 percent of the population professing faith in Islam. Religious identity is an obligatory feature of Indonesian citizenship. All citizens are legally required to hold identity cards stating their religion as Islam, Protestantism, Catholicism, Hinduism, Buddhism, or Confucianism. Belief in a single God is enshrined in the country's philosophical foundation of Pancasila, and a lack of religious affiliation is equated with atheism, which, in turn, Indonesians commonly conflate with communism. The latter label is a deadly serious one in a country where the army led civilians to murder somewhere between five hundred thousand and 1 million alleged communists in 1965–66. These killings followed an alleged communist coup attempt, in which six army generals were assassinated. General Soeharto's role in orchestrating retribution paved the way for his toppling of the left-leaning President Sukarno, and Soeharto's New Order regime thereafter consistently invoked the communist specter to justify its oppression over the course of its thirty-two-year rule.

Suspicious of Muslim "extremists" and militant groups that had sought to establish an Islamic state, the New Order regime initially endorsed a form of "statist" Islam with only a restricted public role. In the late 1980s, however, the government began courting leading religious figures and organizations more openly, as well as supporting Qur'anic recital competitions, Islamic art, and the Islamic reform movement then evident in the increasing numbers of mosques, religious schools, and pious forms of dress (Brenner 1996; Gade 2004; George 1998, 2010; Hefner 2000; Jones 2010b). Soeharto himself went on the hajj in 1991.

In 1998, while the Batu Hijau mine was under construction, Soeharto was ousted from power following widespread popular protests and violent state reprisals. Part of the general fallout from the broader Asian financial crisis that began in 1997, the protests were triggered by the Indonesian rupiah's steep devaluation against the U.S. dollar, which had led to skyrocketing prices for basic goods, capital flight, and crippling unemployment. The period after Soeharto's fall saw the outbreak of long-simmering ethnic and religious tensions, many of which had been brought about—but also contained—by the New Order regime's policies (e.g., the transmigration program that resettled millions of Indonesians from more to less densely populated islands). The popular independence movements of Aceh, West Papua, and East Timor gained new vigor (with only the last of these being ultimately successful). Conflict between Muslims and Christians broke out on various islands, with violence in Sulawesi and Maluku attracting a great deal of attention and support from Muslim and Christian communities elsewhere in the archipelago, including the emergent Laskar Jihad, a Muslim militia organization with a presence in Java, Sulawesi, and Maluku.

As the center of Indonesia grew "loose" (Kusno 2010), vigilante gangs and youth groups formed across the country, with many rallying around particular ethnic and religious identities. On the island of Lombok, west of Sumbawa, an Islamic civilian militia organization named Amphibi formed to control crime, although it soon gained its own reputation for criminal activities and for violence against Hindu Balinese (MacDougall 2003; Tyson 2013). Amphibi operated mainly in Lombok, but members established an outpost of the organization on Sumbawa in the village of Maluk, near the mine.

Sumbawans historically have had the reputation of being relatively homogeneously and staunchly Muslim,[24] although some highland communities of the island converted to Islam only after the introduction of national identity-card laws, and transmigration projects have brought significant numbers of Hindu settlers from Bali to parts of the island (Hildebrand 2009; Just 2001). The mosque forms a focal point of social life in villages near the Batu Hijau mine, and residents feel it is important that a place of worship be conveniently located in relation to their homes, close enough that the mosque loudspeaker, typically set near full volume, is easily audible to those at home. In addition to being used for the call to prayer and for broadcasting sermons, the mosque loudspeaker also functions as a public address system for secular village matters.

Islam is also central to the marking of everyday time and annual cycles in villages. Most Sumbawans pray five times a day, whether privately in their homes or communally in the mosque, and they organize other activities in relation to this time devoted to prayer. Men and older women are more likely to carry out their daily prayers in the mosque, and on Fridays the majority of men in villages and many of the more senior women attend the mosque sermon. In the evenings, many children go to the homes of local *kyai* (religious teachers) to learn how to recite the Qur'an. Throughout the year, village residents follow the Muslim calendar, with days devoted to fasting, feasting, pilgrimage, sacrifice, and grave-clearing.

Some religious activities assume a highly local cast, such as a day spent preparing and consuming a special rice dish called *me sura*—a ritual expressing love for the prophet, as well as empathic recognition of the cravings of his pregnant mother. These cravings are also recognized in the preparation and empathic consumption of special sour foods during the ritual belly-washing ceremonies held for pregnant women under the supervision of shaman midwives.[25] The agricultural cycle involves religious activities related to planting and harvesting paddy. Local residents frequently prepare, distribute, and consume ritually consecrated meals for these events, as well as for events in the life cycle, such as births, marriages, and deaths.[26]

Southwest Sumbawan village residents generally lean toward what academic scholars have called a "traditionalist" rather than "modernist" approach to Islam (Bowen 1993). When villagers mentioned Muhammadiyah, a large modernist Indonesian religious organization that supports individual learning, translation, and interpretation rather than reliance on traditional interpretations and intermediaries, they often did so in suspicious tones (e.g., describing in a half-whisper how someone in another village was Muhammadiyah, or mentioning that the organization would forbid some local ritual practice). One imam explained to me that Sumbawans in the Sekongkang region held on to and perpetuated the accreted wisdom of their ancestors, "throwing nothing away" (tidak ada yang dibuang). This traditionalist orientation is compatible with an attunement to national and global events affecting the larger Muslim community; in mosque sermons and everyday conversation, people often expressed concern and outrage over the plight of Palestinians and fellow Muslims as the United States waged its global "war on terror."

With this historical and geographic context in mind, let me turn to the religious policy of PT Newmont Nusa Tenggara, which its president, Robert Gallagher, dubbed a "mosque-r-us" approach during an interview. The company actively donated to and supported Islamic activities and events in villages and on company grounds. This stands in significant contrast to the policy of PT Newmont Minahasa Raya; the Newmont subsidiary—which owned and operated a now closed gold mine in northern Sulawesi, where there are significant populations of both Muslims and Christians—made no religious donations. If we think of the capital-intensive mine as having a secular interest in recovering a profit as quickly as possible on the enormous outlay of labor and capital involved in building and operating the mine (Marx 1992, chap. 15), then PT Newmont Nusa Tenggara's policy makes perfect sense. A secular corporate-interests perspective would also support downplaying an association of the company with Christianity and with U.S. policy. In an era when the

Bush administration was invading Afghanistan and Iraq and pursuing a "war on terror" that many Indonesian Muslims saw as a war on Islam, it was better to cultivate a local identity and not be seen as a symbol of U.S. capital.[27] Indeed, a village preacher (*khatib*) told me that he and others attended a meeting after 9/11 in which senior executive Tom Enos told them not to confuse America with the mine: "America is America and the mine is the mine." Finally, from a corporate-interests perspective it makes sense that Newmont would support a version of Islam that was market-friendly, liberal, tolerant, and, in general, consistent with fostering what Mahmood Mamdani (2004) has described as the "good Muslim," imagined against a militant "bad Muslim."

Yet there is no singular capitalist "Newmont" actor who went about doling out religious donations, supporting "market Islam" (Rudnyckyj 2009a), and gathering intelligence on potential threats, isolable from the actual heterogeneous set of people who brought distinctive and sometimes contradictory practices and beliefs to the project of Islamizing Newmont.

Inside Batu Hijau's gates, Newmont Islamized by providing Muslim workers with the time and facilities for worship and by reducing output during Ramadan. The mine's main mosque was large and well appointed, and there were also smaller *mushollas* (prayer congregation spaces) in various sites, including a portable one kept near the mine pit so that workers' prayer breaks would be shorter. The Community Relations Department (which, in keeping with local practice, I will shorten to "Comrel") had oversight of many of the programs that made Newmont's religious sponsorship visible in villages. Comrel made donations for the construction and repair of village mosques, mushollas, and *pondok pesantren* (religious schools); sponsored communal meals for breaking the fast during Ramadan; contributed to the annual Qur'an recital competitions in local districts, and subsidized local participation in the regency-level competition. Around the Day of Sacrifice (Hari Korban or Idul Adha), Comrel (and some Newmont subcontractors) donated bulls for slaughter and distribution in villages and periodically gave religious accoutrements (e.g., prayer mats) to senior village men. Batu Hijau's mosque committee regularly invited local village khatib (preachers) to deliver sermons (*khutba*). When renowned khatib from other islands were invited to the mine, Comrel invited senior village residents to attend and ensured that they had transportation and permission to enter Newmont's facilities.

I never heard village residents question or criticize the existence of these flows of money, construction supplies, food, prayer materials, and invitations to hear and be heard speaking about Islam.[28] If anything, village residents seemed to expect and welcome these flows, which brought Newmont materially out into the villages and village residents inside Newmont's gates. The head of an Islamic middle school suggested that Newmont provide more religious support to counteract the morally corrosive effects of the mine, which bore responsibility for bringing alcohol, bars, prostitutes, brothels, and nonbelievers into the region, as well as for making people more materialistic. These examples illustrate that Newmont was partible, subject to external claims and extractions in support of religion, as well as permeable, able to assimilate, at least provisionally, ideas and substances from the outside.

Yet Newmont was also composite, made up of heterogeneous parts and persons, including those deeply ambivalent about the Islamization of Newmont and their own role in and relation to this project. Comrel officers, for example, were supposed to gather intelligence for the company on potential Islamic militancy, a function that complemented their efforts to cultivate positive relations with village residents. As "Pak Comrel" ("Mr. Community Relations"), the manager of PT Newmont Nusa Tenggara's Community Relations Department told me, rather apologetically, one of the functions of his department was to be "like the FBI." On Fridays, Comrel officers tried to fan out across the mosques in the region so that they could hear the sermons as well as take part in the social interactions that went on before and after. "Trouble," one expatriate miner's wife told me, "usually starts on Fridays after prayers." These Comrel officers were themselves all Muslim and Sumbawan, mostly hailing from villages around the mine. Thus, they went to the Friday congregation both as members of the Muslim community (*ummat*) and as potential corporate informers.

With their Muslim identities, Comrel officers could also potentially be coded as threats themselves. In Laidlaw's terms (2010), Comrel officers had the potential to shift from being simple "intermediaries" who acted out corporate interests in a transparent and predictable way to becoming "mediators" who might play an independent causal role in a chain of events.[29] One Comrel officer signaled awareness of this possibility when, before PT Newmont Nusa Tenggara's president arrived for a village meeting, he slipped off his *peci* (a round black cap that is part of Indonesian men's Muslim dress and commonly worn on Fridays) and tucked it away, making a little joke about not wanting the president to confuse him with al-Qaeda. Others found humor in the idea of a militant Muslim identity within Newmont. A translator told me with a grin that Newmont had paid for the visit of one religious speaker who was a bit more radical in his views than the speakers Newmont's management normally endorsed. She obviously took pleasure in the idea that Newmont had sponsored someone who was, from a conventional Western perspective, a potentially dangerous or "bad" Muslim. On another occasion, I was sitting with some friends on the side of the road in Tongo village when an acquaintance pulled over to say hello. I asked what he was up to. "I'm looking for an American to kill," he responded. "Here's a hardliner [*orang garis keras*]," responded one of my companions with mild disapproval. As we continued to chat, the "hardliner" told me that he had begun working for an agricultural nongovernmental organization that received most of its funding from Newmont, noting that the organization was still small and could not afford to be too critical of its sponsor at this point. Before remounting his motorbike and heading off, he extended a friendly invitation to me to attend a wedding taking place that weekend. The joke was ludic, experimental, not personally menacing but politically pointed. His play with this "could-be-terrorist" identity (Ahmed 2004) should be understood in relation to a deep ambivalence he probably felt in being financially dependent on a company associated with the United States in an era when the torture and killing of Muslims in Afghanistan and Iraq featured frequently in mosque sermons and everyday village talk.

Non-Muslim (predominantly Christian, Hindu, agnostic, and atheist) Newmont employees and their family members held views of the Islamizing project that did not always coincide with the corporate-interests perspective outlined here. Some resented the visibility and audibility of Islam and felt the company was being too conciliatory. One Australian miner's spouse complained about the volume of the Townsite mosque's loudspeaker, saying that multiple attempts to have it lowered, particularly during the dawn call to prayer, had met with little success; someone always turned the volume back up to full. In offhand comments and observations, some non-Muslim Newmont employees expressed, at times in highly visceral terms, their concern about and dislike of various expressions of Muslim piety. Some of these were coded as "extremist," such as the dark mark (*zabiba*) that developed on some men's foreheads, indicating the vigor of their prayer practices, or the increasing prevalence of veiling by women and younger girls in villages (one American employee expressed concern over a village wedding attended by women from northern Sumbawa wearing burqas, and the militant tenor of the preacher's remarks). Other complaints, such as those about the "bad breath" and "poor work performance" of mine employees fasting during Ramadan, focused negative attention on more routine expressions of piety.

Newmont's highly visible official support for Islam in Sumbawa contrasted with more muted and ambivalent support for Christian employees who wished to engage in public religious practice. Christians could use the Community Hall building in Newmont's Townsite for worship on Sundays. The building was meant to be available for any community purpose, but informally many workers called the building a church (*gereja*), noting that it was built in the shape of a cross and seemingly associated with Christian activities. One Newmont official told me that managers had to actively dissuade some Christian expatriate miners and their spouses (who often had quite a bit of spare time on their hands due to the availability of cheap domestic labor) from proselytizing in villages. He expressed concern that any identification of Newmont with Christianity and proselytizing could prove inflammatory. Indeed, many Sumbawan village residents feared they were potential targets of covert attempts to convert them to Christianity. I heard several preachers cautioning their audiences on the risk posed by Christians living among and befriending them and claiming a neutral interest in the religion while, in practice, seeking to convert them. Other residents expressed concern that a dance craze associated with the Christian island of Ambon, called the *poco-poco,* or images of churches in English textbooks, might represent covert attempts at conversion. Although Newmont managers might rein in Christian employees seeking to proselytize, they had no control over the presence of several Christian preachers who spontaneously migrated to Sumbawa during the construction era and then stayed on in the villages of Benete and Maluk to pursue a dream one preacher described as "opening Sumbawan hearts" to Christianity. The preachers were not enjoying any obvious success in recruiting converts, and Muslim residents regarded them with some suspicion.[30] Unofficial Christian prayer locations in Maluk were attacked and stoned in 2001, during a time when church burnings were taking place on the neighboring island of Lombok and in northwest Sumbawa. At this time, rumors spread that a price of 35 million rupiah had been placed on the heads of individual pastors in Maluk.

Fears of local religious conflict (possibly fueled by national and global processes and events) intersected with fears that broader terrorist networks might target Newmont employees or facilities. In October 2002, when two nightclubs in Bali were bombed, killing over two hundred people, a large number of Newmont employees, contractors, and family members happened to be there for a rugby tournament. Many were staying at a hotel just down the street from the bombings. One described the windows on the bottom floor of their hotel shattering, and disoriented, bleeding, and burned tourists subsequently wandering into the hotel compound asking for help. She and others felt they could easily have been victims of the bombing, having tried to get into Paddy's Pub (one of the two targeted) just the previous evening.[31]

Newmont employees' fear of falling victim to a terrorist attack receded little in subsequent years. In 2003, Newmont moved its office in Jakarta to a supposedly more secure location. But the new office tower was directly across from the Marriott Hotel, which was bombed in August that year. Newmont employees, who were sitting down to lunch at the time of the explosion, suddenly saw part of their roof cave in from the force of the bomb. One Jakarta executive emailed me after the "barbaric" (*biadab*) bombing, remarking sarcastically on the decision to move to the "more secure" building: "Good choice by Batu Hijau & Denver." Various bombing incidents (the bombing of Newmont's Mataram office in 2000,[32] the 2004 Australian embassy bombing, and a second Bali bombing, in 2005), as well as evacuation rehearsals and "credible intelligence" threats (see chapter 6), all stoked fears that company personnel, offices, or other facilities might be the next target of terrorism.

CORPORATE INSECURITIES

Surveying their field, economic geographers Nigel Thrift and Kris Olds observe growing appreciation of the "disorganization of organization" (1996:319–20).[33] No longer depicted as enclosed shells through which transactions with the outside world take place as the organization steadily works toward preset goals, the contained and directed organization model gave way to a focus on ongoing action, *organizing*, revealing the tentative, temporary, practical, ad hoc, and improvisational manner in which actors talk organizations into being at every moment as they "fashion informal solutions to formal goals" (320). Corporations, like humans, should not be approached as actors whose mental plans and models direct physical action, or whose active intentions structure passive execution (Ingold 2000:415; Suchman 2007). New interests may be produced alongside or as a consequence of particular strategies pursued in specific contexts. What is intrinsic and extrinsic to the corporation, what corporate obligations and interests are, and how these obligations and interests ought to be carried out will all be seen as contested, as coordinates in motion, in the coming chapters.

Just as the business case for CSR is malleable and protean, allowing morality to be economized in various ways (Rajak 2011a; Shamir

TABLE I   DEBATING CORPORATE STRATEGIES

We need to give the Uzbekistan project a go. If we're successful, we'll be well placed to exploit new opportunities across the former Soviet Union.	Uzbekistan is a terrible idea. We might be able to cut a good deal at first, but who knows what the government will do in the future?
These demonstrations are illegal. Why don't we just get the army in with their guns and clear out the demonstrators?	We can't do that; next thing you know, the army will be mowing us down. Can't we just figure out who's behind the demonstrations and pay them off?
Based on what we've been spending, we'll probably be looking at a budget of $6 million minimum for community development next year.	That's way too much. We need to lay off funding the big infrastructure and work on building community and government capacity. Our budget should be closer to $1 million.

2010:538, 543–44), so too are corporate interests themselves. Even when the goal is profit maximization, that goal forms a large and loose target, an imprecise orienting device rather than a clear roadmap prescribing a fixed route for corporate managers and staff to follow. When Newmont managers faced decisions about whether to pursue a joint venture with the newly independent state of Uzbekistan, how to deal with demonstrators in Sumbawa, or how much they should spend on community development near the Batu Hijau mine, they could invoke the same goal—the pursuit of profit—to justify quite contradictory strategies. Table 1 is based on later accounts by managers involved in these debates, and it illustrates some of the opposing logics represented in negotiations.

The people on either side of these debates can claim that their strategy is in the interest of securing corporate profits. History sometimes pronounces one side right. Even before the Uzbekistan government nationalized Newmont's assets in 2006, one Newmont executive had described the firm's Uzbek venture as a "fiasco" (Morris 2010). In Indonesia, the army might have helped to quell protest quickly, at the risk, however, of attracting unwanted scrutiny from human rights activists. Spending less on community development obviously reduces expenditures but can also generate community opposition, costing the company more in the long term. Whether Newmont invested in Uzbekistan or did not, shot demonstrators or paid them off, spent more or less on community development, one could potentially view the company as acting in the interest of profit maximization. To say that the company took a particular course of action dictated by the profit motive or because this course served its own interests, then, does not actually take us very far analytically.

In the chapters that follow, I emphasize that corporate decisions are made by people engaged in negotiations and struggles over complex issues rather than by a metaphysical corporate actor that unerringly acts in the interest of profit-making (on the making of capitalist interests, see Hirschman [1977] 1997). As Latour (2012) has pointed out, organizational interests are often generated in the wake of organizational action. Indeed, it is precisely at moments when organizational members are confronted by difficult choices that they may be inclined to invoke an organizational essence that is supposedly dictating their actions. Attributing their decisions to this essence rather than to their own improvisations, they enact the organization as entity.

A brief look at Newmont's own history shows that the company is more the product of ad hoc responses to historical events than the gradual emergence of some unified metaphysical actor. Newmont's founder, Colonel William Boyce Thompson, originally incorporated the Newmont Company in Maine in 1916, deriving the name from a combination of *New York* and *Montana*.[34] He used that company to invest in "everything from Knox hats to Indian motorcycles," but primarily to promote and trade in mining stocks (Ramsey 1973:28). In 1921, Thompson incorporated the Newmont Corporation in Delaware. It was a family-owned and -run enterprise, with the bulk of its shares held by the Thompson family and a smaller amount distributed among officers, board members, and Thompson's friends. With a portfolio of mining and oil stocks as its principle asset, Newmont existed largely as a vehicle for promoting and trading shares. In 1925, the company went public with a listing on the New York Curb Exchange (later the American Stock Exchange), adding *Mining* to its name later the same year. In 1939 Newmont Mining Corporation was listed on the New York Stock Exchange. Becoming a publicly traded company allowed for the segregation of ownership and control deplored by Adam Smith ([1776] 1937) and theorized by Berle and Means ([1932] 1968), and it set the stage for Newmont's transformation into a large managerial firm (Chandler 1977). For several decades after Thompson's death in 1931, the firm retained traces of its initial family character, with Thompson's wife, daughter, granddaughter, and grandson successively serving as board members (Ramsey 1973:166).

As a stock-trading company, Newmont was hit hard by the 1929 Wall Street crash and its aftermath. Shares trading as high as $236 sank to a low of \$3.875 by 1932. Buoyed by a 1934 New Deal measure fixing the price of gold at \$35 per ounce, Newmont began developing gold-mining properties in California. At the same time, because of New Deal measures protecting workers and regulating business, Newmont executives decided to seek mining properties outside the United States.[35] With the outbreak of World War II, a more mutualistic partnership developed between Newmont and the U.S. government, with a revolving door cycling executives through government offices to establish incentive programs for mining strategic minerals. Strategic metal stockpiling continued with the Korean War and the Cold War.

The 1950s through the 1970s were decades of commodity diversification and geographic expansion for Newmont. The company became involved in cement, uranium, coal, asbestos, oil, vanadium steel, lithium, and fertilizers. It established mining properties in Peru, Canada, the Philippines, South Africa, and Algeria and carried out exploration work in Canada, Mexico, Nicaragua, Chile, the Philippines, Indonesia, Papua New Guinea, Burma, South Korea, Lesotho, Botswana, South Africa, Algeria, Spain, and Portugal. During these decades, the nationalization of extractive industries in various postcolonial countries provided a powerful rationale for Newmont to concentrate on domestic production. At the same time, increasing social and environmental regulations in the United States served as a rationale for pursuing opportunities overseas. Newmont's commodity diversification was typical of U.S. business trends of the era, which saw a corporate merger movement that led to the formation of conglomerates.[36] Neil Fligstein (1990) argues that as firms began selling unrelated products, managers increasingly came to view firms not as producers of particular goods and services but as "bundles of assets" or "diversified portfolios" open to investment strategies and experimentation. Such views of corporations were conducive to the shareholder-value perspective that became hegemonic in the United States during the 1980s (see Welker and Wood 2011). Newmont was subject to multiple hostile takeover attempts during the decade, including one by the famous corporate raider T. Boone Pickens. The latter prompted the board to fund a large, defensive dividend distribution to shareholders, taking on massive corporate debt in the process.[37] Newmont subsequently shrank its operations and, by 1990, had crafted a "core business" identity around gold, which had peaked at \$850 per ounce in 1980. In 2002, Newmont acquired the Australian firm Normandy Mining and the Canadian firm Franco-Nevada Mining to become, for a brief time, the world's largest gold producer.

These corporate transformations, along with the relatively high rates of personnel turnover common to U.S. firms (Jacoby 2005), perhaps help account for my finding that many executives knew little about Newmont's history prior to its incarnation as a gold-mining company with a limited international profile in the late 1980s and early 1990s.[38] Discussions of corporate responsibility had waxed and waned in previous decades, growing prominent in response to public outrage over the South African apartheid state, as well as to increasing U.S. civil rights legislation and environmental regulation (shareholder reports alternately condemned new regulations as draconian and lauded the corporation for its performance in these domains). These debates fell silent in the later 1980s, as the shareholder-value movement swept up Newmont along with much of corporate America. Unaware that the firm had produced copper, zinc, cobalt, oil, uranium, and cement as recently as the 1960s and 1970s, some executives described the Batu Hijau mine, which produced copper as well as gold, as a new and anxiety-provoking phase for Newmont. Similarly, a Normandy property in Ghana that Newmont acquired with the 2002 takeover of that company spelled for many a brand new corporate presence in Africa, rather than a return to a continent where Newmont had a significant ownership stake in several mines until the 1980s.[39]

This relatively shallow institutional memory is evident in chapter 1, which begins at Newmont Mining Corporation's headquarters in Denver among newly appointed CSR executives striving to moralize the corporation by reworking its boundaries and responsibilities across time and space. The executives drew on divergent strategies to render Newmont more responsible: a humanistic approach meant to induce moral consciousness by fostering the ability to see and critique a corporate self through the eyes of others, and a risk management approach closely tied to the "business case" for CSR and promising to secure shareholder profits over the long term. My analysis shows that profit maximization and risk management are claim-making devices that people deploy in particular contexts in order to justify or support particular courses of action. They correspond imperfectly to what corporations actually do.

Moving to the context of Sumbawan villages, chapters 2 through 4 dramatize the debate between contradictory models of how the corporation and its responsibilities should be enacted: the sustainable development model, which encourages local residents to seek economic opportunities beyond the mine and be independent of it, and the patronage model, which constitutes the mine and villages as interdependent subjects with mutual obligations. By erecting frequent roadblocks and carrying out demonstrations, residents of Sumbawan villages demanded that Newmont act as patron. These strategies were partly successful in extracting concessions from the mine, but they also prompted Newmont managers to classify villagers as security threats. I examine how Newmont managers and staff oscillated between sustainable development and patronage models in their approaches to the state (chapter 2), local village elites (chapter 3), and farmers (chapter 4).

In chapter 5, I examine different enactments of the corporation and their ethical entailments by analyzing an incident in which village residents attacked environmental activists. Environmental activists enacted Newmont as environmentally destructive ("Newmonster"), mine managers enacted it as environmentally friendly ("Goodmont"), and local attackers enacted Newmont as a patron under their protection. Each of these enactments entailed specific ethical stances among its adherents and motivated them to different kinds of action.

The final chapter follows social auditors in Sumbawa as they conduct an annual social assessment of Batu Hijau shortly after corporate headquarters made such assessments mandatory for all mines. Bringing the universalizing and transcendent aspirations of CSR together with local understandings and commitments, the assessment highlighted competing conceptions of how the corporation should perceive and act upon its interests and responsibilities, and how its performance should be assessed.

Questions of corporate security are threaded through these chapters. The prominence of this theme reflects, in some ways, the time and place of much of this research: post-Soeharto, post-9/11, post-Bali-bombing Indonesia. But it also reflects a basic vulnerability of extractive industries, which sink great sums of fixed capital into particular sites, often exacerbating existing political instabilities and increasing economic inequality in the process. Like state security, corporate security is configured as an always ongoing and incomplete project, never an achieved, fixed, or final state (Masco 2006:54). This self-perpetuating logic renders corporate security a useful lens if we are to see corporations as relations and processes, always shifting, unstable, and insecure, rather than as instantiations of *Homo economicus* who know just what they want and how to get it. A person or piece of equipment that acts predictably as an intermediary in today's mine might tomorrow become a mediator, revealing an unexpected capacity to produce effects that disrupt continuous ore production. The haul truck driver might prove to be part of a terrorist sleeper cell. The Christian homemaker wife of a miner might start proselytizing in villages. The pipeline channeling 160,000 tons of tailings every day into the ocean might spring a leak (as it did, in fact, on several occasions).

The enactments that I analyze in the coming chapters are rooted in social relations and material practices. The "environmentally friendly mine," for example, is not just a freestanding ideology that corporate managers and PR representatives, channeling corporate interests, implant in people's heads but is continually enacted in material and embodied practices, including, as we will see in chapter 5, the ingestion of tailings, the "rescue" of endangered sea turtles, and the organization of Earth Day beach cleanups. The risk-managing, responsible, and "auditable" corporation discussed in chapters 1 and 6 materializes in acts of documentation and inspection meant to link everyday practices—community donations, proper use and timely retirement of safety harnesses, and distances maintained between vehicles in the mine pit—to overarching and universal principles summarized on glossy business cards that Newmont managers carry in their wallets. The largesse-distributing patron of chapters 2 through 4, materialized in mine jobs as well as in schools, clinics, markets, and dams bearing Newmont's logo, came into being because village residents exploited essential transportation routes and mobilized their own bodies, machetes, and stacks of burning tires to demand them.

The material practices and struggles involved in enacting the corporation lend it thickness and durability but also render it vulnerable to contestation and competing enactments.

CHAPTER I

"We Need to Newmontize Folk"

A New Social Discipline at Corporate
Headquarters

Chris Anderson's administrative assistant escorted me to the thirty-sixth floor of the Wells Fargo Center for my first appointment with Newmont's Social Responsibility group executive in June 2003. We emerged from the elevator into a festive scene. A set of paintings Newmont had commissioned from Warlpiri artists had just arrived from Australia, addressed to Anderson under his adopted Warlpiri name. Executives and consultants were trying them out in their offices and on hallway walls, and Anderson was explaining the importance of the flying ant motifs in the paintings, the cosmology of places they contained, and how one renowned artist could sing her paintings as women's stories and men's stories. Noting Newmont president Pierre Lassonde's zeal for the paintings, he joked, "We better get these out of the way before he sees them." Shocks of vibrant color against the subdued blues and grays of the office décor, the paintings seemed to represent a new, unexpected, and disruptive presence. Anderson was appointed to lead CSR at Newmont in 2002, as part of the corporate restructuring that followed Newmont's acquisition of the Australian company Normandy Mining and the Canadian Franco-Nevada Mining Corporation. Those takeovers left Newmont the world's largest gold producer, raising its profile for both investors and environmental activists.[1] The paintings were material traces of Anderson's biography and the relationships he had cultivated with Australian Aboriginal communities and artists as a doctoral student in anthropology doing his fieldwork, as a curator and director at the South Australian Museum, and as executive general manager of Public Affairs for Normandy.

At that time I had only a vague sense of the shape my research at Newmont's corporate headquarters would take, since much would depend on the level of access granted me. I was disappointed to find that the corporate library and centralized archives I had hoped to explore did not exist, but my access to daily life at headquarters was better than I had expected. My initial plan was to interview executives and shadow Anderson and his close colleague Helen Macdonald, director of Community Relations and Social Development, in the occasional meeting. This took on the livelier complexion of fieldwork when Anderson and I sat down together and he said, "I don't want to tell you how to run your research, but, as a fellow anthropologist, I think it makes sense for you to get a cubicle so you can really be among the natives." My timing was fortunate. Both Anderson and Macdonald, who holds a doctoral degree in applied philosophy and had been Normandy's community relations advisor, were willing to let me observe their daily activities and follow them in meetings as long as other participants did not object to my presence (Newmont lawyers were the only ones to do so).

It was not a given that Anderson and Macdonald's academic training would encourage them to open their office doors to a graduate student they knew little about. Anderson had encountered academic anthropologists who shunned him for taking a job with a mining company and asked him how much he had been paid to "go over to the dark side." But being the subject of ethnographic scrutiny was not a novel experience for him: in his previous role as a museum curator, Anderson had received nuanced but not uncritical treatment in an article by American anthropologist Fred Myers (1994). Whatever other factors may have contributed to Anderson and Macdonald's openness to an independent academic shadowing them for several months, I believe they saw the potential for an experiment in enacting Newmont as a transparent corporation.

If so, this was an experiment that Anderson and Macdonald undertook from a position of weakness, not strength. Their newly prominent place in the corporate hierarchy was tenuous, and the future of CSR was as uncertain at Newmont as it was then in the mining industry and indeed the corporate world more generally.[2] This chapter is about Anderson and Macdonald's struggle to acquire authority, resources, and legitimacy in order to enact Newmont as a responsible mining corporation. Though "responsible mining corporation" may strike many of us as oxymoronic (Benson and Kirsch 2010b), my goal here is to hew closely to my interlocutors' terms rather than produce yet another rearview-mirror critique of corporate responsibility as simply serving corporate interests. As I discussed in the introduction, this critique itself bears a striking resemblance to the "business case" that CSR proponents use as a forward-looking marketing device to promote their field, and both models overstate the seamlessness of the meld between responsibilities and interests.

Within the office towers of corporate headquarters, executives disagree, sometimes vehemently, about the appropriateness of CSR values and practices. The notion that CSR is in the "corporate interest" is not a given; advocates must continually make the case for it by framing and reframing the boundaries, interests, and responsibilities of the firm. Were CSR executives little more than empty vessels channeling preset corporate goals, if indeed their activities originated in the will of a metaphysical corporate actor or neoliberal capitalism writ large, then there would be little point in examining their ideas and behavior. If, however, no corporate actor exists independent of its ongoing enactments, then the practices and subjective experiences of those trying to "responsibilize" the corporation must be worthy of examination and thick description. Rather than treat CSR agents as ciphers, critics interested in reorienting corporations must take executives seriously as complex, thinking subjects who, like us, are also engaged in analyzing, interpreting, theorizing, and criticizing capitalism (Miyazaki 2013:6–7, 9, 13, 23).[3] These executives are engaged in a project of reform rather than revolution, but the nature of that reform—and of the corporation itself—is never fully predetermined.

"We need to Newmontize folk!" declared Alan, a manager with oversight of land and permitting, at a planning meeting. "We've got all the programs to draw on from Batu." At issue was Newmont's start-up gold mine project in Ghana. With significant social and environmental problems already on the horizon, Alan was stressing the need to instill Newmont's standards and values in contractors in Ghana. Behind this statement stood the assumption that Newmont itself was unevenly responsible or "Newmontized." Depending on one's perspective, some mine operations, such as Batu Hijau in Sumbawa, could serve better than others as models for enacting an aspirational and idealized conception of the responsible mining firm.

In their efforts to frame the corporation as responsible, managers shift—sometimes rapidly—between a pancorporate identity articulated around the firm as a whole and more partisan identifications with their fields of expertise ("disciplines") or their mine sites. These identifications are often articulated in contradistinction to other industries, corporations, disciplines, mine sites, or corporate headquarters. They enact the corporation in ways that frame it as a whole or as separate parts, expand and contract corporate boundaries, and embrace or estrange various actors and responsibilities.

DENVER, COLORADO, AS CORPORATE HOME ADDRESS

In 2003, Newmont's headquarters occupied floors thirty-four through thirty-six of the Wells Fargo Center, an imposing structure and—with its cash-register shape—an iconic part of the downtown Denver skyline. The firm's geophysical, metallurgy, microbiology, analytical, and mineralogy departments were housed in the Malozemoff Technical Facility, named after a former Newmont CEO, in an office park in Englewood, on the southern outskirts of the city.[4] Newmont relocated its corporate headquarters from New York to downtown Denver in 1988, moving its exploration, engineering, and computer services from Arizona and Connecticut to Denver as well. The consolidation was meant to integrate management and bring it closer to Newmont's U.S. assets and areas of exploration (Newmont 1989:4).

Leaving Manhattan was probably a money-saving maneuver, and it positioned the company in a state that had long embraced the mining industry. Colorado's growth in sectors ranging from mining and agriculture to tourism has long depended heavily on fossil fuels (Andrews 2008); natural resource exploitation was likely facilitated by the lack of formal recognition for American Indian land rights in the state.[5] Extraction is economically welcome, politically nurtured, and culturally celebrated. The Colorado School of Mines, a state institution founded in the 1870s in Golden, west of Denver, promoted in its early decades a masculine culture around the notion of the western frontier and the technological mastery of (feminized) nature (LeCain 2009:56–60).[6] State and national mining history is commemorated in local museums and old mining towns,[7] which shed light on a harsh industrial past and in some cases parlay it into romantic kitsch for tourist consumption. Colorado's coal mines saw some of the bloodiest labor battles of the past century (Andrews 2008), and mining has contaminated the state's streams, lakes, groundwater, and soil. Although Newmont no longer has any active mines in the state, it operated several there in the past. In 1983, Colorado sued Idarado Mining Company, a Newmont subsidiary that operated near Telluride, under the Superfund Act, forcing the company to carry out environmental remediation in the 1990s.

FIGURE 1. Supervised by mine booth volunteers, children and adults pan for gold at the "A Taste of Colorado" festival, August 31, 2003. Photo by author.

Although I heard executives complain that Newmont ought to do more to raise its local profile, the company was engaged with and embraced by a range of local institutions. For example, Newmont speakers made regular appearances at the Denver Mining Club, which describes itself as "the oldest active organization of its type in Colorado" and brings together largely retired miners for a weekly lunch and mine-related talk or film.[8] I accompanied Chris Anderson to one such speaking event at a local Country Buffet restaurant. We were both promptly and jovially inducted into the club (which automatically included membership in the "Colorado Chapter of the International Order of Ragged Ass Miners") and presented with certificates to that effect. Newmont employees also help run the mining booth at the annual "A Taste of Colorado" festival in Denver. At the booth, children can play at panning for gold (figure 1), while informational displays and brochures created by the Colorado-based Mineral Information Institute educate the public on the hazards of old mines (emphasizing individual education and responsibility for staying clear of them), contemporary reclamation practices, and the millions of pounds of minerals, metals,

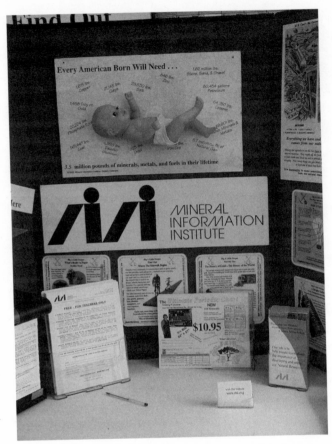

FIGURE 2. According to a mine booth display at the 2003 "A Taste of Colorado" festival, every American requires 3.5 million pounds of minerals, metals, and fuels across her or his lifetime. A 2011 version of the poster reduced this number to 2.96 million pounds, suggesting how mineral, metal, and fuel needs can be reassessed and reduced ("Every America Born Will Need . . .," Mineral Education Coalition, 2012, www.mii.org/pdfs/baby.pdf). Photo by author.

and fuels every American supposedly needs in her lifetime. One display with a baby doll depicts minerals, metals, and fuels nourishing human life rather than, as environmental critics would claim, destroying it (figure 2). The display addresses "every American," but the baby doll with which it invites identification is racially coded as white. The Mineral Information Institute furnishes teachers with curricular materials to recruit young children, not only as potential miners, but also as citizen-consumers cognizant of their implication in and dependence on extractive industries. Promoting similar themes, Newmont has hosted a Science Day for schoolchildren at its technical facility.[9] The company has won various social and environmental awards from local media, and its CEO has also been accorded various honors by local universities.[10] Local critics (Gordon 2003; Lewis 2007) question on principle the granting of these awards to a mining company and its top executives and voice concerns that such awards consolidate potential conflicts of interest (through the reciprocities of corporate donations, academic consulting, etc.).

Newmont's chief critic in Colorado during the period of my fieldwork was Global Response, a nonprofit environmental action and education network located in Boulder. Global Response coordinated letter-writing and media campaigns in response to issues such as Newmont's plan to mine in Ghana's national forest, and it helped to organize an activist presence and protests at Newmont's shareholder meetings. In 2003, the organization mobilized people to write thousands of emails and hundreds of letters to CEO Wayne Murdy opposing Newmont's proposed mine in Ghana.

CSR AMONG THE CORPORATE DISCIPLINES

Organization theorists have called attention to a tendency among academics to treat management as monolithic by neglecting power relations among managers and lumping executives together as if they shared common views on strategy and policy arising from lockstep fealty to firm interests (Anteby 2013; Jacoby 2005:4). In the United States at least, executives often identify more closely with their domain of expertise, with what Anderson and Macdonald referred to as their "discipline."[11] This term, more familiar in academic settings, connotes distinct epistemological fields within a corporation, each with its own distinct history, set of canons, and social conventions. Geology, metallurgy, engineering, investor relations, security, and human resources are among the disciplines at Newmont. The executives at headquarters who were in charge of a particular discipline set policy for the global mine sites, but they were linked only "by a dotted line" to their disciplinary counterparts who served as on-site managers and reported to the general manager or president of the subsidiary company. Annual meetings (known as "collegiates") brought together managers of the same discipline from operations around the globe.

An excerpt from notes I took during a meeting over a planned mining project will give a sense of the disciplinary divisions at corporate headquarters. CSR-aligned managers (Helen, Kwabena, and Alan) and engineers from the Projects and Operations Departments (Bill, Ilana, and Tim) here debate the project's construction start date.

Bill (Projects engineer): Can you promise to get some of the land more quickly? Like for the construction camp. We're only talking about the size of a football field. Like two hundred by two hundred meters.

Alan (land manager): No. We're not promising anything like that more quickly.

Kwabena (CSR manager): Even if you're only talking about ten by ten meters, someone might live there.

Alan: There's no way I'm going to promise you a single case. That could jeopardize the whole negotiation process. Don't forget we are creating our own cost increases as we go along. Soft issues are hard issues.

Ilana (mining engineer): Maybe there's a problem of resources that needs to be addressed here. If it costs us a million per month to put off a project, and it would cost less than that to speed up negotiations considerably, maybe we should just put more money into negotiations.

Alan [voice raised and visibly annoyed]: There are too many inconceivables in negotiations to assign a date. More resources? What do you want? Six negotiators? That will only lead to confusion. We need to have two chief negotiators who will control everything and write everything. You cannot maximize negotiating resources. When you balance an artificial deadline of going into production in the third quarter of 2006 against doing the job right and going into production in fourth quarter of 2006, you have to ask yourself what the difference is. . . . Let's ask Wayne [CEO] or Pierre [president] what they think. I don't care about the money that you could be making by starting six months earlier. I don't care. You can put it on the back end or take it out somewhere else.

Helen: By doing any construction before the end of the negotiations we would also violate the IFC [International Finance Corporation] principles by putting pressure on people. . . .

Bill [joking]: You guys are harder to negotiate with than the community. We'll give a few more months.

Alan: Now listen, we need money to do our work, and we can't worry about an extra twenty or thirty thousand dollars here or there.

Tim (Operations director): OK, we'll open the checkbook a little on this one.

Helen: Keep this in mind, the IFC would say the schedule is still aggressive.

Bill: All right, we'll move the construction start date back two months.

Bill's "you guys" captures the fractious relationship between corporate managers, who are often far from being "diligent souls work[ing] contentedly towards a universally accepted goal" (Fleming and Spicer 2007:11). Through their hard-line posturing and jokes, participants in this exchange relate and interact "via a set of conventionalized role expectations" (Mazzarella 2003:27), with engineers wanting to get the project up and running fast, and CSR managers wanting to slow it down, to keep the start date flexible in order to "prepare the community." Alan anticipated this dynamic before the meeting, telling the CSR executives that Projects would want to "hold a schedule up and say, 'Look [CEO] Wayne, I'm a hero!'" Macdonald later explained to me that Alan was particularly defensive because this was the first time he had been given a real say on the project start date in a meeting of this kind; he had been accustomed to having deadlines determined by others, and his own work ignored or devalued.[12]

At Newmont, CSR executives were not alone in their sense of being embattled or marginalized. They had a close alliance with the disciplines of Health, Safety, and Loss Prevention and Environment.[13] Of the three disciplines, CSR was relatively junior; the others had a longer history in mining and enjoyed greater legitimacy (land manager Alan referred to safety as Newmont's "sacred cow").[14] I would call all three ameliorative disciplines insofar as their role is to mitigate the negative social and environmental consequences that mining routinely produces. Financially, they are regarded within the corporation as cost centers rather than profit centers. Representatives of ameliorative disciplines are thus under pressure to justify their activities in a way that, say, geologists or engineers in a mining company are not. Although these disciplines may help mining companies comply with laws and garner environmental and social awards, which in turn support employee morale and serve a public relations function, for the most part they have relatively low visibility in the absence of breakdowns (such as worker deaths, toxic spills, or human rights scandals). They have a counterfactual dimension, working effectively when no problems are visible. A trained anthropologist and CSR executive at the London-based mining giant Rio Tinto told me how easy it is to get management to spend on social issues when a mine has lost its "social license" (a key CSR term and concept for extractive industries, registering the agency that local communities and NGOs can exercise over the ability of extractive companies to operate in a particular region). It is much harder, she said, to get the budget you need to maintain the social license when all appears to be well.[15]

For these reasons, executives in the ameliorative disciplines are under constant pressure to document their practices and relevance. For example, I attended a lengthy meeting between a senior Health, Safety, and Loss Prevention executive and a National Lightning Safety Institute representative investigating the death of a contractor killed by lightning at a Newmont site in Sumatra. The executive told me afterward that he had learned nothing from the meeting, but the fact of having convened it would be useful if he wanted to recommend changes. Similarly, a communications consultant instructed Anderson to document all external meetings for potential value added, warning him, "If you're holding a meeting with a government official like the prime minister of Tartar Land that might produce future benefits, you need to document this. If I was the CEO and didn't hear good evidence for why such meetings were being held, I'd say, 'You are an expense, goodbye!'"

CSR practitioners' ambiguous status with respect to basic corporate production and profit-making functions is expressed in the stereotypes attached to them and in their responses to these. Like Environment Department managers, whom I heard jokingly referred to by other mine officials as "hippies" and "tree-huggers," CSR practitioners risk being seen as having "alternative" and politically progressive ideas, identities, and lifestyles. Discussing a CSR report commissioned by the company, retired Newmont Investor Relations vice president and corporate biographer Jack Morris (2010:327) remarked on "the leftist orientation of the CSR fraternity." The report, he wrote, "left no doubt that indigenous rights should trump corporate rights; that it is the company's responsibility to address every need, every want, and every perceived slight within miles of its mines; and that dialogue is the only option for resolving differences. There was no acknowledgement that some demands have been outrageous or that protests were staged by outside organizations." Morris's published views, although not directed at Newmont's own CSR executives, suggest that they might be seen and see themselves partly as outsiders, members of an alien and potentially unwelcome fraternity imposing impractical and unwanted ideas and pandering to the excessive demands of NGOs and indigenous communities.

CSR practitioners alternately emphasized and suppressed their epistemological and political distinctiveness. During a collegiate meeting that brought together CSR managers from Newmont's sites around the globe, Anderson rejected an image of feminized piety by asserting, "We don't want to be like nuns, always saying 'Thou shalt not . . .'"[16] An Australian manager concurred, adding, "We don't need to emphasize

that we're so special and different and act like bleeding heart liberals."
One afternoon I accompanied Max, a communications executive, and
Kwabena, a CSR manager from Ghana, on an excursion to Boulder, a
progressive university town northwest of Denver, to take part in a radio
interview involving several environmental and social justice NGOs.
Alan, the land manager, drolly asked us to return with some granola, as
well as some of that soap whose name he struggled to recall. (I supplied
the name, Dr. Bronner's, confirming my own political Otherness.)

A relevant analogy here would be the experience of diversity workers
in university settings, who find diversity constantly invoked as an institutional value even as the institution resists the work they are charged
with carrying out (Ahmed 2012:17). Sara Ahmed (15, 22) notes that
diversity practitioners "simultaneously experience themselves as working 'for' and 'against' institutions"; they "do not simply work *at* institutions, they also work *on* them given that their explicit remit is to redress
existing institutional goals or priorities." Diversity, Ahmed shows, is a
multivalent resource, deployed to challenge social injustice, organize
commitment, and go beyond compliance and legality, but also to construct an aesthetic and moral order, provide comfort, suppress histories,
celebrate and valorize "digestible difference," and gain institutional
advantages (rather than to challenge disadvantage). Like diversity
workers, CSR managers are engaged in a fundamentally ambivalent
form of work, often caught in what Jane Guyer calls the "midstream-
ness" of open-ended and indeterminate processes and the ethical dilemmas that emerge as projects deviate from their blueprints. Under these
circumstances, Guyer (2011:S21) reflects, both meanings of "perseverance" resonate: "one—perse*ver*ance—implies a positive endorsement
of staying power and the other—per*sever*ance—an annoying and inappropriate hanging on and continual return to a project in life or topic of
conversation that has outlived all possibility of bearing fruit."

Financial resources signify and constitute power within a corporation and, therefore, merit close attention from CSR managers striving to
enact a responsible corporation. Like other corporate officials, CSR
managers at Newmont at times expressed an ambition to enlarge their
department's operating budget, as well as to be recognized as a core
part of the overall corporate operating budget, not a discretionary
expense that could be trimmed in hard times. They wanted to rid CSR
of its "air of contingency" (Ahmed 2012:29). Yet budgets were only
one way that CSR executives might measure corporate recognition of
their discipline. CSR managers also struggled to ensure their inclusion

in meetings and strategic decision-making processes. They met with some success: Anderson, for example, was a member of the powerful Operations Committee and was included in board meetings and functions. CSR executives evaluated their positions in organizational charts and reporting structures and frequently took stock of the CSR presence at mine sites, how much discretion they had in hiring and firing, and whom they could count as allies among the company's senior executives.

THE CHARISMA AND ROUTINE OF CSR

To enact Newmont as a responsible corporation, Anderson and Macdonald deployed tactics that I characterize in loosely Weberian terms as charismatic and rationalizing. The charismatic mode of CSR depends heavily on individual personality, storytelling, and performances that stage and elicit emotion as a way of mobilizing moral and affective dispositions. Working in this mode, CSR proponents seek to touch, recruit, and transform individuals. Weber (1946b:249, 251–52) portrays charisma as particularly appealing in conditions of warfare. Charismatic power springs from "faithful devotion . . . born of distress and enthusiasm" and entails openness to "the extraordinary and unheard-of, to what is strange to all rule and tradition."[17] In the mining context, charismatic authority might be especially appealing at times when executives find a company has lost its social license to operate.

The rationalizing mode of CSR, by contrast, is devoted to the selection, installation, maintenance, and monitoring of standards and codes of conduct, which in turn are linked to public statements and incentive and disincentive mechanisms built into departmental and individual performance reviews. The rationalizing mode operates at the level of the organization, enveloping individuals in a system that should steer their conduct toward compliance with universalized ethics and rational resource allocations. While the charismatic mode acts upon intrinsic human consciousness and motivations, the rationalizing mode develops extrinsic rewards and punishments. Although I describe the two modes in binary terms, in practice they are copresent, often complementary, and arguably both requisite for the CSR discipline to take root.

In the pages that follow, we will see Anderson using a charismatic approach and Macdonald deploying more routinizing tactics in order to make Newmont more socially responsible. In some respects, Anderson's and Macdonald's distinctive approaches fit with their academic backgrounds. Anderson the anthropologist was attuned to cultivating interpersonal relations, improvising, delivering theatrical performances, and converting empirical evidence into memorable vignettes containing moral lessons. Macdonald, trained in the more universalizing discipline of philosophy, which prizes abstraction and reason, sought to establish mechanisms that upheld universal values and ensured continuous compliance with them.

Gender roles and stereotypes played into their contrasting approaches in complicated ways. "You talk, you walk," a senior vice president wryly instructed Anderson and Macdonald, respectively, shortly after meeting them. On the one hand, this fits with dominant gender conventions: for him the public posturing and glory, for her the details. On the other hand, affect and qualitative reasoning are conventionally coded as feminine, and metrics, standards, and quantitative, abstract, and rational reasoning as masculine. Yet the very existence of such stereotypes grants male executives greater latitude to emote. Scholars have shown corporate settings to be zones of passionate engagement where masculine identities are shaped and staged in complex ways (Allison 1994; Collinson and Hearn 1996; Roper 1994; Schoenberger 2011). For female executives, however, the range of permissible comportment is much narrower; at both ends of the emotional spectrum from impassioned to impassive, professionally perilous stereotypes abound: trivial "cookies" and "fluffheads," supportive "pets," nurturing "mothers," dangerous "seductresses," or coldly ambitious "calculating bitches" or "iron maidens" (Jackall 1988:56; Kanter 1977:233–36).[18] Macdonald (and I) were often the gender minority in meetings. Reflecting the pattern of most large corporations (and perhaps exaggerated by the association of mining with masculinity), Newmont's upper executive ranks were dominated by men—with the exception of Human Resources, a marginalized and feminized discipline in the United States, and one scholars have described as among "the lowest-prestige divisions in most major companies" (Khurana 2002:124) and "normally the wasteland of the corporate world" (Jackall 1988:36).[19]

Anderson strove in various ways to highlight the human dimensions of the company rather than allow it to be faceless. He hired a consultant to make a video for the firm's website (since removed) in which he and fellow executives discussed the company's approach to community relations. He acknowledged criticism from colleagues about the expense of the video, and for his starring role in it, but insisted this was not so much an act of self-aggrandizement as an attempt to get Newmont's human faces seen

FIGURE 3. An interdisciplinary meeting to discuss Newmont's participation in a voluntary industry code for cyanide management brings together executives from the Operations; CSR; Environment; and Health, Safety, and Loss Prevention Departments. Photo by author.

and voices heard. Notwithstanding the gender convention associating women with affect (Shever 2010), it was he who embraced the view that it could be appropriate and strategic to publicly display emotions, whether these were sorrow, concern, humility, and contrition for mistakes made, pride over goals achieved, or measured anger and righteous indignation over what corporate officials saw as false activist claims about the social and environmental harm caused by mining operations. Speaking at a CSR collegiate to CSR managers from mine sites around the globe, Anderson said, "We need to let [NGOs and activists] see our vulnerability and weakness so they see the process we go through." They needed to rhetorically relinquish control, Anderson continued, "because we never really had it in the first place." A recurrent theme for him (and others at corporate head-quarters) was that Newmont's legal team was always trying to stifle attempts to reach out to and engage the public out of fear that any public statements might be used against the company in court.[20]

If Anderson had a theory of affect, Macdonald had a theory of risk, as we will see. Yet neither executive operated exclusively in either the rational or the charismatic mode. Anderson believed in signing on to standards and codes of conduct that could improve Newmont's practices and confer credibility. At one interdisciplinary meeting I observed, he enthusiastically supported Newmont's adoption of the cyanide code, saying that as the world's largest "goldie" (gold producer) Newmont should beat out other companies and sign on first (figure 3).[21] The business case for CSR, which I described in the introduction, and which fits well with the rationalizing mode, also ran through many of the stories he told, providing a structuring device for "lessons learned" and a bottom-line rationale for "doing the right thing." Similarly, Macdonald worked hard to build personal relationships with industry actors and NGOs and appreciated that this aspect of her work was crucial to the success of CSR. She also served as a public speaker in forums such as the annual Business for Social Responsibility meetings. But humanizing Newmont's public persona constituted a smaller part of her everyday work, which focused instead on building global human-rights standards and "best practices" for community relations into Newmont's management systems.

REINING IN A ROGUE DISCIPLINE

Do company geologists act in the firm's interests? The answer depends on how these interests are defined. Much talk of exploration work among CSR officials revolved around the figure of the rogue geologist, a reckless and culturally insensitive cowboy. At Newmont's international CSR collegiate, one manager noted that geologists sometimes "seriously misbehave"—for instance, by using drill rigs on a farmer's land without requesting permission. An American CSR manager from Newmont's Peruvian mine commiserated: "One of the nice things about coming to these meetings is reassuring yourself that you're not alone." To the larger group, he recounted how an exploration contractor was "run out of town by the community" for going on someone's land. The contractor knew he was violating proper procedure but "just wanted to go another fifty meters," later saying, "We thought we'd do it and run." Another manager shook his head and added, "They just go wherever they want to after getting information. Some do ninja exploration at night, trespassing and sampling on property where they aren't allowed; refusing to reveal results to property owners, when in fact it should be the property owner's data; stealing rocks." Another chimed in, "Sometimes you have to hold their hands, and other times you have to put your hand over their mouths."

The "value driver" behind geologists' bad behavior, CSR managers agreed, was reserve replacement: the need to replace the gold reserves mined each year with an equivalent (or preferably greater) quantity of fresh "booked" reserves.[22] This is the basic capitalist imperative of perpetual growth applied to nonrenewable resources. As the CSR manager for Peru put it during a conference call following the collegiate, "The bonus structure of geologists depends on how many ounces of gold they find, not on how well they maintain the social license." During the collegiate, however, Macdonald noted that with Newmont's new management systems (described later in the chapter) more than half of the performance questions posed to employees were about values, violation of which could be cause for firing. Anderson recounted firing an exploration team member in Sumatra who had responded to his insistence that he remove his shoes before entering a community member's home with: "You've got to show them who's boss." Note that Macdonald's hypothetical firing of a worker results from a violation of the system, whereas Anderson's story centers on personally firing an employee. "The question," an Australian manager said in response to this exchange, "is how do we get those values to penetrate?"

Anderson and Macdonald had a chance to do this when they were invited to address the exploration collegiate meeting. Before we walked into the room full of geologists, Anderson reminded me that Lévi-Strauss (1992) had found geology to be one of the most humanistic of natural science disciplines, drawing inspiration from it alongside psychoanalysis and Marxism. Speaking to the assembled geologists, Anderson drew on a stock of cautionary tales: the twenty-four-year-old man in Turkey who showed up demanding the job that a geologist had, over a decade earlier, promised his father would be held for the young boy when he grew up; the guys in Turkey who brought in busloads of prostitutes on company buses and put them up in company housing; the drill contractor in Ghana who said he went on someone's land by accident because he did not have a map ("That's odd for a geologist!"); and the "perhaps apocryphal" story of the young geologist who went onto a dairy farm in West Australia while the farmer was away, then left the gate open afterward, allowing all the cows to escape. In a more uplifting register, he played with the moral and economic connotations of value in describing how "values can create HVOs: high-value opportunities. The opportunity to take on projects that other companies can't crack. . . . We can go where it doesn't seem possible because we do things the right way." Anderson sought to confront the geologists with an image of themselves seen through the eyes of others, and then to frame their actions in terms of corporate interests that they could threaten or advance. In the process, he temporally reframed "corporate interests," supplanting the short-term goal of replacing reserves as quickly as possible with the longer-term goal of accessing high-value opportunities by "doing things the right way." Seen in this light, the "cowboy" approach was myopic, discipline-specific, and self-serving rather than an expression of loyalty to corporate-wide interests.

The exploration managers acknowledged Anderson's critique to some extent. One admitted, "In the past, in the eighties, we were the worst. Did you take the time to sit down with a mayor when you went exploring? No, you just snuck on to the real estate." Another quipped, "We have seen the enemy and it is us." Yet some pushed back, putting the CSR executives on the defensive. One remarked, "I just got back from Ghana, and I heard that there are already lots of social problems. Are you community guys there, doing anything?" Anderson responded, "At Ahafo there are twelve pits spread over thirty kilometers with twenty adjacent villages. So that's thousands of people, and of course there will always be social issues there. We just need to know what they are and manage them intelligently. Kwabena [a CSR manager in Ghana] is like the Dutch boy holding his finger in the dam, keeping expectations at bay." This prompted another to ask, "Is Kwabena the guy with the black BMW?" "No," another responded, "he has the Mercedes. The one with the BMW is Kwabena's assistant." The subtext of these remarks was that Kwabena, a CSR manager as well as traditional leader and trained lawyer, and his assistant were inappropriately wealthy. Anderson shot back: "I don't care what sort of car Kwabena has; he's doing a good job and deserves compensation." Macdonald added that the problem in Ghana was the lack of "money or the leeway at this point to do what needs to be done." In arguing that CSR was insufficiently resourced in Ghana, Anderson and Macdonald's defense of their mine-site CSR counterparts allowed the geologists to lose sight of how CSR was supposed to be everyone's responsibility.

After the meeting ended, a manager from Peru took Anderson aside and told him that his section had been "assigned one of the Social Affairs guys" for an exploration project. The presence of this "community guy" near one village had deeply upset the locals, who had issued an ultimatum: "Either you get him out of here right now or we will take his shoes and make him walk back barefoot, because we won't allow him to get in your truck again." One of their geologists, he added, had great relations with locals, while Social Affairs was despised. He mentioned an incident in which a fifteen-year-old had used a rifle to fire upon an exploration helicopter. Anderson suggested that the team take carefully selected local leaders along on future rides. "Then, in the future, they won't be so afraid of the whole process, because it has been demystified, and they'll know who's in the helicopter. They will also be less likely to fire on a helicopter if they know their uncle might be in it!" If the helicopter represents the company, Anderson's suggestion implied, then put some of the community inside it, making it no longer wholly foreign and threatening, and blurring the distinction between an attack on the company and an attack on the community. Enacting the corporation as part of the community is a security strategy, one I elaborate on in greater detail in chapter 5. In offering this suggestion, Anderson here showed his ability to improvise and stage events bringing together opposed sets of actors, as he had done earlier, at Normandy Mining, by coordinating a news event that involved executives playfully bathing in a tailings dam in Turkey.

BEFORE AND AFTER CHOROPAMPA

Newmont's past and ongoing social controversies ranged from its ownership stake in mines in apartheid-era South Africa to its joint venture with the government of Uzbekistan (which stood accused of human rights violations and employed prison labor in the project). But Newmont's 2000 mercury spill in Peru was especially resonant.

Emphasizing the sense of rupture the spill generated at corporate headquarters, a security executive told me, "We talk about BC and AC: Before Choropampa and After Choropampa." For practitioners of Newmont's ameliorative disciplines—Health and Safety, Environment, and CSR—Choropampa was shorthand for a collective trauma that had to be remembered and prevented from recurring. Early in my time at Newmont's headquarters, an open screening of *Choropampa: The Price of Gold* for Newmont employees took place on Anderson's initiative. The scathing 2002 documentary on the spill and its aftermath (by independent filmmakers Ernesto Cabellos and Stephanie Boyd) was then being screened at Sierra Club chapters and film festivals in the United States and abroad, winning acclaim and multiple awards for its powerful portrayal of campesinos claiming they had been poisoned by—and demanding justice from—a large U.S. corporation.[23] Newmont's Communications Department had obtained a copy of the film through the public relations firm APCO.[24]

The spill occurred on June 2, 2000, as a truck driver made his way down the mountain roads from Newmont's Minera Yanacocha mine warehouse in Peru with a load of mercury. The mercury, a marketable by-product of Newmont's profitable gold mine, was destined for Lima. Had it arrived there, it might have been marketed to the informal mining sector (which Newmont managers frequently condemned for polluting the environment with mercury; see chapter 5).[25] Unbeknownst to the truck driver, two of the containers he was transporting were leaking, dribbling a trail of 330 pounds of mercury along a twenty-five-mile stretch of road. The mercury pooled under the truck in the small towns of Choropampa, San Juan, and Magdalena, where the driver, who happened to be suffering from intestinal distress that day, had stopped. Campesinos gathered the strange liquid from the highway, bringing it into their homes. Some boiled it in the hope of recovering gold. Children divided it among their friends. In warm homes with little ventilation, the volatile substance easily vaporized. Because mercury has an affinity for organic matter and clay, it also burrowed deep into dirt floors and attached to wooden beams, roofs, walls, clothing, and household goods.

A day after the spill occurred, it came to the attention of mine officials. Using ambulance loudspeakers, they attempted, with little success, to persuade campesinos to part with the mercury they had collected. Officials' claims that the mercury was toxic were met with slammed doors and suspicion. Some campesinos still hoped that gold was in the mercury and might be recovered. Taking another tack, officials offered to pay campesinos to relinquish the mercury. This strategy proved more effective but introduced fresh risks: some people imported mercury to sell to the mine, often handling it with few precautions. Close to a thousand people developed symptoms of mercury poisoning.

During my one brief meeting with the CEO, Murdy told me he had only learned about the mercury spill four or five days after it occurred, which "really upset" him. Cutting short his trip to Indonesia and flying immediately to Peru, he had visited the hospital room of the victim worst afflicted. He displaced Newmont's responsibility for her dire condition— she was unlikely to recover and regain a normal life—by noting it might have been caused by a severe allergic reaction to the medicine administered to treat her. Murdy had also met her two brothers, describing the whole encounter as "a very powerful human experience."

In his talk at the Denver Mining Club, Anderson rhetorically minimized the scope of the spill as well as Newmont's responsibility, claiming rather improbably that the amount of mercury spilled could have fit into two large coke bottles,[26] and underscoring that it was a contractor rather than a Newmont employee who spilled it. But in the next breath he brought the accident back within Newmont's purview, noting that "communities will see to it that the mining company is held responsible for contractors, and this is, in fact, how it should be." Emphasizing the point, he added, "Almost all of Newmont's fatalities in the past ten years have been contractors."

Anderson's goal in screening *Choropampa* for Newmont staff and executives was to foster organizational introspection and openness to transformation, which he saw as a prerequisite to "moralizing" the corporation.[27] As Webb Keane (2010:73) observes, "The cognitive capacity to take another's perspective—both to see things from his or her point of view and to see oneself from the outside—is often taken to be an essential precondition for morality." Newmont executives were critical of the documentary, but also disturbed by the mercury spill and its consequences and by some of the behavior the film documented among Newmont's Social Affairs workers in Peru. In one unflattering scene, a Newmont official tells impoverished campesinos to hire a lawyer if they have a problem with the company.[28] Anderson told me that when Newmont's top executives watched the film they had an "aha moment." One declared, "We're racist." A senior vice president subsequently called Anderson to his office and proposed that Newmont "audit our people who are out there and figure out who shouldn't be there, and whether we should fire or rehabilitate them." In the idealized construction of the moral corporation, what cannot be reformed should be excised. But this is easier said than done. Finding and firing the offending individuals can be difficult; relations may be hard to sever and a better replacement is not necessarily easily available. Years after the spill, complaints about the Yanacocha mine's Social Affairs officers remained widespread.

Some Newmont executives saw the corporation as a whole—"us"—as racist. Others demanded the "bad apples" be identified and removed. The work of recognizing institutional or individual racism raises fundamental and fairly intractable dilemmas (Ahmed 2012:44–48, 150). On the one hand, when people recognize institutional racism, it becomes easy for individuals to excuse themselves or disidentify with this racism. A "before-and-after narrative" can also emerge in which the act of recognizing and confessing to racism is seen as exorcising it, moving the institution into a new place. On the other hand, the identification of individual racists within an organization (bad apples) makes it easy to underestimate the scope and scale of the problem and to fail to account for how it is institutionally reproduced.

In addition to exposing racist beliefs and practices in the company, the mercury spill was expensive.[29] But this very expense was useful to representatives of the ameliorative disciplines, who could invoke it in support of the business case for corporate responsibility. Beyond its direct costs in the form of remediation and compensation, the accident galvanized local opposition to Newmont's plans to expand operations to nearby Cerro Quilish and, later, Conga. In his talk at the Denver Mining Club, Anderson noted that the community had warned the company that there would be "blood on the streets," that the company would only mine Cerro Quilish "over their dead bodies." Newmont executives and geologists had hoped to add the gold deposit to company reserve estimates, thereby boosting stock prices. Anderson guessed that with "very intelligent, targeted, and strategic work with the community" over two to three years the company might "earn the social license" to mine Cerro Quilish. His assessment proved too optimistic. In 2012, after Newmont announced that it would move forward to mine Cerro Quilish and the $4.8 billion Conga mine, demonstrations and bloodshed ensued. Police fired live ammunition on protestors, killing five (Wade and Aquino 2012).

The mercury spill had attracted unwelcome international attention as well. A communications executive told me that high-volume institutional investors began asking questions they seemed to be pulling off the website of the activist organization Project Underground. Rumors circulated in Denver that Erin Brockovich, whose role in a pollution lawsuit against Pacific Gas and Electric Company was made famous in a movie starring Julia Roberts, planned to help launch a massive lawsuit against Newmont. Renowned investigative reporter and television news producer Lowell Bergman (who was played by Al Pacino in *The Insider*, a tobacco industry exposé based on a true story) devoted an episode of the acclaimed Public Broadcasting Service show *Frontline* to the mine. The episode implied that Newmont paid bribes to Vladimiro Montesinos, the notorious right-hand man of Peruvian president Alberto Fujimori, in order to get a favorable court settlement in a dispute with a French state-owned company that had partnered with Newmont (*Frontline* 2005).

Newmont, it seemed, was increasingly playing the role of villain in a movie script over which executives exercised little control. Peruvian campesinos began showing up at annual shareholder meetings to protest, and the CEO's elderly mother began asking her son what all the criticism in the papers was about.[30] Executives smirked a bit at the idea of the CEO being interrogated by his mother, but she clearly registered as a kind of moral barometer and proxy for a broader public. If seeing oneself through the eyes of others is a precondition for morality, those others may be distant, abstract, and mediated, or as near as loved ones whose questions—in bedrooms and over breakfast tables—demand that executives account for themselves and for the collective subject of the corporation.[31] Producing these accounts can, in turn, generate questions: Why did it take so long for me to hear about the accident? Why were we using that contractor, or those containers, to move mercury? What are our procedures for communicating and handling accidents, for transporting mercury, and for selecting contractors? Could this happen with another toxin or at one of our other mines?

Disasters, as Fortun's 2001 study of Bhopal shows, have no fixed beginning or end point and often recur and reverberate in different registers. They are like wounds that will not heal, as the 2012 deaths of mine protestors in Peru may have reminded some Newmont executives. At the same time, disasters like the *Exxon Valdez* spill can be mobilized as an "origins myth for internal reform and redemption" (Coll 2012:603). "Organizational encounters with risk," Hutter and Power (2005:24–25) write, "problematize the meaning and identity of organization itself, a process in which the possibility of rational management is placed in question, where promises of control and existing orders are broken down and challenged, where the distinction between experts and non-experts is no longer clear, and where the social permeability of organizations is increasingly apparent." For Hutter and Power (25) this is "the organization's encounter with itself. And in this self-encounter, ambivalence is usually tolerated only temporarily before it demands the restoration of order via re-organizing." For executives in Newmont's ameliorative disciplines, Choropampa was a piece of corporate history and identity that could be invoked for the project of enacting Newmont as a moral corporation. It was a tool for rethinking—and getting others to rethink—the nature, boundaries, interests, and responsibilities of the corporation.

Creating aha moments and converts did not simply generate a sense of affirmation for Anderson and Macdonald; it was also crucial to cultivating alliances and strengthening CSR's position within the corporation. But this strategy has its limits. To the extent that CSR depends on the personal values of company employees, it remains weak. Converts' commitment to and grasp of CSR might be incomplete, they might "backslide" or cave in to deep-seated older tendencies, and they might at any moment retire, die, or leave the company for positions elsewhere. It was impractical to try to individually convert all relevant Newmont employees, much less every contractor on whom the company relied. To cement the place of CSR within Newmont, Anderson and Macdonald sought instead to institutionalize it in corporate-wide management systems. The development of such systems was also crucial for enhancing CSR's legitimacy throughout the corporation—in the eyes of Newmont's CSR critics and proponents alike.

THE SOCIAL LICENSE TO OPERATE

Newmont's restructuring in the wake of the Normandy and Franco-Nevada acquisitions in 2002 served as the catalyst for rationalizing CSR initiatives. With this restructuring, senior management charted an official course for corporate transformation inspired in part by the program for change outlined in Jim Collins's *Good to Great: Why Some Companies Make the Leap . . . and Others Don't* (2001). The business best-seller struck a chord with CEO Wayne Murdy, who made it mandatory reading for managers at Newmont's mine sites around the world (although by the time it reached their bookshelves Murdy's enthusiasm had reportedly moved on to other titles).[32] *Good to Great* encourages companies to understand what they can do better than anyone else in the world and to engage in a disciplined pursuit of this objective. To forge a unified identity, Newmont developed a new logo, vision ("Creating Value with Every Ounce"), and set of values that Murdy encouraged employees to "live" and hold one another accountable to.[33] The values were printed on business cards and distributed to employees. While speaking at the CSR collegiate (and showing his support for the discipline with his very presence), a senior vice president of operations fished out his card from his wallet and read from it as if to demonstrate how these values ought to structure the thoughts of executives who encounter ethical dilemmas. Though Anderson later remarked on the awkward, staged quality of the gesture, he grasped its intent, which hewed to one of Collins's research team's findings: successful companies instill well-articulated and strongly held values in employees.[34]

Alongside this makeover of corporate image and values, Newmont was meant to undergo a corporate-wide "wave of transformation" titled the "Social License to Operate," defined as "the acceptance and belief by society, and specifically, our local communities, in the value creation of our activities, such that we are allowed to access and extract mineral resources" (Murdy n.d.). The social license concept underscores that the corporation must meet not only government regulations but also the expectations of various nongovernmental actors who may facilitate or impede mining. The notion was that Newmont continuously had to earn from local communities the social license to operate. The adoption of the Social License to Operate program, moreover, was supposed to usher in a wider transformation of corporate practice.[35]

The principal mechanism for ushering in this transformation was the Integrated Management System (IMS) for Health and Safety, Environment, and Community and External Relations (which focused most closely on CSR issues). A revised version of the system developed at Normandy, the IMS was a complex system for corporate-wide collection, management, and analysis of data on performance and compliance with social license standards. The system had multiple components. The first was a set of corporate-wide standards for Health and Safety, Environment, and CSR derived from risk management studies and voluntary corporate responsibility codes in which Newmont participates (described further in chapter 6). Along with these standards, Newmont implemented a process for assessing adherence by various units. This was known as the Five Star Integrated Assessment (see chapter 6).

Second, the IMS instituted a data acquisition program requiring that regional sites record social license data in data acquisition workbooks (following a standardized format on Excel spreadsheets) that were submitted to, and required signatures from, various executives in the corporate hierarchy (discipline-specific manager, site line manager, mine general manager, headquarters). At headquarters, executives could aggregate data from multiple mine sites, compare those to one another, and scrutinize their individual trajectories over time. Combining data from the Five Star Assessments and these data acquisition procedures, headquarters could also produce public reports on Newmont's performance in the domains of Health and Safety, Environment, and CSR (see chapter 6).

Third, the IMS introduced Rapid Response, a training program and set of procedures designed to enable corporate staff to use a "severity matrix" to assess safety, environment, or community "incidents" that might attract negative public scrutiny and to formulate the appropriate response, rapidly deploying mine site, regional, and corporate teams to mitigate and manage such incidents. In these rapid-response trainings, executives role-played various scenarios: in one, a miner has gone missing and is presumed to be underground; in another, which takes place in "a developing country," a car accident occurs near a mine, killing five villagers from the same family and injuring the mine site's general manager. Finally, the IMS included discipline-specific programs, such as equipment maintenance or leadership in the Health and Safety Department, reclamation in the Environment Department, and social impact assessment in CSR. CSR's discipline-specific programs included training in the use of Peter Sandman's licensed software and manual (Sandman 1993) for developing corporate plans to predict and manage "community outrage."

The Integrated Management System promised to constitute and legitimate the ameliorative disciplines by bringing new rigor to documentation and risk management practices. Speaking at the CSR collegiate, Macdonald said, "In order for our department to be taken seriously, we need management systems like every other part of the business. We need to document our work and deliver a consistent performance, like the safety department does." The turn to documentation also involves the production of numbers, recalling Porter's 1995 insight that quantitative reasoning is a way to shore up the power of a disciplinary field that is weak. Ahmed (2012:75) similarly notes how the use of data "aids the production of the competent self."

The various components of the Integrated Management System constituted an explicit attempt to hold the transnational corporation together as a unified and responsible entity, to turn it into something more than "a complex tangle of remotely related parts" (Fortun 2001:93). The difficulty and scale of this project underscores just how heterogeneous corporations are. The system was also meant to centralize knowledge, to render mine sites more legible and amenable to control from headquarters, as well as to foster better self-governance. Disputes over the Integrated Management System that appear here and in the final chapter reveal struggles over the place of CSR itself in the corporation. Ideally, the Integrated Management System would help install and expand the standards of the ameliorative disciplines across space (to mine sites in North America, South America, the Southern Pacific, Central Asia, and Africa), time (over the lifetime of a mine, from ore discovery to closure monitoring), and epistemic divides (encompassing all the mining disciplines). From the early stages of mine planning, for example, a closure standard was meant to ensure a local staff's proper anticipation of the problems and costs of mine closure. From a CSR perspective, this could serve as a safeguard against general managers' historical practice of slashing CSR budgets during closure in order to earn a bonus for completing the process under budget. The system was supposed to be transparent in both input and output—requiring no esoteric knowledge to operate nor any to interpret its findings.

The Integrated Management System was poised to strengthen the position of CSR within the corporate hierarchy insofar as it rendered explicit CSR's role in the management of risks and benefits. Not everyone was completely comfortable with the underlying logic of this. Anderson, for example, once remarked that he found it "offensive" when communities were described as risks. Macdonald, by contrast, was unruffled; for her, the link between CSR and risk was an open and unembarrassing fact, not some dark or problematic secret that should be kept hidden.[36] When I asked Macdonald how she performed social risk analysis, noting that it seemed to me a potentially vast and nebulous terrain, she replied that it was actually quite straightforward. Whereas the technical side of mining assesses "hazards," she explained, on the social side "we start by laying out the stakeholders, then the potential problems, like land and unemployment. Then we perform conventional risk analysis by estimating the scale and possible consequences."

The assumed link here between stakeholders and risk calls to mind Michael Power's analysis of the rise of a narrow and strategic concept of the stakeholder as any party that can influence, or be affected by, the advancement of a firm's objectives. The "normative operational task is to know ex ante who these stakeholders might be," and this "requires a broader view of the potential *boundaries* of a business or project" (2003b:152–53). While "stakeholders may not enter the corporation through the front door of legislative reform, they are entering via the back door of risk management and 'reputation assurance,'" altering in the process the boundaries between business and society (154). Instituting practices that account for stakeholders involves reframing business activities in order to internalize externalities (Callon 1998; Foster 2007:710).[37]

Morality, Michael Power (2003b:147) suggests, is increasingly processed through risk management systems because "the project of internalizing ideals of social and environmental responsibility is as much about embedding micro-systems and categories of information gathering as it is about appealing to individual morality or economic self-interest." A data acquisition worksheet soliciting information on each mine's community expenditures, for example, was designed to be comprehensive, capturing data on community projects that were not necessarily managed by community departments; operational and capital expenditures; outside funding sources, amounts, and purposes; and community investments that were direct and in-kind, with estimated monetary values given for the latter. A footnote clarified: "The word investment is now used to describe donations." The word *investment* was supposed to make explicit the expectation of "returns," in contrast to *donation,* which sounds charitable and altruistic. Macdonald showed me the template of a new form for recording such "investments," which solicited information on primary and secondary beneficiaries, as well as short- and long-term outcomes of the investment for both the company and recipients. She said in another conversation that she did not want to see any more "donations" but desired instead the "creation of partnerships that could be leveraged."

For adherents of the view that morality should be organizationally embedded, it makes better sense to pursue ethical outcomes by controlling the routines and habits of organizational life rather than the intentions of individual participants (Power 2003b). Corporate social responsibilities can be linked to corporate risks, with tools like risk maps serving as powerful symbols of this rational integration (151). In the rationalizing mode, CSR does not depend upon the moral fiber and good intentions of individual managers and staff, which therefore do not need to be constantly cultivated or displayed. What the corporation should display is its organizational standards. The emphasis falls on formal rationality oriented toward organizational goals, rather than on substantive rationality, concerned with critical, reasoned reflection (Jackall 1988:80; Weber 1978:85–86).

ROLLING TRANSFORMATION UP AND OUT

It is one thing to develop a new management system, and another to persuade people to comply with it. In corporate parlance, the wave of transformation called the "Social License to Operate" had to be "rolled up" to senior executives and "rolled out" to the salaried workforce; people had to develop a sense of "investment" and "ownership" in the system. It would reach hourly workers only in a more limited fashion. To demonstrate his backing of the Integrated Management System, Newmont's CEO sent out a memo (Murdy n.d.) to all employees exhorting them to participate in earning Newmont's social license and describing himself as "particularly excited to be a part of the Rapid

Response Program," so much so that he had "asked to be the first person at corporate headquarters" to be trained in it. Corporate headquarters required that each mine site establish a high-level "change council" responsible for aligning its existing data collection system with the new one, overseeing a gap analysis to check what was missing, and developing an action plan to fill those gaps.

Even at headquarters, support was not assured, despite the CEO's professed enthusiasm. Executives of the Health and Safety, Environment, and CSR Departments formed a "Five Star Shadow Steering Committee" devoted to expanding, refining, and promoting the system. The executives hoped to graduate from "shadow" to formal committee status, commanding a budget for their activities. Even they seemed daunted at times by the scale of their ambition for collecting knowledge and gaining control. "It's growing bigger and bigger, like *Ben-Hur*!" exclaimed an executive at one meeting, gaping in horror only half-feigned at a massive Excel spreadsheet illustrating the extension of Five Star Management Standards to early project phases. In another meeting over Newmont's public reports, communications and CSR executives expressed concern about their ability to handle the new influx of data sent in from mine sites around the world. The land manager, Alan, likened the transformation to "a wave: overwhelming!" Helen Macdonald assured fellow executives that the system was not so bad, and that once it was in place it would essentially "run itself."

Other executives expressed skepticism about the motives of top executives in organizing the transformation, explaining that having vastly overpaid for its acquisition of Normandy, incurring in the process reorganizational expenses (involving employee terminations, new trainings, alignment efforts, and legal costs), they were now trying to "add value" in the form of a new management system. One operations executive in Denver approved of it as a public relations maneuver, an instance of Newmont matching its "talk" to its "walk" (he thought Normandy excelled at public relations, but that Newmont was better at actual corporate responsibility performance). An Indonesian executive, by contrast, dismissed the "social license to operate" concept and program as an obvious attempt to "hypnotize" investors. Even those who felt enthusiasm for the Integrated Management System did not necessarily like the Social License to Operate concept attached to it. A veteran Environment executive in Denver said he hated the social license concept but "bought into" IMS because, with the takeovers, Newmont now operated so many mines that "I just can't keep track." Anderson called the social license concept "flimsy," while Macdonald conceded it had become "a dirty word." Having poured resources into attaching Newmont's name to the concept through the transformation program and a guidebook on the theme produced by the organization Business for Social Responsibility (BSR 2003),[38] the executives resigned themselves to living with it.

Attitudes toward the transformation were much more mixed at the mine sites. At the CSR collegiate, managers expressed joint concerns about the burden of documentation imposed on them by the Integrated Management System, arguing that this was eating up employee time. They also called the Five Star Assessment into question with their concerns that it was insufficiently independent. "We're measuring ourselves," one American manager complained. An Australian manager concurred, asking, "Shouldn't we be benchmarking ourselves against other companies?" Macdonald vigorously defended the system, arguing that it was "light-years ahead" of the systems other mining companies were using. She felt that the site managers were confusing the function of IMS—a profound reworking of management systems and the establishment of new monitoring regimes—with the "popularity contests" run by various institutions that ranked social and environmental performance but were essentially based on self-reporting.

Macdonald's response to the charge that the Five Star Assessment lacked independence was complex. On the one hand, she had been a chief architect of the system at Normandy. She initially developed the Integrated Management System with Kurt Hammerschmid, an environmental auditor in Australia, by translating the environmental management standards developed by the International Organization for Standardization (ISO 14001) into social standards that were later extended to safety. Deriving these standards from the ISO quality-control approach, Macdonald noted that they might have been extended to any discipline. The innovative part of the systems approach, from Macdonald's perspective, was the social standards that she developed along with several Australian consultants, one of whom was social auditor Richard Boele (see chapter 6). Macdonald's role in creating the Integrated Management System helps explain why she found it less intimidating than others did. From the moment of its adoption she enjoyed a level of comfort, familiarity, and dexterity with it that was unrivaled at Newmont. Her presence was probably crucial in adapting the system to its new corporate setting and in convincing various executives of its workability. On the other hand, in order to promote the system's universalizing character and credibility, she had to distance herself from her own authorial role and diminish its significance. When mine site managers identified her with the system even as they called its validity into question, she emphasized that it was designed to capture universal ethical codes, not her own beliefs and values.[39]

Though they demanded a system with universal legitimacy, mine site managers seemed to fault the Five Star Management Standards for being at odds with local obligations and commitments. At the Batu Hijau mine site, for example, External Relations had to commission an annual social impact assessment in order to meet Indonesian government requirements. After the Five Star Management Standards were introduced, Newmont's social auditors began evaluating these social impact assessments, finding them overpositive and questioning their quality and utility. Batu Hijau managers noted that they had chosen researchers from the University of Mataram to carry out the assessment as part of their commitment to hire (and cultivate) local experts rather than rely on more established and credentialed consultants from the top universities or NGOs in Java (who might have applied the latest research methods and offered more constructive critique).[40] The commitment to local expertise seemed at odds with the auditors' demands for optimal quality standards.

The Integrated Management System was meant to generate a more durable and positive "economy of care" (Prentice n.d.) for measuring, monitoring, and ameliorating mine effects on the environment, workers, and local communities. As conceptualized at headquarters, this economy of care reflects liberal, secular ideals and a generalized concern for the "human," or distant strangers (Boltanski 1999; Bornstein and Redfield 2011; Sontag 2003). The "structure of feeling" that energizes it is indifferent, indifference signaling here not neglect (Herzfeld 1992) but rather the abstraction and universalism that population-level intervention requires (Stevenson 2012:593).[41] Such indifference entails technologies of calculation, with the success or failure of care measured in infant mortality rates, maternal health outcomes, literacy rates, and so on. These systems are indifferent to precisely which infants live and die, or who learns to read and who does not. What matters is finding evidence of a trend consistent with universalizing understandings of development and progress, or an increase in a set of abstractly conceived goods: life, education, gender equality, health (Metzl and Kirkland 2010). Stasis or backsliding signals institutional failure and defeat. CSR executives are involved in a quest for metrics that render progress, stasis, and backsliding visible, and in the broader CSR industry a competitive marketplace exists for the production and sale of such metrics (Rajak 2011a:7; Shamir 2008).

Such abstract care is more easily managed from a distance. Studying the humanitarian organization Médecins Sans Frontières (Doctors Without Borders), anthropologist Peter Redfield (2012) formulated a useful distinction between the "light" volunteer expatriates of the global North, who maintain a passionate but general and abstract commitment to universal humanity, and the "heavy" national staff in the global South, who are subject to personalized and partisan claims related to "self-interest" and particular others (relatives, friends, those of the same ethnic group). For my purposes, it is important to consider how "lightness" and "heaviness" inhere in fluid circumstances and can shift across space and time: a single individual may be "heavier" (more subject to social expectations) in one setting and "lighter" in another. The executive at headquarters is "light" compared with the CSR manager at a mine site who must confront specific petitions and dilemmas. This reflects, in part, the distance of upper management from sites of operation. Jackall (1988:22) writes, "Because they are unfamiliar with—indeed deliberately distance themselves from—entangling details, corporate higher echelons tend to expect successful results without messy complications." Executives at corporate headquarters can see themselves as more progressive and enlightened than the managers and staff of mines in relation to various categories of subordinate actors with whom they do not actually interact, as, for example, when senior executives were perturbed by the "racism" of Newmont's Social Affairs staff in Peru.[42]

If bureaucracy itself "facilitates an abstract rather than a concrete view of problems," and "the abstractness of one's viewpoint increases as one ascends the hierarchy of an organization," the "austere, uncluttered perspective" of top executives results from their "social distance from the human consequences of [their] actions" (Jackall 1988:131). Yet it also reflects an ethical understanding among executives like Macdonald that their professional duty is to act "as receptor sites for standards evolving in wider environments. Indeed, they have something of an obligation to betray the interests in the local setting in preference for putatively universal principles" (Meyer 2010:13).

In a conversation with a new Social Development manager from Ghana who was visiting corporate headquarters, Macdonald laid out the new disciplinary terrain as she saw it:

First, I'll be driving stakeholder engagement. Decisions can't be made without consultation with local stakeholders. It's not just me saying that. It's in the corporate standards. Second, as much as possible, programs in social development must be about building capacity and changing expectations. This will enable the communities to sustain new economic expectations in the postclosure era. Anything that creates dependence and entails buying goodwill—I don't want to go near it. We want to be seen not as a pot of money but as a set of skills.

Macdonald asserted her authority ("I'll be driving stakeholder engagement"), aligned it with the interests of local stakeholders (without whose input decisions cannot be made), and then displaced her authority by insisting that the corporate standards were doing the talking. Her second point honed in on her understanding of social development, which has a meaning, appearance (capacity, expectations, and skills, not a pot of money), and temporal orientation (the postclosure era) that conform to a "sustainable" model and are articulated against a conventional patronage model. I explore the dynamic relation between the two models in greater detail in the next three chapters, which turn to the Sumbawan context. The sustainable model is easier for the "light" executive to articulate in Denver than it is for the "heavy" manager or Community Relations officer near a mine site to follow, even if the latter understands and values the rationale for the sustainable model. The interests of the corporation and its stakeholders look different depending on whether one is "light" and invested in producing universal, humanitarian benefits (e.g., improved human development indicators) or "heavy," more directly invested in social relations with, and subject to the claims of, those who stand to suffer or benefit from a mining project.

CONCLUSION

An American CSR manager for Newmont in Sumbawa told me he hated driving through a certain village. He always wanted to accelerate as he approached the home of the village head, who invariably recognized his car and tried to flag him down with some request. Having little choice but to listen and respond in such scenarios, the expatriate manager in Sumbawa is heavier than Macdonald in Denver, who argues that the company must not be enacted as a "pot of money." But two years after I finished my fieldwork in Denver, Anderson was given a new appointment in Ghana, and Macdonald followed a few years later. Moving from lightness to heaviness, neither followed the "natural" course of executive ascent in Denver. Newmont appointed new CSR executives at headquarters, but they reported lower down the "food chain," to an Environment executive under the new umbrella rubric of Environment and Social Responsibility, constituting a demotion of CSR as an independent discipline.

I am not sure what happened to the Warlpiri paintings I saw that first day in Newmont's headquarters. Newmont moved its headquarters offices, and the last time Macdonald visited in 2011 they were nowhere to be seen. The Integrated Management System that was part of Macdonald's legacy had been partly undone, too. The standards and policies remained in place, but the corporate-managed annual assessments of sites (examined in chapter 6) had been suspended and nothing was put in their place other than audits required to meet government standards. Some sites, such as Ghana, voluntarily continued the annual assessment process.[43]

Although Macdonald may have been particularly well suited to work at headquarters, she had had direct contact with "local stakeholders" before her time in Denver. Her remarks during a meeting with an Environment executive made it clear that the experience had stayed with her. In response to his characterization of the Australian mines inherited from Normandy as "challenged from an environmental perspective" (owing to their high sulfur dioxide emissions and the company's inability to track possible cyanide seepage from refilled mine pits), Macdonald recalled interacting with traditional owners (TOs): "It's really horrible taking TOs to a site like the refilled pits. The women will start crying and wailing for their country, going on for hours."

Ameliorative disciplines cannot prevent the destruction of land, the pollution, and the waste production that are inherent in all mining. At best, they can mitigate these effects and help ensure that those affected are compensated. At worst, they facilitate more mining and the destruction that goes with it by overcoming resistance and unlocking "high-value opportunities." In the end, there is little these disciplines can offer those who, like the wailing traditional owners, object in principle to what mining companies are doing. Like all CSR practitioners, Anderson and Macdonald were engaged in a project of reform, not revolution. They sought, for example, to enhance compliance with "best practices" for involuntary resettlement rather than to end the practice of involuntary resettlement itself. They worked to develop tools to help mining corporations better listen to and serve the interests of local communities rather than to help communities resist mining. They wanted to institute mechanisms to restrain police, military, and private security forces that guard mining operations and to instill human rights principles, rather than to do away with an industry that requires armed protection. They train their attention on some social responsibility issues and not others.[44]

As reformers, CSR executives fit into a much-maligned type: apologists for capitalism. In Žižek's words (2006), such apologists belong to the corps of "liberal communists" who keep global capitalism going, those who—we should have no illusions—stand as "*the* enemy of every true progressive struggle today," tinkering to fix all the "secondary malfunctions of the global system." Such typecasting allows us to articulate a critique, to pass judgment on CSR practitioners. But it also encourages us to caricature and dehumanize them, to treat them as the obedient foot soldiers of neoliberalism, simple structural effects rather than complex thinking subjects in their own right, and ones who are, moreover, often regarded in corporate headquarters as the enemy. Our efforts might therefore be productively channeled away from critiquing reform for its obviously reformist character, and toward thinking about its content and about how, in shifting contexts, this content is generated, structured, rolled out, and rolled back.

CHAPTER 2

"Pak Comrel Is Our Regent Whom We Respect"

Mine, State, and Development Responsibility

One rainy evening in January 2002, the head of the regency (*kabupaten*) of Sumbawa, an administrative territory then covering the western half of the island, paid a rare visit to the subdistrict where the Batu Hijau mine had been operating for around two years. Newmont's Community Relations manager, whom, following local conventions, I will call Pak Comrel (Mr. or Father Community Relations), introduced the regent (*bupati*) to an audience seated in gender-segregated rows of plastic chairs under a tent erected in the elementary school courtyard of Sekongkang Atas village. Pak Comrel and the regent exchanged the mutual praise that tends to accompany the public meeting of two important officials, and the regent gave a speech urging local people to seize the opportunities afforded by the mine to pursue local development. After the speech concluded and the floor was opened for questions, the head of an Islamic middle school in Tongo stood. Not mincing words, the *ustadz* (Islamic teacher) forcefully upbraided the prominent government official for neglecting the region.

> We once asked for and were promised wells. "Make a note of that," you said [to your assistant]. But, perhaps because you were otherwise preoccupied, it was forgotten. Perhaps, with this occasion, it might be recalled. Little people—please try to experience the fate of the little people. Perhaps once or twice you could travel via the government road, such that you wouldn't go via Newmont's road each time you come to Tongo, SP1, and SP2, and you would be a little more understanding toward the community aspirations. All the more so if you went to Tongo, in this [rainy] season, maybe taking a

regular car. Within two meters you'd be stuck. This is a recommendation from our community, first the road. We have not yet experienced independence [belum merdeka kita ini]. . . . Especially in the community of Tongo, if they see the development that's taking place, what stands out is Newmont. They see the health post [posyandu]. Who built that? Newmont. They look at the drains on the side of the road. Who built that? Newmont. Look at the school. Who built that? Newmont. "Well then, where's our government?" they ask. So Pak Comrel is our regent whom we respect.

The ustadz invoked Newmont's provisioning of local infrastructure less to praise the company than to condemn the state.[1] When the ustadz finished speaking, the regent sharply retorted that Newmont only engaged in development because the government required this of the company; he sought thereby to take credit on behalf of the government for Newmont's local development projects. The regent might have found the ustadz's words shockingly insolent while Soeharto was still in power; but in post-authoritarian Indonesia, government officials had grown accustomed to such public rebukes.

Situating the Batu Hijau mine in this context of national transformation, I use the term post-authoritarian to signal that dramatic changes took place after Soeharto fell in 1998: electoral reforms, decentralization of fiscal and governing authority to administrative regencies, increased press freedom, and more general freedom of expression for those marginalized, repressed, and targeted for violence under Soeharto's New Order regime (e.g., organized labor, Chinese Indonesians, West Papuans, and Acehnese; see Heryanto and Hadiz 2005; Kirksey 2012; Kusno 2010; Sai 2006, 2010; Strassler 2010). At the same time, the legacy of Soeharto hung heavily over Indonesia—in the limited social acknowledgment and redress of historical violence, the forms of ongoing violence both extraordinary and mundane, and the decentralization of predatory dynamics.

Against this backdrop, in southwest Sumbawa the village residents, company officials, and government officials tried to work out their roles, rights, and responsibilities in relation to one another. In Newmont, this task fell primarily upon the External Relations Department, which was headed by a senior manager and former U.S. Army colonel and military attaché. The departments under External Relations included Government Relations, led by a manager from Lombok; Security, led by an Australian manager; Community Relations, led by a Sumbawan manager; and Community Development, led by a manager with a hybrid Indonesian and North American identity. This chapter and the two that follow focus on competing but copresent modes of enacting the company as an agent of development, which I characterize as patronage and sustainable development (and which loosely correspond to Helen Macdonald's distinction, in the previous chapter, between local views of the company as a "pot of money" and a "set of skills"). The Community Relations Department and its manager, Pak Comrel, were more closely tied to the patronage model, whereas the Community Development Department and its manager, Ibu Comdev (again, following local conventions, I use this title, which translates to Mrs. or Mother Community Development), were more closely associated with the sustainable development model. These models have distinct implications for the role of the state.

In the largesse-distributing-patron model of the corporation, the company acts as a surrogate state providing jobs, tangible welfare, and infrastructure to local communities. Central to this book's argument is a critique of the corporation as liberal subject (self-contained, metaphysically prior, coherent in identity and intentions), so I should stress here that whatever the casual connotations of the term *patronage,* the model presented in these pages does not presuppose a one-way flow of rational munificence and agency; rather it is coproduced by local residents through requests, demonstrations, and threatened mine shutdowns, and by Newmont employees such as Pak Comrel and his all-Sumbawan staff who selectively supported local demands. Pak Comrel made keeping the mine running the primary motto and mission of his department. He and other managers and senior staff in the External Relations Department routinely invoked the estimate that any work stoppage would cost the mine $1 million per day. The significance of this figure lies less in its necessarily fluctuating relationship to a financial truth than in how External Relations managers used it to elevate their own status within the company and lay claim to bureaucratic resources.[2] The capital-intensive mine was meant to operate nonstop to pay down debts and accumulate profits under conditions of political uncertainty and exposure to changing commodity prices. To the extent that patron-client relations cultivated through local development projects were requisite to nonstop mine operations, patronage—like kinship, affect, sentiment, and other social ties and gifting practices—must be seen as constitutive of capitalism rather than as residual in or opposed to it (Cattelino 2011; Dunn 2004; Granovetter 1985; Rajak 2011a; Shever 2008; Yanagisako 2002). Patron-client relations foster attached, entangled, and symbiotic conceptions of corporate-community relations.

From a financial perspective, however, other Newmont executives asked why the firm should behave as a surrogate state while also paying to the Indonesian government—which Indonesians and expatriates alike widely saw as corrupt—millions in taxes and royalties that ostensibly were meant to enhance the welfare of the Indonesian people. (This perspective indeed prompted a managerial experiment, one I explore in further detail in this chapter: publicly disclosing mine revenues paid to the state in order to pressure the government to act more responsibly.) For proponents of "sustainable development" such as Ibu Comdev, the "conventional development" (patronage) model was morally problematic as well. It involved enriching elites while ignoring the marginalized, focusing on buildings while overlooking what actually goes on inside of them, and fostering local dependence on a company that would depart once the ore body was exhausted, with the infrastructure left behind destined to slowly crumble after the company departed if neither the government nor the local people "invested" in or took "ownership" of it. From this perspective, the proper goal of a mining firm—the approach that best serves the interests of the community as well as the firm—should therefore be to foster a state attached to and responsible for local people and to keep the company itself detached from such entanglements.

Talk of sustainable development in the mining industry—which by definition extracts nonrenewable resources, generating large-scale destruction and pollution in the process—sounds patently oxymoronic (LeCain 2009). Stuart Kirsch (2010b) traces the evolution of this oxymoron as a function of progressive redefinition of the term *sustainability* since the early 1970s, when it referred primarily to environmental preservation. In the early 1980s, the term began appearing as a modifier of *development* (89), and in 1987 the UN established the Brundtland Commission, which defined "sustainable development" as "development that meets the needs of the present without compromising the ability of future generations to meet their own needs."[3] The 1992 UN Conference on Environment and Development in Rio de Janeiro endorsed a growth-centered version of sustainable development comprising three pillars: economic, environmental, and social. While ideally all three pillars should be present in development efforts, they are discursively detachable. CSR experts in mining often give the economic pillar primacy, thinking in terms of economic growth and a capitalist future. Social and environmental aspects remain significant, however, and confer positive connotations on the idea of sustainability. Given these connotations, I wish to stress that I use "sustainable development" here not as an analytic category (that is, I am not making a positive judgment that CSR experts in mining actually achieve "sustainable development") but rather as an actor's category or category of practice (Brubaker and Cooper 2000), an emic term that occupies an important place in the mainstream CSR vocabulary. What I refer to as the "sustainable development" model might also be labeled the "neoliberal model," insofar as it embraces programs that cost less than those of the patronage model and transfers responsibility for community welfare from the company to community members themselves or the state. I use the actor's category "sustainable" rather than the critical analytic category "neoliberal," because the latter flattens out the more complex ethical understandings and motivations (including those related to social justice and the environment) that animate actors promoting sustainable development through mining capitalism. Moreover, *neoliberal* is often conflated with reduction and retreat of the state and privatization of state functions; sustainable development proponents at Newmont sought, by contrast, an enlarged role for the state with regard to local citizens' welfare.

In their review of the anthropology of mining, Ballard and Banks (2003) note with approval that anthropologists are increasingly attentive to the internal complexity of communities, states, and corporations. This chapter shows that community, state, and corporation are not only internally complex but also often (by no means always) inextricable from each other in their interests, responsibilities, and material operations (see also Golub 2014). Dynamic practices of attachment and detachment (Cross 2011), entanglement and disentanglement (Appel 2012b), connection and disconnection (Gardner 2012), coproduce communities, states, and corporations, simultaneously producing complex ethical dilemmas.

FORMING PT NEWMONT NUSA TENGGARA

Natural resources, according to Indonesia's constitution, are to be maintained under the powers of the state and used "to the greatest benefit of the people." Constitutionally prevented from directly selling off mineral assets to foreign investors, President Soeharto, with the help of a subsidiary of the U.S. firm Freeport, developed a workaround to this constitutional provision during his first year in office: the Indonesian government would contract private firms to conduct mining exploration, construction, and production. Soeharto and Freeport signed the first "Contract of Work" in 1967. That same year, Soeharto's New Order regime passed the Basic Mining Law (UU no. 11/1967) and the Basic Forestry Law (UU no. 5/1967), which expanded state power to regulate natural resources. Under these laws, around 70 percent of Indonesia was designated as "forest" land, to be administered by the state without regard for complex local land uses and property rights systems (McCarthy 2011:96–97; Peluso and Vandergeest 2001). Throughout the New Order period (1966–98), Soeharto used exclusive land concessions for natural resource extraction to underwrite what scholars have described as his "patronage machine" (McCarthy 2011:97) or "franchise system" (McLeod 2011).[4]

Newmont's existence in Soeharto-era Indonesia hinged on a partnership with Jusuf Merukh, who served as a deputy minister of agriculture under Soeharto and later became chairman of the Indonesian Democratic Party in the House of Representatives. An important political ally and client of Soeharto, Merukh controlled exploration rights to multiple regions of Indonesia with good mineral prospects and was often described as the king of mining concessions. In 1986, President Soeharto signed a Contract of Work with PT Newmont Pacific Nusantara, Newmont Mining Corporation's Indonesian subsidiary. The contract granted the company broad exploration rights across the islands of Lombok and Sumbawa, and exploration work eventually led to the Batu Hijau mine. The mine is under Newmont Mining Corporation's operational control and appears to many in Indonesia as a symbol of either U.S. imperialism or U.S. enterprise. As a subsidiary, it conforms to Indonesian law and is at a sometimes strategic remove from corporate headquarters. At the time my research began, Batu Hijau was owned by several partners under the parent company PT Newmont Nusa Tenggara (PT NNT).[5] Newmont Mining Corporation owned 45 percent of NNT through PT Newmont Pacific Nusantara, the Japanese Sumitomo Corporation owned 35 percent through its affiliate Nusa Tenggara Mining Corporation, and Jusuf Merukh's Indonesian firm PT Pukuafu Indah held the remaining 20 percent.

Although Newmont could not have operated in Indonesia without ties to Merukh and his company, some Newmont officials were at pains to distance Newmont from its business partner. A senior vice president in Denver described Merukh to me as a "shady type" who was "as crooked as a dog's hind leg."[6] The executive claimed that although Newmont had fronted the money for Pukuafu Indah's 20 percent stake in both Batu Hijau and Newmont's Minahasa Raya mine in Sulawesi, Merukh was unsatisfied and regularly approached the company with demands as urgent as they were disparate: "The Muslims are after me in Lombok; I need $350,000 to build them a new mosque immediately or else they'll kill me," "Newmont needs to buy the governor a Land Rover," and so on. The executive told me the official response from Newmont was always: "Let these parties come to us themselves with their requests, and we'll see," but the direct requests never came. PT Pukuafu Indah and Newmont were embroiled in multiple lawsuits against one another and, in 2011, sought international arbitration from courts in Singapore (Tan 2011). Such lawsuits are, of course, mainly battles over money, efforts to seek an outside authority to adjudicate a dispute. But they also perform the important work of separating out and isolating individual actors that otherwise would be subsumed under the larger collective actor, PT NNT.[7]

By labeling Merukh a crook and suing his company, American executives sought to enact Newmont as a clean and law-abiding company in opposition to the firm's greedy and corrupt Indonesian partner. Yet Newmont was and is an Indonesian state contractor; and Jusuf Merukh, with his close connections to the Indonesian state, not only owned 20 percent of the mine but also was essential to its existence. No clear and distinct boundary separated the American company from the Indonesian state.

EXPLORATION

Newmont began exploring for minerals on Lombok and Sumbawa in 1987, a year after signing its Contract of Work. In 1990, Newmont geologists discovered a green creek, indicating copper, in southwest Sumbawa, and in 1991 the company began drilling in the region. Newmont's early exploration teams encountered small, sleepy lowland villages and hamlets connected to one another by rough roads.[8] The rhythm of daily life in southwest Sumbawa was dominated by the demands of the Islamic faith and the agricultural cycle. While the agrarian economy centered on paddy production, village residents made use of a strikingly heterogeneous natural resource base, cultivating a variety of crops in fields, gardens, and orchards as well as engaging in animal husbandry, fishing, and marine and forest foraging.[9] Most lived in traditional elevated houses (*rumah panggung*). Recalling how idyllic it seemed back in 1994, one Australian contractor remembered saying to another expatriate as they walked along a beautiful beach: "You're really going to put a dirty copper mine here?"

Despite its rugged tropical beauty, southwest Sumbawa was marked by rural poverty and government neglect. Access to formal education and health care was extremely limited, and life precarious, all too vulnerable to droughts and treatable diseases. A national survey in 2004 ranked West Nusa Tenggara Province, encompassing the islands of Lombok and Sumbawa, at or near the bottom among Indonesian provinces across a broad range of social indicators. Out of thirty provinces, the survey ranked West Nusa Tenggara at twenty-six for poverty, twenty-nine for gender development, and thirty for human development (BPS, BAPPE-NAS, UNDP 2004). The province had high infant mortality, short life expectancy, low rates of high school graduation, and a lack of public health professionals, infrastructure, and access to clean water. Historically, southwest Sumbawa was among the least developed parts of the province. Farthest from the regency capital of Sumbawa Besar, the mining district fell at the dead end of a road connecting largely coastal villages. In state development discourse, southwest Sumbawan villages were isolated (*terasing*) and left behind (*tertinggal*), having never reached the ideal trajectory toward rural modernity.

Between 1991 and 1996, Newmont employed an average of 110 local workers in exploration and preconstruction activities (PT NNT 1996:F-5). The majority came from the village of Tongo-Sejorong.[10] Former exploration workers spoke to me of their early work for the company with bitter nostalgia. Hired as day laborers, many nonetheless worked for several years, carrying core samples through the forest, felling trees with chainsaws, digging trenches, and generally assisting with surveying and bore-drilling work. With only rudimentary infrastructure in place,[11] Newmont relied heavily on these workers. The pay was meager,[12] and much of the work was physically arduous; but relations with supervisors were personal, and former workers told me they felt proud of the future they were building. They imagined themselves to be an integral part of the coming mine, with the company and local community potentially crafting a joint future rather than separate trajectories. Far from an idle longing, Sumbawans' nostalgia for their early encounters with Newmont form part of a critique of subsequent Newmont practices that pushed local people away from the company and framed their "dependence" upon the mine as a problem (on nostalgia as critique, see Boyer 2006).

LAND DISPOSSESSION AND MINE CONSTRUCTION

Before mine construction began in early 1997, Newmont had to conduct feasibility studies, gain necessary government permits, secure

approval from the board of directors in Denver, conduct an environmental impact assessment, and buy land. Several American Newmont
managers told me that during this time both President Soeharto and his
daughter Tutut tried to get their "fingers in the pie" of the project (e.g.,
claiming a 10 percent share) by holding up the necessary permits. They
spoke with pride of how Newmont had held its ground against these
shakedown attempts, allowing the project to be delayed by several years
and threatening to simply walk away from it, noting that Batu Hijau
was projected to be "a marginal mine" in terms of potential profit anyway. According to this narrative, Newmont secured its permits without
paying significant bribes, holding at bay the most powerful and corrupt
Indonesians.

During this preconstruction phase, new company representatives and
consultants arrived in southwest Sumbawa, as did land speculators and
other fortune seekers. "Team Nine" (Tim Sembilan), charged with
overseeing "land acquisition" (pembebasan tanah), included various
members of the state apparatus: village heads, the subdistrict head, soldiers, and police. Because the actual mine was located in the mountains
northeast of Tongo-Sejorong, Newmont did not directly displace people from their homes, instead buying mostly agricultural or swidden
land for mine infrastructure (e.g., the mine's Townsite and road corri-
dors).[13] Tongo-Sejorong residents who lost access to forest resources
closer to the mine itself, including huts where they engaged in palm
sugar production (figure 4), were not formally compensated, because
Newmont officials adhered to a government determination that local
residents lacked the status of indigenous people with customary rights.

The preconstruction period unleashed a frenzy of land sales, seizures,
expropriations, and exchanges; ignited conflicts among families; and
created enduring rancor toward village heads who had negotiated with
the company and helped some, but not others, formalize their land
claims. Years later, scattered parcels of land remained derelict or half
developed, still mired in competing claims. Some Sumbawans told me
outright it was better not to talk about what happened during this era.
Others who had brokered land sales spoke with regret and remorse.
One former village head admitted to me that he had failed to support
Tongo-Sejorong residents who lost forestland, but excused his inaction
by pointing out that it had, after all, been the Soeharto era, so he had
not had much choice.

The construction period was also a time of fantasy, when people
could imagine possible futures that bore only a vague resemblance to

FIGURE 4. A Tongo-Sejorong resident making palm sugar in the forest in a *jalit*, a structure built especially for this purpose. Photo by author.

the eventual realities of village life near a large mine.[14] Pak Ramli, a contractor from Taliwang, told me that during that time he had taken community leaders (*tokoh-tokoh masyarakat*) to Senggigi, a resort area on Lombok island. He showed them hotels, bars, and prostitutes and told them that Maluk village could be just like Senggigi. He urged them to "socialize" (*sosialisasi*) the mine in villages—that is, to promote it to local community members and convince them it was in their best interest. He recalled Newmont representatives screening footage from mine sites in Nevada showing workers welding and performing other mine-related tasks. "This is what we thought it would be like," he said. "Then Newmont built the mine so fast, we didn't know anyone anymore." Variations of this complaint were common; other residents recalled promises made by early Newmont staff who later departed, only to be replaced by staff who were harder to reach and who did not feel bound by the promises of their predecessors.

Newmont contracted Fluor Daniel, a Texas-based engineering construction firm, to build the mine facilities. Construction began in 1997,

coinciding with a deepening of the Indonesian economic crisis that cata-
lyzed social protest and culminated a year later in the toppling of Soeharto and the New Order regime (1966–98). During the period of the
mine's construction, which lasted close to three years (early 1997 until
late 1999), the region became a bustling hub of economic activity.
While the rest of the country suffered crippling poverty and unemployment, the southwest Sumbawan economy was booming. Fluor Daniel
and other subcontractors employed up to twenty thousand Indonesian
workers to build the $1.9-billion mine, which was at the time the
world's largest start-up operation.

Maluk village became a key site of construction activity and was
dubbed "Little Texas" for its bars, brothels, and Wild West atmosphere. A doctor who set up his practice there during construction told
me he had had to duck out of the crossfire of a police shootout, and an
elderly imam recalled withdrawing into his home in the evenings, never
knowing when he might be shocked in the streets by a sprawling drunk
or some stabbing incident.

Overwhelmed at first by the more experienced workers and savvy
and well-capitalized entrepreneurs who arrived from outside the region,
local residents soon came to participate in the construction economy.
Many let their remaining agricultural land lie fallow or leased it out to
migrants from Java or Lombok. Men found work as laborers for Newmont's construction contractors, while women worked for its catering
contractor, PT Prasmanindo Boga Utama, which employed twelve hundred workers during construction. Local residents also set up small
kiosks,[15] and some rented out rooms to workers, while those who could
afford it built blocks of simple one-room accommodations (*kos*) to rent
to workers. Job seekers sought to rent from village heads, hoping that
the connection might lead to employment.

A local elite came to prominence during this period, seeking to channel
mine-related economic opportunities to fellow village residents and their
own fledgling businesses, which supplied transportation, housing, temporary labor crews, construction materials, and food. The economic success
and political power of this predominantly male elite were tightly linked,
and they blurred the boundaries between community, state, and corporation. Many were already part of the *aparat desa,* the village governing
apparatus (e.g., village head, secretary, representative councilperson), or
otherwise held the coveted status of civil servant.[16] In Indonesia, civil
servants enjoy job security, pensions, and formal fringe benefits but are
poorly paid. Most nonetheless pay hefty bribes for their positions, with

the expectation that these will yield lucrative opportunities through which they will recover their initial outlay (McLeod 2011:58). As members of the civil service and village governing apparatus, many local elites retained the conservative outlook promoted by the Soeharto regime, which began with the 1965–66 anticommunist massacres and purging of teachers and other civil servants with leftist sympathies (Cribb 1990).

In the *reformasi* era that followed the regime's collapse, elites were still conventionally referred to as community leaders, or tokoh-tokoh masyarakat, but were frequently denounced in public and private for enriching themselves while claiming to work on behalf of the community. They came under the most intense public pressure for failing to distribute their gains widely enough. Family members, friends, and other would-be clients all viewed public office as a source of valuable development goods and pressed officeholders for access to Newmont's largesse. Rumors constantly circulated about how village heads distributed development goods; in one case a woman accused a village head of charging villagers for rice that was meant to be distributed free to poor people (*beras miskin*). (In fact, he was charging the appropriate subsidized government rate, but selling the rice to his clients, Newmont employees among them, rather than the poorest village residents.) Some women tried to deter their husbands from assuming public office, knowing the suspicion their families would confront. One told me she would not allow her husband to take a position that would have put him in charge of irrigation water distribution, because she did not want to hear his name besmirched (*menjelekkan namanya*) by neighbors. In one popular play on words, village heads (*kepala desa*) were described as leaders of sin (*kepala dosa*).

Village residents expected their leaders to play a mediating role similar to the one described by anthropologist Peter Goethals. Based on fieldwork conducted in a highland village near Sumbawa Besar in the 1950s, Goethals (1961:38, 46, 48, 75–76) claimed that village residents chose their leaders for their perceived ability to both maintain beneficial connections to the outside world and protect the village from that world by mediating and softening external demands. In the early postcolonial period, villagers favored younger men for these positions owing to their literacy in the new national language and perceived ability to cope with changes.[17] In the context of a mining megaproject, however, the power this mediating role conferred on village leaders was extraordinary, easily abused, and frequently called into question (similarly, see Turner 1995).

In the mine construction economy of southwest Sumbawa, for example, local elites organized villagers to demonstrate against large Newmont contractors such as Fluor Daniel to extract jobs, wage and benefit increases for those already working, and contracts for small businesses they themselves had a share in. Demonstrators sometimes created roadblocks by burning tires, and at times they stripped drivers of their keys and threatened them with machetes. As tools for extracting economic concessions, the demonstrations were effective. Contractors stood to reap significant monetary rewards for completing contracts ahead of scheduled deadlines and, for this reason, usually acceded to at least some of the demonstrators' demands. As we will see, local elites organizing demonstrations to force Newmont or its contractors to hire local workers and contractors continued well after construction ended; this indeed became the familiar pattern of an ongoing symbiotic relationship.

MINE OPERATIONS AND THE END OF THE CONSTRUCTION BOOM

The Batu Hijau mine began operating in late 1999, and commercial production proper began in early 2000. No longer a work-in-progress involving nearly all local villagers in this or that aspect of construction, Newmont suddenly seemed detached and self-sufficient: a self-contained, self-constituting, and self-governing subject. It had its own power plant, sewage system, garbage dump site, roads, helicopters (and later an amphibious plane), boat, port, docks (both in Sumbawa and on the island of Lombok), fire station, health clinic, mess halls, commissary stocked with Indonesian and imported goods, and award-winning international school. One needed a badge to enter Newmont's Townsite or the company's administrative and port facilities in Benete, and vehicles that passed through Newmont's gates had to be registered and annually inspected. Newmont had its own private security guards from the Jakarta-based contractor 911 and an Indonesian police mobile-brigade unit. Trucks regularly watered down Newmont roads to control dust, and speed limits were enforced.

Examining an expatriate-only enclave of a major American oil company in Equatorial Guinea, Hannah Appel (2012b:451) argues that the firm's separation from its local setting is a work-intensive project that allows firms to abdicate responsibility for those beyond the walls and creates a ring fence as a prophylactic against "corruption" from outside. She found that those within the enclave walls saw themselves as upholding the "discursive and procedural regimes of the global, the standard, the compliant, the objective, to be differentiated from the arbitrary, the personalistic, the incomprehensibly local beyond their walls." I part ways with her regarding the discreteness and agency of companies that she describes as "creating and policing" a line of distinction between themselves and the government, or of an industry that "works furiously to perform a distinction between itself and that which is 'outside' its walls, despite their utter intercalation" (2012b:445). If corporations, as I have been arguing, are not metaphysically prior subjects but instead are always provisionally and materially enacted through ongoing struggles (Fleming and Spicer 2007), then the vision of them planning and implementing the effect of their separation from corrupt or immiserated places and persons is revealed as a mirage. Corporate entanglement and disentanglement from the state and local communities is a more dialectical and contested product of human activities. The material qualities of offshore oil deposits and extraction technologies allow for extreme enclaving practices (Appel 2012a; Ferguson 2005; Rogers 2012). In contrast to the strict segregation of expatriate and national lives Appel found in the context she examines, at Newmont's Townsite the majority of residents were nationals rather than expatriates.

When the mine began operating, Newmont no longer needed 18,000 unskilled construction workers; instead, the mine required only around 4,000 workers, most of them highly skilled. Competition for these jobs was fierce, and would-be workers demonstrated frequently. Those who had sold land to Newmont demonstrated for jobs, claiming that they had been promised actual positions and not simply preferential hiring. Caving in to these demands, Batu Hijau agreed to hire one member of each documented ex-landowner's family who successfully passed the company's physical and mental tests. This resurrected simmering disputes over land sales. And given the low levels of health and formal education in the region, it was not always easy—even for those recognized as landowners—to place a family member among the ranks of Newmont employees.[18] Would-be workers were excluded for common medical conditions such as eardrums ruptured by childhood infections, or testing positive for (often latent) tuberculosis. Many resented what they saw as overstringent requirements for entry; after all, there had been no comparable requirements for early exploration and construction work. Facing further protests, Newmont adopted a more accommodating stance and lowered some of its requirements, while investing more in building up the company training department and programs to compensate for the lack of formal job skills. In 2002, 28 percent of Batu Hijau's 3,942 employees were categorized as *lokal-lokal* (local-local), meaning they came from the districts of Sekongkang and Jereweh, and a further 31 percent were *lokal*, defined as from the province of West Nusa Tenggara, which includes the islands of Lombok and Sumbawa. One senior manager claimed the mine hired 600 more workers than initially estimated, 300 of whom were really unnecessary. At Batu Hijau and Denver, I heard managers describe overhiring as indicative of an inability to withstand community pressure.

As at many large mines around the world, mine workers at Batu Hijau were organized into an "ethnotechnical hierarchy" (Hecht 2002:699) correlating class, ethnicity, and job description. Expatriates constituted around 3 percent of the workforce and occupied the top managerial and technical positions at the mine, followed in descending order by nationals, lokals, and lokal-lokals, with the latter generally occupying the least skilled and lowest paid positions. The vast majority of lokal-lokals held positions classified as "nonstaff," working as drivers and manual laborers in mine operations, infrastructure, maintenance, transportation, and environmental reclamation. In 2002, of 701 Batu Hijau workers from Jereweh and Sekongkang, only 9 (1.3 percent) were "staff" workers. The hierarchy among employees was evident in everything from the letters on their badges and the mess halls they ate in to the health and housing benefits they received and even the order in which electricity was restored to their living quarters after a power outage.[19] In villages, those with Newmont jobs were accorded prestige and regarded with envy, but once inside Batu Hijau's gates they were made keenly aware of their subordinate position within the company hierarchy. One driver told me he always opted for the boxed lunch, even though it was not as good as a mess hall meal, because he hated to be seen walking into or out of the mess hall reserved for "nonstaff."

For landowner families who failed to get a member hired at Batu Hijau, the company offered a choice of "packets" that were supposed to allow the landowner to pursue an alternative livelihood. The packets that landowners could choose from, each valued at roughly 15 million rupiah, included four water buffalo and plowing instruments; a mechanized hand tractor; a water pump; a farm-supply-store setup; a kiosk setup; tools for a mechanic's workshop; or a motorbike and accoutrements for becoming a motorbike taxi driver (*ojek*). Most opted for the last, but few actually went on to become ojeks.

This failed attempt to engage local people in alternative occupations—to attach them to new economic livelihoods and thereby detach them from the mine—points to a larger problem faced by mine managers. Recruiting and maintaining an army of proletarian workers, once a major challenge for large mines back when they were more labor-intensive and involved more underground rather than open-pit operations (Ferguson 1999; Nash [1979] 1993), had been relatively easy for Newmont during the construction phase. Once production had begun, however, a major challenge was keeping the workforce small while ensuring that the now redundant "surplus population" that was "superfluous to capital's requirements for its own valorization" did not turn against Newmont (Marx 1992:782). Michael Denning (2010) notes that, like the peasant class from which they often emerge, those condemned to not being exploited, to "wageless life," occupy an ambivalent position in scholarship on class conflict; they are a volatile group—potential supporters of revolutionary or reactionary movements (Gramsci [1926] 1994; Holmes 1989; Marx 1964; Paxton 1997). Denied jobs in the mine, the wageless demanded indirect wages, and Newmont was forced to at least partly comply.

DEVELOPMENT AS PATRONAGE

Having built up assets and inventory during construction that became superfluous once the mine was complete, many local contractors found themselves saddled with large debts as the mine began operating. They began organizing unemployed men to demonstrate and demand public infrastructure projects that would generate contracts for themselves and work for the unemployed. Responding to these demands, Newmont paid—in piecemeal and indirect fashion—wages to the wageless, containing their feared revolutionary potential and enacting Newmont as a patron of local development. Newmont hired local contractors for a range of public infrastructure construction projects, including markets, schools, health outposts for midwives (*posyandu*), new clinics (*puskesmas*), and new village and district government offices. Newmont paid for the construction and repair of roads, ditches, irrigation systems, and public toilets, and for the provision of potable water. Many of these projects had small plaques affixed to them or nearby signage bearing the company logo and the words "bantuan (assistance of) PT Newmont Nusa Tenggara." These constituted small reminders, for those who needed them, that Newmont was providing much of the basic infrastructure supporting everyday life in villages.

The ustadz's remarks to the regent that opened this chapter point to Newmont's success, and the state's failure, to act as a patron in this domain. An elementary school teacher echoed this sentiment when he told the regent, "Our government is Newmont" (*pemerintah kita Newmont*). While the regent claimed that Newmont built local infrastructure only because the government required it to do so, village residents generally saw things differently. As a village head and local contractor told me, there might be government requirements to this effect on paper, but it was demonstrations by village residents that had actually "opened the faucet" of Newmont jobs and development projects. From this perspective, Newmont's patronage strategy was coproduced by village residents and by Newmont staff who were either sympathetic to village demands or felt the company had little choice but to comply with them.

The enactment of Newmont as a largesse-distributing patron producing tangible infrastructure fit well with the dominant understanding of "development" under Soeharto's rule. Soeharto had promoted it as the paramount national project, styling himself the generous but stern Father of Development (Bapak Pembangunan) capable of mobilizing vast quantities of capital and labor toward the creation of impressive physical infrastructure (Heryanto 1988, 1995; Robison 1986; Shiraishi 1997). The Indonesian word for "development," *pembangunan*, also means "building," reinforcing the association between development and construction (van Klinken and Aspinall 2011). Like the rural Lao residents discussed by Holly High (2009:75, 83), southwest Sumbawans apprehended "largesse and provisioning as the hallmarks of a successful [development] project and legitimate state," even though they were more accustomed to actually experiencing the "non-provision of services, or rare and inadequate provisioning." Like other rural subjects who experience citizenship as neglect, southwest Sumbawans express a desire for more and better access to state services and for more thorough incorporation into the Indonesian state (High 2009:85–86; Li 2007). With the opening of the mine, however, southwest Sumbawans could bring their demands for this form of development to Newmont instead of a distant and unresponsive state.

As an agent of development, Newmont differed in important respects from the state and NGOs. The financial and political authority of the state is at a geographic remove from southwest Sumbawa, and even the provincial and regency governments are relatively distant. It is difficult for residents of isolated villages to hold distant government officials accountable for their actions (or inaction). On the rare occasion of a visit from such an official, however, they gamely lobbied for better roads, medical supplies, electricity, teachers, and so on, as we saw at the beginning of this chapter. When members of the national People's Representative Council (Dewan Perwakilan Rakyat) visited southwest Sumbawa in 2003, local residents blockaded Newmont's road to force the parliamentarians to use public roads. The blockaders, including a village head who theatrically exposed his chest and announced that someone would have to shoot him before he would allow the distinguished guests to travel on Newmont's road, wanted the Jakarta officials to experience for themselves the visceral—and sometimes frightening—sensation of driving on the local government roads.[20]

If important government officials are typically too far away to be held accountable, multilateral organizations and NGOs are hard to pin down for a different reason: they usually run projects for fixed periods. Extensions may be granted, but donors expect projects eventually to be declared successes or failures, allowing them to move on to other parts and programs. With $1.9 billion sunk into the infrastructure for a mine with an initially estimated twenty-year-year lifespan, Newmont was not leaving the region anytime soon. Because local people perceived the firm as more responsive than the state (Hill and Irvine 1993; Laidlaw 2010:162), they held the former responsible for development projects that might legitimately be seen as the responsibility of the latter. In order for what Gillian Hart (2001:650) calls the "little d" development of capitalism to proceed, then, Newmont had to become an agent of "big D" Development. Big D Development is a continuation of the "post–second world war project of intervention in the 'third world' that emerged in the context of decolonization and the cold war," and which, as Cooper and Packard (1997:9) put it, held out to decolonizing countries the "liberating possibility" that "modern life and improved living standards could be open to all."

As the key mechanism for opening Newmont's faucet, demonstrations merit closer examination. Newmont managers and local residents alike tended to take a cynical view of them, but the cynicism of each had a somewhat different focus. Managers saw demonstrations as inauthentic expressions of popular will. Demonstrations, from their perspective, typically had an overt pretext (e.g., demands for a market or dam) and the appearance of popular support, beneath which lurked the real instigator and motive (e.g., a contractor wanting to build a market). They saw hidden motives everywhere. Apparent expressions of religious concern, for example, were sometimes actually motivated by business interests (e.g., a brothel burning was a means of eliminating a competitor). When a mysterious fire damaged the wooden bridge on the Sekong-

FIGURE 5. Workers building irrigation channels in a Newmont-sponsored community infrastructure project generate contracts for local businesses and temporary wage-labor opportunities for the unemployed. Photo by author.

kang-Tongo road, for example, Pak Wahid, a Community Development officer, told me it had been the work of a contractor who had been angling for Newmont to fund a new concrete bridge.

Local residents also saw demonstrations as having been provoked (*provokasi*) and engineered (*rekayasa*) by local elites, but their concern lay less with the authenticity of the demonstration and its rationale than with how its fruits were distributed. Most believed that benefits resulting from demonstrations, such as wage labor opportunities (figure 5), should be widely shared, and that too often they were not. One man likened the experience of demonstrating to pushing a car that will not start. Once it gets going, the driver leaves you tired and sweaty in a cloud of dust and exhaust fumes, not even turning to give a wave of thanks. Another man explained, "When you demonstrate, you might not eat for the whole day while standing around in the blistering heat. Then the demonstration leaders get invited into an air-conditioned office for a talk. They get jobs and the rest eat shit. Those up front get jobs, while those in the back are just bait, victims."

Many blamed the resulting unfair distribution of gains from Newmont on fellow village residents and on those most visible at the interface between mine and village: the mostly Sumbawan officers from Newmont's Community Relations and Community Development Departments, as well as officers from Newmont's foundation Yayasan Olat Parigi. In Peter Redfield's terms (2012), discussed in the previous chapter, blame fell on those who were "heavy," enmeshed in local relations and obligations, rather than on those who were "light," who cared about local people in a more distant, indifferent, and impartial fashion. Extending this logic further, some local residents claimed that Newmont, or Newmont's expatriates, were essentially good and not responsible for how Sumbawans distributed Newmont's largesse among themselves.

One resident insisted that Newmont's upper levels were clean (*bersih*), but that Newmont's "hands and feet," like the Community Relations officer in villages, were dirty (*kaki-tangan yang kotor*). A neighbor similarly told me that Newmont's white people (*bule*, also meaning "albino") were very honest (*paling jujur*), that it was the black-skinned whites (*bule hitam*), Newmont's Indonesian employees, who were the problem. A preacher (*khatib*) similarly complained about how Newmont's aid was always distributed to those who were already wealthy, such as schoolteachers, while the poor got nothing—the opposite of what Islamic principles dictate. Newmont, he explained, wanted to give thanks with the people (*Newmont ingin bersedekah sama masyarakat*); the calamity (*musibah*) that instead transpired was that "those who are already full will not stop eating." Citing the cast-off Newmont mattresses that Community Relations officers gave to village heads to distribute to the poor, he accused the village heads of instead selling or hoarding them or giving them to those who did not need them. He suggested bitterly that it would be better to throw the mattresses in a heap and burn them than to keep enriching the wealthy.

Though some village residents saw particular expatriates or Newmont as a whole as corrupt, the view that Newmont had good intentions at its core served an important function for those who subscribed to it. Like the expatriate narrative of Indonesian corruption and American virtue, it helped create the effect of a Newmont standing above and separate from the forms of exchange that are actually constitutive of the corporation and capitalism more broadly. If one could only get unmediated access to this "good" Newmont, to its heart rather than its hands and feet, then distribution of development goods would be equitable. Concerns over how village elites might be benefiting from Newmont's soiled mattresses or snack contracts could draw attention away from larger questions of corruption and equitable distribution arising from the mine.[21] Even so, these concerns were always embedded within a larger moral expectation of generosity from Newmont.

Senior Newmont officials, meanwhile, viewed as acts of extortion the threats of local elites to shut down the mine if they were refused construction contracts. From this perspective, such actions are part of a wider political phenomenon in post-Soeharto Indonesia: the rise of a *"preman* state," or the "gangsterization" of local politics, in which semi-criminal gangs, vigilantes, bureaucrats, and business elites that had incubated under Soeharto's rule reconstituted themselves and seized power (Barker 1999; Hadiz 2010; Sidel 2004). Such practices cannot be written off as asocial criminality. Southwest Sumbawan elites' actions were underwritten by a sense of moral entitlement to a better life based on the presence of Newmont in their territory and the assistance they had extended to the company over the years.

Village elites, in fact, used the threat of violence to protect as well as to menace Newmont. They pacified the wageless with temporary day labor jobs, policed local villages for threats against the mine, shared intelligence with Newmont officials on potential foes, and orchestrated public demonstrations of local support and protection. After militant Muslim groups threatened to kidnap Batu Hijau's U.S. expatriates in the wake of the U.S. invasion of Afghanistan, for example, elite-organized groups hung banners over public buildings declaring, "The people of Jereweh reject the sweeping [targeted search and expulsion] of foreigners around the mine." They also preempted a planned port blockade by fishermen from Lombok who claimed Newmont's tailings were destroying fish stocks, attacked visiting environmental and social justice activists (see chapter 5), and expelled a labor union attempting to make inroads in the mine and catering workforces.[22] Newmont officials gratefully accepted such protection and even interpreted it as evidence of success in their relationship-building efforts. Some told me with pride that in defending Newmont, villagers showed that they regarded it as "part of the community." Elites deployed violence both for and against the mine with the express purpose of extorting wealth and protecting its source (Schneider and Schneider 2003:31–33). In the process, they set out to entangle the mine in long-term relations of reciprocity, to enact it as a powerful yet vulnerable patron. At the same time, through revenue transparency and other efforts to involve the government in southwest Sumbawan development projects, Newmont officials were trying to devise ways to detach the local community from the company and attach it instead to the regency government.

REVENUE TRANSPARENCY

In a press release sent out by PT NNT's Media Relations Department soon after the Batu Hijau mine began commercial production in 2000, President Director Tom Enos proclaimed, "Based on our commitment to be transparent, the royalty payment reporting will be one of our ongoing efforts to provide the public with accurate information on the development of the company's operations, particularly in its financial obligations." Announcing that the company had deposited $2,518,567.10 into the coffers of the Finance Department of the Republic of Indonesia based on production levels in the first quarter of 2000, the press release clarified that annually the government would earn roughly $10.5 million in revenues from royalties, $70 million from operational taxes, and $6.2 million from income tax levied on employees (*Sumbawa Ekspres* 2000).[23] By publicizing these revenue payments, mine managers reasoned, they would make it more difficult for corrupt officials in Jakarta to pocket the money, and they would provide local government officials with a powerful tool for demanding their fair share. Local citizens, so the theory went, would then turn to local government representatives, rather than Newmont, with their requests for infrastructure and jobs. Newmont executives in Denver watched this novel experiment with keen interest; no other mine under Newmont's operational control had previously attempted to use revenue transparency to foster more responsible government.

Gary MacDonald, Newmont's Social Development executive in Denver at the time, presented the case at a meeting in Berlin—"Corruption Issues in the Mining and Minerals Sector"—that was part of the broader, industry-sponsored Mining, Minerals and Sustainable Development Project, overseen by the U.K.-based International Institute for Environment and Development. At the Berlin meeting, which was cohosted by a prominent NGO, Transparency International, MacDonald described how revenue transparency had exposed the fact that money was not returning to the local community, starting with the central government's failure to pay the province its share. Rather than stimulating government responsibility, however, revenue disclosures had "had the effect of shifting the focus onto the company itself": they generated "a perception of Newmont as a rich 'cash cow,' and demands for large payments rocketed from other groups, such as the military" (IIED and WBCSD 2002:4). The regional autonomy laws passed in 1999 by the administration of President Bacharuddin Jusuf Habibie, Soeharto's vice president and successor, promised to further complicate matters. Under these new laws, regencies in extractive industry zones were to enjoy far greater shares of royalty and tax revenues than historically had been the case.[24] The meeting report summarized the effect of the laws: "Instead of increasing the local share of mineral revenues and investments, corrupt practices were 'dispersed to the local level'" (4).

The events unfolding around Batu Hijau did nothing to derail the broader revenue transparency movement gathering steam at that point. The movement gained a central place in CSR agendas in the extractive industry in 2002, when hundreds of NGOs banded together to launch the Publish What You Pay campaign and U.K. prime minister Tony Blair launched the Extractive Industry Transparency Initiative at the UN World Summit on Sustainable Development in Johannesburg. The intuition driving this movement was that transparency could break the "resource curse," the so-called paradox of plenty in which citizens of resource-rich countries are condemned to sluggish economic growth, poor human development, corruption, authoritarianism, and violent conflict.[25] Back in Berlin, responding to the Denver executive's presentation of Newmont's policy at Batu Hijau, other conference attendees suggested the company's transparency project was naively unilateral, foregoing, in its attempt to be an honest actor, the sine qua non of successful anticorruption efforts, coalition-building (4).

In Sumbawa, meanwhile, both village residents and Newmont officials continued to express frustration with the Sumbawa Besar–based regency government. When the regent received the first revenue checks from Batu Hijau, he supposedly went on a shopping spree, buying a fleet of new Toyota Kijang vehicles for each district head (*kepala camat*) in the regency—except for those in Sekongkang and Jereweh, the mining districts, which he saw as Newmont's responsibility. Similarly, the regency provided garbage trucks for each district except Sekongkang and Jereweh. The regency government had long neglected Sekongkang and Jereweh in the first place because they were so far away. When Newmont held a training for cooperatives and invited officials from the regency cooperative agency to speak, some trainees voiced their suspicion that cooperatives closer to Sumbawa Besar were the only ones receiving regency support. One woman remarked, "Those who are far from the fire don't get any smoke" (*kalau yang jauh dari api tidak kena*

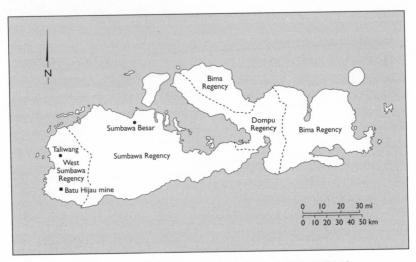

MAP 3. The new administrative regency of West Sumbawa. Credit: Bill Nelson.

asap). The official insisted this was untrue and complained that he and other civil servants were very poorly paid compared to Newmont workers. When the regent's top assistant came to Sekongkang to meet with villagers, he openly advised them in a mixture of Indonesian and Sumbawan that if they had unmet needs, then they could easily make their requests to the wealthy company (*Nyaman tu ngeneng, perusahan peno pipus. Tu lo kekurangan, tu ngeneng*). The head of the regional infrastructure agency complained that the community had become "difficult" because whatever the government did for them was no longer good enough; Newmont built better infrastructure. Through their words, actions, or inaction, Sumbawa Besar regency officials indicated that the mining districts were clients of Newmont, not of the regency government.

Popular frustration with the Sumbawa Besar–based regency, fanned by Newmont's revenue transparency disclosures, led to a movement for a new administrative regency that would control regency-level mine revenues. Pak Kyai Haji Zulkifli, the leader of a *pondok pesantren* (Islamic religious school) in Taliwang, headed the Committee for the Formation of West Sumbawa Regency. The movement had been in the works for a while when he took it over, but he quickly gained the support and signatures of key local government officials. Various maps of the potential regency had been debated; he ensured that the smallest one would prevail (see map 3). As in other extractive-industry regions, the proliferation of new administrative territories reflected attempts to prioritize some while excluding and deprioritizing others (Bubandt 2006).

While waiting for a ferry from Lombok to Sumbawa, I ran into the *kyai* and his family, who gave me a lift as far as Taliwang. He told me that he would be writing to Newmont shortly to request support for the movement. Indeed, Newmont managers soon spoke of pressure from Zulkifli to provide financial support. A senior American executive told me Newmont had refused to contribute directly to the movement for a new regency but had paid for a visit by members of the national People's Representative Council, an expensive undertaking that included business class airfare, bus and car rentals, local resort accommodations, and lavish meals for the Jakarta politicians and their entourages. An official in Newmont's Government Relations department told me he thought these expenses were inappropriate. He blamed Pak Comrel for insisting Newmont pay for the junket and speculated that the head of Community Relations might be envisioning himself as future regent. As he shared his concerns with me, the official received a call from Pak Comrel; the large trees in front of the regent's office in Sumbawa Besar were disrupting electrical lines, so Newmont needed to send a vehicle with a ladder to trim them. The officer promised to make the necessary arrangements. I was struck by the contrast between village residents' struggles to get corporate or government attention and the regent's palpable—and apparently warranted—air of easy entitlement to Newmont's resources.[26]

One of Newmont's public relations consultants told me it was clear that Zulkifli and his supporters were paying enormous bribes, mortgaging away future mine revenues in order to expedite the approval process for the formation of the new regency. He wondered where Zulkifli got the cash to pay these bribes and to whom he might be beholden. One American executive had previously described Zulkifli to me as "a very bad boy" who had "orchestrated" large and sometimes violent demonstrations against the company in the mine's early days. In an attempt to win him over, Newmont had hired his wife in the External Relations Department. Discussing this maneuver, one American consultant winced, dryly adding that it had yielded "unsatisfactory results." Through a close family member, Zulkifli was already part of Newmont.

After the new regency of West Sumbawa came into being in late 2003, Zulkifli indeed became the new regent. Many residents had been skeptical of the benefits it would bring to the mining districts in the first place; those with high hopes were disappointed. Although the new regency's support for the subdistricts closest to the mine did increase relative to historic levels, they remained among the least-served by government infrastructure. Those in Tongo-Sejorong and transmigrant villages closest to the mine still lacked government-provided electricity years after the new regency's formation. It did not take long for the usual accusations of corruption to emerge—this time against the new regency. Meanwhile, in Taliwang, the new regency capital, which lies at some remove from the mine, lucrative land sales and construction contracts flourished as spectacular new buildings were erected to house the new government offices. Newmont's annual community development budget (discussed in the next chapter) underwent no appreciable declines, suggesting that the company was no more successful in shifting the financial burden of development to the new regency than to its predecessor.

Zulkifli was on a new footing in negotiations with Newmont, and the regency he led actually came to own part of PT NNT. Article 24 of Newmont's 1986 Contract of Work contained provisions requiring the international owners of PT NNT to gradually divest shares to Indonesian owners, so that by 2010 Indonesian investors would hold at least a 51 percent share of the company. As discussed earlier, PT Pukuafu Indah originally owned 20 percent of PT NNT. Jusuf Merukh sought control of the remaining 31 percent, which would have made his company the majority owner. Eager to avoid this, however, Newmont officials insisted that the Indonesian government was first in line for the remaining 31 percent. Newmont's divestment efforts proved messy and protracted, with the company offering shares to government buyers in 2006 and 2007 but failing to close a deal.[27]

The issue came to a head in 2008, when the Indonesian government threatened to cancel its contract with Newmont. This led to international arbitration proceedings, and Newmont called into question the integrity of its government negotiating partners—West Nusa Tenggara Province, West Sumbawa Regency, and Sumbawa Regency—after discovering that negotiators for the three were serving as fronts for Bumi Resources, which was controlled by the family of Aburizal Bakrie. Bakrie was then Indonesia's welfare minister and later became the leader of Golkar, Soeharto's party. In the end, Newmont and Sumitomo went to court in Jakarta and then Singapore to fight off PT Pukuafu Indah's claims, ultimately selling 24 percent of their PT NNT shares to Multi Daerah Bersaing, a joint venture of the provincial and regency governments, and to Multicapital, a unit of the Bakrie Group's Bumi

Resources. In 2011, the West Sumbawa Regency government threatened to shut down the mine unless Newmont sold the final 7 percent to the regency. Newmont's workers' union threatened demonstrations against the regency. In the end, Pusat Investasi Pemerintah, a sovereign wealth fund under Indonesia's Ministry of Finance, purchased the remaining shares.

ENGAGING THE STATE

While the revenue transparency initiative and the movement for a new regency were unfolding, the manager of Newmont's Community Development Department and her staff were engaged in their own efforts to make the regency government in Sumbawa Besar more responsive and responsible. For them to successfully enact Newmont as an agent of sustainable development, the cooperation of state officials willing and able to commit resources was crucial if rarely forthcoming. Ibu Comdev emerged as an important and controversial figure in this struggle, gaining both admirers and detractors in the process. Her approach was shaped by her background. Born to Javanese parents and raised in North America, Ibu Comdev had worked for various international development agencies before taking a job at a prestigious management consulting firm. There, she missed development work and grew tired of "making the superwealthy wealthier." When she was recruited by Newmont, she at first resisted the idea of working for a firm she automatically classified as an "evil mining corporation." She told me how, during an early visit, she had smiled and expressed polite interest in the programs but had been privately shocked by what she saw as an amateurish and ad hoc approach to community development. She told me she ended up taking the Newmont job over several other "clean job offers" because it seemed like the most intriguing challenge, and that she came to Sumbawa not to support the mine but "to have access to a lot of money to help people." At the same time, reducing and reallocating Newmont's community development budget was part of her agenda. Sustainable programs should, from her perspective, be modest rather than flashy. At the Freeport mine in West Papua, she said, "everything is Cadillac, but I want a Chevy."[28]

Ibu Comdev conceived of herself as an "inside provocateur," identifying with Debra Meyerson's characterization (2001) of the "practical" or "tempered radical." She also considered herself a "patriot" for returning to work in Indonesia. There was much she disliked about post-Soeharto

Indonesia: the replication of conservative social hierarchies, "stunted" political thinking, the "jilbabization" (increased veiling practices) of women, and the stifling of individualism. Watching rows of uniformed students conduct their marching exercises along the road in preparation for the August 17 National Independence Day celebrations while trucks rumbled past, perilously close to their small bodies, Ibu Comdev sighed and remarked, "This is how they make people like robots in Indonesia." Her personal "will to improve" (Li 2007) appeared relentless, manifesting itself not only in large and ambitious programs but also in the most mundane of interactions. These she seized upon as occasions to upgrade and professionalize even the most innocent of bystanders, down to the wait staff in restaurants, who found themselves urged to hone their marketing skills by making recommendations from the menu.

Ibu Comdev told me that when she had joined Newmont, the company had been "rightly criticized" for not working with the government. Newmont would charge ahead building schools and clinics and, upon completion of such projects, would organize ribbon-cutting ceremonies attended by mine and government officials. More than just conventional photo opportunities, these were meant to signal a transfer of authority, marking the moment at which Newmont took credit for the new construction while relinquishing to the government future responsibility for cleaning and maintaining the building and stocking it with well-trained civil servants (e.g., teachers, administrative staff, nurses, doctors) and supplies (e.g., furniture, medical equipment, medicine). The government met only some of these new responsibilities. Ibu Comdev sought to change this, embedding in her department's long-range strategic plans the goal of getting the government to assume ownership of—and maintenance responsibility for—all Newmont- and government-built facilities by 2010, and full government responsibility for all infrastructure in the region by 2020 (PT NNT 2002).

Ibu Comdev tied this strategic plan to a budget. One day she told me she needed to go to the regency capital of Sumbawa Besar to present a detailed version of it to regency officials. "I know what they really want," she said. "The budget figures for each sector. But I'm going to make them work for it." She planned to run the officials through Newmont's entire twenty-year plan, going over each sector, starting with the least interesting. "At the end of each sector, in small print, will be the figure they were hoping for." She believed regional government officials never engaged in such long-term planning, and wanted to demonstrate to them how it works.

To increase government participation in local development projects, Ibu Comdev was willing to countenance direct payment of officials. At times when the regency budget did not allow for agriculture or fisheries field staff in Sekongkang and Jereweh, Newmont paid for them, a practice Ibu Comdev said allowed her to "demand quality" because she could send back unsatisfactory officials and request replacements. Indeed, I heard one Javanese Community Development officer upbraid a fisheries official, whose position Newmont had subsidized, after his failure to support farmers when they had questions and when their fish died. Ibu Comdev resolved to send the man back. But it was often hard to get field staff to stay in the first place; southwest Sumbawa has a long-standing reputation as a place of exile (*tempat buang*) for civil servants who have fallen into disfavor or disgrace elsewhere. Local residents often lamented how hard it was to keep government officials content (*dipetahkan*),[29] and one woman even suggested they be forced to marry locally.

Runaway or absentee regency field staff proved a significant stumbling block to the "revolutionary" collaboration Ibu Comdev sought on a project to construct a weir and irrigation channels that would serve the transmigrant villages SP1 and SP2. With Ibu Comdev, Pak Wahid, and Adam, an Australian technical advisor, I visited the weir in its final stages of construction. Adam went around the project studying the work that remained, such as smoothing out cracks and burying wires. In addition to insisting that Newmont would finish the project on time and under budget ("even if only by one rupiah"), he wanted high quality, saying they "had to do this perfectly so it will be self-maintaining once it starts running"—as if perfect technology could compensate for imperfect government. Rather than contracting a third party to carry out the project, Newmont and the regency Infrastructure Department (Prasarana Wilayah, or Praswil) agreed to manage it entirely themselves (*swakelola*). A few days earlier, stories in the local press had quoted an official from the regency Infrastructure Department claiming that Newmont did not know how to run a self-managed project and should have supplied tactical funds (*dana taktis*). Irritated by these statements, Ibu Comdev said government officials were the ones out of their league, being both inexperienced in "dealing with locals, especially Sumbawans who get quite angry," and unaccustomed to "NNT's very disciplined working style." She said she had given the government officials wiggle room to write miscellaneous costs into their budget—some "slush funds" or "funny money," in her translation of the official's "tactical funds"—but the costs had to be "accounted for in a transparent fashion" (e.g., described under accepted categories such as "transportation" and "honoraria"). She heard the government official's media statements as a complaint about the insufficiency of these slush funds, an interpretation seemingly borne out by the sudden alleged sickness and swift departure of four technical staff members provided by the government. (One of them contracted malaria, leaving for what Ibu Comdev saw as a genuine complaint, but then failed to return.)

On another occasion in 2002, I accompanied Ibu Comdev to a development coordination meeting (*rapat koordinasi pembangunan,* or *rapkorbang*) with the government in Sumbawa Besar, the regency capital before the formation of the West Sumbawa Regency. I arrived at the gates of Batu Hijau's Townsite before 6 A.M., but the assigned driver for the day was late, annoying Ibu Comdev, who felt that arriving on time was important for setting an example for government officials. Later on, with the driver swerving around and crashing through deep potholes, Ibu Comdev told me how the previous year the senior manager of External Relations had called her, demanding that Community Development fix the road immediately because Benete residents were threatening to demonstrate. She had insisted they wait for the government to repair the road and had exerted pressure on the government to do so for several months. The government finally repaired the road but, she noted ruefully, did such a shoddy job that it was already falling apart again. She had also insisted, once again against the strident objections of her superior, that Newmont get the government to contribute to a potable water project in Sekongkang by paying for pipes. "Again," she sighed, "it's taken a long time."[30]

When we finally arrived in Sumbawa Besar, the head of the Agency for Regional Development (Badan Perencanaan Pembangunan Daerah, Bappeda)—after a lengthy preamble about whether he should address Ibu Comdev as Bu or Mbak (she was unmarried)—opened the meeting by acknowledging that people had come to believe (*percaya*) in Newmont more than in the government. This was changing, he added, citing the government's contribution of 750 million rupiah for the water pipes for the potable water project in Sekongkang. Yet the rest of the meeting reinforced the notion that Newmont, and not the government, should serve as patron for the mining districts. The farming agency official, for example, said that of thirty water pumps to be distributed, only two were for the mining area, and of seventy field staff, only two were for the region. When one of Ibu Comdev's staff pointed out that Newmont had built a health clinic, but that the government had yet to supply it with water and electricity, the kepala bappeda responded, "We are too spoiled now by technology. We're born naked. Civil servants like me used to use bicycles and bathe in the rivers. If civil servants have a sense of moral responsibility, they can withstand anything." Water and electricity, of course, have important uses in a medical facility besides enhancing the comfort of doctors and nurses. Representatives from the tourism, education, and infrastructure agencies were similarly unforthcoming.[31]

When the infrastructure agency official said they had received only one request for infrastructure from Sekongkang and Jereweh, he drew an immediate and outraged response from an NGO member who was attending the meeting to seek Newmont and government assistance for an agroforesty project: "It is a complete lie [*sangat bohong*] that we have never asked for this development assistance. We often make demands upon the village and district government, as well as in written and oral form to the regent. This is coming purely from the community. We are thrown back and forth [*saling melempar*] between Newmont and the government." He was not alone in expressing the latter sentiment. The head of an agricultural cooperative similarly complained that they were "like ping-pong balls": "When we go to Newmont for assistance, the company says, 'Go to the regency government; we've already paid our royalties.' Then the regency sends us back to Newmont." Appel (2012b:444) describes a similar situation in Equatorial Guinea, in which an American oil company and African state each pass on responsibility to the "demonized other," either the evil oil company that steals resources and saps state sovereignty, or the corrupt state that robs bread from the mouths of citizens. This leaves ordinary citizens caught in "an impasse of mutual abdication" of responsibility.

Making more durable relations between the regional government and local citizens (relations literally cemented in infrastructure) was seen as a virtue by those (like Ibu Comdev) seeking to enact Newmont as an agent of sustainable development. But waiting for the government was not without moral costs. One village resident and worker in Newmont's Transportation Department told me NNT stands for *nunggu-nunggu terus,* "perpetual waiting." Pak Sukri, a Community Development staff member who embraced the sustainable development model, told me he nevertheless felt occasional frustration with Newmont's priorities. A father with children getting an elite education in Newmont's International School, he looked at the Sekongkang middle school and said he could not fathom why his department was not doing more to improve it. For him, Newmont's inaction was directly implicated in producing another lost generation. "Why," he asked, "do we spend so much on the irrigation system when the education system is in shambles?" Answering his own question, he said, "When people get hungry they get angry, so irrigation gets priority. But when they're stupid it's not really a problem for mine security." Responsive government may be in the long-term interest of local people, he felt, but well-educated children were too. The patronage model, in its haste to "open the faucet" of development and generate visible results, did not impose this waiting. Largely coproduced by village elites and supportive Newmont staff, the patronage model tended to engage teachers in business deals with the company, rather than focusing on the quality of their training and support or their basic pay as civil servants.

CONCLUSION

Thomas Hobbes (1886:152) famously declared corporations to be like "lesser commonwealths in the bowels of a greater, like worms in the entrails of a natural man." Parasite metaphors seem particularly apt for the complex interrelations between PT NNT and the state. In successful parasitism, it can be difficult to determine which is the host and which the parasite. Indeed, which is which is very much a matter of one's perspective. It can also be difficult to determine where one organism ends and another begins; rather, they must be viewed as mutually constituting one another and a broader ecology of relations. So, too, with Newmont and the state. It is true that each draws sustenance from the other. However, even to put it in such terms takes for granted the distinctness of each. In fact, as we have seen, the two are inextricably linked. Many government officials were, and are, simultaneously Newmont contractors, sometimes even employees. Regency, provincial, and national governments are now all part owners of the company. Even those local government officials not working for Newmont were often able to transform corporate practice by manipulating the local ecology of relations. And Newmont officials, too, transformed local government in profound ways.

CHAPTER 3

"My Job Would Be Far Easier If Locals Were Already Capitalists"

Incubating Enterprise and Patronage

When I interviewed Mark, a manager for Batu Hijau's catering contractor, PT Prasmanindo Boga Utama (PBU), he launched straight into the numbers and statistics he figured I was after. PBU employed 619 people to staff Batu Hijau's mess halls and commissary. Five were expats, 80 percent were lokal, from the province of Nusa Tenggara Barat (which includes the islands of Lombok and Sumbawa), and 40 percent were lokal-lokal, defined as from the region stretching from the town of Taliwang to the village of SP2. One hundred ninety-eight women, 421 men; 401 single, 218 married. The numbers were up to date, Mark assured me, because PBU reported them on a weekly basis to Newmont, which reported them to the government's Human Resources Division. Under the contract it signed with Newmont, PBU was obliged to hire local people and to gradually increase the proportion of Indonesian managers. In 2002 when we met, Indonesians occupied 20 percent of the senior managerial positions. "After Newmont, PBU is the largest employer of local people, which is something to be proud of," Mark claimed, then qualified the boast by adding, "but it's largely because almost all our staff is unskilled."

Having covered the employment figures, Mark moved on to procurement. He pulled out some pie charts and explained that the bulk of PBU's supplies consisted of food. In 2001, PBU sourced 18 percent of its supplies from Mataram, the provincial capital on the neighboring island of Lombok, and 21 percent lokal-lokally. Sixty-one percent of PBU's supplies originated from outside Nusa Tenggara Barat Province. In 2002, over 40 percent came from the province. Mark offered an example: "We get all of our rice from NTB. That's fifty thousand to sixty thousand kilos of rice per month, for nine thousand meals a day, 90 percent of which are for Indonesians." PBU was spending 3.5 billion rupiah per month on supplies, which meant almost U.S.$1 million per month, in the local economy.

Local hiring and procurement was a mandatory, contractual obligation stemming from the Contract of Work that Newmont signed with President Soeharto in 1986, which required that the company try to hire locally and "make maximum use of Indonesian subcontractors," giving "first preference . . . to landowners in and other people originating from the area of the Enterprise" (CoW 1986:61). Newmont passed this expectation on to its own subcontractors. Local hiring and purchasing could be calculated, quantified, and visually represented in various ways (meals served, kilograms of rice consumed, workforce percentages, and so on). Such quantifications and visual expressions of data were part of mandatory reporting requirements, but they also served a public relations function. Mark cast local hiring and purchasing as positive achievements, "something to be proud of," and the more the better. But his words and charts showed that local residents were, for the most part, getting the opportunities at the bottom of the barrel: the less skilled, lower-paying jobs and the least-lucrative supply contracts.

I asked Mark to describe how relations with local businesses worked. His frank response reflects the jaded perspective of the hard-boiled resource-extraction expatriate.

> *Mark:* Purchasing locally is a nightmare. It's better now. Now at least they know what delivery orders, purchase orders, and invoices are. And we have a contractual obligation to achieve a certain quality standard that we can use when there's a problem. . . . But everyone wants a contract with PBU, and as these multiply it leads to additional administrative costs. Some people force contracts on us at exorbitant rates, but these only last for two months. People who give us good offers get two-year contracts.
>
> *MW:* How do they force their supplies on you?
>
> *Mark:* They demonstrate; they create a roadblock and don't let PBU trucks pass. But we have a contingency plan. We order supplies from Surabaya on boats. So when they realize targeting PBU isn't working, they expand to [the mail carrier] DHL, NNT, everyone. Then we have to give the one person behind it a contract. Back in February the village head of X and his thugs held three of our guys hostage in the DPR [People's Representa-

tive Council] building in Sumbawa Besar after PBU terminated his bus contract and gave [a rival bus company] the tender. Fortunately [the External Relations manager] was there right then, meeting with the *kapolres* [regent police chief]. He had the helicopter and all. He took care of it. Now PBU has a lawsuit against those who orchestrated the hostage taking. The problem with local people is they lack longevity in their thinking.

Mark went on to describe how local businesses would deliberately "bungle" orders—for example, arriving with twice the quantity actually ordered and insisting the company buy the whole lot. He said they also put pressure on PBU for not running halal mess halls around the time that tender offers were due.

Mark's exasperated depiction of local people suggests that local hiring and business relations, portrayed in brochures and presentations as unambiguously positive, involved elaborate threats, plots, intrigue, and brinksmanship. He also implied that local businesspeople might outgrow this behavior, both by assimilating proper business norms and mastering technicalities (such as what a purchase order is and how to fill it out properly) and by a kind of natural selection, with those who flout protocols being denied the plum contracts.

I question such implicit evolutionism, exploring the possibility that the dynamics Mark deplores may be more deep-seated, constitutive, and resilient than his words suggest. One Javanese labor activist told me that PBU itself was an unsavory company formed by a politically powerful Soeharto-era navy admiral, adding that the contractor had leverage over Newmont. At any rate, it is essential to understand the broader historical and geographic context out of which local business dynamics emerge. This entails an examination of how Batu Hijau's community programs have worked to foster and channel—as well as to suppress—patronage dynamics. I also develop a view of local residents as actors engaged with (and not simply acted upon by) CSR business development initiatives. Their perspectives on what the corporation is and what it owes them shape Newmont's community development plans and programs, creating flows of money, materials, ideas, and persons across mine boundaries. These flows and dynamics are constitutive of rather than marginal to everyday mine operations; thuggish though they may seem, they are not, per Mark's suggestion, evidence of entrepreneurial inexperience or immaturity in relationship building. They challenge us to make sense of how corporate managers variously claim integration with, distance from, and control over their trading partners—to understand how and why they essay rhetorically and materially to gather them in and hold them at a distance.

The contradictory patronage and sustainable development models that I discussed in the previous chapter also structure corporate responsibility programs that promote local economic enterprise. In the patronage model, Newmont, by providing a range of business projects to village political elites who are also contractors, cultivates allies who defend the mine and quell potential protests by the unemployed. In contrast, from the sustainable development perspective, mines are by definition ephemeral as markets, so development projects should focus on cultivating flexible entrepreneurs capable of selling primarily to external markets. Sustainable development proponents view mine-village interdependence as negative and myopic. In this view, detachment is both a guide to conduct and a positive ethic in corporate-community relations (Cross 2011). The sustainability model is "neoliberal" insofar as it supports rendering locals responsible for their own economic fate and assigns a positive value to a small mine budget for local development.

Newmont's business programs vacillate between the sustainability and the patronage models. This is not because a metaphysical Newmont is calibrating with precision what dose of neoliberal "sustainable development" must be combined with what amount of "patronage" to maximize profits and minimize community disruptions. Instead, the lurch between approaches reflects power relations in villages, between villages and the mine, and among Newmont's own staff and management. The resulting tension is evident in a casual remark by Greg, PT NNT's External Relations senior manager: "You have to compromise, but not until you have no sustainability at all." From a cosmopolitan CSR perspective, sustainability occupied the moral high ground; but in the local moral economy, a patronage approach formed a political and practical necessity.

ANTICIPATING THE END: SUSTAINABILITY

By late 2000 a consensus was emerging that PT NNT's External Relations Department was, overall, not handling the local community very well. A financial auditor from Newmont's Denver headquarters told me Batu Hijau had sunk some $15 million into the External Relations office during the mine's first year, with little to show for it. He reserved special criticism for two expatriates, one of whom was earning roughly twenty thousand dollars a month as a consultant and appeared to have faked his credentials. The mine was facing weekly demonstrations, he told me, and its development projects were misguided. He cited the example of a paving block factory (part of a company Newmont had set up called PT Industri Batu Hijau) that was producing European-grade roof tiles and bricks at three times the cost of similar local products. It could still generate income because it had one loyal customer: Newmont.

The Community Development Department used PT Industri Batu Hijau products for a range of projects, such as building health outposts (posyandus) for village midwives. These small buildings were constructed at about ten times the cost of a house of similar size. To judge by the piles of droppings appearing around them, the buildings were more keenly appreciated by village goats than by midwives; the latter found them too remote, too exposed, and too liable to pique the jealousy of village heads, whose offices looked shabby in comparison to the posyandus with their nested, bamboo-shingled roofs evoking the Sumbawan palace. In Tongo-Sejorong and Benete, in fact, the village heads went so far as to appropriate and repurpose the buildings as their own offices. These buildings were a striking example of construction carried out for its own sake.

Meanwhile, the head of Yayasan Olat Parigi, Newmont's local community foundation, had deposited the foundation's money into his personal bank account and was drawing interest on it, which he used as a stream of personal income. Recipients of the foundation's "revolving" credit and livestock programs—which were supposed to generate returns for other villagers—interpreted cash and livestock as handouts or gifts. One resident of Jereweh, newly returning from Java, recalled the chaotic and festive scene after goats were distributed: some were being cooked into satay, others were running loose and suffering diarrhea.[1]

Newmont decided to end the party by firing the expensive expatriates and installing Ibu Comdev (whom one of the departing expatriates had worked to hire) as leader of its Community Development Department. In Ibu Comdev's view, the existing mine managers lacked familiarity with current best practices in development and were letting local people run all over them. Having done postconflict aid work for several years in Cambodia at a time when possession and use of firearms was common, she claimed to be less alarmed than other managers by the machetes, threats, and shouts of local demonstrators. When she saw the company facing a demonstration, roadblock, or bomb threat every week, Ibu Comdev said, she quickly got over her "misconceptions about corporations trampling hapless victims. Locals were holding the company ransom, and the company was too stupid to do anything about it." The $6 million community development budget, from her perspective, was way too large, more than the region could "properly absorb." Under her oversight, the 2002 budget was slashed to $2.4 million, which she felt was still on the high end and expected to whittle down in future years.

Ibu Comdev was committed to sustainable development, a discourse with a mixed view of the moral and economic benefits of local hiring and purchasing. All mines have a limited lifespan; when Batu Hijau opened, it's lifespan was estimated at twenty years.[2] Mine-village economic relations being by definition unsustainable, what local people really needed, according to Ibu Comdev, were the skills and capacity to take advantage of economic opportunities that lay outside the mine economy. Mining, from Ibu Comdev's perspective, was not the only game in town: Sumbawans were blessed with abundant natural resources she felt could better be used for agriculture and tourism. In an early conversation with me, she compared Newmont to a spaceship: "After the spaceship landed, everyone wanted to get on it. What they didn't understand was that it was going to leave and wouldn't be taking them along. Locals should forget the spaceship and think about other opportunities they have, like farming and tourist potential."

Ibu Comdev had a feminist conception of, and commitment to, empowering women, but she noted the need to "pick your battles" in the gender-conservative mining industry. Other mine managers were concerned that any perception that the mine was trying to impose Western feminist norms might provoke opposition from powerful men in villages. After a conversation on these themes between Ibu Comdev, several managers, and the company president broke off, Ibu Comdev looked at me and said, "Thank God you're here. See what I'm dealing with?" While direct beneficiaries of the programs under Community Development were mostly men, at Ibu Comdev's request Newmont contracted two NGOs from Lombok, one to carry out women's literacy work and the other to support existing government programs for midwives and maternal, infant, and children's health (figure 6). This arrangement permitted Ibu Comdev to enact Newmont as a company that cared about local women, albeit indirectly (through NGO labor rather than development of in-house expertise) and in domains conventionally coded as feminine (education and health). Indirect delivery of care allowed managers to strategically distance Newmont from this work when it was called into question, such as when men in certain villages challenged the presence of the NGO doing women's literacy work.

FIGURE 6. Transmigrant women from Lombok learn literacy skills with help from an NGO contracted by PT NNT's Community Development Department. Photo by author.

The hiring of Ibu Comdev and the turn toward sustainable development give the superficial appearance of a transformation of Newmont's CSR programs in Sumbawa, along the lines of what Elana Shever (2010) has described in relation to Shell's refineries in Argentina. Shever depicts a regendering of the corporate face, from normatively masculinized to feminized care, after a suave young woman took the place of a gruff older man. Whereas the latter had embodied the older *patrón* ideal—a stern, distant, financially necessary father figure—the new community representative embodied neoliberalism. She adopted a motherly approach to nurturing and building affective bonds with Shell's "neighbors" but portrayed the company role as that of educating local people and NGOs to take responsibility for their own health and welfare rather than that of providing paychecks and infrastructure. "While he provided things, she nurtured relationships," said Shever (35). The transformation from the patronage to the sustainability model in Sumbawa was far less complete, however, with Ibu Comdev's department working alongside and sometimes in opposition to the patronage model rather than supplanting it.

Pak Comrel, the Community Relations manager whose persona and approach to patronage we glimpsed in the last chapter, found his department at times pitted against Ibu Comdev's. Pak Comrel, who came from Taliwang and had decades of experience in extractive industries, routinely served as the mine's public face, such as when he hosted the regent from Sumbawa Besar in a tour of villages around the mine, or when he opened the Qur'an recital competition. His office oversaw local philanthropic initiatives, from providing soccer teams with uniforms to donating materials for mosque construction or repair. Business experts claim corporate philanthropy should strategically reflect corporate interests and generate a competitive advantage; it should not be an ad hoc effort to generate goodwill, or a capricious reflection of the hobbies and pet causes of executives or their spouses (Porter and Kramer 2002). The act of giving has an inescapably personal dimension, however, and local people at times expressed gratitude to Pak Comrel (as opposed to Newmont) in personal ways. At the close of the district Qur'an recital contest, for example, a schoolteacher thanked Newmont for material support of the event to great applause and then, as the applause subsided, added that Pak Comrel deserved especial praise, but that only God could repay him.

An expatriate who formerly consulted for Newmont told me that in the early days at least, Pak Comrel enjoyed access to a store of discretionary cash that was dubbed the "Panadol [painkiller] fund." When problems arose in the community, Pak Comrel would administer a "Panadol" (cash infusion) to relieve the pain. In one conversation, Pak Comrel described the mine-community dynamic in related terms, likening the mine to a boat out at sea and locals to sharks. "First we see one shark, swimming around, but it can't really affect the big boat. Then a whole bunch of sharks swim up, and the boat starts to rock back and forth, and it gets a bit dangerous. So we throw a bunch of fish out at the sharks, and then they go off with their fish. But then they come back after a little while and there's even more of them. So you have to keep throwing them fish." Newmont not only "fed" money and projects to people who threatened the company but also frequently hired them or their close relatives, as we saw in the last chapter, with the hiring of the wife of Zulkifli, the man who would become regent. Newmont also hired men whom a former Newmont consultant characterized as "New Order thugs," citing in particular a Community Relations officer who headed a local chapter of the notorious Pemuda Pancasila, a vigilante-style youth group notorious for violently defending the Soeharto regime (Ryter 2001).

The ostensible aim in hiring those who threatened the company was to turn them to useful and productive purposes, to channel their leadership and energies in new and more positive ways. But this sometimes also meant internalizing their logics. Both Indonesian and expatriate Newmont employees of different ranks told me that Pak Comrel himself had been hired because the company feared him, and that managers above him in the company hierarchy were still afraid to challenge his views on how mine-village relations should be run. Aware of such rumors, Pak Comrel once asked me if I had been warned by a Denver executive that he was a thief (*maling*). Rather than try to judge the veracity of these rumors, I use them here to underscore the complex ways in which corporations are constituted. To use Pak Comrel's own analogy, it was not always clear whether various persons, including Pak Comrel himself, were part of the boat or one of the sharks circling it.

Rumors of rivalry between Ibu Comdev and Pak Comrel also circulated in the mine and village communities. Greg, the senior manager of External Relations, told me that relations between the two had improved, that they "acted civil" toward one another after being chastised for their "uncompromising and backbiting" behavior. Their differences were reflected in relations between junior members of their respective departments; one argument between staff members apparently came close to blows. When I asked Ibu Comdev herself about her differences with Pak Comrel, she diplomatically said they shared the same goals and commitment to the community but had different ideas about how to realize these. Both sought—and found—affirmation that they were doing the right thing and that their work was succeeding. For Ibu Comdev, hearing people make requests she deemed smaller and more rational constituted a sign of improvement. For Pak Comrel, non-stop operations, fewer demonstrations, and villages with modern infrastructure and a cleaner appearance were signs of positive change. Ibu Comdev also acknowledged that they had different trajectories: whereas Pak Comrel was from the region and "would probably become the *bupati* [regent] one day," her only ambition, she joked, was to become president of PT NNT so she could implement real change. To put this in Peter Redfield's terms (2012), Ibu Comdev was motivated by a "lighter" commitment to improving Indonesia in the ways espoused by the sustainable development model, whereas Pak Comrel, subject to personalized and partisan claims, was motivated by a "heavier" commitment to southwest Sumbawa. They enacted the corporation and its interests according to their divergent perspectives and commitments.

VALUES FOR REFORM

From the sustainability perspective, the purpose of mine-sponsored development is to "incubate capitalism" by equipping villagers with tools for "independence," including market rationality and entrepreneurial virtues. As Yanagisako (2002:13) argues, capitalists do not engage in capitalist activities as a direct and natural expression of their objective interests. Rather, through a cultural process, capitalists are "sustained, nurtured, and endowed with the sentiments and motives to pursue capitalist goals." To put this differently, enterprise, like land, labor, and capital, is a factor of production that cannot simply be assumed (Skillen 1992).

"My job would be far easier if locals were already capitalists," Ibu Comdev said to me in one of our first conversations. She readily grasped the implicit telos of Newmont's economic development efforts, but her formulation also cut to the core of a perception widespread among Newmont officials, including some Sumbawans, that the latter were frustratingly "difficult" to develop because they lacked a strong work ethic and were often stubborn, irrational, emotional, lazy, and undisciplined. Managers usually attributed these traits to Sumbawan culture—and found support for this in cultural and linguistic research commissioned by Newmont (Mahsun, Ruhpina, Sulaimi, Rahmandayani, and Hamzah 1998:38–43)—or to the Sumbawan environment, the natural abundance of which supposedly freed Sumbawans from worrying about the future. Newmont's environmental impact assessment (PT NNT 1996:D-128) had already identified the (absent) Sumbawan work ethic as a "constraint" to more productive land use. Like the original "lazy native" myth of colonial domination (Alatas 1977), Sumbawan "indolence" was consistently invoked to criticize villagers for their not-yet-capitalist behavior as entrepreneurs, wage laborers, or farmers, and so on.

Newmont-sponsored business trainings and religious lectures attempted to impart entrepreneurial values. In September and October 2002, Newmont's Community Development Department sponsored two training sessions for small business owners, each lasting five days. Polished consultants from Java facilitated both trainings. The first day of training was devoted to teaching the underlying values that ought to guide entrepreneurial action. In one exercise, for example, we were instructed to connect nine points, arranged in a square, with only four straight lines, a feat possible only by "thinking outside of the box." The points, one facilitator explained, form something like our value system:

it restricts us, and we must move beyond it to achieve success. He cautioned entrepreneurs: "Our value system ties us down. There are those who are paralyzed by their values. Only if they can break free or move outside of their values can they become pioneers. Farmers say that *gotong-royong* [mutual assistance] is very good, and it is indeed good, but we can't progress if we constantly gotong-royong."

In condemning gotong-royong, which connotes a "general ethos of selflessness and concern for the common good" (Bowen 1986:546), the facilitator attacked one of the centerpieces of official Indonesian national ideology. Early nationalists treated gotong-royong as the quintessential embodiment of agrarian Indonesian values (546), while under Soeharto it was routinely invoked to marshal "voluntary" labor and supplies for official development projects. The facilitator's critique of gotong-royong was also at odds with the fifth principle of the national ideology of Pancasila: social justice, the goals of which are economic and social egalitarianism, and collective rather than individual well-being (the other principles are belief in God, national unity, internationalism/humanism, and a commitment to a democratic process that incorporates *musyawarah* [deliberation or consultation] and *mufakat* [consensus; Ramage 1995:13–14]).[3] Understandings of Pancasila and gotong-royong furnished norms for evaluating development, although Sumbawans knew well that in practice these ideologies could be used coercively, and that state programs justified in their name often failed to measure up to their ideals.[4] Within this ideological matrix of national development, *capitalism* remained something of a dirty word. In spite of Soeharto's avid pursuit of profit and foreign investment, *capitalism* had to be euphemized. A Government Relations manager from Lombok responded with surprise to a casual statement I made about Newmont's development programs aiming to expand capitalist values. For him, *capitalism* had negative connotations that were not consonant with "development." He had learned the word *capitalism* in school, and it had a negative resonance like that of other terms he had learned alongside it, such as *feudalism, colonialism,* and *imperialism.*[5] Although the facilitators critiqued national ideologies inherent in gotong-royong and Pancasila, entrepreneurs in the trainings and in everyday life still had recourse to the values embodied by them, which served as resources for enacting Newmont as a patron.[6]

By the end of the first day of training, we had isolated a set of key entrepreneurial traits, which the facilitators recorded on the flip chart:

1. Take moderate and calculated risks.
2. Manage yourself and take personal responsibility.
3. Use your experiences as feedback and think positively.
4. Always work creatively and innovatively.
5. Always feel that you are pressed for time.
6. Enjoy that which is complex and offers many choices.
7. Exercise initiative and frequently survey and study your environment.
8. Engage in relations with people not only for friendship but also to acquire knowledge.
9. Always seek out opportunities.

These entrepreneurial traits clearly celebrate the notion of the rational, autonomous capitalist, combining the systematic self-control (punctuality, frugality, industry) of Protestant asceticism (Weber 1992) with Romantic ideals of choice, freedom, creativity, individualism, initiative, and risk (Marquand 1992). The foil to this energetic entrepreneur is the equally universal figure of the risk-averse, subsistence-oriented, progress-inhibiting peasant embedded in a moral economy of sharing and gotong-royong (Popkin 1979; Scott 1976). The training proceeded as if Sumbawans, like all not-yet-capitalists, were naturally endowed with inner entrepreneurs just waiting to be liberated from the illogical shackles of cultural oppression (Rankin 2001).

As the Newmont-sponsored business training unfolded, however, it was clear that facilitators were having a hard time convincing trainees they were better off chasing external markets than cultivating close business relations with Newmont. Consider, for example, this excerpt from a dialogue between one of the facilitators and a local contractor:

> *Facilitator:* We obviously need to be careful [*jeli*]; we need to conceive of new opportunities and can't invest all our capital in one business.
>
> *Local contractor:* We already have a market, but it is exclusive. We cannot see sociocultural values in Newmont. We are in fact really distributors, not producers.
>
> *F:* If we are distributors we must know what the market wants, our consumers. Can we continuously provide the product? There must not be any stoppages. What is our system for distributing products; what is our method of payment?

LC: We want to be a satellite town of Newmont. We need a starter from Newmont, and our first customers should be domestic tourists from Newmont. Newmont workers have a kind of passport or visa—the badge—as if they live in a different country.

F: But we must remember that consumers have criteria like suitability and security.

LC: We want to be on intimate terms with Newmont.

The two men speak at cross-purposes. The facilitator scrupulously avoids using the word Newmont, speaking instead as if entrepreneurs were producing for abstract consumers, and he directs attention to local entrepreneurs' (lack of) technical capacity. By contrast, the entrepreneur levels a moral critique against Newmont for erecting barriers between the company and local villages and for failing to build proper social and economic relations with the latter. Their speech, while mutually intelligible, is underwritten by incompatible moral logics. When I spoke with entrepreneurs after Newmont's business training, several complained that the training had produced no results (tidak ada hasil). The only people they felt had been enriched by the training were the facilitators. The icebreakers and games they played were sometimes infantilizing (one businessman cheerfully noted the training reminded him of kindergarten), but the message they conveyed—grow up and be independent of Newmont—was not. This very message reinforced a sense of defeat among many participants, whose hope for the training was that it would deepen and extend their relations with Newmont, not urge them to cut themselves loose from it.

Toward the end of one training session, the facilitators divided us into small groups and asked us to draw pictorial representations of our ideal version of business. My group turned the marker and flip chart over to me. Producing imagery I figured would appeal to the facilitators, I drew a picture that showed a stick figure who transformed over time from a walking vendor to one with a bicycle, a motorbike, then a truck, and finally a house. This won praise from the facilitators, who pointed out how it illustrated appropriate growth and progress, not a leap straight to the big house. My drawing also depicted the individual entrepreneur growing without external assistance. The facilitators were less impressed by the other drawings. One group displayed a drawing of a circular, unbroken chain like a bracelet. Its artist explained that the chain showed how we were all tied together, linked and united. Further, he expressed his hope that, as a businessman, he could keep working with Newmont, not just for ten or twenty years but sustainably (berke-

lanjutan), forever. Another depicted a cow in a field with a fish and chicken below. The artist explained that he meant to illustrate how we are all connected to one another, and even the droppings of the cow could be made use of to benefit the other animals. These drawings, presented at the conclusion of the business training, suggested how imperfectly its lessons in entrepreneurialism and individualism had sunk in.

About the same time as the training session, Newmont began conveying similar messages in other venues, to other audiences, and in other rhetorical registers. The Community Relations Department began sponsoring Pak Ustadz Nur, a religious leader from Taliwang, the nearest large town, to deliver religious lectures in the near-mine villages. He reminded his village audience that the Prophet Mohammed was first a merchant, "empowered" by Khadija, who gave him precious silks and capital. The prophet kept his books well, multiplied Khadija's investment several times over five years, and then married her.[7] The ustadz went on to explain that according to the Qur'an, the concept of empowerment (*pemberdayaan*) is about people gaining independence (*kemandirian*). Rallying behind the Community Relations project of improving the Sumbawan work ethic, the ustadz observed that work is spiritually fulfilling and pure, a form of religious devotion, because "Allah surrendered the earth to those who would work—and He did not say [this] only to those who are Muslims—and because of this we must work." As with their religious devotions, the ustadz sternly intoned, Muslims must work alone and be disciplined in their use of time; it is the burden of the individual to sacrifice, pray, and undertake the hajj. Thus, the ustadz gave religious sanction to the entrepreneurial logics of commerce, individualism, autonomy, and hard work we saw promoted in the secular business training.

Such values, however, were not central to *sedekah*, the core religious ceremony in Sumbawa that accompanies marriages, belly-washing ceremonies for pregnant women, circumcisions, hajj departures and returns, funerals, successful harvests, and important events in the Muslim calendar. In these ceremonies, village residents prepare food (centering on a sacrificed goat or water buffalo, depending on the means of the host and the significance of the occasion) with communal donations of material and labor, especially by women. Senior religious men consecrate the meal, which men then consume communally, followed by women. After the meal, women and men distribute the remaining food throughout the wider community. Participants take special steps to see that the poorest villagers and orphans get a share of these meals. Through their communal

FIGURE 7. Tongo-Sejorong residents butchering a sacrificed bull on Idul Adha, the Day of Sacrifice. Photo by author.

production, distribution, and consumption, Sumbawan villagers might give thanks to Allah for blessings (e.g., a bountiful harvest or a child's recovery from a life-threatening illness), supplicate Allah (e.g., for the health of an unborn baby), or engage in empathic consumption (e.g., following the cravings of the Prophet Mohammed's pregnant mother, as discussed in the introduction). Through meritorious activities such as giving to the poor, villagers attempt to communicate with Allah on behalf of deceased kin. Sumbawa village residents, like Gayo Sumatrans described by Bowen (1993), also sacrifice bulls or water buffalo on the Day of Sacrifice (at the end of the month of hajj), sometimes designating seven kin members who will seek passage together using the sacrificial animal as an "afterlife vehicle" (figure 7).

These Sumbawan rites of sacrifice and redistribution—which deliberately echo and recall the Prophet Mohammed's own acts of redistribution and concern for marginalized groups (e.g., slaves, orphans, the impoverished)—stand in stark contrast to the Newmont-sponsored religious lectures emphasizing the Prophet's acts of accumulation and his professional skill as a merchant. Moreover, while the ustadz stressed that individuals alone are responsible to Allah, Sumbawan villagers often seek to transact with Allah on behalf of others in need. These differences in emphasis do not necessarily reflect incompatible positions on religious doctrine, but they can be drawn on to support quite different moral assessments of social action. In his religious lecture, for example, the ustadz made of economic independence and self-sufficiency a moral goal very much in accord with Newmont's efforts to foster independent entrepreneurship. By contrast, the Sekongkang preacher quoted in the last chapter ascribed a different moral aim to the company when he said Newmont wanted to give thanks with the community, by which he meant show gratitude for the ore body and redistribute the wealth gained through its exploitation.

After the ustadz's religious lecture, Pak Comrel read a short poem to those assembled. The poem reproduced the great cliché of sustainable development: the goal is not to give the people fish but to teach them how to fish. A subtext of this now hackneyed idea is that gift exchange is morally inferior to commodity production and exchange. Newmont officials claimed subtle progress in their efforts to foster entrepreneurship by noting that villagers were slowly becoming more hardworking, more oriented to opportunities outside of Newmont, and "more rational" in their expectations of the company (i.e., they now expected less).[8] But gift exchange was hardly a thing of the past. As if to emphasize this point, Pak Comrel concluded his reading of the poem by presenting the village head with a framed copy of it reproduced on a scenic background.

IMPLEMENTING THE REFORM AGENDA

In addition to value-centered trainings, Ibu Comdev instituted other measures aiming to reform local business practices and relations with Newmont. She pursued the liquidation of PT Industri Batu Hijau, converting the company into three separate cooperatives: a sawmill, a paving block factory, and a container-servicing unit. Over the ensuing years, none found much of a market outside of Newmont, and the sawmill's monthly operating costs were frequently double its income, with the shortfall made up by loans from Newmont (Basuki and Yuyud 2002; KSU Somil Jaya 2002, 2003).[9]

Among the cooperatives, the sawmill was the most successful in finding outside buyers, but its non-Newmont customers often defaulted on their payments. I suspect that customers did not feel obliged to pay for the sawmill's products in part because they saw the cooperative as a part of Newmont, the patron. From this perspective, the cooperative was just another conduit for the distribution of development goods. This was true not only for the cooperative's customers but for its member-workers as well. Ibu Comdev observed that, were it not for the threat of demonstrations, Newmont could move to privatize the cooperatives so that they might be run according to market principles. The cooperative "members," she complained, behaved as "employees" entitled to wages from Newmont. Many of those who worked at the sawmill did indeed feel entitled to wages from Newmont as compensation for their exclusion from the mine workforce. Newmont defended its limited number of lokal-lokal jobs in the mine by subsidizing wage labor outside of its employee ranks, providing a range of inferior substitutes for the direct wage labor relations many village men sought with Newmont. By encouraging the cooperative management to institute time-discipline measures and make members' income directly dependent on sales, Newmont tried to steer the cooperatives toward production of commodities for sale on the open market; but progress along these lines was fitful and incomplete.

More in accordance with rational capitalist principles was a tailoring cooperative established with Newmont's support. Yet Newmont managers and village residents alike were perturbed by this. Although the cooperative membership was almost entirely female, the head of the cooperative was a male schoolteacher, and his wife, also a schoolteacher, was the treasurer. When Newmont awarded the cooperative large purchase orders for workers' uniforms, the cooperative head and his wife reorganized the local village cooperative branch into what one American consultant dubbed a "sweatshop," using cheap male labor hired from Lombok and excluding local Sumbawan women. The Sasak men from Lombok, separated from friends and kin, could work full time in a central location under close supervision; with cooperative branches and members in multiple villages, it would have been far more difficult to exert comparable control over women's piecemeal labor. For most female cooperative members, sewing took a backseat to the pressing priorities of caring for children, husbands, parents, and in-laws. The "sweatshop" clearly did not embody the communal ideals that first led the early Indonesian nationalist Mohammed Hatta to see in German cooperatives an attractive model for economic development. Most of the "community" benefits of Newmont's decision to purchase uniforms locally were going into the schoolteacher's new house or being sent to

Lombok in the form of remittances. Although some cooperative members complained, Newmont officials were reluctant to intervene. The cooperative was officially independent, after all. In addition, they saw the politically well-connected teacher as a potential threat, whereas disgruntled female cooperative members posed no apparent danger to the company.

A fellow schoolteacher condemned the actions of the cooperative head, claiming that the latter was initially selected for the job because he was religious and came from a poor family, but that he had turned out to be "worse than anyone could have imagined." When the cooperative head was hospitalized for an illness, his colleague remarked that his sickness was a symptom of his single-minded pursuit of money, which made him stop eating and grow perilously thin. Ibu Comdev told me that following several "unpleasant" interactions with the cooperative head, her staff had contemplated cutting off contracts for Newmont uniforms or bringing the regional cooperative agency into the picture; ultimately, however, they facilitated a dialogue among the cooperative members and improved the distribution of contracts.

In yet another program, PT NNT in February 2002 formally established the Local Business Initiative (LBI) as a subdivision of the Purchasing and Contracts Departments to facilitate local purchasing on a company-wide basis. Ibu Comdev said she wrote the LBI contract in a day, but it took a long time to get local entrepreneurs and senior managers to sign on to it. The creation of this separate system, overseen by an expatriate from Singapore (whom another manager described as an unfortunate choice, given his "allergy to the community" and his fear of traveling without the company of a senior Community Development staff member, who had his own important work to do), added substantially to Newmont's administrative overhead for purchasing. Newmont began channeling smaller contracts through the LBI, which issued invitations to local businesses to tender secret bids for contracts.

Local purchasing was more complex than the data cited by the catering company manager at the opening of this chapter suggests. Just as not all the lokal-lokal workers were what they claimed to be, some lokal-lokal businesses were actually fronts for outsiders. As of July 2002, LBI had 135 "lokal" businesses registered with the company, 72 of which had addresses in the subdistricts of Jereweh and Sekongkang.[10] Many of the owners of these, however, were newcomers. The terms lokal and lokal-lokal were often assigned discrepant meanings internally and by Newmont's subcontractors (e.g., for some, lokal-lokal included the town of Taliwang, whereas for others it was limited to the districts of Sekongkang and Jereweh). Purchasing from lokal-lokal businesses, moreover, did not necessarily benefit a very large—or for that matter, particularly Sumbawan—segment of the village population: for example, when a business was a distributor rather than a producer, importing goods from other islands, then the economic infusion was very limited in its local scope. As we saw in the case of the tailoring cooperative, many small enterprises preferred to hire wage laborers from Lombok. With high rates of landlessness on Lombok, laborers from the island were typically willing to work for lower wages and were more accustomed to wage-labor discipline. It may have also been easier for Sumbawans to extract labor from workers with whom they shared no ties of kinship. Local purchasing, then, may have been a widely shared ideal, but often in practice its protocols were circumvented and its principles subverted.

Contractors also complained that with the LBI they were frequently expected to compete for humiliating and absurd contracts. A tale I heard repeatedly—though probably apocryphal, it was highly illustrative—centered on the nickel-and-diming alleged to be pervasive in LBI contracting. PBU, Newmont's catering contractor, supposedly ordered twenty forks. Because forks were sold in one-dozen packs, the suppliers would either have to sell them to PBU at a higher price (reflecting the four extras), and thereby risk rejection, or themselves be saddled with the remainder. Perhaps, one contractor suggested, these were games played by those within Newmont who wanted to steer genuine, lucrative contracts to their cronies from Java.

Through the LBI, Newmont established rigid rules for engaging with local entrepreneurs. LBI representatives at the business training made it clear that the entrepreneurs should carefully read the tender invitations, provide written responses, familiarize themselves with filling out forms written in English, and get accustomed to thirty-day waiting periods for invoice payments. The English-language requirement was especially daunting; a local middle school teacher (of English, no less) requested my assistance one evening in filling out one of Newmont's maintenance supplier forms. The LBI system incorporated multiple mechanisms for training new entrepreneurs to achieve "principles of professional competitiveness" and for exacting compliance with "Newmont's stringent quality, quantity, and delivery requirements" (PT NNT 2003). LBI representatives held "one-stop shops" for the entrepreneurs, three days a week, when a representative was available to help match them with potential opportunities. The representatives told the entrepreneurs to show up regularly and behave in a courteous and restrained fashion, avoiding irrational displays of anger and frustration. In the training, one LBI representative insisted, "You cannot force your desire to win a contract upon us by slamming your fist on the table or by organizing a demonstration." These messages seemed to be sinking in the day I observed the one-stop shop in action and witnessed Pak Jamal paying the LBI supervisor a visit. Usually swaggering and assertive, Pak Jamal adopted a subservient demeanor, unlike anything I had ever witnessed in Sumbawan villages. Eyes lowered, he responded to the LBI supervisor's statements with a deferential "Sahaya, Pak." When the supervisor got up to get some forms, Pak Jamal instantly dropped his meek demeanor and greeted me.

Several contractors I interviewed welcomed the LBI, seeing it as expressive of Newmont's concern with assisting local businesses and as a system that—whatever its failings—did improve upon its predecessor by leveling the playing field. Some also noted that it relieved them of the burden of orchestrating demonstrations each time they sought a project. Most, however, felt the LBI still had serious flaws. Although LBI representatives insisted publicly that they followed "best practices" and were "afraid of" corruption, collusion, and nepotism, rumors still circulated that LBI awarded contracts based on personal relations, bribes, and threats of demonstration. Studying the distribution of government construction contracts in the eastern Indonesian town of Kupang, Sylvia Tidey (2013) notes that concerns about corruption, collusion, and nepotism accompanying Soeharto's fall and the rise of neoliberal discourses of transparency, accountability, and good governance led to intense focus on adherence to proper form in documents. Rather than diminishing corruption, this multiplied opportunities for public officials to charge for their expertise in bureaucratic forms, and for fee-sharing among entrepreneurs who established fictive companies to generate the mirage of meritocratic competition around a fixed winning bid. One of the chief complaints I heard from contractors was that the LBI's closed tender system was destroying their relations with one another and leading them to run their businesses into the ground as they vied to outbid each other and gain a track record as Newmont's trusted partner. They complained that Newmont judged their bids upon the sole criterion of price. Moreover, they believed that the company had a secret figure budgeted for each contract, and that when bids arrived with budgets still below that, they would accept the lowest, leaving the contractor with no profit at all.

Laborers recruited for local projects often bore the brunt of this "self-exploitation." One contractor explained,

> Analyzing the situation from 1999 to now, it is the workers of contractors who suffer the most. They can still feed their families and smoke cigarettes, but that's about it. The problem is that when a tender comes up, Newmont takes the lowest price. Doesn't Newmont have an idea of how much a project should cost—for example, a million rupiah? Why would they give the contract to someone who offered a much lower price? The problem is that if contractors put a higher bid in they lose, but if they put in too low a bid they are screwed.

Another said that under these circumstances their businesses would fail unless they lied, hiring workers from Lombok for only 12,500 rupiah per day rather than paying locals 20,000 rupiah per day plus food. On another occasion, I heard a Community Relations official upbraiding a colleague because local contractors in his area were not paying their workers the minimum 20–25,000 rupiah a day.

Many of the contractors agreed on measures that might form the foundation of a more ethical and just way of doing business with Newmont. They felt that LBI should utilize standard budgets and prices, like the government does in purchasing different products in different geographic regions. Second, they wanted LBI to hierarchize businesses (as strong, medium, and weak) so they could compete with their peers rather than all entering the same tender process. Third, several entrepreneurs suggested that contract opportunities should be revolving (*bergilir*), so each company would have its turn, rather than distributed in a lumpy fashion (*kelompokan*), allowing one company to win several contracts at once. I heard contractors remark approvingly on instances when Newmont—after encountering business protests—had broken up and redistributed individual contracts (e.g., a school furniture contract) to several companies spread across multiple subdistricts, thus dispelling social jealousy.

Given the fairly high degree of consensus on what ought to be done, it may seem surprising that contractors felt they were unable to influence LBI's competitive, capitalist "best practices." They did in fact meet among themselves to organize strategic (sometimes threatening) approaches to LBI and even formed consortiums to effect a better distribution of opportunities—for example, by creating a rotating system (*arisan*). Such efforts were however typically short-lived. One contractor claimed a consortium dissolved once its leader got a purchase order. Another observed, "There is no unity among my friends." This suggests two important consequences of the LBI. First, by treating the entrepreneurs as individuals competing with each other through a tender process, the initiative made it more difficult for contractors to forge a collective voice and orchestrate demonstrations. Second, by making prices more competitive and tender processes secretive, the initiative made it more difficult for local contractors to mobilize demonstrators who might stand to benefit from wage labor opportunities. But the LBI did formulate mechanisms for ongoing economic exchange between local businesses and Newmont, perpetuating the patronage model.

THE MORAL PROPRIETY OF PATRONAGE

In 2002, former exploration workers posted flyers around Maluk village illustrated with a drawing of men digging the earth and carrying supplies. Part of a larger lobbying effort to get jobs or compensation for these workers, the flyers read, "PT NNT has no sympathy. The sons of the region have been abandoned. The exploration pioneers are now suffering. . . . Former exploration workers request justice: the boat is already full, take off some passengers, board the passengers who once served to get the boat going." The exploration workers' boat metaphor contrasts with Pak Comrel's depiction of the mine as a boat at sea, with locals surrounding it like sharks. It contrasts as well with Ibu Comdev's analogy, in which the mine is a spaceship that locals are clamoring to board, unaware that it will be leaving without them. The metaphors have divergent temporal orientations: Ibu Comdev's anticipates Newmont's future departure, while Pak Comrel's examines escalating claims to Newmont in the present. Both overlook history. The exploration workers instead look to the past to assert a moral claim in the present, declaring that their work in constructing the vessel in the first place confers on them a prior and rightful claim to a berth on it. They regard it as disingenuous when community development officials say the villagers' central problem is their dependence on Newmont, when it was Newmont who had, in recent memory, depended on them.

When critiquing Newmont, village residents often pointed to the company's aloofness and reluctance to engage with locals. As one man—a Newmont contractor as well as a critic, with ties to prominent environmental advocacy organizations—bluntly put it, "Newmont eats here, shits here, and sends the gold to its home." Another contractor, a village head angry and humiliated after being ordered around by Newmont security guards when he approached mine gates with an expired vehicle permit sticker, complained bitterly that Sumbawans were now treated as "guests in their own home." At a district-level meeting about how health cadres would administer polio vaccines and vitamin A to village children, a village head grumbled that they ought to run the program in Townsite as well and inject children there. He and others felt that residents of Townsite should have to apply in villages for their local identification cards. The village head took issue with Townsite's existence as a zone of privileged exception, run as if it fell completely outside the local territory and jurisdiction (a visiting spaceship), and indeed another Sumbawan contractor complained that Townsite was like another country, with special passports.

In a separate conversation among contractors, the same man protested that, with special boats and transportation arrangements for its workers to visit the more developed island of Lombok, Newmont moved not just its tailings but also all of its goods and labor force through pipelines, diverting to the neighboring island the "multiplier effect" that should have stimulated demand and created new jobs in Sumbawa.[11] In 2003, along with other contractors, he successfully lobbied Newmont to implement a policy giving workers larger housing allowances for living off-site rather than in company housing, encouraging them to live, eat, and spend their rupiahs in local villages. Feeding and housing Newmont workers in villages may not have been "sustainable," but it was desirable in the eyes of various local residents who could rent out rooms and sell food (figure 8).

Local residents were also successful at getting Newmont to take a measure of responsibility for the social jealousy caused by the mine. The term *social jealousy (kecemburuan social)* is Indonesian, not Sumbawan, and appears in corporate records as an explanation for antimine demonstrations as well as in local residents' proposals to Yayasan Olat Parigi (Newmont's community development foundation) as a justification for why Newmont should allocate resources to villagers. Sumbawan residents successfully wielded this discourse to get jobs, contracts, and funding for small development projects. The status of social jealousy as an accepted rationale for community development projects is evident in a Newmont-commissioned 2010 social impact assessment, which notes that PT NNT had implemented a program to renovate seventy-five homes in each village for families without any member employed by Newmont or Newmont contractors. At that point, work had already been completed on seventy-five houses in Tongo as a measure to "appease jealousy" (AMEC Geomatrix 2010:xii, xv, 72). When PT NNT's president director, Robert Gallagher, met with village

FIGURE 8. A Maluk businessman preparing to convert his property, which included a thriving nightclub during the construction era, into rental units for Newmont workers after PT NNT increased housing allowances for employees living outside of mine facilities. Photo by author.

officials in Tongo, he too made reference to local "social jealousy" as an important issue. Taking social jealousy seriously means going against capitalist notions of meritocratic wealth achievement and distribution. Whether or not Newmont's managers privately believed social jealousy was a legitimate rationale for community development programming or simply a security concern, it had become part of their vocabulary and was validated by Newmont's housing renovation practices.

In my own experience, social jealousy indeed figured prominently in everyday village life, and everyone regarded it as a serious matter. Village residents often claimed that physical ailments (e.g., stubborn respiratory infections or sudden, sometimes fatal, illnesses) were inflicted upon them or family members via witchcraft by neighbors jealous of their good fortune. One woman told me her family had reoriented their house toward a hillside, away from neighbors, after her son was killed by a leg infection caused by a jealous neighbor. Repressed jealousy— which can be dangerous, a threat to individuals and the social order— can be addressed through generosity and redistributive practices. The parents of Newmont workers often instructed their children to be generous with their newfound wealth, to lend their motorbikes to those who had no jobs. My own relationship to goods was subject to similar scrutiny. One day, when I was talking to friends at a kiosk, one asked if he could borrow my motorbike to get some mangos from an orchard. As I handed over the keys, he also requested my sunglasses. I was more reluctant to lend those to him, saying that I might be using them shortly when I walked home—and thinking that if I loaned them to him I could hardly refuse requests from other friends to borrow them. He returned later with a swollen face, absolutely furious with me. He had been stung by a bee and was certain that my reluctance to loan him my sunglasses was to blame. Everyone glared at me, seeming to concur that I was at fault for not meeting the expectations of generosity that go along with friendship. Applying a Sorcery Perception Index to complement Transparency International's Corruption Perception Index, Nils Bubandt (2006) correlated a rise in accusations of sorcery-related deaths in North Maluku with the increased opportunities for local wealth accumulation that came with a nickel mine and the establishment of a new regency.

As a moral critique of uneven development, social jealousy has a logical foundation in national discourse; the New Order development state was ideologically (albeit not practically) grounded in communal goals, social justice, and economic egalitarianism.[12] Sumbawans believed that because Newmont had created the conditions for socioeconomic differentiation, the company was responsible for managing the social jealousy it had created—that it should redistribute wealth through contracts and employment, thereby restoring good social relations.[13]

Sumbawan villagers assess their economic circumstances in a social context. I asked one married couple whether they were better off economically now than before Newmont's arrival. They remained farmers but had sold some land and used the proceeds to build their (still unfinished) brick and concrete home (*rumah batu*) and buy a motorbike, which the husband used as a taxi service (*ojek*) for villagers needing transport. In government prosperity reckonings, this family had enlarged its disposable income and property assets. But, contrasting his fortunes with those of neighbors who had established formal links to Newmont (through jobs or business contracts), the ojek driver argued that he was worse off than before Newmont. This assessment stood at odds with government indicators because he considered his family's economic well-being in a social context rather than in the abstract. Before Newmont, his lot was roughly comparable to the next villager's. Now, it was not.

FIGURE 9. A typical elevated home (*rumah panggung*) largely constructed of wood and bamboo. Photo by author.

Some villagers spoke nostalgically about a time when they were all equally poor (*sama-sama miskin*)—but it was the relative equality, rather than a state of poverty, that they missed (see the contrast between village homes in figures 9 and 10). There is nothing uniquely Sumbawan about conceiving of one's wealth or poverty in socially relative terms, but Sumbawans have the accepted idiom of "social jealousy" in which to express these feelings.[14] As Indonesia's first president, Sukarno, noted, seeing others with material objects like refrigerators or motorcars can create a sense of deprivation, expectation, and aspiration that holds revolutionary potential (Strassler 2010:97–98).

The head of an Islamic middle school in Tongo village stated numerous times in both private conversations and public forums (where he called for greater Newmont support of religious activities) that villagers were losing their values, becoming more materialist, individualist, capitalist, and atheist. Claiming that gotong-royong had undergone a dramatic decline, he asserted, "If the social feeling [*rasa sosial*] here used to be 100 percent, it is now 10 percent." A successful merchant from Taliwang similarly joked that Maluk, the village where mine-driven eco-

FIGURE 10. The luxurious-looking new brick-and-concrete home (*rumah batu*) of a village resident who works at Newmont. Photo by author.

nomic growth was most concentrated, was an acronym for "humanity that has forgotten family, village, and friends" (*manusia lupa keluarga, kampung, dan kawan*). "You might think," he admonished me, "that people are more prosperous here than they were in 1990. The opposite is true. Back then you could come here and eat for six months and never pay anything, whereas now everyone is in debt." Measured in terms of reciprocity and mutualism, villagers' wealth had shrunk. With greater inequality, generosity becomes more necessary as a leveling mechanism. But the increased capacity for generosity among some villagers was accompanied by the diminished capacity to reciprocate among others, making gift exchange more fraught with anxiety, reluctance, embarrassment, and mistrust.

Schneider and Schneider (2003:284) note that although antimafia activists in Italy, armed with Green and feminist ideology, opposed the "hypermasculine" construction industry that had "buried every tree in sight under a load of cement," the activists proposed no economic alternatives for the lower-class working people who depended on the mafia-controlled industry for their livelihoods. Similarly, those in Newmont who advocated that the company do less for local people in order to foster more sustainable development sometimes took too little account of the precariousness of the present. Although patron-client relations generally, and figures like Pak Comrel specifically, might appear corrupt within a moral framework valorizing rationality and autonomy, Schneider and Schneider (282) remark that "one can appreciate in [clientalist] practices the 'connectivity' that obligates kin and friends to look out for each other in a continually shifting and insecure world." For many Sumbawan villagers, exclusion from patron-client relations is indeed a worse fate than the uneven distribution of goods already assumed in these relations. Rather than view Newmont through the artificial equality of "partnership," then, they sought to underscore the dominant status of Newmont, an entity they saw as having the capacity, and thus the obligation, to mediate the radical socioeconomic inequalities it had introduced.

CONCLUSION

From the perspective of many PT NNT staff and managers in External Relations, local entrepreneurs did not get business quite right. Often they were hypocapitalists: lacking a proper work ethic, untutored in proper contract form, using brute force to try to win contracts, and averse to genuine competition. At other times they behaved like hypercapitalists: exploiting workers, monopolizing contracts, and generally making it hard to present their work as exemplary of local development. Through various training programs and contract procedures such as the Local Business Initiative, Newmont managers sought to turn contractors into ideal neoliberal agents of sustainable development. Contractors, for their part, sought to transform Newmont into the ideal patron. Neither group succeeded completely; yet both were, at times, able to force important changes that enabled them, for a while at least, to enact Newmont in ways they saw as socially responsible.

In 2003, Ibu Comdev emailed me the "juicy news" that she was resigning. I received an email from one of her staff soon after, expressing concern over the future of Community Development programs. He said he knew of no one else of Ibu Comdev's caliber, given both her vision and willingness to fight with management. He asked me if I had any suggestions (I did not). Pak Comrel was promoted and put in charge of both departments, which he swung back toward the patronage model. The shift is strikingly evident in the Community Development annual budget as reported in a 2010 social impact assessment. In 2000 it was $6.1 million, including administrative overhead. It reached a low in 2002 of $2.4 million, the year that Ibu Comdev was most firmly in charge. It crept up to $3 million during 2003, the year Ibu Comdev left, to $4.1 million in 2004, $5.2 million in 2005, and close to $6.8 million in 2008 (in the intervening years hovering around $5.6 million).

Newmont's Community Relations Review recommended that Batu Hijau take steps to "improve the sustainability of development programs," consider the "vulnerability of traditionally neglected groups," and develop clear plans to collect community input in order to "remove a large part of the pressure applied to community relations staff to acquiesce to demands with discretionary actions" (Newmont Mining Corporation 2012:40). A subsequent social impact assessment found that the representation of "marginal groups (e.g., women) [was] still below adequately representative levels," and that Community Development, "in accordance with the expectations of community leaders," was focused "predominately on infrastructure projects which are tangible and perceived as higher value than more intangible capacity development programs" (40–41). The report found that the Community Development Department had yet to shift from a focus on short-term infrastructure to longer-term capacity building and development, from a reactive response to social incidents to "a strategic approach focusing on sound social research, program prioritization and delivery," and from a mind-set of "keeping the mine operations running" to a mind-set of "sustainable development" (42). The consultants who wrote the report sought to expand the definition of *stakeholders* from one that focused on "'elites' and influential people of the community" to one that would "include marginal groups such as women and non-Muslims" (43). In sum, in southwest Sumbawan villages Newmont still looked more like a patron distributing largesse than like a supporter of more modest and democratic sustainable-development agendas.

Rather than assuming that distant and calculated "corporate interests" determine the shape and practices of CSR, I have underscored the people involved and their struggle over whether to enact Newmont as patron or as facilitator of neoliberal subjects. This struggle involved not just economic calculation but also social and phenomenological relations formed through dense ties and emotions, including fear (miners' fear of locals armed with machetes, demonstrators' fear of corporate security and the police, young unemployed men's fear of not being able to reproduce themselves socially, and Newmont workers' fear of not showing solidarity with fellow villagers by joining in demonstrations) and religious and consumerist desires (to buy a motorbike, to live in a brick-and-concrete home with tiled floors, to send one's children to high school or a relative on the hajj). In struggles over how to enact a socially responsible Newmont, local residents asserted that the company was obligated to them by virtue of their mutual proximity to the ore body; the company's causal role in generating, and presumed ability to mediate, social inequalities; and their historical ties and interdependence.

CHAPTER 4

"We Identified Farmers as Our Top Security Risk"

Ethereal and Material Development in the Paddy Fields

Prospective entrepreneurs were not the only ones invited to Newmont trainings. In July 2002, twenty residents of villages in the Sumbawan sub-district of Sekongkang embarked on a Training of Trainers, a Newmont-sponsored ten-day agricultural program. By day, under the simple bamboo-and-palm-frond structure that was part of a farmers' "laboratory" constructed by Batu Hijau's Community Development Department, facilitators led participants through a packed program beginning with games, role playing, and icebreakers, moving on to social, historical, and biological analysis exercises and then on to tutorials on composting, making organic pesticides, and pH testing of soil. By night, the participants were supposed to sleep in simple huts in the rice fields surrounding the lab, which was located several kilometers from the nearest village. This immersion in an agricultural setting and isolation from regular village and family life was supposed to heighten the training's intensity and foster bonding among participants as they slept, ate, and performed Muslim prayers together. The training was supposed to remake participants, to alter their beliefs, capacities, desires, and identities, to inspire them to both become more exemplary farmers themselves and recruit and encourage others to become more environmentally conscious and productive agricultural subjects. In Foucauldian parlance, the training was supposed to create new subjectivities.

The training exhibited a logic scholars have tracked in a range of liberal institutions aiming to "transform structures of consciousness," "govern souls," produce "new subjectivities," and "create self-regulating" or "governable" subjects (e.g., Agrawal 2005; Cooke and Kothari 2001; Dean 1999; Leve 2001:119–20; Paley 2001:4; Rankin 2001; Rose 1999). This line of analysis is deeply indebted to Michel Foucault's insights (1978, 1979) into how power works in positive ways—rather than simply as a repressive force—to govern individuals and populations through technologies that foster the agency or capacity of human actors to autonomously make "free," rational, and calculated choices and take responsibility for the consequences of their actions (see also Foucault 1991, 1997; Lemke 2001). Foucault's governmentality analytic offers a powerful approach for exploring effects of neoliberalism at the level of subjectivity, a project that complements political-economy-inspired critiques of neoliberal agents, policies, and rhetoric that promote market mechanisms, roll back state welfare functions, and consolidate class power (Harvey 2005). Yet the linkage between the rationality, technics, and subjects of government (Inda 2005) has also been challenged by scholars who, while still operating within a Foucauldian framework, argue that the *projects* or *rationales* of rule that Foucault's concept of governmentality has illuminated should be carefully distinguished from, rather than conflated with, the messier *practices* of rule (Li 1999a, 2007; Moore 1999; O'Malley, Weir, and Shearing 1997). The practices of rule often lack coherence and always run up against limits (Ferguson and Gupta 2002; Hart 2004; Watts 2004). Rather than reconfirm neoliberalism's triumph, its conquest of hearts and minds everywhere, such critiques support a more open-ended ethnographic exploration into systems of power and subject-formation. They also support exploration into these systems' unintended consequences—that is, the contingent forms of agency and contestation to which they give rise.

Trainings and related pedagogical programs such as workshops, retreats, and fee-based self-improvement courses are fruitful sites for the investigation of deliberate subject-formation (Cruikshank 1999; Elyachar 2005b; Jones 2010a; Kondo 1990; Martin 1994; Rudnyckyj 2010). They articulate, in a distilled fashion, "before" and "after" qualities for their subjects (corporate employees, unemployed youth, state welfare recipients, aspiring middle-class consumers, etc.), who are supposed to undergo a deep transformation (e.g., from dependent to enterprising, from low to high self-esteem) over the duration of the program. Transformative as they can appear to be midperformance, however, such choreographed pedagogies of the self are vulnerable to subsequent slippage, redirection, recidivism, and critique (e.g., Kondo 1990; Rudnyckyj 2010) and can ultimately prove evanescent in their impact on participants.

I endeavor here to look more systematically at moments of failure in farmer trainings—to explore how pedagogic technologies can elicit the "wrong" ideas and behaviors, and how they at times reinforce the very subjectivities and intersubjective relations they are supposed to replace. The trainings were meant to "responsibilize" individual farmers, but instead farmers sought to "responsibilize" Newmont. I make an argument that parallels Paul Willis's 1977 discussion of how working-class youth wind up in working-class jobs. Against the Marxist view that schools were simply succeeding in their aim of molding young subjects along class lines, Willis argues that, ironically, it was the lads' own resistance to school that prepared them for their role as laborers in the capitalist system. Similarly, Sumbawan program participants often misapprehended and critiqued the participatory and empowering rhetoric of Newmont's trainings, insisting instead that they were entitled to— and dependent on—conventional development assistance. In so doing, they enacted two kinds of interdependent, nonliberal subjects: themselves as clients and Newmont as patron. Before turning to Newmont's Farmer Field Schools, Training of Trainers program, and participatory rural appraisals, I will briefly situate Sumbawan agriculture in its geographic and historical context and, in doing so, discuss the Green Revolution and integrated pest management, which are key to making social sense of the trainings.

NEW ORDER DEVELOPMENT LEGACIES

Mine construction, which lasted from early 1997 until late 1999, had important implications for local agriculture. First, it reduced the amount of land available for farming. Newmont bought over eight hundred hectares of land from more than four hundred landowners. Moreover, the prospect of the mine unleashed a frenzy of land grabbing, trading, and speculating, which in turn left an enduring legacy of unresolved disputes, overlapping land claims, and bitterness toward the village officials, and particularly the village heads (kepala desa), who presided during this era. Questions of landownership in one village, Maluk, were further complicated by the fact that it had become part of the government's controversial transmigration program in 1983. Transmigration was meant to resettle poor, landless, dispossessed, and displaced people from more to less densely populated islands, simultaneously developing Indonesia's hinterlands and containing the threat of a growing class of urban poor. Existing Maluk residents had to cede enough land to accommodate 240 families from Lombok, Java, and elsewhere in Sumbawa. Malaria and severe water shortages led many families to abandon their new land; but mine exploration and construction brought a number of them back to reclaim it.[1] In the mid-1990s, the Indonesian government also established SP1 and SP2, two new transmigrant villages east of Tongo-Sejorong village (whose residents, too, were forced to relinquish agricultural land) and directly adjacent to the coming mine site.[2]

Besides "freeing" a number of farmers from their land, mine construction altered local residents' perceptions of labor and their broader desires and expectations for the future. Before mine construction began, agriculture was the undisputed economic mainstay. Jobs in the civil service, police, or army represented alluring and prestigious alternatives to farming, but such careers were out of reach for most, owing to limited schooling and the high cost of bribes necessary to secure government positions. Although a growing number of women had been traveling to the Middle East on two-year contracts to work as domestic laborers, they typically used their earnings to construct a new home or purchase paddy fields rather than as capital for some new enterprise. With the construction of Batu Hijau, however, Sumbawans began to act, and envision themselves, as wage laborers and the owners of small business enterprises. For younger men in particular, the farmer's hoe lacked the prestige of the miner's vest, boots, and helmet or the contractor's sport utility vehicle. Agricultural land was left fallow or leased out to migrants from Java or Lombok. Once Batu Hijau began commercial production in early 2000, however, things changed dramatically again, as described in the previous chapters, with fierce competition for a place on Batu Hijau's roster of four thousand employees and numerous demonstrations for jobs and infrastructure contracts.

As noted earlier, Batu Hijau's External Relations Department identified disaffected local farmers as the mine's top security risk; getting local people "back on the land" became a far more pressing and challenging problem than assembling a workforce. Newmont managers wanted to turn would-be mine workers, whom they saw as a threat, into a different kind of subject: farmers who knew their place (on the land). Yet Newmont programs pursued the goal of making farmers in several ways that were deeply inconsistent with one another; indeed, they often reproduced the very inconsistencies and contradictions already existent in state-led development programs.

Newmont's first model for agricultural development was the Green Revolution. Indonesia's Green Revolution programs were initially developed in the 1960s. Facing domestic Indonesian rice shortages, the left-wing administration of President Sukarno, Soeharto's predecessor, created the Bimas program (Bimbingan Massal, or Mass Guidance) to modernize agriculture by improving rural infrastructure, supporting agricultural extension, and providing farmers with high-yielding rice varieties, pesticides, fertilizers, and credit (De Koninck 1979; Winarto 2004). As another subject-making endeavor, Bimas was meant to transform "the mentality of the farmer" from "traditional" and "instinctive" to "rational" (McVey 1990; Rieffel 1969:105, 113). On September 30, 1965, just as agricultural students were preparing to introduce Bimas in rural villages, six Indonesian army generals were killed in an alleged communist coup attempt. The aforementioned wave of army-backed massacres against alleged communists swept Indonesian cities and the countryside, and then-General Soeharto used the alleged coup to consolidate control and oust Sukarno from power. Bimas went forward despite the massacres (Rieffel 1969:115), and over the ensuing decades the New Order expanded the Green Revolution through a series of Mass Guidance and Mass Intensification (Intensifikasi Massal, or Inmas) programs. Shorn of Sukarno-era land reform goals and revolutionary passion (113),[3] Bimas was carried out in partnership with the International Rice Research Institute in the Philippines and "foreign chemical companies [that] conducted aerial spraying and fertilizer distribution for entire blocks of farmland, whose farmers were frequently coerced into planting high-yielding rice varieties and charged automatically with a debt for the inputs" (Bowen 1986:553; see also Rieffel 1969).

In Indonesia, as elsewhere in Southeast Asia, the Green Revolution disproportionately benefited wealthier rural residents, who used the new technologies to increase production and shed traditional obligations to women and poorer neighbors, who were pushed onto more marginal land or off the land entirely (Franke 1974; Scott 1985; Stoler 1977; Winarto 2004:14). The resulting agrarian class differentiation, Gillian Hart and colleagues (1989) argue, reflected the state's assiduous cultivation of patron-client networks rather than neutral interactions between technology, land, and capital. Ruling national parties supplied rural elites with agricultural subsidies; rural elites, in turn, acted as the state's "agents in the countryside," policing villages, distributing development goods to loyal followers, and preserving the preternatural rural stability over decades of authoritarian rule (Antlöv 1995; see also Gupta 1998; Scott 1985).[4]

The Green Revolution, and conventional top-down New Order approaches to agricultural development more broadly, provided a ready-made template for mine managers to adopt for use with local residents they wanted to convince to farm. Starting in 2000, Newmont's Community Development Department set about using bulldozers to clear land that had fallen into disuse during mine construction, so farmers could resume cultivation; the department also went on to construct dams, weirs, and irrigation channels for agriculture. Newmont's nominally independent development foundation, Yayasan Olat Parigi, began dispensing chemical pesticides and fertilizers along with microcredit, water pumps, fish, livestock (water buffalo, chickens, goats, cows), and seeds and seedlings. While the foundation nominally provided these goods to farmers through loans, more often than not, local residents, following long-standing patterns of interaction with state authorities, interpreted credit and supplies as gifts and failed to repay the foundation. The tangible technologies and "can-do" approach appealed to Batu Hijau managers with backgrounds in engineering. For other managers and employees, it also made sense that agricultural inputs could be used to build alliances or, to put it in a different idiom, cement patron-client relations. Mine managers refashioned the state practice of cultivating rural elites through development inputs as a corporate strategy for addressing mine security risks and needs.

But the Green Revolution was not the only model of development to which Newmont officials turned. In 2001, Ibu Comdev (Batu Hijau's newly hired Community Development manager, whom we met in previous chapters) began trying to steer the mine's programs onto a more participatory course. She drew on her background at the U.S. Agency for International Development to find consultants and NGOs who could train local residents in participatory approaches and alternative development models. From her perspective, if local people's actions were governed by reason rather than emotion, they would begin to meet the company halfway in generating local progress and development, rather than demonstrate to demand jobs. Over the course of a year in the company, she reported progress in villagers' attitudes as they realized that they were "only hurting themselves by demonstrating" and preventing fellow villagers from getting to work in the mine. Increasingly, she added, villagers had begun to sanction their own "troublemakers."

Although the participatory integrated pest management (IPM) programs to which Ibu Comdev turned had been developed in explicit opposition to many of the technologies of the Green Revolution and the ideology that undergirded it, these programs too had their origins in Soeharto's New Order. The Green Revolution produced spectacular increases in rice production but also increased pesticide resistance, leaving farmers vulnerable to pest epidemics.[5] In 1986, with brown planthopper outbreaks devastating rice crops, President Soeharto signed a presidential decree banning fifty-seven insecticide varieties from use in rice cultivation, eliminating pesticide subsidies, and pledging to train 2.5 million farmers in IPM with support from the United Nations' Food and Agriculture Organization (see Fox 1991:75–76). The IPM framework promotes "natural" biological, physical, and chemical pest controls, including weather, habitat modification, and the protection of "natural enemies" (predators and parasites; see Winarto 2004:20–21).[6] To train farmers in IPM, the organization created its first Farmer Field Schools in 1989, drawing heavily on participatory development models, discussed in greater detail later in the chapter. These "schools without walls" ran for one morning a week over twelve weeks, in parallel with the cycle of paddy planting, transplanting, and harvesting.[7] IPM temporally succeeded the Green Revolution model but by no means eclipsed it, reaching only a fraction of the farmers who had already adopted Green Revolution techniques. The incomplete and inconsistent shift in Indonesian agriculture toward IPM makes sense if one approaches the state not as a monolithic entity but as a complex set of processes and actors whose actions are not well coordinated, and at times even work at cross-purposes to one another. Much as conventional Green Revolution and IPM models coexist in state policies, they coexist in Batu Hijau's approaches to farmers.

PARTICIPATORY TECHNOLOGIES, INTEGRATED PEST MANAGEMENT, AND THE CULTURE OF FACILITATION

The participatory turn initiated by Newmont's Community Development manager was neither surprising nor unprecedented. Participation was in the air, having become "the new orthodoxy of development" by the early 1990s, with every major bilateral development agency emphasizing participatory policies (Henkel 2001:168). By the late 1990s, CSR managers in extractive industries saw participatory technologies as part of the best practices tool kit for community interactions and development programming. Over the course of my research, I observed and gathered materials from multiple Newmont-supported Farmer Field Schools, Training of Trainers programs for farmers, and participatory rural appraisals. Newmont also carried out participatory wealth rankings, participatory school assessments, and participatory health assessments. When a conflict brewed in one village over who should be village head, Batu Hijau managers even discussed running a participatory political assessment to resolve the crisis. The Indonesian state was hardly immune to this trend. As one Indonesian government official wistfully remarked during a meeting with Newmont managers over the next year's budget, the horseback-riding, pistol-toting days of "commando government" were over; Indonesia had entered an era of "participatory government."

If conventional approaches to development treated people as objects, as "abstract concepts" or "statistical figures to be moved up and down in the chart of 'progress'" (Escobar 1995:44), participatory technologies were supposed to restore agency to people as subjects of their own development.[8] Further, by incorporating anthropologists and ethnographic methods, development planners hoped to make their programs more cost-effective and culturally appropriate.[9] Critics depict participatory technologies as having a "patina of radical politics" (Francis 2001:75; Hailey 2001:99; Leal 2007) derived from the work of Ivan Illich (1971) and Paulo Freire (1970), thinkers who sought to create a model of education that supported political transformation, valorized and worked inductively from the knowledge and insights of the oppressed, and countered the conventional hierarchical relationship between teachers and students.[10] In keeping with participatory principles, the Newmont staff and consultants who led agricultural trainings were called "facilitators," signaling that they facilitated the knowledge and consciousness of participants, rather than teaching them from a position of hierarchical authority.

Most of the consultants, NGOs, and field staff from Newmont's Community Development Department who led trainings hailed from outside the mining region: five were from the regency branch of the Indonesian Integrated Pest Management Farmers' Association (Ikatan Petani Pengendalian Hama Terpadu Indonesia); several were from the neighboring island of Lombok; and the most senior were two Javanese men with backgrounds at the Food and Agriculture Organization. An exception was Pak Nur, a village resident who had recently graduated from a university in east Java, where he also had been briefly imprisoned for political activities and affiliation with the leftist People's Democratic Party (Partai Rakyat Indonesia). Although he formed an NGO that partnered with Batu Hijau on various programs, such as the trainings, he was ambivalent about Newmont's presence in southwest Sumbawa and acutely aware of the irony involved in teaching lessons in political empowerment and IPM with mine support. Other facilitators sometimes felt this irony, too. When Pak Amir, one of the Food and Agriculture Organization–trained facilitators, toured the mine and saw its vast expanse, he was reduced to tears. The benefits of bamboo drip irrigation systems and pesticide reduction seemed environmentally trivial next to the impact of the mine itself.

The Food and Agriculture Organization model adopted by Newmont's facilitators conjoins IPM and participatory technologies. The model's scope of concern extends beyond the environment narrowly construed. Facilitators promoted the analysis of structural violence (Farmer 2004); principles of social justice and collective rights; democratization of economic and scientific tools and analysis; and a natural, informal, and simple aesthetic. They believed in and performed a "hybrid agronomy" of scientific and economic rationalization, romantic nostalgia, and radical pedagogy.[11] IPM facilitators used exercises and discussions to stimulate recollections of the past and to shape and classify farmers' memories. Much of this "memory work" (Delcore 2003) centered on the participants' experiences in adopting and using the pesticides, fertilizers, and high-yield rice varieties of the Green Revolution.

Facilitators cast violence, dispossession, and disempowerment as central to the farmers' Green Revolution experience, while framing the era preceding it in a positive and nostalgic light. In one activity, facilitators asked participants to catalogue—using the markers and flip charts that are the obligatory accoutrements of such trainings—the rice varieties, pesticides, and fertilizers they had used since the 1970s. Facilitators could anticipate the participants' lists of rice acronyms and foreign-sounding commercial compounds because the same succession of seed, pesticide, and fertilizer "input packets" had been distributed across, and beyond, Indonesia.[12] Imbuing rice with agency (similarly, see Gupta 1998), participants described the acronym-titled varieties as "spoiled" (manja) and "greedy" (rakus) because they demanded large quantities of expensive inputs and water. Asked what kinds of paddy they had planted before the Green Revolution, participants recalled varieties with colorful names like hairy rice and copper rice, each with its distinctive characteristics and growth cycles.[13] Facilitators asked participants to plot this type of data on a historical analysis chart showing the numbers of human illnesses, rice varieties, pesticides, fertilizers, and pest species over the past four decades. The facilitators sought to correlate the shrinking number of rice varieties and the growing use of pesticides and fertilizers with outbreaks of pests and new human illnesses, but in order to do this they had to intervene to rework the tables drawn up by the farmers. Thus the era before the Green Revolution appeared to be a golden age of abundant rice varieties, low fertilizer and pesticide use, and limited human diseases and pest afflictions.

Facilitators used these data to open up discussion of the numerous environmental impacts of Green Revolution technologies. They screened a documentary on the devastating potential consequences of pesticides. When farmers called pesticides *obat* (medicine), something that should be routinely applied to rice (as to a body) as a form of preventive care, the facilitators corrected them, insisting that pesticides should instead be called poison (*racun;* Hansen 1971:71; Winarto 2004). The participants were horrified by the footage of Javanese farmers severely and permanently debilitated by pesticide exposure, and unsettled by the familiarity of much of what they saw. They too had been approached in their paddy fields by corporate-sponsored "formulators" peddling pesticides. They too had opened, used, and disposed of pesticides without safety precautions. Several recalled instances of nausea and headaches associated with pesticide use. One remembered a time when he sprayed his fields then staggered home, told his wife not to bother him, and passed out for several hours. They began thereby to link what had seemed to be merely individual experiences to larger processes.

Facilitators also focused on questions of agency. They asked participants: "What happened to the Sumbawan process of seed selection and breeding [*sanklek*]?" "Where did all your paddy go? Is it in a bank in the Philippines?" After suggesting that the rice varieties had not disappeared but had been appropriated, Pak Amir appealed to nationalist sentiment: "Why doesn't Indonesia have a bank like that?" Linking the historical analysis of environmental impacts to a structural analysis, IPM facilitators sought to demonstrate that attempts to increase food supplies were not politically innocent, that, indeed, the farmers had been disempowered systematically, not accidentally. As Pak Nur darkly warned, "Everything in our environment is moving, while we just stay quietly, awaiting our fate. Everything is in motion; we too must move. We are the objects of a conspiracy between the Agriculture Ministry and the seed corporations. We have been humiliated. In the past we had such variety, then the *koramil* [military commander] came and said, 'You must plant this and that.'" Pak Amir explained that universities and other research institutions, the government, credit institutions, the

World Bank and the Asian Development Bank, the International Rice Research Institute, and European and Japanese corporations created input packets with no regard for local ecological variation, the maintenance of long-term ecological integrity, and the economics of small-scale farming.[14] He told them,

> We must pray [zikir], reflect deeply [tafakkur]. For example, BRI [Bank Rakyat Indonesia, the People's Bank of Indonesia]—we see only its hands and feet in the village; it comes also from Jakarta, from the World Bank. Bayer, Monsanto—these are giants, they have monthly meetings, and they enter the village systematically, in a fashion that is hardly felt by us, and they have computers where they keep data on villages. They feel it when Pak Nur appears. Now if farmers are busy, each just thinking about himself, we can't fight them. Pak Nur said that we must police the traffic in information. Newmont has interests, too, so we cannot have too much faith in them.

Using rousing rhetoric, facilitators urged farmers to see that they suffered a shared predicament created by larger forces. To judge by their nods, murmurs of agreement, and exclamations of disapproval, the participants largely found this conspiracy narrative compelling and disturbing.

Facilitators then prompted participants to reproduce this narrative through social analysis exercises diagramming their relations with state and private actors. The size of the circles representing designated actors indicated their significance, and the thickness of arrows linking each actor to the peasant indicated the ratio of give and take in their relations of exchange. Constructing these diagrams, participants grew animated. They criticized Yayasan Olat Parigi (Newmont's foundation) for "using the community's name to enrich itself" and the national electricity company for "not being social," for providing service as sporadic as it was expensive and for being punitive in charging for it. Through this exercise, facilitators sought to impart the understanding that participants were objectively exploited by most if not all the institutional actors with whom they dealt. The single figure labeled "farmer" at the center of these structural analysis diagrams suggested their homogeneity as a class, the essential similarity of their experiences of exploitation (Kearney 1996), just as it obscured relations of exploitation among them; class, gender, and ethnic differences; and finally the fact that a single farmer may occupy multiple subject positions (e.g., civil servant, village head, or merchant).

The facilitators implied that farmers adopted Green Revolution technologies because they were either duped or forced into it. One farmer affirmed this with his admission that, as a young government agricultural officer in the 1970s, "I had to chase farmers down and force them to use the new rice. It was like forcing people into family planning at first." His analogy was not uncommon—one Green Revolution rice variety was even dubbed "family planning rice" (*padi KB, keluarga berencana*; see Fox 1991:68)—and it had a material basis: rapid population growth had made agricultural self-sufficiency, which Sukarno had failed to achieve, an increasingly urgent goal of the Soeharto administration (Hansen 1971:74–75). Although coercion and fear figure in their social memories of state interventions into agricultural production and human reproduction, Sumbawans had in fact viewed these programs with ambivalence. Agricultural inputs and contraceptives had at times been forced upon people, but, often enough, local demand for these government-subsidized products had actually outstripped supply, allowing local authorities to consolidate their power by regulating access to them (see also Tsing 1993:108–9; Winarto 2004:25–26). Many Indonesian farmers had been interested in trying new Green Revolution technologies but wanted pesticides without fertilizers, or vice versa, and had disliked being forced to accept a whole package of inputs on credit. Throughout the Green Revolution period, credit repayment rates had been extremely low, and farmers indeed took the program as a (not necessarily desirable) government handout rather than a loan (Hansen 1971:65; Rieffel 1969:119). Newmont's IPM facilitators ignored such complexities in their narrative of farmer disempowerment at the hands of the state.

The facilitators then sought to reveal a path through which farmers' agency—and the environment—might be restored. They urged participants to seize their rights to improve their fields; access government services; play a role in determining prices; receive correct information; work in a healthy environment; develop seeds; manage water; market products; create formal organizations; and enjoy linguistic, cultural, and artistic expression (IPPHTI n.d.). Although facilitators cultivated nostalgia for the past, they did not encourage participants to return to barter relations or subsistence farming. They proposed they become enterprising farmers rather than static traditional peasants—even as they criticized contemporary "free" market conditions (and policies of international institutions such as the IMF, WTO, and World Bank) that allowed developed countries to heavily subsidize agriculture while forcing developing countries like Indonesia to dismantle their agricultural protections. *Transnational agricultural capitalism is a rigged game, so you better get good at it* was more or less the message. Facilitators reminded participants that their produce could be turned away from developed countries for excess levels of toxic pesticide residues; urged them to focus their energies on something other than poultry if they could not produce Indonesian chickens more cheaply than those imported from New Zealand or Thailand; and encouraged them to consider tapping into distant European markets for organic tropical medicinals or cultivating information networks and infrastructure allowing them to store produce rather than sell it off when prices bottomed out after the harvest.[15]

In addition to encouraging participants to be savvy market players, facilitators sought to impart to local agriculture a scientific idiom. With bought and donated land, they created "laboratories" where field schools were held and "experiments" conducted in accordance with scientific principles, using test and control plots to measure variations in productivity and insect density resulting from variations in technique (timing, spacing, watering, etc.), seeds used, and other inputs (Winarto 2004).[16] Through practical experiments in laboratories, facilitators sought to convey to participants the merits of creating and controlling their own knowledge rather than relying on external authorities for it (figure 11).[17] After the results had been measured from harvested test plots planted with IR-64 and several organic varieties of rice from Java, this conversation ensued:

> *Pak Amir:* Should we buy rice with a label or without a label? Who makes the label?
>
> *Participants:* A company!
>
> *Pak Amir:* If a company makes a label do we believe what they say? What they are interested in is making a profit. Of course the PPL [government agricultural extension officer] recommends that you buy the labeled rice, but from our research the ones that don't have a label are better. Companies like to use farmers too. It is better if we use our minds. . . . We eat rice, not brand names.

The facilitators also invoked an economic logic in urging participants to consider alternatives to industry-produced pesticides and fertilizers, comparing the cost of pesticides to what a farmer might expect to earn selling rice, and calculating the probable costs (in rice) of not spraying. When a similar calculus was brought to bear on fertilizers, one Sumbawan farmer spoke of how he still made his own fertilizers. Fearing his homemade fertilizer would be seen as a sign of poverty (commercial

FIGURE 11. Farmers taking part in an integrated pest management training. Photo by author.

fertilizer, conversely, being associated with wealth and prestige), he usually spread it on his fields at dusk when no one was around. By this point in the workshop, he had reframed his homemade fertilizer in positive terms.

More generally, the facilitators sought to revalorize farming in comparison to higher-status activities such as working for the civil service or Newmont. Several local men and women had told me they were ashamed (*malu*) to be seen going into their fields and farming, and that they disliked planting and harvesting in the hot sun. One training participant explained he wanted to do well in farming so that his children could be raised for something greater than just holding a hoe (*pegang cangkul*). Facilitators in turn emphasized the foundational role of farming in feeding the nation. If not the farmers, they asked, who would feed (then-president) Megawati? Describing farming as the purest (*paling murni*) form of work, they praised myriad details of the training setting—many of which were otherwise unremarked parts of everyday life for farmers—as indices of the aesthetic pleasures of peasant simplicity, informality, earthiness, and intimacy. They called attention to how the farmers and facilitators sat on leaves spread on the ground under bamboo structures, used their hands to eat, wore torn clothing, took their shoes off, and prayed together. And they noted farming's inextricable link to Sumbawan culture: "If we reopen our history we find that all of our culture is connected to our farming. . . . If *basiru* [mutual aid] disappears in farming, how much more in other aspects of our culture? The destruction of farming represents the destruction of our culture."

THE LIMITS OF TRAININGS

It often struck me as ironic that a mining corporation was sponsoring programs in which participants were being radicalized, taught to value their knowledge and use it to think critically about their relations with corporations and government authorities. Yet it soon became apparent to me that the trainings were not taking hold among participants in the ways they were supposed to. This might be attributed to the fact that the ideas of Paulo Freire and other radical thinkers used in the trainings had been diluted and deradicalized, first by a development industry seeking, in a neoliberal era, to put the onus for development on citizens rather than states or international institutions, and second by a mining corporation. Indeed, Batu Hijau's Community Development manager had cautioned one facilitator to not be too inflammatory in exhorting participants to transform their structural conditions. For reasons explored in the following pages, this fear of radicalized subjects may well have been unwarranted. I focus first on the mundane limits of the trainings, and then show how participants criticized normative training assumptions, casting themselves instead as subjects entitled to material forms of development assistance from Newmont.

To begin with, the selection processes that produced Newmont's participant rosters curtailed the reach of its participatory programs. Newmont facilitators and members of the village governing apparatus were responsible for selecting participants, and their selection criteria were often inconsistent with broader participatory goals of social, political, and environmental transformation. One Javanese sharecropper taking part in the Training of Trainers program, for example, suspected his selection had been a political favor by a village head, on whose land he lived and worked. Because he resided well outside of the village and interacted little with other village residents, he was unlikely to motivate other villagers to adopt IPM. Two other participants, Pak Jamal and Pak Saleh, speculated that the village head had selected them as participants because they had been publicly organizing former workers from the mine's exploration era to demand compensation from Newmont (on the grounds that the mine had paid them low wages as day laborers and had not hired them on as permanent workers once production began). They regarded the training as an effort to distract them from their political goals.

Participants were also overwhelmingly male, despite the emphasis in participatory development materials on the significance and benefits of women's involvement. Indeed, Newmont terminated the contract of the one female facilitator from the regency capital early on, leaving exclusively male facilitators. I suspect this gender bias may be widespread in participatory programs, rather than simply reflecting the particular conditions of West Sumbawa.[18] As in other Newmont programs, the absence of women tended to go along with other exclusions. The poorest village residents, landless farmers, and non-Sumbawan transmigrants were largely absent. The trainings reached only a limited number of participants and tended to exclude the socially and economically marginalized. In this way, the trainings followed rather than subverted the ruling order.

The trainings also entailed activities that could be viewed as culturally inappropriate for mixed-gender groups, further reinforcing the gender bias. The very structure of the Training of Trainers program, which entailed an eight- to ten-day commitment, during which time participants were supposed to sleep away from their homes, made it unfeasible for most women. Further, in southwest Sumbawan villages there is a sufficient degree of gender segregation in social life that many of the games—which involved physical contact, dancing, and one-on-one partner activities—would have been uncomfortable or even unseemly for a mixed-gender group. Part of my own experience during these trainings involved learning when to step out of such games to avoid provoking the discomfort of male participants; sometimes when I was not quick enough to excuse myself, older men would instruct me to do so.

At times the trainings went beyond being culturally inappropriate to become culturally unintelligible. A discourse must be recognizable in order to be persuasive (Keane 2005:721), and participants clearly did not always grasp what facilitators were talking about (Winarto 2004). Participants were not always equipped with the tacit, class-based cultural knowledge and behavior that would have enabled facilitators to pull off their activities successfully. I was frequently struck by the fact that I found the trainings and the implicit narratives that ran through them more compelling than did my fellow village participants. Although participatory pedagogy is supposed to work inductively from the knowledge of participants, Hull (2010:263) shows that participatory speech technologies are at once "objective and suggestive," blending "dialectic or conversation used to uncover truth" with "oratory, intended to persuade interlocutors to act in a particular way." IPM is embedded with scripts (e.g., about the Green Revolution's negative impacts) and norms (e.g., respect for nature) that were already instilled in or obvious to me (someone with an undergraduate degree in environmental biology who worries about pesticide residues in food and the larger political economy of agribusiness) but which eluded many of my fellow participants. For example, when the facilitators set up the historical analysis I discussed earlier, it was immediately apparent to me that the objective was to show a set of related trends: more synthetic pesticides, fewer rice varieties, more human diseases. This was not evident to the other participants, however, who produced lists with the number of human diseases declining over time. The facilitators obtained the results they wanted only by adding diseases such as colds to the list (likely experienced before the Green Revolution too) and cancer (rates may well have gone up, but so has diagnosis). I already believed in the scientific correlation between these trends, but, for the participants making up these charts, it was not obvious what the facilitators wanted them to show, ostensibly from their own experiences. Similarly, Daromir Rudnyckyj (2009b:111) found that Emotional and Spiritual Quotient trainings at Indonesia's Krakatau Steel had profound appeal for "an educated audience of middle- and upper-middle-class participants" but met with "less success" among employees at lower levels of the company, such as foremen and operators.[19]

When facilitators had to shoehorn what participants said into the dominant IPM narrative, the gap between their pedagogical model and their conviction that they (rather than the participants) knew the real story of the Green Revolution became painfully apparent. Today, most farmers plant IR-64 rice, one of the high-yield varieties developed in the Philippines. Some have retained stocks of older varieties, which they have grown on the side for their families and consider more nutritious than IR-64—an approach that accords with the IPM narrative. Other farmers however saw things differently. Some, for example, proclaimed that they had abandoned older varieties that took five to six months to grow and, although strong enough to outcompete weeds, tasted terrible. Despite several pest outbreaks over the 1990s, many southwest

Sumbawans saw an overall advantage in planting varieties that grow in three months and allow for two crops per year. Living in Indonesia's driest region, Nusa Tenggara, Sumbawan farmers could vividly recall past periods of drought-induced famine and intense hunger when their rice stores ran out and they were reduced to eating sago, boiled bananas, and corn as starch (similarly, see Delcore 2003:72–73; Ellen 2007:4, 24–28; Monk, De Fretes, and Reksodiharjo-Lilley 1997:69, 494).

The facilitators' attempts to manage games and icebreakers were also vulnerable to breakdown, particularly as they transitioned between the phases of setup, execution, and exegesis. Uma Kothari has noted that participatory development involves very contrived performances "where the . . . facilitators act as stage managers or directors who guide, and attempt to delimit, [the participants'] performance" (Kothari 2001:148–49):

> The development practitioner initiating a PRA [Participatory Rural Appraisal] is asking participants to adopt and play a role using certain techniques and tools, thus shaping and, in some instances, confining the way in which performers may have chosen to represent themselves. The stage and the props for the performance may be alien to the performer. The tools provided can limit the performance so that the performers are unable to convey what they want to; the stage has been set by others and the form of the performance similarly guided by them. The resulting communication or dialogue [is] then fraught with confusion and ambiguity.

While Kothari emphasizes the control of facilitators, I instead underscore the "confusion and ambiguity" that emerges when they fail to fully control the performance. When, for example, facilitators had participants do the trust fall (in which one participant falls backward from a standing position into the arms of a waiting partner), they did not get the results typically elicited in group trainings in the United States (e.g., the unnerving moment of letting go and the relief upon being caught; see also Martin 1994, chap. 11). Several spotters allowed their partners to fall to the ground, occasioning laughter, shock, embarrassment, and a little bruising. In another trust-building game, which involved steering a blindfolded and perambulating partner, a number of participants took the opportunity to slam their charges into the poles holding up the palm roof or into other pairs of participants. Any message conveyed by these activities was quite different from the one intended.

Role-playing games also misfired when participants themselves introduced evaluative criteria incommensurate with the intended "take home message." In one activity meant to demonstrate that better guidance produced better results, for example, we were divided into groups of six, assigned leaders, and asked to construct towers and boats out of straws. The facilitators took the leaders aside and told them to role-play a certain kind of leader: one was to be a good, supportive leader, the other two were to be bad leaders—demanding and aggressive, or lazy and apathetic. Hull (2010:278) traces such simple oppositions in leadership types in participatory trainings to World War II–era research on speech technologies for changing politically pathological subjects—the German "autocrat" and "its complement, the passive or submissive subject"—into American democrats. As one of those asked to be a bad leader, I disparaged my group's efforts as they worked, producing a rather pathetic, small, lopsided tower that one participant joked looked like the handiwork of a Newmont subcontractor. The other group with a "bad leader," however, made a tall tower creatively festooned with origami cranes (which we had made earlier as a lesson in the value of learning by doing). While the latter made it hard to argue that bad leaders generate poor results, my group, not wanting to compare unfavorably to other groups, insisted that as a leader I had made them feel safe, good, and proud.

Trainings also fell short of their mark when, as one of Newmont's Community Development workers wryly observed, they put participants into a state of *asbun. Asbun* is short for *asal bunyi,* denoting the production of noise simply for the sake of noise, without real interest, effort, or regard for content and meaning. Echols and Shadily (1989:31) translate this as speech without forethought. The mental disengagement of asbun can be a consequence of over-routinized participation. For example, the facilitators frequently employed a didactic technique that involved asking questions such as "What is an ecosystem?" "What did we learn from playing that game?" or "What is a motivator?" Participants' answers would be used to generate a brainstorming list, from which facilitators would draw the group toward a sound conclusion. But once the facilitator had affirmed the correct tenor of the response, by noting it approvingly on the flip chart, for example, participants would continue with responses that largely reiterated the same theme, often gaining momentum as they went. It often took an effort on the part of facilitators to stanch the flow of resulting platitudes (e.g., an ecosystem would be described as depending upon one another, loving one another, etc.). Whereas some of the confusion resulting from the games described earlier derived from a lack of cultural relevance, *asbun* emerges instead from participants being overpracticed and only marginally engaged. Their hyperobedience—whether it was rooted in deliberate parody or in support combined with incomplete engagement and understanding—could have a subversive effect on the training's objectives (Boyer and Yurchak 2010; Heryanto 2006).

MATERIAL MICROPOLITICS

Many critics of participatory development have viewed it as an insidious process for remaking subjects, a process ultimately embedded in relations of power that go largely unremarked by facilitators and participants.[20] The analytic burden of such critiques then becomes the revelation of insidious relations of power supposedly concealed from those taking part. Several critics have lauded resistance on the part of participants but portray it as intermittent, unconnected, unsystematic, fugitive, deviant interruptions.[21] In my research, by contrast, I found resistance to the training and the lessons they were supposed to impart to be widespread and systematic. I devote this section to analyzing this resistance, attending to how it often appears in a material register that may be neglected in studies focusing on interiorized transformations of subjectivity. I do not attach an *a priori* positive valence to expressions of resistance and critique. As feminist scholars have noted, in resisting one form of authority (e.g., traditional patriarchal power), subjects often assume subordinate roles within other forms of power (e.g., state or capitalist authority; Abu-Lughod 1991; Ong 1987). In this case, I show that resistance to participatory programs was not necessarily politically progressive and could in fact be rooted in a desire to foster closer relations with Newmont or to defend ideologies central to the Green Revolution and legacies of Soeharto's New Order rule.

Critics have correctly pointed out that participatory development models tend to suppress and deny hierarchies and relations of power within trainings and among community members. I found that participants themselves were acutely attuned to how the trainings were related to—indeed, enacted—broader relations of power. At a basic level, participants expressed this concern by publicly estimating how much the trainings must cost and how the budget was allocated, factoring in the wages of facilitators, honoraria for participants, supplies, and daily meals and snacks. Some speculated that the facilitators inflated participant rosters to extract more money from the company. Participants also complained about the quality of the food, with some voicing suspicion of foul play on the part of the (usually Javanese) caterers, perhaps in collusion with the training's organizing committee. This kind of conflict was not limited to corporate-sponsored events. In post-Soeharto Indonesia, suspicions about corruption (and phenomena like faked and inflated participant rosters and even billings for facilities rentals and refreshments for nonexistent trainings) were rampant. A teacher who attended a government-sponsored training on the neighboring island of Lombok told me that he and others had banded together to expose the training committee's misappropriation of snack funds, leading to a melee that left one committee member with a bleeding head wound.

A participant asked in one training how much he and his fellows might expect to earn in honoraria (*uang duduk*, lit. "sitting money") for their participation. A Newmont facilitator responded by ribbing them about their "cash obsession," at which a generally mild-mannered Sumbawan farmer sharply retorted, "Don't always oppress us!" Another facilitator attempted to defuse things by suggesting that they carry on with the training, promising he would later whisper the sum into the farmer's ear. I suspect that in light of the shared interests, goals, and altruistic motivations that were supposed to characterize participation, the facilitator found explicit discussion of honoraria vulgar and embarrassing. For participants, however, these payments represented the only material benefit they could truly count on after spending more than a week away from their normal lives. They wanted, moreover, to assure local kiosk owners that they would be able to pay them for the cigarettes they were purchasing on credit during the training.

Participants found other ways to underscore the hierarchies internal to the training (amounting, in the eyes of some, to an undercurrent of oppression running through it). They were keenly aware that the facilitators, like other agents of development they had encountered, owed their conditions of material privilege to their claim to be assisting villagers. They did not take facilitators' simple dress and demeanor as a sign of poverty or shared status with farmers.[22] During a break, Pak Jamal, one of the farmers who suspected he had been selected to participate in the training as a means to distract him from his grievances over Newmont's handling of exploration workers, complained of the infantilizing nature of the games and pointed out that the facilitators were all younger than him. Tugging at his hair, he added, "Look, I'm already going gray, and they're making me play like a child, mocking me."

Participants also grew annoyed when facilitators did not translate their ideas into plain speech. At one training, a participant irately insisted that facilitators stop using words like *productivity, commitment, management, monev* (monitoring and evaluation), and *lab* because farmers did not understand what these words meant. When a facilitator responded by trying to explain what *paddy management* meant, he was immediately silenced by a chorus of calls for him to "sit down." Another farmer explained, "We don't go to the office, and in the paddy fields there is no such term as *management*. It has no meaning or place." Facilitators themselves were sometimes uncertain of the meanings of the words they used, and called upon me to explicate terms like *demplot* (demonstration plot) or *gender,* noting that these words originated in "Marina language" (i.e., English). Yunita T. Winarto (2004) meticulously documents the failures (as well as successes) in processes of IPM knowledge production. Such knowledge failures—which scholars have noted are often neglected in Foucauldian approaches (Graeber 2006; Mathews 2005)—are related in turn to failures in the production of new subjectivities.

Participants' critiques of the facilitators and their modes of learning and teaching went deeper than hostility to jargon. After a highly technical discussion of random sampling during a training, Pak Hajji Razak, a soft-spoken but authoritative participant, criticized the discussion in particular and, in general, how the training aimed to turn them into something called "guides" as opposed to conventional "leaders":

> I am a farmer. Perhaps not by the measure of a guide [*pemandu*], but what is really important is that one is capable of doing everything. If you start looking at papers, then there are grades, and then we have to go to school like Pak Nur. . . . I, personally, am a farmer. Perhaps with this training you could say I've become a guide. But I am a farmer. I—as a farmer—was invited to join this training. It's not that we don't respect important people [*yang tinggi*] like Pak Nur. I am just a lowly person [*orang rendah*]. But as a farmer my success is beyond doubt.

All of the facilitators and participants knew that through his farming success this man had become a hajji, with the means to undertake the pilgrimage to Mecca. With his statement, he questioned the entire exercise, asking what utility it would hold for him, a successful farmer, to be taught by facilitators younger than he and whose skills derived largely from formal education.

Other participants questioned even these skills. One farmer told a facilitator that he and his neighbors did not want any more guidance, that the facilitators should leave since they just eat and drink and ride around on nice motorbikes, not teaching farmers anything useful. On another occasion he suggested to me, "Perhaps we should expel our friends from Sumbawa [Sumbawa Besar, the regency capital], who get lots of money even though they can't farm as well as I can. . . . They sell the people's heads, writing their little reports." Another participant remarked to me that as impressive as their farming techniques might be on paper, many facilitators appeared to know little in the fields. Several farmers also insisted during our conversations that they too could be successful if only they had access to the seemingly unlimited supply of capital that Newmont used to furnish its experimental field labs with generators, concrete-lined fishponds, seedlings, and the like.

A story told by another senior male villager further illustrates such critical takes. He spoke out after sitting down while the rest of us engaged in one of our more undignified icebreakers (the theme was "Titanic" and we danced around the room in a circle, singing "Hallo-Hallo Bandung" and clapping until a facilitator called out a number, upon which we would rush to assemble the right number of friends in a lifeboat). The man was a somewhat imposing former village head and stalwart of Golkar, the government party that had supported Soeharto's thirty-two years of authoritarian rule; he stood up and delivered his story unbidden:

> A youth from Jereweh went to Lombok [the neighboring island] for six years, where he obtained a religious education. When he returned to the village, he was wearing the clothes of one who had gone on the hajj. No one recognized him anymore, but he explained who he was, and he was well received. He offered to deliver a sermon at the mosque. On the appointed day the mosque was packed with listeners. He stood up, opened al Qur'an, and proceeded to read. He read his sermon from start to finish. As he read, much of his audience disappeared, walking out of the mosque, while those who were left behind were lulled into a deep sleep. At the end of the reading the young man said, "Thank you, all you gentlemen." An old man stirred awake from his slumber and responded, "Thank you for your reading."

After listening attentively, the audience, including the facilitators, erupted in hearty laughter at the man's story. In contrast to facilitator-led activities, however, we did not pause for any exegesis. Instead, the facilitators steered us nervously toward the next activity on the program agenda. Yet the man's story, alongside his refusal to participate in the song and dance of the training, constituted a profound commentary on participatory methodologies. Like the learned religious scholar, facilitators at times regurgitated participatory development dogma and methods without reflection or a process of translation that would make their ideas relevant or useful to Sumbawan villagers. They read their scripts from start to finish. Just as the young man who wore the trappings of a hajji could not make a meaningful contribution to villagers' religious understanding, facilitators' inability to make themselves understood called into question the superiority they were often accorded by virtue of their formal education credentials or position as facilitators.

At times, participants also explicitly rejected the roles marked out for them as village motivators and guides who would altruistically adopt the charismatic facilitator role and propagate participatory values and IPM technologies. We engaged in games and role plays to grapple with the supposed difference between the conventional leader (*pemimpin*) and the village motivator (*penggerak desa*): Whereas a leader is formally elected and motivated by a desire for prestige, for example, a motivator is informally selected and works voluntarily for the people, motivated by shared interests. Whereas a leader barks out orders and is obedient to higher authorities, a motivator asks questions, works with people, and sets an example. Whereas a leader is stiff, formal, and clad in a government-issue uniform, a motivator is informal, approachable, and indistinguishable from fellow farmers in appearance. As examples of leaders, facilitators cited a regent, village head, or tribal leader (*kepala suku*, a formal administrative position since the Dutch era), while citing the Prophet Mohammed as an example of a motivator. The motivator is a cross between the "big man" in anthropological literature, who leads by example rather than by issuing orders, and Gramsci's "organic intellectual" (1971), who is part of a community of fate, developing consciousness from practical labor.[23]

Participants, however, questioned the notion of working uncompensated for the community's benefit. At one training, Pak Saleh, another of the critics of Newmont who had been demanding more compensation for former exploration workers, raised the issue several times, asking whether participants were truly capable of voluntarily working for the community. One of the facilitators converted his question into a slogan that the participants yelled in unison at the end of the day, punching the air with their fists and crying out, "We can become voluntary motivators!" (*Kita sanggup menjadi penggerak sukarela*). Pak Saleh went through the motions of this rousing finale but complained afterward that his question had been pushed around "like a billiard ball." Others believed Newmont was actually training them to create a pool of replacements for the company's expensive Javanese facilitators. In a conversation with me and another participant one evening, one man confided that he was already fantasizing about how he would go around telling farmers what crops to plant in their fields after he was hired by Newmont; his words invoked the pleasures of conventional leadership, of telling others what to do. According to his calculations,

Newmont would be able to pay the wages of twelve Sumbawan agriculture officers with the sum that they were paying each month to a single Javanese consultant. Thus, instead of embracing the role of motivator championed by the facilitators, he embraced that of the leader.

The facilitators attempted to make the motivator's voluntarism appealing by explaining it as behaving unselfishly (*dengan ikhlas*) or being like an ustadz (religious teacher) without selfish interests (*tanpa pamrih*). Several of the participants were in fact ustadz, teaching children in the villages how to recite the Qur'an, with no direct remuneration. Yet this did not mean that they were eager to apply the same logic to farming, especially when the facilitators urging them to do so were being paid by Newmont. One participant disconcerted a facilitator on precisely this point, asking whether he would be doing his facilitating work without the security of a generous paycheck.

In retrospect, the ideas expressed by participants as they entered the trainings were fairly accurate harbingers of the challenges, subversions, and rejections they would unleash in due course. At the beginning of the Training of Trainers, for example, facilitators elicited from participants a list of their hopes and fears for the program. Many of the responses were highly specific in nature. For example, the hope lists included water bores; water pumps; vegetable seeds and an explanation of how to market vegetables globally; knowledge of how to raise grapes, seedless watermelons, and *karper* and *nila* fish; and seeds for long-term crops like cocoa, mango, durian, coconut, cashew, and various sorts of teak (e.g., *jati super, jati mas*). More generally, the participants listed goals such as increasing their knowledge about agriculture and integrated farming, controlling pests, reducing unemployment, improving their marketing of crops, strengthening relations between farmers, dealing with the strong winds near the shore, and irrigation. Several expressed concerns of a personal nature, such as the risks they incurred by leaving their wives and children for an extended period to join trainings, their need to return home for village duties, the possibility of falling ill, unexpected calamities, their meals not arriving on time, and compromising their health by sitting down too much.

One recurrent theme on the hope list was that the training would lead to follow-up activities (*tindak lanjut*) and sustained guidance (*bimbingan yang kesinambungan*). The corollary fear was that there would be no follow-up at all. One participant declared that if there were no follow-up activities, then this would be the last training he attended. He said he was developing an allergy to trainings, which had begun making him nauseous. This was, he estimated, the sixth or seventh he had attended. It was expensive to stage these trainings and some were even held in fancy hotels, but none had yielded any real benefits. Like other participants, this man looked to trainings with the expectation that they should lead to longer-term material transfers from the host institutions to the participants rather than serve as stand-alone opportunities for self-improvement. Participants could pursue their interpretations because the Batu Hijau mine retained mechanisms for providing conventional development inputs, from dam infrastructure to fertilizers, IR-64 rice, and synthetic pesticides. Coming out of Newmont's IPM trainings, I was at first surprised to see staff from Batu Hijau's community development foundation, Yayasan Olat Parigi, unloading large sacks of synthetic fertilizer and IR-64 rice to distribute in villages. I gradually realized that both IPM and conventional development were parts of the complex and contradictory processes through which Batu Hijau's managers, workers, and local residents understood and constituted one another.

CONCLUSION

Experienced facilitators had no illusions that their efforts would convert all of the participants into a cadre of true believers. I talked with Pak Amir at the end of one training, asking him if he ever felt disappointed when IPM failed to take root among participants. His face sagged in exhaustion as the adrenaline that had sustained his charismatic stage performance ran out of him. He recalled how his own mentor had told him that a facilitator should expect to really reach only one out of every fifteen farmers he trains, but that that one farmer who is transformed is crucial.

This candid assessment of the fragility of participatory projects calls into question narratives about how easily or completely neoliberal development and conservation programs transform their targets into autonomous, responsibilized neoliberal subjects (see also Cepek 2011; Li 1999a, 2007; Moore 1999; Mosse 2005; Shever 2008). According to such narratives, the surplus population that Newmont cannot employ would—once suitably "trained"—stop making demands on the mine and "acting out" with demonstrations for jobs. No more burning tires in the road, no more holding machetes to the throats of mine personnel and contractors. Instead, much like the Javanese peasants of *Agricultural Involution* (Geertz 1963), local residents not employed at the mine would lavish ever more toil upon their shrunken plots of land with "sustainable" and "appropriate" practices (e.g., planting neem trees and distilling organic pest repellents from them, making manure from the droppings of chickens and horses, plowing their fields with water buffalos, etc.). Not only would farmers displaying the proper subjectivity refuse shortcuts like synthetic pesticides and fertilizers and mechanical tractors that belch out exhaust, but they would also abandon as misguided and excessive their expectations of modernity and material progress (Ferguson 1999). They would adapt instead to living modestly "in ways that are neither environmentally nor politically disruptive" (Kearney 1996:107).

Where others have illuminated how technologies of government work to fashion new kinds of environmental, entrepreneurial, and spiritual subjects (Agrawal 2005; Cruikshank 1999; Dean 1999), what I saw in Sumbawa suggests the need for a more systematic exploration of failure in subject-making. If the trainings failed, over the period I observed, to turn farmers into neoliberal subjects, they also failed in their potential to turn farmers into radicalized subjects who might turn IPM discourses against Newmont. Much as Willis's study (1977) found that working-class youth produced themselves as future workers through their own resistance to education, I found that training participants—through incomplete comprehension of and resistance to participatory pedagogy—produced themselves as subjects entitled to and dependent on increased support from Newmont. Participants misapprehended the content and criticized the structure of trainings that preached less Green Revolution. Some farmers headed over to other units in Newmont's community development apparatus to demand more Green Revolution: more dams, credit, high-yield seeds, and fertilizers. Batu Hijau's hybrid approach accommodated these desires and demands, even as its trainings tried to foster independent and enterprising subjects. To the extent that farmers were successful in making Newmont responsive to their demands, they produced themselves as dependent and entitled subjects and the mine as the classic paternalistic provider. Such subject positions are constantly negotiated rather than fixed and finalized. In this sense, while the trainings certainly sowed new ideas and left marks on the beliefs and practices of their participants, to speak of "a new subjectivity" emerging as a consequence is misleading. As Ken George (2010:115) observes, "The who and what of subjectivity are precarious and improvised standpoints, and always vulnerable to the circumstances into which we are thrown." Consciousness has multiple and distinct sources of inspiration (Galt 2013;

Nash [1979] 1993:xxx). Participants who entered trainings were neither "fully preconstituted" (Sharma 2008:xxv) nor tabulae rasae that would exit trainings as enterprising and autonomous liberal subjects. As they brushed against opposing corporate logics about who they should be, training participants affirmed their dependency upon the mine, responsibilizing Newmont as a collective subject and insisting it owed them more than just a sense of enterprise, empowerment, and autonomy.

CHAPTER 5

"Corporate Security Begins in the Community"

The Social Work of Environmental Management

In June 2002, around thirty environmental activists from across the Indonesian archipelago convened a Women's Empowerment Workshop in the village of Tongo. Workshop participants gathered to discuss the environmental hazards of large mines, their differential impact on men and women, and tactics for transforming village-mine relations. After the activists concluded the workshop, twenty men from nearby villages wielding machetes and other weapons confronted them on the dirt road leading out of Tongo. The men forced the activists out of their vehicles, warning them their cars would be burned if they failed to comply, then ripped rolls of film out of their cameras and robbed them of their personal journals, notebooks, and documents. Although the attackers did not inflict serious physical injuries, they verbally abused the activists for close to an hour before allowing them to continue, paying no heed to one activist's hysteria or to the presence of several children and an eight-month-pregnant woman in the group (MinergyNews 2002b). Another group of men again halted and intimidated the frightened activists farther down the road as they made their way through the village of Sekongkang Bawah. Two policemen watched the second confrontation but made no move to intervene.

In this chapter, I analyze the attack in terms of three enactments of Newmont. The first, sharply at variance with the other two, is the activist enactment of Newmont as "Newmonster," an environmentally and socially destructive entity. Newmont managers produced a counterenactment, "Goodmont," which figured the company as environmentally friendly and socially responsible. The local elites and unemployed men who attacked the activists treated Newmont as an important and vulnerable patron for which they bore responsibility. By exploring the actions and commitments of the latter groups who defended capital against activists, I seek to complement the extensive anthropological literature on transnational advocacy networks supporting indigenous rights, social justice, and environmentalism against extractive industries.[1] Understanding the emergence and coherence of the moral commitments of "political Others" who violently defend capital is critical for anthropological accounts of how, in the face of significant social and environmental challenges, global capitalism is constituted and sustained.[2] I situate the attack on environmental activists in relation to constructions of corporation and community as interdependent.

CSR AND CORPORATE SECURITY

The militarized enclave represents one approach to securing extractive industry operations (Ferguson 2005, 2006). Cleared of local residents and fortified with guns, watchtowers, high walls, razor wire, attack dogs, and armed guards, such enclaves are reachable only by corporate infrastructure. Batu Hijau has elements of this security model in place. The mine's first community infrastructure project involved constructing a police station; company facilities are fenced in and patrolled by private guards; a color-coded flag system alerts employees to the ambient social threat level; and for years Newmont paid an Indonesian mobile brigade police unit (Brimob) to remain on-site as a backup force. Yet Newmont's approach to security is hybrid, partly militarized but also cognizant of the permeability of the mine terrain and of threats that cannot be seen or countered through conventional techniques of surveillance and force.

In 2002, Newmont became a signatory to the Voluntary Principles on Security and Human Rights, a centerpiece of CSR in extractive industry.[3] Drafted in 2000 by an international group of NGOs, corporations from the global North, and government leaders seeking to avoid the kinds of human rights abuses by state and private security forces that have made the extractive industry notorious, the principles were intended to "guide Companies in maintaining the safety and security of their operations within an operating framework that ensures respect for human rights and fundamental freedoms."[4] In keeping with the spirit of the principles, Newmont had long ensured that villagers could make use of certain forests within the mine area, and the company had shrunk the number of Brimob guards over time and largely confined them to mine facilities. Only thirty Brimob guards were on-site in 2004, and a few years later Newmont ceased maintaining a standing Brimob force altogether. What is more, Newmont's private guards bore no firearms, underwent human-rights training with their morning drills, and wore laminated cards with the UN Declaration of Human Rights around their necks.

Although downplaying militarized approaches to security, the CSR industry implicitly endorses drawing civilians into the sphere of corporate security through community development. "Corporate security," as an expatriate Batu Hijau manager explained to me, "begins in the community." He drew on his experience as a U.S. Army colonel and military attaché, deploying in a corporate context the long-standing U.S. foreign policy logic of using development aid as a means of realizing strategic security objectives such as cultivating allies, gaining territorial access, and establishing lines of intelligence communication (see also Atwood 2002:335). The view that community welfare projects are useful for conflict management is echoed in the Voluntary Principles,[5] and in Newmont Mining Corporation's official line that "the most effective way of maintaining the security of our operations and employees is to have good relationships with local communities and governments" (2005:11). Although CSR initiatives such as the Voluntary Principles have partly demilitarized corporate security, they also legitimate the role and involvement of local communities in promoting corporate security, to mixed effect.

FROM NEWMONSTER TO GOODMONT: MORAL NARRATIVES AND COUNTERNARRATIVES

Involving the forcible detention of people, theft, and bodily threats, the attack on activists breached both legal and ethical codes. I argue that its supporters and perpetrators nonetheless embedded their actions in moral commitments bound to particular enactments of Newmont. On the managerial side, I depart from two standard analytics of corporate behavior. The first, the "bad apples" approach, singles out deviant individuals. For example, psychologists have claimed that many successful chief executive officers are subcriminal psychopaths who channel their manipulative, narcissistic, and ruthless psychopathic tendencies into corporations rather than becoming serial rapists or murderers (Stein-berger 2004). Singling out CEOs for blame when things go wrong is a corollary to the specious tendency to lionize them when share prices are rising (Dudley 1994; Khurana 2002); either way, CEOs are treated as all-powerful beings. The second standard analytic is an institutional approach. Legal scholar Joel Bakan (2004:50) argues that corporate managers are largely "good people, moral people" who behave unethically because they are under a legal obligation to maximize shareholder profits. Both the legal foundation and the influence of this narrative of legal determinism for harm (which does not explain harmful behavior in privately owned or state-owned firms) have been called into question (Stout 2008), as noted in the introduction. My story differs from both the deviant-executive and profit-maximizing explanations. The mine managers who supported the attack were invested in a particular enactment of Newmont that ensured ongoing profits and mine security, but their actions were not determined in a reductive way by the profit-maximization imperative.

Corporate managers construct their moral self-narratives in active dialogue with the beliefs and tactics of their most vociferous critics. My starting place is an advocacy critique from a comic book story of "New-monster" produced by Project Underground, a Berkeley-based social and environmental advocacy NGO (PU n.d.).[6] Although Project Underground ostensibly produced the comic book for community members affected by Newmont mines (it appears in English, Spanish, and Indonesian), I never saw a copy of it circulating in Sumbawan villages. Rather, I came across it on the Internet and in the Jakarta headquarters of Jatam, an Indonesian network of NGOs opposed to the social injustice and environmental damage that accompanies large-scale mining.

The Newmonster narrative unfolds as follows: (1) large mines destroy the environment, scarring the earth and dumping waste, (2) large mines destroy the health and environment of local communities, (3) this is an ancient imperialist evil, (4) greedy, amoral men are responsible for this evil, (5) these men are able to carry out this evil because they are backed by police and military violence, (6) communities want to educate themselves to fight mines, and (7) the struggle is transnational, and you can be a part of it. My aim here is not to dwell on the oversimplification of geography, history, community,[7] and corporation. As a story it incorporates a set of standard leftist assumptions about how U.S. mining corporations operate abroad. Newmont managers engaged these assumptions in developing alternative narratives and practices through which they could contrast "environmentally friendly" mining with various foils: backward mines, poor Indonesians, and activist NGOs. As I shift between these three groups and the practices through which corporate actors construe them, readers may detect an accompanying shift in register—from a seemingly healthy sense of competition as a company aims to position itself at the forefront of mining's "best practices," to a patronizing sense of environmental superiority in relation to poor villagers, to, finally, the outright vilification of activist NGOs.

The Batu Hijau managers I spoke with unanimously compared the mine's social and environmental performance favorably to that of other mines they had worked for, Indonesian state-owned enterprises, and informal mining operations; the latter they insistently called "illegal mining." Newmont managers often described Batu Hijau as a "model mine"; from an environmental and social perspective they regarded it as the star performer in Newmont's portfolio, the apex of "best practices." A public relations consultant who had worked for both Newmont and Freeport-McMoRan Copper and Gold quipped that the term "Goodmont," for Newmont, stood in contrast to "Badport," for Freeport. Freeport is infamous for corrupt ties to the Soeharto regime, large-scale environmental destruction, land expropriations, and complicity in military abuses of human rights (Leith 2003); that it should figure as the prototypical socioenvironmental "monster" from which Batu Hijau managers differentiate themselves is unsurprising. In contrast to the "ancient evil" of the Newmonster narrative, Goodmont's "environmentally friendly" mine as portrayed by Batu Hijau officials is a departure from past practices. CSR experts claim the future belongs to "responsible" mining companies— which will become the "miners of choice" for states, communities, and lending agencies while setting on the path to extinction the "dinosaurs" that pollute and neglect their social responsibilities.

Newmont managers from a range of fields expressed pride in Batu Hijau's environmental and social accomplishments and initiatives. An Environment Department executive in Denver who worked in Batu Hijau during mine construction told me he "loved" the mine and was so certain that it was the best in the world that he might not be objective about it. Several officials tried to impress me with the cost and state-of-the-art design of Newmont's water management system (which they referred to as "the eighth wonder of the world"), offering it as evidence of environmental commitment.[8] Other officials pointed out special features like the channels that transported surface water runoff from the

FIGURE 12. A member of PT NNT's Environment Department showing visitors from an environmental NGO Newmont's revegetation work and, in the background, the channels that divert rainwater from forests to the local river system. Photo by author.

forest surrounding the mine into the Sejorong River, which runs through Tongo village (figure 12). On the community front, Newmont managers expressed pride in the company's local hiring efforts, infrastructure projects, development programs, and NGO collaborations (figure 13).

In constructing a positive corporate identity, managers also addressed Batu Hijau's practice of submarine tailings disposal. The mine is permitted to expel up to 58 million tons of tailings per year into the ocean, or 160,000 tons per day. Although executives may have initially reacted with abhorrence to the idea of such disposal (Shearman 2002), many have come to regard the practice as minimally disruptive to the environment. Its impact can be ideologically neutralized in part by technoscience. Newmont documents acknowledged that submarine tailings disposal extinguished the life of every nonmobile bottom-dwelling deep sea creature in the path of the tailings, but they dismissed as negligible its impact on biodensity and biodiversity. Newmont brochures compared tailings' toxin levels to those of harmless dirt and sand samples. Under lab conditions, moreover, Newmont's environmental scientists have found that benthic organisms can colonize tailings.[9]

FIGURE 13. The office of Aspirasi, an NGO in Taliwang, whose members both criticized and collaborated with Newmont. Photo by author.

Beyond the realm of technoscience, Newmont managers perform their conviction that tailings are inert in other ways. Before various audiences of NGO representatives, government officials, journalists, village elites, village schoolchildren, and Indonesian university students, Newmont officials flamboyantly demonstrate the supposedly benign nature of mine tailings by licking and drinking tailings (figure 14), as well as by covering their hands, faces, and arms with the mudlike substance. Metropolitan visitors and village elites witness such performances during the mine tours that are part of Newmont's public outreach and stakeholder dialogue efforts, and through which Newmont managers showcase CSR initiatives and cultivate new alliances. Mine officials staged a lower-budget, road show version for local villagers and schoolchildren. Enjoined to eat and play with the tailings, audience members typically reacted with a mixture of awe, horror, curiosity, or skepticism.[10] The Batu Hijau mine has no monopoly on such practices. At the Ovacik mine in Turkey, senior mine officials donned bathing trunks and frolicked in a tailings dam before media cameras to assure the public the tailings were harmless. In West Papua, Freeport invests

FIGURE 14. Environment Department officials encourage NGO visitors to taste tailings during a visit to the mine. Photo by author.

heavily in projects demonstrating that agricultural products can survive on a substrate of mine tailings and even ships off bubble-wrapped, tailings-raised cantaloupes to government officials in Jakarta. Leaving aside questions about the authenticity of these performances (activists expressed skepticism to me about whether the substance officials drank was actually tailings), they impart no actual scientific knowledge on the short- or long-term impacts that millions of tons of tailings have on the deep-sea marine ecosystem (scientists are still in the early stages of exploring the complexity of this ecosystem and its ties to human bodies and health; see Bond 2013, Helmreich 2009). Yet by ingesting tailings, Newmont officials not only demonstrate but produce their belief in the harmlessness of tailings. By dramatically portraying their faith in the neutrality of the tailings, managers attain this faith (Althusser 1971:168–70; Geertz 1973:114).

In addition to symbolically neutralizing Newmont's dumping of mine waste in the ocean, Newmont managers also engaged in various practices aimed at protecting the environment from local practices they saw as environmentally destructive. Newmont's environment officials stocked a small turtle hatchery with eggs collected from local beaches and from a subdistrict to the east (Lunyuk). From the perspective of Newmont officials, local villagers, who consider turtle eggs a wonderful delicacy, are a significant threat to the sea turtles. These charismatic, endangered turtles—unlike the scientifically unknown and uncharismatic benthic organisms smothered by mine tailings—elicit from many Westerners and some upper- and middle-class Indonesians a sense of wonder and a desire to nurture and protect. As in its tailings-ingestion practices, Batu Hijau is not unique in its focus on protection of an endangered species; corporations at other mine sites have also cast themselves as saviors of iconic species (Macintyre and Foale 2002:3; Rio Tinto 2001:10–11). Newmont held events at the beach resort close to its gated Township in which family members of senior company officials hand-released young hatchery-raised turtles. Such interactions, as Susan Davis (1997:242) suggests in her Sea World study, create a powerful sense of relationship and communion with nature that "feels good, [and] may even feel like social action," all the while anesthetizing participants to the political and economic dimensions of serious environmental problems.

Other Sumbawan marine foraging practices troubled Newmont managers. Village residents turned out en masse every year to net *nyale*, the colorful marine polychaete worms that can be caught near the shores at dawn for two days during their annual reproductive cycle (figure 15).[11] One manager told me villagers must be driving nyale into extinction. Company officials were convinced that villagers were, moreover, destroying the reefs with their *remada*, a practice whereby groups of villagers, often dominated by women, combed the reefs at low tide, using knives and crowbars to spear fish and octopus and gather shellfish and seaweed (figure 16). At low tide, men also fished in the surf with cast and gill nets. From the perspective of Newmont officials, who expressed awe at the flora and fauna they recorded on underwater digital cameras, villagers were consuming the biodiversity and crushing it underfoot. This perspective has roots in conservation ideas and practices, where there is a long history of criminalizing subsistence activities (Jacoby 2003; Peluso 1992; Walley 2004; Williams 1973).

For the most part, managers blamed villagers' "environmental destructiveness" on a combination of poverty and ignorance. In conversations with Newmont executives in Sumbawa, Jakarta, and Denver, I grew familiar with the refrain that "the biggest enemy of the environment is poverty."[12] One manager cited an apparent decline in marine

FIGURE 15. A Tongo-Sejorong resident holding *nyale* (sea worms) caught at dawn. Photo by author.

foraging as evidence of increasing village prosperity, which he attributed to the economic opportunities brought by the mine.[13] Based on my own participation in village activities, however, even the wealthiest villagers enjoy seashore foraging and raw seafood meals out on the reefs; it is an important social activity in addition to meeting subsistence needs (figure 17). Although barter relations and gifting between neighbors sharply declined after Batu Hijau's construction began, village residents continued to pass along turtle eggs and seafood to one another (and even to distant relatives) as gifts. Newmont managers nevertheless saw marine foraging as a problem to be remedied by developmental and environmental initiatives.

FIGURE 16. Using crowbars, a Sekongkang resident pries an octopus from the reef at low tide. Photo by author.

FIGURE 17. Sekongkang residents preparing raw seafood *sepat,* a Sumbawan dish, for seashore consumption. Photo by author.

Batu Hijau's beach cleanups, organized by the mine's Environment Department every year around Earth Day, represented an occasion for disseminating environmental messages. Newmont officials and surfer tourists alike were revolted by the garbage that had become a constant feature of local beaches since the construction of the mine had brought in both a larger population and increased access to disposable cash and industrial goods. Most of this garbage originated in the villages, where residents disposed of trash by burning it, dumping it in shallow depressions, or throwing it into the rivers or on the riverbanks. Rain carried the trash out to sea, wind and tide washed it back upon the beach. This went on for years while Newmont unsuccessfully petitioned the regency government to establish landfill sites and pay for trash collection.[14] The annual beach cleanup addressed one symptom (dirty beaches) of village waste disposal problems by, once a year, gathering trash to be carted off in Newmont trucks to the company's landfill. In the run-up to this event, Newmont organized environmental appreciation activities for villagers, particularly targeting elementary and middle school students by sponsoring art and poetry competitions. Newmont's environment officials gave lectures in village schools, where they explained how local harvesting of marine resources destroyed marine ecosystems.

Because Newmont managers constructed themselves as enlightened, scientific, and responsible environmental custodians in contrast to villagers, who abused the environment, they gave little credence to local residents' observations and concerns about the mine's environmental impacts. Newmont managers did not see "environmentally degrading" local practices in isolation. Rather, managers interpreted these practices as corroborative evidence that the "ecologically noble savage" myth is the romantic construct of Western activists.[15] Thus they connected Sumbawan marine foraging, waste disposal, and swidden cultivation to environmentally damaging practices far more common elsewhere in Indonesia, including illegal logging, the use of poison or bombs to fish,[16] and the use of mercury in small-scale mining. These diverse Indonesian practices share several characteristics. First, they are in fact often linked to poverty. Second, they either compete directly with transnational mining interests for resources or constitute a potential threat insofar as mining companies can be blamed for their detrimental effects (reef destruction, fish stock depletion and species endangerment, forest erosion, introduction of toxins).[17] Issues like greenhouse gas emissions (closely connected to the extractive industry) were conspicuously absent from the list of environmental problems regularly cited by corporate managers.

Newmont managers also constructed a positive corporate identity through contrast with activist NGOs, but here their discourse assumed a darker tone. Not content to simply refute the Newmonster narrative, some managers actually turned it back against activist NGOs, seizing the moral offensive and accusing them of being greedy, corrupt, violent, and insincere. Organizations that don the mantle of social virtue and environmental consciousness are particularly vulnerable to such allegations. As Kim Fortun (2001:51–52) notes, advocates are widely seen as embodying modernist ideals. Motivated by unwavering and altruistic purpose, the ideal advocate is never distracted by "personal desires, secondary issues, or simple doubt" (51). A perfect fit always exists between standards and practices, universal and particular, behavior and ideals, world and theory, micro and macro. The ideal advocate "is never seen enmeshed in discrepancies, ambiguities, and paradox. Nor is he seen trying to force fit the world into available political ideologies" (52). Advocates, like "ecologically noble savages," are thus always poised to fall from the moral high ground either claimed by or imputed to them.

Newmont managers sought out gaps between activist theory and practice, exploiting them to frame established environmental organizations as not only hypocritical but also obstructionist and counterproductive. In a letter to the editor of the *Jakarta Post* disputing accusations by two Jakarta-based NGOs that Newmont's Minahasa Raya mine in Sulawesi polluted the environment, one Newmont consultant presented a familiar managerial critique: "Why have [NGOs] Walhi and Jatam done nothing about illegal mining, which is the real environmental issue in northern Sulawesi? Illegal mining dumps anywhere from 15 to 60 tons of raw mercury into the waterways of northern Sulawesi every year." The consultant insisted that "Newmont does not use mercury or arsenic to process its ore,"[18] and, moreover, that it had "been working on pragmatic solutions to the problems created by illegal mining (since Walhi and Jatam aren't)" (Pressman 2001). Newmont managers have also sought to stoke public concern over "illegal mining" by helping journalists write critical accounts (Schuman 2001).

Some Newmont managers went further and attempted to impugn individual activists and NGOs. For example, various officials told me a Walhi representative tried to extort money from Newmont (reversing the activist's own claim that Newmont had tried to bribe him), acted as a "heavy" trying to provoke violence at a UN conference in Bali, had links to Abu Bakar Ba'asyir (the cleric convicted of conspiring in the 2002 Bali bombing), and supported the presidential campaign of

General Wiranto, who was implicated in massive human rights abuses. These same officials closely followed, and fostered, allegations that Lembaga Olah Hidup (LOH), an NGO based in Sumbawa Besar, had embezzled foreign donor funds. Newmont managers explained to me that environmental activist NGOs in Indonesia focus on Western corporations because this attracts overseas funding organizations, which are far less interested in addressing problems caused by domestic or Asian companies. They also insisted that it is NGOs rather than publicly traded corporations that lack transparency and oversight in the form of good governance policies, annual reports, and accountability to shareholders.

Newmont officials consult with public relations firms that offer—in addition to CSR services—clandestine research on advocacy NGOs, and strategies for destroying them (see, e.g., Dezenhall 1999; Nichols 2001). A senior Newmont executive, seeking to illuminate for me the dark underbelly of environmental advocacy networks, furnished me with two documents apparently produced by such consultants. He archly dodged the question of their origin by saying they "fell off the back of a truck." Fortun (2001:104) describes similar documents in the possession of Union Carbide in the 1980s. Their "old-fashioned paranoia about environmentalism" contrasted bizarrely with Carbide's "proactive embrace of environmental stewardship." She concluded that Carbide "was caught up in a time warp, exhibiting postures of times past concurrently with postures demanded by the future. The 'corporation' was undergoing an identity crisis that brought divergent personas to the surface." At Newmont, similarly disparate perceptions of activists and the best strategies for dealing with them existed in the face of widely shared views about what the core environmental problems were and who was competent to resolve them.

CSR experts with a background in social science, development, and activism, for example, tended to favor letting "extreme" NGOs die out by natural selection. PT NNT's Community Development manager considered some of the NGOs opposed to Newmont as old-fashioned (*kuno*) but claimed she defended the Indonesian environmental network Walhi—and praised it for its diversity—before other managers. She strongly disapproved of using secret intelligence practices to find out about activist activities, and she told an American consultant she did not want to know about the fruits of his clandestine information gathering. Other managers expressed similar embarrassment and even disdain for what they dubbed the "cloak and dagger" techniques and "NGO jihad" impulses of managers with engineering or military backgrounds. Despite these important differences in approach, however, the company's "doves" and "hard-liners" largely shared the same moral framework and narrative when it came to identifying the real environmental issues and actors.

"Fell off the Back of a Truck," Part 1 Indonesian Antidevelopment LSMs and Their International Support Network

An excerpt from the *Project Green Shield* report produced by a public relations firm commissioned by Newmont:

> The national-level and international LSM's [NGO's] methods of identifying local activists, recruiting, training and deploying them are not unlike those used by intelligence agencies around the world. The LSM recruiters spend time in the local communities and learn about people who may be disgruntled, angry or dispossessed. They then recruit the person, direct their anger towards the investor [mining company] and provide the recruit with direction and orders to carry out. The local LSMs then carry out the larger program directives of Walhi and Jatam, which are formulated almost exclusively in conjunction with the international anti-development LSMs. This strategy, as implemented through Walhi and Jatam by the international LSMs, allows for the appearance of grassroots resistance to mining, oil and gas investments. In most specific instances, the "local resistance" amounts to nothing more than a handful of vocal, trained cadres of the national level LSMs. But because of the layers of activities by the different LSMs, it appears that many groups are working to "represent a large group of local people."
>
> In actuality, it is the international LSMs and their national level partners (Walhi and Jatam) who are setting the agendas for the campaigns, not the local people appealing to the LSMs for help, as the LSMs often profess. The agenda of these LSMs is almost always very different from the desires of the actual communities they claim to represent from around the projects or the sites of potential investment. The communities themselves are often seeking benefits from the projects[,] including jobs, local infrastructure enhancement and other social and economic benefits.

The report goes on to profile the Mineral Policy Institute, an Australian environmental advocacy organization, concluding with this statement:

> It is important to note . . . that the MPI web site makes absolutely no mention of the massive problem with illegal mining in Indonesia. This, combined with the efforts of Walhi and Jatam to attack internationally regulated and financed mining companies[,] belies their true nature. MPI, its

international friends, Walhi and Jatam[,] are not environmental LSMs, but anti-development groups seeking to shut down investment in Indonesia while ignoring critical environmental problems such as illegal mining, illegal logging, and illegal fishing practices.

"Fell off the Back of a Truck," Part 2
White Paper on Project Underground
(1998)

An excerpt from a document implicating NGO Project Underground (the Berkeley-based NGO that produced the Newmonster comic) in instigating the large-scale civil violence that occurred around Freeport's operations in 1996.[1]

> Not one dollar of Project Underground, WALHI, or IRN [International Rivers Network] funds has been directly expended on the welfare of local people of Irian Jaya. Project Underground claims that it seeks to "introduce corporate accountability into [mining, oil, and gas] sectors." Yet, Project Underground is itself a business, not a registered NGO. Questions have been raised about how it handles its own corporate accountability. Project Underground has no membership, no readily identifiable constituency, no legally binding charter nor mission statement, and no corporate officers who can be held accountable for the thousands of dollars it spends solicited from legitimate organizations. Questions have also been raised about the group's true agenda. Project Underground's key leaders have committed their organization to challenge every aspect of support provided to international mining operations. They also plan to conspire to undermine the sellers' markets for products derived from mining operations. . . . Thus, the organization's true agenda becomes apparent— to bring international mining companies to their knees.

> 1. I have not included here the relevant excerpts implicating NGOs in violence (the document is six pages long). Suffice it to note, the argument is reductionist and leaves unexamined the roles of Freeport and the Indonesian military.

A further set of documents that "fell off the back of a truck" illustrates how corporate attacks on NGOs are planned and justified. In 2002, the Sumbawa Besar–based LOH demanded a government investigation into allegations that tailings strewn ashore by an ocean upwelling had afflicted crops near Tongo, the village closest to Newmont's tailings pipeline. Batu Hijau contracted the Jakarta office of an international, award-winning PR firm to conduct clandestine research and develop strategies for dealing with LOH. The firm's report, *Project Green Shield,*[19] featured a detailed stakeholder map.

Stripped of the typical CSR references to vulnerable, marginalized, or underrepresented groups, "stakeholder" refers here in a nakedly instrumental fashion to those who can advance or impede corporate interests (Conley and Williams 2005; Power 2003b). The report covered stakeholders at every level, from village residents to international actors, and characterized the positive or negative potential of media outlets (print, television, radio), academics, NGOs, international funding organizations that could be concerned about the credibility of donor recipients, and government officials. The report described stakeholders with adjectives like *vocal, emotional, aggressive, passive, proactive,* and *cooperative but unclean.* Besides tracking relations among stakeholders (through kinship, friendship, and financial ties), the consultants amassed sordid, potentially useful details of stakeholders' personal shortcomings, vices (philandering, drug abuse), and predicaments (e.g., a son accused of embezzlement).

The consultants also formulated a plan of action for Newmont. The report cautioned Newmont against suing LOH for libel, noting that this course of action would generate a "David and Goliath" impression. Moreover, the consultants noted, it is difficult to look good carrying out litigation within a tainted government system. The report proposed that Newmont instead pay the consulting firm close to $1 million to elevate Newmont's reputation while tarnishing LOH's. The consultants offered, first, to educate the "oblivious . . . floating mass" about Newmont's good works,[20] by carefully orchestrating town-hall-style public meetings, providing television media with flattering B-roll footage of Newmont's operations, and sponsoring trainings for local journalists at a journalism school where they could learn the principles of objective journalism. Indirect sponsorship would ensure "the appearance of independence." Second, the consultants proposed to lobby through "third parties" for reform of the Indonesian Environmental Management Law (Undang Undang 23/1997), which had allowed LOH to prompt the government investigation without financial risk to itself (which the consultants portrayed as acting "irresponsibly and without accountability"). Finally, the consultants proposed destroying LOH's reputation by rendering the NGO "transparent."

Project Green Shield recommended tapping nascent Indonesian movements for both NGO transparency and an NGO code of ethics to frame LOH as unethical and lacking in transparency. The consultants wrote, "Reputable national and international NGOs will be approached (through third parties) to obtain their support for a move to advocate standards for NGO accountability." The report identified the Indonesian Society for Transparency, Indonesian Corruption Watch, and Civil Society Support and Strengthening Program as potential supporters. They also suggested that an influential NGO that had collaborated with various corporations (including Newmont) might conduct workshops and seminars, make talk show appearances, and develop "NGO Watch" lists of "responsible" and "irresponsible" NGOs. "Efforts must be made," the report asserted, "to ensure that LOH is included in a list of irresponsible NGOs." The report proposed "positioning" LOH as a workshop "case study" in NGO irresponsibility, and it offered ideas for "placing" op-eds about transparency in the media and for prompting the government to "monitor and sanction" NGOs as well as use existing laws to regulate and potentially dissolve nonprofits. This strategy shows some of the coercive and, ironically, concealed ways in which corporations can use moral discourses about transparency and accountability against activists, fostering a popular groundswell of disappointment and disaffection with NGOs.[21]

An American senior manager told me Newmont had rejected the consultant's proposal, complaining that the PR firm was too expensive and had added little new information to what they had learned from company spies (euphemized as "research assistants") placed in villages and in NGOs such as LOH. Yet Newmont managers continued to build on the strategy of making activists transparent.

NEWMONSTER IN SUMBAWA

In May 2002, activist NGOs opposed to corporate mining sponsored Bu Halimah, a Sumbawan woman, to attend three linked events: the International Mining Workshop, the Indonesia People's Forum, and a meeting of the Preparatory Committee for the UN World Summit on Sustainable Development. The Indonesia People's Forum, convened by NGOs to coincide with and critique the UN event, produced several small newsprint bulletins with critical perspectives on globalization and mainstream UN agendas. One of these, titled "Local People Swept Away by the Newmont Dam" (Nilhuhdian and Wawi 2002) was devoted to Bu Halimah's criticisms of Newmont and featured a photo of her with shoulders slumped and staring despondently at the camera. The bulletin was freely available to anyone taking part in the forum, and the Jakarta-based NGO Jatam also posted the article on its website.

It was an unremarkable advocacy document, the product of a network of alliances between international and Indonesian NGOs, Bu Halimah, a printing press, and the Internet. International activists may have read it as the voice of an indigenous Sumbawan woman speaking truth to power and exposing Newmont's Sumbawan activities to global disapproval. Yet for those more familiar with the mine setting, the article was riddled with inaccuracies. Newmont managers, who were out in force at the UN meeting and maintained a more subdued and even clandestine presence at alternative events, carted a stack of bulletins back from Bali to southwest Sumbawa. They then used Community Relations field officers and village offices to circulate copies of the article among village elites who benefited from Newmont's development projects.

Newmont managers strategically circulated the article among elites precisely because of its inaccuracies, which they saw as tangible and persuasive evidence of the malfeasance of advocacy NGOs, of their tendency to put lies in the mouths of local people like Bu Halimah in order to attract foreign donor money. Other explanations could be offered for these inaccuracies (for example, the authors' haste in producing the article against the deadline of the scheduled forum). For all its faults, the article offered an account of Newmont satisfactory to an external audience of activists who had already internalized a generic narrative of bad corporate behavior but looked for specificity—a certain place, the particularities of environmental destruction, a photograph of a sad or defiant face, poignant details, and personal touches. For Newmont managers and village elites, however, the inaccuracies themselves became the central focus.

The article's dramatic headline, "Local People Swept Away by the Newmont Dam," drew power from the collective memory of a tsunami that had indeed washed a local hamlet away—but in 1977, two decades before Batu Hijau's construction. Although the article describes Bu Halimah leaving Tongo, the village nearest the mine, to resettle in Benete village after the Newmont "disaster" struck, her husband told me that Benete was his family's village, and that they had moved there around 1991, when Newmont's exploration had barely begun. The article suggests Batu Hijau precipitated a population exodus, when in fact the local population had doubled since the mine was built. It also describes Newmont appropriating land with no compensation, although hundreds of local residents sold land to Newmont. The article claims that all palm sugar production, pandanus mat weaving, and river fishing had disappeared. Local residents, however, continue to engage in these activities, if less than before. The article also states that Newmont employed only thirty-two locals, but if the ten villages near the mine are considered, the true figure was close to seven hundred.

Although the article correctly points out that Newmont's nominally independent community development foundation, Yayasan Olat Parigi, had been discriminatory and exclusive in making loans, the claim that the foundation withheld money from Newmont critics is unfounded. Newmont and Yayasan Olat Parigi staff used the foundation to dispense gifts—officially loans—to both the company's supporters and its critics. Indeed, many local residents felt that vocal criticism or threats against Newmont were the only effective mechanisms for accessing its goods. Bu Halimah's husband served as the Benete village representative for the foundation, and Bu Halimah herself had presided over a twenty-five-hundred-dollar loan it made to a women's group. Newmont's Community Relations manager invoked the latter fact to discredit Bu Halimah in front of fellow villagers when she led an activist demonstration in the regency capital (*MinergyNews* 2002b, 2003). Newmont staff may not succeed in buying off corporate critics when they extend assistance to them through the mine's community foundation, but they do thereby gain the ability to compromise or neutralize them later. Several Newmont managers and Community Development officers told me Bu Halimah was "not trusted" by local residents and had been beaten on at least one occasion for misusing community funds disbursed by Newmont.

Despite its shortcomings, the article did deal with a set of environmental and social problems of grave concern to local residents, highlighting issues felt most acutely by villagers marginalized by their geographic and social location. Bu Halimah focused on the predicaments of people in her natal Tongo because, relative to other local residents, they had suffered the greatest impact from the mine on forest, freshwater, and marine resources.[22] Owing to their proximity to Batu Hijau's mine, dams, and tailings infrastructure, they bore the brunt of the environmental risk.[23] Geographically as well as socially, however, Tongo's isolation meant residents had greater difficulty accessing Newmont's community development programs, a problem compounded by villagers' lack of formal education and by prejudice among Batu Hijau managers and field staff.[24] Bu Halimah explained to me that in Bali she deliberately wore shabbier clothes because she went to speak for the poorest and most marginal families, those whose sons—unlike her own— did not get Newmont jobs. She sought to underscore environmental problems, poverty, and inequality as salient features of Newmont's impact on villages. These insights fell outside of the interpretive framework Newmont managers brought to bear on the article.

Newmont managers' decision to circulate the article among village elites must also be understood in relation to managers' and villagers' unequal ability to access and evaluate information. As critics of globalization discourse have noted, capital and commodities "flow" not of their own accord but through the actions of various agents, institutions, and technologies that may enable, direct, reverse, constrain, and block movement (Cooper 2001; Ferguson 2006; Tsing 2005). Information, like capital, is "lumpy" (Cooper 2001), accumulating among certain people in some places and remaining sparse elsewhere. Within Batu Hijau's offices, all Newmont-related articles appearing in local, national, and international news were clipped; photocopied; condensed into bilingual summaries; labeled good, neutral, or bad; and filed chronologically. Workers with email accounts received Newmont's bilingual summaries of media coverage. These daily missives often fueled internal ire over "NGO lies." In southwest Sumbawan villages, however, few people read or subscribed to newspapers, and only a handful of individuals were in possession of advocacy materials, which usually tended to be worn and dated. Print media trickles fitfully and selectively, rather than flows, into villages, and never circulates in an egalitarian fashion within them (Tsing 2003). Without Newmont managers' deliberate and selective intervention, which was tied to their perception that "Goodmont" was coming under unfair attack, the bulletin would not have reached village elites, whom it activated in defense of the mine they viewed as a patron.

GOODMONT UNLEASHED

Bu Halimah was one of the conveners of the ill-fated Women's Empowerment Workshop in Tongo, held after the UN meeting and associated advocacy events in Bali had concluded. One Sumbawan mine worker told me he and others had received advance information that the activists' "demonstration" would take place and even descriptions of the number, type, and colors of vehicles that NGO members would drive. Some had mobilized to defend the company, but the NGO group managed to slip in unnoticed. Once the group had arrived in Tongo, however, a Community Relations officer had become aware of their presence and put his office and Tongo residents on alert. Newmont workers in Tongo, meanwhile, had taken a day off to monitor, restrict, and intimidate workshop participants. To my knowledge, Newmont managers did not reprimand them for their absence (as they might have in the event of labor activism), suggesting at least tacit approval. It was not until the activists were on their way out that they were attacked in the fashion described at the beginning of this chapter.

There were two doctors among the activists, one of whom later told the national media that Batu Hijau was poisoning the local environment with arsenic. Dr. Aidarus predicted that a "generation of idiots," Newmont's victims, would soon appear (*NTB Post* 2002c). In *Tempo*, a widely read and well-respected Indonesian magazine, Aidarus explained that he had inspected forty villagers with symptoms of arsenic poisoning, including low blood pressure, itching, a burning sensation in the throat, and foot cramps (Maha Adi and Khafid 2002). When I asked village residents about these reports, only the few with advocacy links had even vague knowledge of these serious allegations.

After the attack, teachers and other members of the village governing apparatus of Sekongkang Atas and Sekongkang Bawah defended their actions in the media and hung banners to alert fellow villagers, Newmont representatives, and outsiders to the fact that the mine was under local protection. Equating environmental activists with terrorists, one banner hung by a resort hotel popular with Newmont's senior miners read, "The Sekongkang community opposes all forms of terrorist action against PT NNT." These villagers claimed that activists had disrespected them by not properly requesting permission and reporting themselves to local officials, from the village to the subdistrict level (*Sumbawa Ekspres* 2002).[25] They insisted that the community behaved "purely," "spontaneously," and out of "concern for the investment world. We must secure regional assets" (*MinergyNews* 2002a; *Lombok Post* 2002a).

In justifying the attack, village elites repeatedly cited the article on Bu Halimah. One village official and teacher explained that "the anger of the Sekongkang community started because of a paper that was published by an institution which asked that PT NNT be shut down" (*Bali Post* 2002b; *Lombok Post* 2002a). Yani Sagaroa, the head of LOH (the NGO examined by Newmont's clandestine consultants and discussed in *Project Green Shield*), who was among the activists, told me that some teachers had produced the Bu Halimah article during the second attack and waved it about as evidence of the nefarious motives of NGOs, mistakenly attributing its authorship to Yani Sagaroa himself. However uncertain the teachers might have been of the article's content, they were sure it meant NGOs were bent on shutting down Newmont.

Various groups with formal titles mushroomed to justify the attack and voice suspicions about Bu Halimah and the NGOs. In a media statement, the head of the Alliance of Near-Mine Communities for Justice cited alleged lies in Bu Halimah's testimonial at the UN event and the Indonesia People's Forum (*Sumbawa Ekspres* 2002).[26] He further accused the NGOs of "easily getting projects with the photos that they took" (*MinergyNews* 2002c). In Indonesia, "projects" (*proyek*) commonly connotes development programs that powerful people appropriate for private purposes (Aspinall 2013). The term is often associated with the triad of corruption, collusion, and nepotism that became a focus of critical public attention in the post-Soeharto era. The Forum of Youth, Students, and Poor Communities of NTB also emerged to take credit for the attacks, explaining,

> It should be known that the study team took lots of photos of women and children; this was very much manipulated such that they could carefully focus on people who were really in rags, exactly like for a soap opera. Thus, we as the community very appropriately questioned this matter. "What do they want to do with these photos of us." After we discussed this with the community, students and youth, it turned out that the photos were to be sold to donor organizations. . . . So right away we chased down LOH's team which took photos and gave us information that PT NNT didn't pay attention to the community. It should be known that we, the community of Tongo Sejorong, Sumbawa, have never felt harmed by PT NNT. (*MinergyNews* 2002c)

These statements resonate well with the Goodmont narrative: the community was never harmed by Newmont, and NGOs in fact are the ones trying to manipulate locals to obtain overseas funding. Newmont managers probably did not have to do much to plant this suspicion among villagers. Every NGO that worked in the region, regardless of mission or funding source, at some point seemed to find itself the object of village suspicions that it was really after money and just "businessing" the community (*kami dibisniskan),* "selling our heads" (*menjual kepala masyarakat*), or "invoking community" for personal ends (*mengatasnamakan masyarakat*). Villagers were thus predisposed to see NGOs as manipulating them. Advocacy NGOs do little to dispel such assumptions when their representatives show up very suddenly, stay only briefly, and shroud their visit in secrecy, even if such measures are taken in the interest of protecting Sumbawans and external activists.

Before the attack, two other emergent groups—ominously named the People's Front for Protecting Investment (Barisan Rakyat Pelindung

Investasi) and the People's Front for Protecting the Mine (Barisan Rak-yat Pelindung Tambang, or Barak Petang, which might be translated as "night barracks")—had issued clear warnings in the *Bali Post* that NGOs would not be welcome (2002a). Nasrum, the head of the People's Front for Protecting Investment, had warned that the community had agreed to reject the NGOs. If they came anyway, he said, they would be asking for trouble from the community, which would confront them (*kami akan menghadangnya*). Published before the NGO representatives arrived, this article undermines the claims of village elites that community behavior was entirely spontaneous.

CONCLUSION

If the violent defense of capital is as culturally meaningful and amenable to thick description as the work of transnational advocacy networks, then it will not do to attribute the attack to the inexorable, expanding logic of capital. This approach would dismiss the agency and intentions of corporate managers and village residents, casting them as "simply pawns" of capital rather than as "social actors and commentators in their own right" (Walley 2004:227) with the capacity "to interpret and morally evaluate their situation and to formulate projects and try to enact them" (Ortner 1995:185).

What we need are modes of analysis that carefully show how the moral commitments of capitalism's defenders emerge and cohere in an era when grassroots approaches to corporate security are nourished by the CSR industry, development projects, and corporate adoption of environmental values and discourse. The attack in Sumbawa was "indisputably a product and expression of powerful forces, national and global," but it also entailed "a significant local dynamic" (Ferguson 2006:99). We saw that in attacking activists, male village elites organized unemployed male youth to barricade roads, halt vehicles, seize keys, destroy property, and yell threats at terrified people who were only trying to get from point A to point B. This sequence of events was familiar to Newmont officials; it was, in fact, identical to the basic plan of attack that villagers had repeatedly used against Newmont and its contractors in the past to secure community infrastructure projects, contracts with the mine, and more accommodating local hiring policies, as described in chapter 2 (PT NNT 2000, 2001).

Some Newmont managers seemed nevertheless oblivious to this similarity. They described villagers who demonstrated against the mine as "still backward," "irrational," "emotional," and "spoiled." Yet when villagers attacked activists using similar tactics, these same managers lauded themselves for persuading local villagers to see Newmont as integral to "the community" and meriting vigorous defense. From this managerial perspective, one might say that villagers engaged in a form of "alternating politics" when they shifted from attacking to defending the company. The activist viewpoint would concur, with the moral valence simply reversed: villagers would be seen as clear-sighted and progressive when they attack a company and demand public goods, and as reactionary dupes when they defend it.[27] In this view Bu Halimah herself would be guilty of political vacillation, first engaging in a progressive alliance with environmentalists and later contracting with the mine to supply village labor.

If, however, we take this appearance of "alternating politics" and apply to it Boas's lesson on "alternating sounds" (1889), the behavior of village elites appears in a different light. As Boas famously showed, what appeared to linguists to be inconsistency in the pronunciations of phonemes among speakers of Native American languages was actually attributable to the bias of the linguists themselves. If we take seriously the village elites' own moral commitments, we find that their apparent alternation between political poles of action originates in a corporate or activist perspective rather in than their own. Within their own moral framework, alternately attacking and defending Newmont was actually part of a consistent strategy. In either case, they constructed themselves as agents playing central roles both in determining whether and how the mine would operate and in creating and maintaining flows of development goods. They certainly had no monopoly on violence, but they sought to use it to exercise greater control over the destiny of villages and the mine alike. Like rural elites elsewhere in post-Soeharto Indonesia, they struggled to assert their continued authority in—and even relevance to—village affairs. Their ability to enact—and defend—Newmont as a largesse-distributing patron was crucial to their authority.

Corporate managers and village elites jointly authored the attack, the former by strategically disseminating information and rewarding its ringleaders, the latter by planning and executing the attack using methods they had perfected against Newmont. Their shared authorship of the attack nonetheless emerged from divergent moral commitments. Corporate managers saw themselves as pioneers of socially and environmentally responsible mining, while village elites sought to implement their vision of development and thereby consolidate their power in the shifting and uncertain political terrain of post-Soeharto Indonesia. As anthropologists grapple with the changing nature of global capitalism, these are precisely the types of hybrid moral and political allegiances we will confront.[28] If we hope to understand how capitalism plays out on the ground, we must tease apart these alliances and attend to the dynamic and diverging political and moral frameworks that animate various actors in defense of as well as in opposition to capital.

CHAPTER 6

"We Should Be Like Starbucks"

The Social Assessment

"I've got better things to do this week than babysit the bean counters," Ivan announced sourly, his voice filled with disgust. It was a sunny morning in late July 2004, and we were waiting for the team of auditors to arrive to conduct the annual Five Star Integrated Assessment that would examine mine performance across the three ameliorative disciplines discussed in chapter 1: Safety and Health, Environment, and the CSR-linked Community and External Relations.[1] As an amphibious Cessna plane owned by the mine and filled with the auditors splashed down in the sparkling waters of Benete Bay, mine managers were reeling from multiple crises. Ivan, an American consultant who assisted the External Relations manager with public relations, was trying to track and manage media representations and public perceptions of these crises. In an accident that had horrified mine workers, a Canadian subcontractor had recently been decapitated by one of the giant haul trucks in the mine.[2] Labor unrest was growing, with Indonesian miners demanding better compensation. In local villages, concerns were escalating about the potential impact of Batu Hijau's submarine tailings disposal. With Indonesia's major television networks airing daily footage of residents of Sulawesi claiming they had been poisoned by tailings dumped in the ocean by Newmont's Minahasa Raya gold mine, residents of southwest Sumbawa began wondering about the safety of fish from their own waters. Meanwhile, news had just arrived from Newmont's start-up operation in Sumatra that a subcontractor had been killed in an electrical accident.

Fresh crises arose as the five-day assessment unfolded. By the time of its conclusion, police in Sulawesi had launched a criminal investigation into PT Newmont Minahasa Raya, Newmont Mining Corporation's Sulawesi subsidiary, and several environmental advocacy NGOs had filed lawsuits against it, which Newmont countered with libel suits. Back at Batu Hijau, a fire on the ore-conveyor-belt system had inflicted three-quarters of a million dollars' worth of damage, and "credible intelligence" emerged that Jemaah Islamiyah, an al-Qaeda-linked militant Islamic group, had made the mine its number one target. One of the architects of the 2002 Bali bombing was supposedly lurking in the vicinity of the mine—perhaps in the hills, since he was rumored to be an avid hiker. The U.S. military attaché and intelligence officials flew in, and there was talk of evacuating the mine site, or at least the expatriate employees, who were seen as most likely to be targeted.

In the midst of dealing with these crises, Newmont managers and staff struggled to answer auditors' questions, retrieve documents for them, and attend to the minute details of their visit, such as whether those who had requested a vegetarian boxed lunch had indeed received one. The juxtaposition of urgent crises and a painstakingly detailed assessment tended to exacerbate mine managers' vexed sense that the latter was entirely irrelevant, divorced as it was from the gritty day-to-day realities of mine operation. For the auditors, however, the very fact of these crises was evidence that mine managers were doing an inadequate job of implementing the management systems the auditors were there to assess. That crises were flaring up across these three domains of expertise—safety and health, environment, and CSR—underscored auditors' conviction that these corporate disciplines were interconnected. Their linked nature formed a central tenet of the "integrated" Five Star Assessment.

As an ethical technology, the assessment is constructed around the very discourses of transparency and accountability we have examined in various guises in previous chapters. The pursuit of accountability and transparency, as other scholars have argued, is always political (Abrahamsen 2000; Hetherington 2011; Li 2007). In chapter 2, we saw PT NNT managers attempting to mobilize citizens to discipline the state through revenue transparency, while in chapter 5 we saw managers rendering environmental-advocacy NGOs "transparent" to stoke internal and public opposition to activists. In this chapter, I examine corporate executives and auditors deploying the social assessment in an effort to enact a transparent, accountable, responsible, and auditable corporation. In the process, they bring to the surface competing perceptions of which knowledge practices support corporate responsibility.

The assessment unfolded over five days, with two auditors delegated to assess performance in each discipline.[3] Opening and closing conferences brought together the mine's junior and senior managers and the assessment team, while auditors spent the rest of the week engaged in desktop and field reviews of the programs in their respective disciplines. I spent the week shadowing the Community and External Relations auditors. To be more efficient, the auditors divided up the standards, working separately with mine staff and translators throughout the day before retreating to the mine guesthouse in the evenings, where they could confer with one another as they converted the information they recorded in their laptops over the course of the day into a score, assigning between one and five stars for each standard. As they went through this process, they asked themselves how each score was justified against the standard criteria, using qualitative and quantitative evidence. They often pulled sixteen-hour days. Within ten days of departing, they submitted draft reports and gave the mine sites two weeks to comment on them. Their final report would be submitted a week later, and the mine site was expected to submit to headquarters an "action plan" addressing problems identified by the assessment.

The assessment was meant to perform multiple functions: supply oversight and evaluation of Newmont's employees and management systems, ensure subcontractor compliance with Newmont standards, bring into the corporation the interests and perspectives of "external" stakeholders (Power 2003b), and generate information for the public stakeholder report (which I discuss at the end of this chapter). As an increasingly popular form of corporate communication, stakeholder reports have already been the topic of significant scholarly critique. Much less attention has been paid, however, to the internal roles and practices of corporate audits. After providing some background on Newmont's embrace of audit techniques for assessing safety, environment, and social performance, this chapter trains an ethnographic lens on the social auditors' fieldwork at Batu Hijau and the interactions with persons, documents, and objects it entailed. In closely following the auditors, this chapter responds to calls from within the critical accounting scholarship for additional ethnographic treatments of "the messy backstage" of audit practice and the particular "exchange processes that construct the transactional reality of regulation" (see Fogarty

1996:262, quoted in Power 2003a:390). In the backstage arena, I found auditors attempting to actualize the reworking of the boundaries of the corporation imagined at headquarters (see chapter 1). They sought to unify the corporation's mine sites in relation to standards rooted in universalizing categories and values (e.g., human rights) while also trying to account for heterogeneous elements in their particularity (e.g., indigenous peoples, environmental activists, social risks).

BACKGROUND

The problem of how a transnational corporation knows and controls itself across dispersed environments is an old one that can be traced back to the early days of empire, when correspondence between metropole and colony could take many months or even years if ships were lost at sea (Cooper and Stoler 1997; Furnivall 1991; Hacking 1990; Litvin 2003; Stern 2011; Ward 2009; White 1991). It would seem logical that with progress in information and communication technologies, executives in corporate centers could make the actions of far-flung agents visible and hold those agents accountable in real time. For executives at headquarters, close management of operations has become ever more necessary in an era of Internet-based activism against transnational corporations (Keck and Sikkink 1998). However, according to the tradition at Newmont, as one environmental executive in Denver told me, mine sites had long been allowed to "operate like fiefdoms. They would get a call from corporate once a year, and corporate would ask the GM [general manager] two questions: how much did you produce, and what was the cost?" Claiming that Newmont had entered a new era, he noted that general managers had begun to be "questioned on environmental performance, social performance, [and] internal audits." Public relations disasters such as the mercury spill at Newmont's Minera Yanacocha mine in Peru justify and motivate the scrutiny and intervention of corporate headquarters, as discussed in chapter 1.

"We should be like Starbucks," a Newmont Investor Relations executive in Denver told me. "If you walk into a store in New York or Jakarta and buy a coffee, you know what you're getting. We shouldn't have a great performance at one site and a poor performance at another." His aspiration was for not only better social and environmental control but also greater centralization and standardization. He elaborated: "I saw a problem in Peru [Newmont's Minera Yanacocha mine] and reported it to [Newmont's president] Pierre. They fixed it at a cost of $25 to $30 million. Their water management system was unacceptable. So you have Batu Hijau, which is barely making any money yet has an excellent system, and then you have Yanacocha, which is supposed to be the crown jewel of Newmont, and they have an unacceptable system. . . . So now Tom Enos has oversight, and they've slowed down their growth and put more expats in place."[4] With Newmont continually under potential scrutiny from investors, activists, and journalists, the Denver executive was impatient with complacency over uneven performance, insisting Newmont should be able to establish and maintain a uniformly high set of labor, environmental, and community standards at its mines—whether they were domestic operations or located in Peru, Bolivia, Indonesia, Australia, New Zealand, Turkey, or Uzbekistan. The assessment seemed to him the key to implementing such uniform standards and evaluating performance.

Before 2002, when Newmont acquired Normandy, Newmont had no corporate-wide system for auditing its health and safety, environment, and social performance. Under instructions from top management, the Health and Safety, Environment, and Community and External Relations Departments moved rapidly to "roll out" Normandy's Five Star Integrated Assessment process and the associated production of *Now and Beyond* stakeholder reports, both of which are part of the Integrated Management System and "Social License to Operate" wave of transformation discussed in chapter 1.[5] While the takeover served as the proximate catalyst for instituting a corporate-wide assessment, social and environmental corporate audits were already on their way to becoming obligatory norms, part of a burgeoning subfield in the CSR industry, with its competitive marketplace for corporate responsibility standards and ideas (Rajak 2011a).[6] Some Newmont executives described their assessment procedures as more rigorous, far-reaching, and innovative than those of other companies,[7] claiming that the standards Normandy had pioneered and Newmont had subsequently refined were proprietary and potentially key to the company's competitive edge as a "miner of choice." CSR and Health and Safety executives even discussed the possibility that some of their standards could be packaged, licensed, and sold. Others were more skeptical, pointing out that similar audit mechanisms had become increasingly standard for global mining companies. David Brereton, a scholar and practitioner of CSR in mining, dismissed secrecy and proprietary claims about standards as "precompetitive," imagining a competitive environment where none actually exist.[8]

While proprietary concerns may favor opacity, companies seek to attach their monitoring practices to established normative regimes that must be explicitly named and invoked. Newmont's 2010 report, for example, claimed that corporate audit standards are rooted in the firm's voluntary participation in the International Council on Mining and Metals' Sustainable Development Framework assurance procedure, the UN's Global Reporting Initiative, the International Cyanide Management Institute's Cyanide Management Code, AccountAbility's AA1000 Assurance Standard, the International Organization for Standardization's 14001 and OHSAS 18000, and the Climate Registry.[9] The proliferating standards, indicators, and metrics adopted by Newmont and other companies tend to bureaucratize, depoliticize, and render technical the social, environmental, and economic impacts of business (Lampland and Star 2009; Merry 2011; Thedvall 2012). Many are developed through consensus-based "multistakeholder" processes; civil society participants lend these processes and their products legitimacy and hegemonic force, even when they may not endorse the results.

Newmont's adoption of the assessment technology exemplifies a broader shift. Since the 1980s, an "audit explosion" has occurred as governments, nonprofit organizations, and businesses have increasingly committed to the technology as the best mechanism for measuring and maximizing quality and value for money (Miller 2003). Auditing practices have made significant inroads into, and transformed, domains previously regarded as bastions of professional and bureaucratic expertise (Miller 1994; Rose 1999), including the environment and higher education (Shore and Wright 2000; Strathern 2000; Tuchman 2009). While many scholars have linked this trend to neoliberal commitments to shrinking the state and applying market mechanisms to ever more spheres of life, Kipnis (2008) points out that audits are rooted in scientific epistemologies and modernizing narratives that enjoy broader political currency.

As organizational reliance on audits has grown, audit practices and the audit profession itself have transformed, acquiring a new emphasis on risk and self-auditing procedures. Faith in time-consuming statistical sampling and testing in low-risk areas has eroded, replaced by the intuition that audits should be conducted in arenas of risk, where they are most needed to generate assurance (Power 1997:76). (To give an example that I discuss in full later in this chapter, social auditors examining Batu Hijau's community relations performance quiz Community Relations officers about risks, scan the visitor logbooks for high-risk entries, and investigate how these were handled, rather than carry out random sampling observations of Community Relations officers in their village offices.) Auditors are now more attuned to identifying and rectifying deficiencies under managerial rather than engineering control and expertise. Once focused on developing technical standards and well-defined measurement parameters such as "defect rates" that could locate problems amenable to engineering solutions, auditors increasingly concentrate on identifying "cultural" arenas amenable to managerial interventions and on devising techniques for measuring abstract and labile qualities such as excellence and commitment (57).

If the audit has exploded outward across new domains, it has simultaneously "imploded" within organizations, fostering self-organizing, self-regulating, and self-auditing capacities, and the construction of an inner organizational world rendered transparent to external scrutiny (Power 2007). Rather than simply verifying the existing system retrospectively, audits are increasingly designed with a forward-looking purpose: to install internal auditing systems that mimic the external audit. The external audit increasingly revolves around checking the systems of self-checking (Dunn 2007; Power 1997:51–52). At the same time that they are constructing auditable and self-auditing organizations, audits are supposed to promote rational, calculating, self-auditing behavior among individuals at various organizational levels (Miller 1992; Miller, Hopper, and Laughlin 1991; Miller and O'Leary 1987). Embedded with centrifugal as well as centripetal knowledge effects, audits push responsibility downward while creating new upward demands for knowledge, bringing distant sites and actors closer to corporate headquarters and enabling "action at a distance" (Latour 1987).

NEWMONT'S FIVE STAR INTEGRATED ASSESSMENT

The emphases on risk and self-auditing are evident in Newmont's interdisciplinary standards (i.e., those applied to health and safety, environment, and community and external relations), which auditors use to judge the systems, performance, and perceptions of its operations. The interdisciplinary standards include: (1) program commitment and leadership, (2) risk and opportunity management, (3) management system documentation, document control, and records management, (4) legal and other requirements, (5) organization and responsibility, (6) training, competency, and awareness, (7) internal communications and reporting, (8) external stakeholder engagement and reporting, (9) accident/incident reporting and investigation, (10) emergency preparedness and response, (11) standard operating procedures, (12) inspections, (13) monitoring and measurement, (14) audits and assessments, (15) corrective and preventative action, (16) change management, (17) contractor selection and management, (18) behavior and observation, and (19) management review (Newmont 2005a:5). Standards 2, 9, 12, 13, and 14 in particular focus attention on risk and serve to catalyze internal audits.

Each discipline has its own standards to meet in addition to the interdisciplinary standards. Under the social assessment, departments focused on community and external relations are audited for their performance on fourteen standards: (1) social impact assessment, (2) human rights awareness, (3) local community investment, (4) local employment and business support, (5) indigenous employment and business support, (6) management of sites with cultural and/or religious significance to indigenous people, (7) management of heritage sites, (8) land access and acquisition, (9) government relations, (10) media relations, (11) staff and contractor behavior, (12) security-forces management, (13) mine closure, and (14) resettlement (Newmont 2005a).

The auditors treated three community and external relations standards as "not applicable" to PT NNT: indigenous employment and business support, management of sites with cultural and/or religious significance to indigenous people, and management of heritage sites. PT NNT managers rejected the notion that local residents could be construed as indigenous or accorded any special privileges (in particular, customary title to forestlands) that would come with the title. Their classification of local residents as nonindigenous reflected the Indonesian government's very limited recognition of indigenous peoples and rights in the country, managers' own understandings of indigeneity (a concept largely forged in the context of settler countries), and an incorrect belief that no inhabitants of the island survived Mount Tambora's 1815 volcanic eruption.[10] Whether because they shared a similar perspective on the indigeneity of Sumbawans, or because they felt it was not their place to question mine decisions about how to apply the category, the auditors acquiesced to managerial perspectives by filling in standards 5–7 with "N/A."

Self-auditing behavioral cues were built into the criteria that underpin the standards. One star was awarded if no systems were yet established to address the standard; two indicated that at least rudimentary ("informal or incomplete") procedures were in place to address the standard; and three, the official minimum, meant proper procedures were up and running ("implemented and functional with general conformance to the requirements of the standard"). Auditors awarded four stars for an effective internal auditing and review system that produced continuous improvement. Five stars were reserved for situations in which such internal auditing and review systems had achieved "sustained continual improvement" and become "integral to site culture." I will come back to what this might look like from the auditors' perspective.

In 2003, on its trial assessment, Batu Hijau's External Relations Department flunked nine out of nineteen management system standards, failing to make the three-star minimum. In the wake of the trial assessment, External Relations managers identified the arenas in which they had scored poorly and generated a list of fifty-eight remedial action items, or "3 Ws," specifying: What must be done, Who was responsible, and When the action had to be completed. These action items included appointing an internal auditor, who had the unpleasant task of trying to get the department's audit procedures in order. Consistent with audit trends elsewhere, a rash of "checking gone wild" (Power 1997:14) spread across the mine, which proceeded to train twenty new internal auditors and had five auditors carrying out an average of four to six audits per week in the first half of 2004. This climate of heightened audit activity and the associated anxiety formed the backdrop to the assessment I observed in 2004 and to which I now turn, beginning with the social identities of the auditors.

THE AUDITORS: IDENTITY, PERFORMANCE, AND PROPS

We are conscious of suspicions that social auditing is just a public relations exercise . . . and do not wish to be the subjects of "corporate capture" or to see our work used as "corporate spin." We will continue to undertake social audit work where it enables us to "make a difference."

Richard Boele, one of the social auditors I shadowed in 2004, wrote these words in an article coauthored with a colleague and published the following year (Boele and Kemp 2005:115). The scare quotes around the phrase "make a difference" wryly admit its clichéd nature, which the authors admit has an "idealistic" ring to it. Boele, like most of his fellow auditors who visited Batu Hijau in 2004, is Australian, reflecting the origins of Newmont's assessment in Normandy Mining. His social-auditing partner, Tricia, has a mixed industry and academic background.

Boele worked for Greenpeace before founding Banarra, a consulting company that provides sustainability assurance and strategic sustainability advice. His activist pedigree could play out in various ways. On the one hand, it could enhance his legitimacy as a professional with an earnest interest in "making a difference." On the other hand, it rendered him vulnerable to hasty dismissal by both corporate professionals (who see him as not properly understanding or representing business interests) and activists (who see him as a sellout).

Hired as agents of institutional reflexivity, auditors also produce reflexive accounts of their profession. In the jointly authored article quoted earlier, "Social Auditors: Illegitimate Offspring of the Audit Family?" Boele and Kemp reflect on the expansion and future of the nascent field of social auditing, which they see as undergoing rapid but not necessarily purposeful or constructive growth. They make a case for social auditing practices that employ hybrid methods, combining qualitative and quantitative approaches drawn both from the social sciences and from financial accounting. They postulate that auditors with activist or academic experience can actually produce richer analyses than those without it. And they suggest, moreover, that social auditors striving for legitimacy should not overidentify with financial accounting and should, in fact, be skeptical of its claims of scientific objectivity and its epistemological indifference to the subjectivity of knowledge producers. They cite inspiration from Flyvbjerg's 2001 *Making Social Science Matter*, which argues, in their words, that "the whole point of social research should be to enter into dialogue with individuals, organisations and societies to assist them to reflect on their values. . . . [It] should not just clarify, but also intervene by generating new perspectives, contributing ideas to a broader social dialogue about what is going on and what could be done differently" (Boele and Kemp 2005:117).

Yet auditors work under significant material and discursive constraints as they seek to put their ideals into practice. In a widely cited essay, Shore and Wright (2000:59) depict auditor and auditee as embedded in a hierarchical relation of scrutinizer and observed. As Kipnis (2008:282) points out, however, those performing audits are not just governing but also governed subjects. As such, they are under significant constraints and are only partly in control of the conditions in which they work and construct their identities as auditors.

An important constraint upon auditors is that they must operate within the standards and grading systems they are given. In his early days consulting with Normandy, Boele had some latitude to influence how standards were written, and auditors could continue to provide comments and feedback on them. As the social audit field professionalized, however, standards increasingly were set in places like Geneva, with normative regimes developed around them. Boele himself was part of this professionalization, having served as president of the Australian Institute of Social and Ethical Accountability. At Newmont, auditors used informal conversations as well as their final on-site presentation as opportunities to convey to company officials important insights and observations that fell outside of the scope of the received standards. Once the assessment concluded, however, auditors had no control over how corporate officials reworked or deployed the knowledge it produced either for internal purposes or for public consumption in stakeholder reports.

While auditors have the authority to sit down in anyone's office and rifle through their computer files and desk drawers (which should be maintained for company interests and therefore be open to unannounced inspection),[11] their ability to command adherence to or belief in the audit system is limited. They must work to elicit cooperation from the Newmont staff and local residents with whom they interact over the course of the assessment. Part of this work entails what Erving Goffman (1959) calls the art of impression management: auditors cultivate varied voices and personae and project these across different encounters. One persona was the seasoned audit veteran who possessed the requisite knowledge, sound judgment, and experience to deal with sometimes uncooperative auditees; such a veteran might, for example, display sternness or impatience with managers. Another persona was more coaxing and parental, suggesting with an eat-your-vegetables tone that the assessment should help identify risks and opportunities and rationalize resource allocations, thereby "paying dividends" and adding "value." They used small jokes at times to take the sting out of a criticism or defuse the nervousness and anxiety of junior staff. The auditors rarely missed an opportunity to remark on hasty or perfunctory performances of managers in response to the audit, using casual asides like: "Last year my fingers got wet on your brand new statements of commitment" or "Oh, you just revised the contracts statement a week ago. OK, just ticking off the boxes, are we?" Through these comments, they implied that they weren't fooled by "ritualized practices of verification" and would do their best not to reward them, either (Power 1997:14).

Increasingly well-versed in scholarly critiques of "audit culture," audit professionals seek mechanisms for ensuring that the audit exercise can strengthen and transform community relations in significant ways, imparting to assessment participants their own commitment to meaningful engagement (Kemp, Owen, and van de Graaff 2012; Macintyre, Mee, and Solomon 2008).[12] Among local village residents who, unlike Newmont employees, did not have to speak with the auditors, the auditors displayed greater deference and gratitude for their cooperation. The auditors were clearly attuned to how their own self-presentation was keyed to ever-changing intersubjective relations and context. Auditors rely upon various identities and must develop the ability to be "multilingual" as they work "among different people of different cultures, with different needs and different issues" (Boele and Kemp 2005:117).[13] Even as they draw on a universalizing discourse of expertise, then, auditors prize the ability to speak in multiple, distinctive languages that reflect the heterogeneity of the subjects they are trying to align with a socially responsible and auditable corporation.

Goffman's dramaturgical metaphor (1959) for analyzing face-to-face interactions helps frame for us the fact that auditors were only partly in command of their own performances. They had to rely on others to select and supply their supporting actors (e.g., translators and drivers) and props (e.g., vehicles). One of the distinguishing features of Newmont's assessment, according to executives, lay in its use of professionally trained, external, and independent auditors rather than in-house staff. While one might justifiably argue that the critical independence of those hired on a consulting-fee basis is intrinsically compromised,[14] what interests me here is how auditors seek to performatively constitute the qualities of "externality" and "independence" in their interactions. Being external and independent, as they well know, is not simply a state of mind or a matter of individual skill and sincerity. Rather, these qualities must be socially and materially produced, and they demand the attention and cooperation of a range of actors and elements.

In order to construct an external and independent as well as gender-sensitive approach to their assessment work, the auditors requested in advance that they be provided with two independent translators, one of them female. A female auditor and a female translator, the reasoning went, could elicit more candid responses from village women. The auditors were deeply annoyed when they arrived at Batu Hijau and were presented with two male translators who normally worked at Newmont's Minahasa Raya mine in Sulawesi. They had placed special stress on the need for independent translators, not wanting a repeat of the previous year, when one translator, a former Newmont consultant, had leaked observations from the audit to a former colleague and friend over drinks. Making a fuss about the two male Newmont translators and flying back to Australia was not really an option, because the assessments—involving the health and safety auditors as well as environment auditors—are extraordinarily difficult to schedule. The auditors proceeded with the Newmont translators while expressing reservations about the latter's skill and professionalism; they soon found their concerns about leaks reinforced when they observed the translators routinely hanging out around the cubicles of Batu Hijau translators, with whom they were clearly on very friendly terms. When mine staff overlooked, misinterpreted, or ignored auditors' requests for specific props and supporting cast, they compromised the auditors' ability to stage and perform audit qualities that the latter valued, such as independence and gender sensitivity.

The problem of the translator points to a paradox intrinsic to the position of auditors: they are supposed to go deep inside the corporation while being external to and independent of it. For the duration of their stay, they are deeply dependent upon their hosts, whom they are also charged with examining. This dependence becomes more evident, or acute, in the setting of an isolated mine in a foreign country. Mine staff arrange where auditors will stay on company grounds; what they will eat; much of their schedule; the roster of managers, workers, and local residents with whom they will meet; their drivers; and their vehicles. Batu Hijau staff sometimes failed to fulfill requests and instructions from the auditors; their food orders, for example, were botched repeatedly, with vegetarian auditors finding meat in their meager boxed lunches. A trivial mistake, it nevertheless rankled in the context of sixteen-hour workdays too tightly scheduled to allow even a hot meal in the mess hall. For auditors, moreover, even small errors may be taken as signs that something larger is amiss.

THE DESKTOP REVIEW

Documents play a foundational role in the social auditing process (Cross 2011). This should not surprise us given that "the ability to create and maintain files is the emblem of modern bureaucracy," serving to establish "the ethical competence to rule" (Riles 2006:5, quoting Osborne 1994:290). It was among the documents that I began to grasp what a five-star rating meant in the eyes of the auditors. Standards were "integral to site culture" when taken up with a view toward comprehensive corporate knowledge and control. In such a world, the auditors would be able to link every single document to every other in a perfectly rational, orderly, and transparent fashion. As one of the auditors explained to a manager, "I'm really trying to draw a line through all the documents to see that they are all relating to each other and supporting a line of decision making and prioritization."

As noted earlier, the social auditors' mandate for written and oral inspections of documents (Hoskin and Macve 1994:75) authorized them to go through anyone's desk, search computers and files, summon missing documents, and demand an audience with the most senior official to quiz him or her on some inconsistency they had uncovered. This authority, along with the guiding aesthetic of rational transparency, may have accounted for the way social auditors behaved while handling documents. It was in that context that they seemed most at home, coming across as confident, secure, in charge: two people who knew what they were looking for, and who, when necessary, could swiftly assess what was missing and why. Though neither auditor spoke Indonesian, with minimal help from the translators they seemed able to speedily make sense of flowcharts, spreadsheets, and byzantine policy and procedural documents that left me bewildered. At one point, when I felt I must be the only one baffled by a statement of standard operating procedure, one of the auditors held it up and confidently pronounced it to be nonsense.

Their mandate included an assessment of document control—that is, of how Newmont staff cared for and safeguarded documents. Staff were expected to guard the material integrity of archived originals by installing a safety system that would, in case of fire, trigger the release of a special gas, rather than water from sprinklers; but they were also responsible for controlling each document's individual existence and relations with other documents. Documents were supposed to be clearly linked to one another in ways that auditors could easily follow. Freestanding documents were a problem from the auditors' perspective. It was also a problem if multiple versions of documents created and modified on different dates were in simultaneous circulation.

An auditor examining an External Relations stakeholder map chided officials for poor document control. Multiple copies of the map from different eras appeared to be in simultaneous circulation. They were out of date, featuring, for example, an NGO that had gone defunct months before (Project Underground, which authored the Newmonster comic book discussed in chapter 5). The auditor reproachfully implied that the problems Newmont was currently experiencing with environmental advocacy NGOs might indeed be related to the poorly maintained stakeholder map, which led managers to jumble priorities and devote significant personnel and budgetary resources to managing government relations in Jakarta while neglecting NGO relations.

The auditors spoke of "drilling down" from their inspection of documents. In doing so, they focused on arenas they deemed potentially high-risk for the mine, such as incidents of sexual harassment or local concerns about mine tailings. Among myriad security "incident" reports recounting speeding violations and petty altercations, for example, one auditor zeroed in on a complaint from a female worker who had been catcalled by a group of men. The auditor noted the woman's name and met with her later in order to verify that "corrective action" had been taken (in this instance, the catcallers had been reprimanded and had apologized). Similarly, a Community Relations logbook entry on a village resident's query over tailings led an auditor to track down the resident and talk to him directly about how his questions had been handled. Through the informal conversations generated by the process of "drilling down," the auditors met with people who had not been preselected by their hosts, and gathered information that potentially fell outside of the scope of the initial inquiry.

In their inspections, auditors repeatedly returned to the theme that the practices they were examining and calling into being should be grounded in a rational and transparent logic. Evidence of this was key to earning a five-star rating. They called out practices and documents that seemed illogical, perfunctory, and designed for the sole purpose of giving an official and strategic veneer to managerial action. While attempting to wade through a mass of forms on community reporting and investigating that half-duplicated one another, an auditor had the following exchange with mine officials:

Auditor: I'm confused; you guys are confused. These procedures don't cross-reference one another. You need one guideline like a street map.

External Relations manager: But this mine would have collapsed if we took all of our actions based on forms.

Auditor: You can make a decision here not to address this standard. But this goes against how community relations is embedded at all the other sites. So have you really got a system to look back and trend issues?[15]

[Community Relations manager pulls out documents with colorful bar graphs and pie charts.]

Auditor: [Pointing to a community relations "inputs" chart on the number of office visits by local people.] So how many of these [inputs] are actually complaints, though? If trending is being used by management, it should be showing up in monthly reports. There is no trending.

External Relations consultant: It can't be found or it's not there?

Auditor: Well, if it can't be found then it's not being used. This is not about doing something wrong; it's about doing it better.

To understand what it would look like if all the elements were "integral to site culture," consider Risk and Opportunity Management, one of Newmont's standards. In evaluating a mine's performance, auditors would examine its risk register and ranking systems, risk assessment workshops, risk register updates and reviews, and so forth. But managerial documents not overtly related to risk—such as objectives, performance indicators, reporting on performance indicators, minutes of monthly managers' meetings, strategic plans, standard task procedures, incident reporting and investigating databases, job descriptions and training programs, budgets, and bonuses awarded—should also relate back to risks. Social impact assessments, stakeholder engagement activities, and stakeholder maps should all feed back into risk assessment and management strategies. For example, Newmont had organized village development councils consisting of several village leaders who would supposedly represent the will of all villagers. According to the auditors, minutes from the council meetings—facilitated by handpicked NGOs that used participatory methodologies—should be processed as risk data. Village representatives would thereby unwittingly contribute to a corporate database that described fellow villagers as "risks" and "opportunities."

The ideal corporate knowledge system would be flexible, capable of destabilizing and responding to unexpected developments and fluctuations in a changing environment (Miller 1994:19), as well as to the unanticipated excesses, perturbations, and overflows that arise in the "congenitally 'failing' operation" of rendering the world calculable and manageable (Callon 1998; Miller 1992:74). Strathern (2006:190–92, 200) describes audit systems as inherently restless, perpetually restructuring and relentlessly refining and improving by co-opting and reformulating criticism and absorbing complexity.

Although Weber's depiction of modern bureaucracy (1946a:228) feels somewhat dated and too mechanical today, contemporary audit practices do share its utopian modernist ideal of a perfectly functioning system operating on a rational, transparent logic that is not tethered to particular

FIGURE 18. A social auditor engaged in a desktop review with PT NNT's Government Relations officials explains how different documents should fit together. Photo by author.

individuals and their personal social relations and agendas.[16] Ideally, the institutional memory of the bureaucratic data processing machine, materialized in a set of rationally created and ordered documents, should render individual staff and managers interchangeable and replaceable. An auditor espoused this bureaucratic ideal of separating offices from persons when asking a manager: "Is there a flowchart outlining what you just explained? If you suddenly left, what would your replacement do?" Another auditor exhorted: "It's about getting the cogs—which we've got now—to fit together like a well-oiled machine." Various metaphors abounded, all to the same point: the mine had "all the pieces of the jigsaw" but just needed to put it together; they had "all the spokes" but needed to fit them on the wheel (figure 18), and so on. But corporations always have in their midst various agents who thwart the fantasy of the well-oiled machine.

MISSING THE POINT

Managers did not passively submit to the logic of the audit. As noted, they did not meet auditors' requests for independent translators. Their response to the audit's demand for enterprising, responsibilized, calculating subjects was also incomplete. Some responded to criticism by blaming junior managers and staff; I saw one manager angrily rebuke a member of his staff who was unable to produce a document the auditors had requested. The fear the audit could induce among junior staff was painfully obvious to me when I accompanied one auditor on a visit to Community Relations offices in the villages. One official sweated profusely as he groped for answers to hypothetical questions village residents might ask about hiring practices, tailings, and contracting. Although it was not his fault that his training had not prepared him to answer basic questions about the mine, he clearly feared that he personally was being tested, that his inability to produce satisfactory answers might incur the wrath of his superiors.

Managers meanwhile found solidarity commiserating with one another. Some noted how easy it is to come and criticize, how much harder to take action and live with the consequences, as mine managers must. This fits with a larger perception at mine sites, that executives and consultants sent from corporate headquarters are, as a communications consultant in Denver put it, just "seagulls" who "fly in, shit on everyone's head, and fly out again." Managers also complained about the ongoing resources they had to commit to the audit and the new management systems it entailed, having been told initially by executives at headquarters that "once you put the system in place it'll run itself."

Managers and staff demonstrated impatience with the audit in various ways. While auditors scrutinized the work of Ivan, the American public relations consultant we saw coping with crises as the auditors' plane landed, he made a show of the fact that he had matters of greater urgency to attend to by indiscreetly reading and composing text messages on his mobile phone. In response to especially urgent incoming calls and texts, he even rushed out of the interview room entirely, stalling the progress of the irked auditors. Ivan repeatedly and rather theatrically made clear that he would tolerate the audit to a point but would continue to attend to "real time" developments in the crises Newmont was facing.

A senior manager of External Relations being quizzed on community development work found a still more egregious way to make the same point, whipping out his laptop to show me spectacular underwater digital photos he had snapped on recent diving trips. The exasperated auditors instructed him to put his laptop away. I felt like an unwilling accomplice while the manager, undeterred, began talking to me about the significance of sea worms, or nyale, in mine-village relations. As discussed in chapter 5, the sea worms can be caught only at dawn for two days every year when they reproduce. Villagers turn out en masse for the event, then spend the next days preparing and eating nyale and exchanging them with family and friends. The nyale came late this year, the manager explained, and if they ever failed to appear, then Newmont would really be in trouble over tailings. Upon subsequent reflection it occurred to me that the manager's sideshow was designed not only to annoy but also to instruct. He was exhibiting for the auditors a piece of local knowledge about which they were ignorant, and the critical significance of which was resistant to capture by five-star categories and procedures for risk management. I already knew about nyale, and he knew I knew. What he hoped would dawn on the auditors was their own ignorance—and the impotence of their vast system—with respect to the key thing: local knowledge. He did not himself believe mine tailings were killing off marine life; but if the nyale didn't show up one year, then local residents would surely blame the mine. That is to say, he understood that risks are socially constructed (Hilgartner 1992), and that even "false" stakeholder beliefs can have serious consequences. What he may not have fully appreciated is the elasticity and omnivorousness of the audit. Indeed, if they had had more time—and been alive to the manager's point instead of frustrated with his insolence— the auditors might well have pushed him to show by what mechanisms potential "false beliefs about environmental and social impacts of corporate activity" might "be taken seriously and managed in the stakeholder economy by 'upstream social analysis'" (Power 2003b:153).

Even acquiescence to the audit could function as a form of resistance to auditors' attempts to "make a difference." Sometimes this acquiescence manifested in an outwardly eager-to-please attitude coupled with strategic diversion. In response to a query on relations with environmental advocacy NGOs, for example, one Sumbawan manager beamed and informed the auditors that an NGO Newmont worked closely with had recently received funding from the Japan International Cooperation Agency, signaling its legitimacy in the eyes of an international aid organization. He leafed through a photo album that documented various "mission impossible" tasks his team had accomplished in local villages: cleaner beaches! a garbage truck! While they had had only one critical performance indicator the previous year—the number of demonstrations—he assured the auditors that this year they had instituted many more. Neither the focus on quantity rather than quality, nor the manager's efforts at self-promotion, left the auditors bedazzled, but his response did protect the manager from having to assimilate the deeper lessons the assessment was supposed to impart.

In another exchange, an American senior manager acquiesced to the notion of being graded by the auditors for his performance, only to haggle with them for an additional half star in the performance monitoring category:[17]

> *Auditor A:* Performance monitoring exists, but it's mostly quantitative. Qualitative monitoring is also required for the standard. In terms of the data that you're trending for your CPIs [Critical Performance Indicators], I've gone through each of them and, say with visitor numbers, you can't determine who is visiting and why. You can't see whether community inputs are positive or negative; same with official correspondence. In Comdev you're tracking expenditures, and that's helpful; but it doesn't tell you whether things are improving. Your data is trended but it's not useful, the number of malnourished children is a classic example.

> *Manager:* I'm reading three [stars], and it doesn't say that *all* monitoring data is formally recorded. You could say, "You're not measuring tire tread." You could carry it to the next step.

> *Auditor A:* I just think it's below the line, and I interpret that as all *useful* information. . . . It must be helpful.

> *Manager:* There is a growing feeling around the site that much of the Five Star is a justification for people to have work. There is a real perception that we're requiring so much paperwork to show this stuff that it's counterproductive.

> *Auditor A:* I'm saying: drop the stuff that's not necessary. Trend the stuff you really need to know to improve. Don't waste your time.

> *Manager:* I understand that, but there is resistance to what should be trended. I did hear that documentation is growing. That's the query: is it useful or not? I think there's nothing unhealthy about people questioning the validity of the report. If they don't understand and value it . . .

> *Auditor B:* The value comes out in performance and monitoring.

> *Manager:* For you, for an outsider it's helpful to see that. For my guys, they can say our top issues are a, b, c, d, e. So I'm putting it on paper not for the site but for somebody else in Denver. Are they in Denver going to tell us what to do? Probably not. It's not obvious what you need to do in the field. So I'm not sure what you're saying is ever going to jump out and convince the people in the field.

> *Auditor B:* Let me give you a simple example: 90 percent of land cases dealt with amicably. Not useful. But your raw data is there, and we're looking for that information more thoughtfully put together to be useful.

> *Auditor A [frustrated]:* You can have a 3 if you really want one; I don't really care.

The manager implies that the audit increases the burden of documentation without enhancing the mine's ability to manage issues, suggesting that auditors were only looking to measure "the level of institutional competence at producing documents" (Ahmed 2012:100). Audits, from this perspective, collect information for symbolic purposes without genuinely enhancing the rationality of managerial decision-making (Feldman and March 1981). The auditors in effect turn this critique against the manager, insisting that the way for officials to make documentation genuinely useful to themselves is to treat it seriously rather than cynically, to treat it as a means for improvement and self-assessment rather than a means of convincing an external authority of their compliance. From the auditors' perspective, nothing gets a manager stuck at three stars quite like ticking off the boxes and wrangling over the number of stars awarded—just as nothing convinces a professor that the B- was deserved, even generous—quite like its recipient's endless haggling over it. While both the student and the manager may wish to learn and improve, as long as grading systems exist to evaluate and judge, to punish and reward, they will be a source of preoccupation in and of themselves.

The auditors did not look forward to their task, on the assessment's final day, of presenting senior managers with the scores for their departments. I was with the auditors each evening as they tabulated their results, discussed them with one another, debated whether the standard criteria were too broad and ambiguous or too narrow and rigid, and finally settled on a score. In the process, auditors also examined the previous year's results and discussed which managers were likely to disagree with what scores and took stock of the evidence that would back up the scores awarded. In some cases, the scores declined because of a change in the five-star standards. (Because the system itself was subject to "continuous improvement" and annual reviews, standards could alter from year to year—making the auditor's job "exceedingly hard," as one of them put it.) In other cases, a lower score was a corrective for seemingly excessive lenience in the previous year's score.

EMPOWERING INTERNAL CHAMPIONS AND AGENTS OF CHANGE

Auditor-manager relations are not always antagonistic. Despite Ivan's negative initial attitude toward the "bean counters," for example, he subsequently became very engaged in a discussion with an Australian security manager and an auditor over the Human Rights Awareness

FIGURE 19. The social auditor quizzes one of Newmont's private security guards on his knowledge of human rights. Photo by author.

standard. Batu Hijau had already introduced a new human rights clause into its contract with 911, the mine's private security provider (figure 19), and had instituted human rights orientations for the mobile brigade police on-site. Ivan was converting the articles of the Universal Declaration of Human Rights and other voluntary norms into items in the risk register. The three had an animated discussion about how to commission a third-party provider to screen the backgrounds of security personnel for involvement in past human rights abuses. If anyone on-site had a problem with more stringent human rights controls, the auditor suggested, they could invoke the "crude business argument": these are international standards; abuses could land the company in a U.S. court on an Alien Tort Claims Act charge, and in the future corporations might well be held accountable in international tribunals. The auditor converted potential human rights violations by the company or its contractors into a future economic "risk" in order to exert moral force over corporate actors in the present. Among the audit interactions I observed, this one felt the most genuinely collaborative, and the least ambivalent. The auditor, consultant, and manager were clearly all enthusiastic about expanding human rights consciousness and preventing human rights violations in the mining context.

In furnishing the consultant and manager with a corporate-wide requirement for human rights performance and a language to convert violations into risks, the auditor was fulfilling the professed ameliorative goal of empowering internal champions of human rights. And yet such moments—in which CSR experts convert ethical issues into business rationales—are often tinged with ambivalence. Kemp and her colleagues (2012:3) note that the concept of risk "currently sits at the very heart of the industry's approach to CSR, accountability and social auditing. It is the dominance of this notion that needs to be challenged for a more relational and dialogically-orientated form of 'new accounting' . . . to emerge." A less instrumentalist accounting would ideally foster critical internal reflection and stakeholder engagement for the purpose of understanding social contexts and revising existing practices, but the emphasis on risk has considerable traction: "Notwithstanding that there are sound ethical reasons for moving away from a risk orientation, it is not surprising that it has such a hold over how CSR is represented organizationally given that its bottom-line appeal would seem to shore up power for vulnerable 'cost centres' like CSR" (Kemp, Owen, and van de Graaff 2012:4).

OUTSIDE THE MINE: "THE COMMUNITY"

If the social auditors seemed at home and authoritative among Batu Hijau's documents, they exuded far less confidence in their interactions with "community stakeholders." This was partly a reflection of their genuine lack of authority in the village context, their inability to command documents or persons the way they did in Newmont offices. But it was also partly deliberate: they sought to cultivate an aura of empathy, sensitivity, humility, and respect in a context where the goal was to elicit perspectives and opinions from people, rather than to judge, influence, and improve them.

One of the auditors confessed to generally disliking community interviews. This might seem strange given that auditors' labor was meant to serve the "idealistic" purpose of "making a difference." Near-mine communities were presumably meant to be important beneficiaries of improvements resulting from the Five Star Integrated Assessment. Anxiety and awkwardness perhaps sprang from this hope, from the auditors' "aching awareness of a distance" between assessment interventions and the "outside" reality they are supposed to express and address (Riles 2000:144).

The auditors relied on the Community Relations department to generate a list of village stakeholders to interview, requiring they be identified as "positive," "neutral," or "negative" in their perceptions of Newmont. They needed such identifications, one auditor explained to a manager, "to demonstrate to external stakeholders that our process is balanced." The interviews were not facilitated by the auditors' lack of Indonesian and their reliance on translators they did not fully trust. The auditors did their best to offset the extractive nature of the rapid interview format by carefully explaining their purpose as they handed out their business cards, and by verifying later that interviewees had received a summary of the assessment results written in Indonesian.[18]

Local residents often brought desires for profound change to the group meetings and interviews. Sometimes they expressed these, sometimes they pulled their punches. Just as the first group meeting was getting started in Tongo, a young man showed up and vehemently denounced Newmont meetings for their exclusiveness; the auditors were not interviewing the real community (*masyarakat*), he protested, but only those who benefited from the company. One auditor entreated the young man to join the meeting, and he seemed mollified by the auditor's conciliatory tone only to turn and walk off. When the auditors called after him, he explained that he was just going home to change out of shorts and into pants, in keeping with the formality and dignity of the occasion. He wound up saying very little; a local storeowner took up much of the meeting with a familiar speech about how Batu Hijau should hire more locals. But the young man's point about the company's tendency to focus on elites came home to the auditors. In a later meeting with a man and two women who were categorized as "negative" stakeholders, both women were silent. One had in the past spoken to me eloquently and expansively of Newmont's social and environmental failings, yet here she sat with her eyes flashing and her mouth clamped shut. Afterward, she intimated to me that she really wanted to speak openly but was afraid to do so because the wife of a staunch Newmont supporter was within earshot; she feared repercussions.

Other interviewees were skeptical of the value of meeting with the auditors at all. Many had extensive experience speaking with journalists, NGOs of various political stripes, the University of Mataram research team hired by Newmont every year to write an annual report, and academic researchers (including me). One auditor heard from several interviewees that they were tired of such interviews and felt they were unlikely to yield results or returns—and their responses to questions indeed became increasingly rote and patterned. Several had met just the previous week with representatives from International Alert (a U.K.-based NGO that was testing a conflict resolution methodology) and showed signs of interview fatigue. Still others were happy to participate, but were pragmatic to the point of cynicism about what was in it for them. One interviewee initially greeted the auditor warmly and arranged for some women to serve us sweet coffee. After the auditor explained that Newmont had hired auditors to conduct an independent assessment, the interviewee insisted that he could not speak to the auditor unless he too was paid. "We should be paid to be audited," he asserted, echoing the logic of the farmers in the participatory trainings I discussed in chapter 4. After the auditor explained that remuneration would jeopardize the integrity of the process, he reluctantly agreed to converse for free.

An auditor interviewing the leader of a local religious school felt a chill when the interviewee turned the tables on him by assuming the role of questioner and asking, "Do you feel safe in Australia?" The auditor interpreted this as a veiled threat, coming as it did at a time when many Australians worried that their government's support for U.S.-led wars in Afghanistan and Iraq had turned their country into a terrorist target. Memories of the 2002 bombing of two nightclubs in Bali, which had killed more Australians than any other nationality,[19] were also still fresh. This made it easier for the auditor to identify, in a direct and personal fashion, with fears of terrorism running through the ranks of staff (especially but not exclusively the expatriates among them) in Newmont offices in Indonesia. While auditors may maintain intact their desire to "make a difference," challenges to their presence and to the assessment process itself could make them feel unsettled and uneasy. Such sentiments could also prove to be a resource of sorts, as is evident in their final oral presentations.

THE AUDITORS' FINAL ACT

The grand finale of the audit was a multidisciplinary presentation by all the auditors before Batu Hijau's managers at Community Hall in Townsite. They raced to complete their PowerPoint presentations beforehand. Auditors from different disciplines sat down together and compared their scores, cheering when there was a match—regardless of the score, because consistency across disciplines confirms their belief in the connections between the disciplines. The mine's general manager opened the event with a gracious and welcoming speech. The auditors couched many of their general comments in the linguistic conventions followed by consultants in such a setting. Deficiencies and serious problems became "opportunities for improvement." As the auditors relinquished control of their findings, releasing them to the company in the prescribed format, their work seemed to shed the social context of its production, with the cacophony of sometimes discordant voices—ranging from those of questionable translators to those of obstructive managers and diffident villagers—subsumed into the euphony of ceremonial etiquette.

There were, however, notable exceptions. Auditors did seize this last opportunity to inject some final criticism in the form of "raw" data, which probably would have lost its impact if processed through the five-star standards. One of the Health and Safety auditors inserted a series of photos into his PowerPoint presentation that documented safety equipment badly in need of repair or retirement, workers wearing improperly fastened and hence useless safety gear, and a haul truck dwarfing—and looking menacingly close to squashing—a regular truck. The auditor accompanied this final slide with a pointed reminder about the subcontractor recently decapitated by a haul truck in the mine pit.

The social auditors meanwhile deployed a different set of raw data, using the "voices" of local community members. They noted a few positive comments, such as "We would like to say thanks for Newmont's assistance" and "Relationships are going well compared to other companies," before delivering, in bullet-point format, the serious critiques:

- We have incredible social jealousy even within families.
- Community Relations is bad; they don't mix with us women.
- Prosperity is only enjoyed by a few, and they are mostly men.
- Comrel [Community Relations] is useful, but the poor are psychologically shy to go to the office.
- When Newmont leaves, this huge hole will be a toxic lake.
- We don't know who we should get angry with, so that's why we close the road, then we get attention.
- We're being kept quiet by Newmont giving us money and programs, but we want to feel these programs and know they are working.
- There is no one from the old Newmont management, so they don't remember their promises.

One of the social auditors added some interpretation for the managers, using the sound bites to "flag the issue of inclusiveness," by which the auditor meant discriminate distribution of community support from Newmont. Inclusiveness was a serious issue, the auditor insisted, because terrorists tend to recruit from the ranks of the excluded and marginalized. By phrasing social inequality in a powerful and, at that time, particularly salient idiom of risk—namely, that of terrorism—the auditor deemphasized its ethical dimensions; like human rights discourse, social inequality can be framed in a way that emphasizes corporate risk. And at this juncture, such reframings of social issues as corporate risks might appear to auditors to be the best way to "make a difference." But such framings were not wholly instrumental. Rumors that one of the Bali bombers was in the vicinity lent immediacy to the otherwise abstract threat of terrorism, and the ustadz's veiled threat left the auditors themselves with a lingering fear for their own safety—even back in Australia.

ADDRESSING THE PUBLIC? THE STAKEHOLDER REPORT

As an oppressive climate of fear came over Batu Hijau with the threat of an imminent terrorist attack, the auditors were glad to be packing their bags. Upon returning home, they still had to complete the final details of their written assessments. They might also take the opportunity to informally debrief the CSR executives in Denver on their observations and concerns falling outside the parameters of their official reports. While Newmont officials in Denver and consultants would use the assessments to write Newmont's stakeholder reports, the auditors themselves had almost nothing to do with this stage of the process. From the auditors' perspective, these reports are not the central point of audits, and their potential impact and ability to contribute to "making a difference" is limited.

In the age of CSR, stakeholder reports generated as part of social and environmental audits have become the conventional complement to the annual shareholder report on financial performance. Often adorned with colorful images of smiling children, productive adults, lush nature, and state-of-the-art, gleaming, and presumably secure laboratories and infrastructure, these reports go by various names: sustainability reports, stakeholder reports, corporate social responsibility reports, and "triple bottom line" reports that simultaneously address people, planet, and profits.

Proponents and critics of CSR alike have accorded these reports considerable weight and significance. Tapscott and Ticoll (2003), for example, champion such reporting and promote the "naked corporation," arguing that given the intensity of public scrutiny, corporations are better off forgoing the strategically positioned fig leaf—with its attendant risk, the accusation and revelation of cover-up. Skeptics of corporate transparency, meanwhile, have argued that voluntary corporate self-monitoring and reporting practices are in fact the fig leaves. Going beyond the reports' appealing visual images, several scholars have engaged in close critical readings to show how corporations define, frame, and circumscribe the salient issues in ways that depoliticize them, portraying themselves as ready to listen to all stakeholders who wish to communicate on CSR (Conley and Williams 2005; Livesey and Kearins 2002). Michael Power (1997:125) notes that voluntary corporate reports are generally written in language that is "sanitized, cautious, and unhelpful." According to Power (127), these bland reports not only fail to empower stakeholders, democratize knowledge, or support public debate but also actually stand as a surrogate for—and deterrent to—external scrutiny and regulation by government actors who can be held accountable through democratic processes. This view, of course, rests on normative assumptions about the liberal democratic state and its ability to develop, monitor, and enforce business regulations.[20]

Many corporate managers, too, accord significance to the stakeholder reports. After all, they spend a great deal of time and money producing them. Newmont began producing its CSR report, *Now and Beyond*, in 2003, initially adopting both title and format from Normandy.[21] In addition to conducting mine site visits and working with mine staff, the editor of these reports used Five Star Integrated Assessment performance-monitoring results, information harvested from data acquisition workbooks that headquarters had begun requiring of all the sites, third-party comments and feedback, and case studies of site initiatives and issues. Newmont later switched from paper reports to an online format and renamed the reports *Beyond the Mine: The Journey towards Sustainability*. This new title invokes distant spatial and temporal horizons and positions the company as engaged in a collaborative and participatory process, a beckoning journey, with the actual destination left unspecified (Li 2009; Milne, Kearins, and Walton 2006).

Many mine managers are quite sensitive about the information that goes into the reports. An executive in Denver recalled that managers at one Normandy mine refused to circulate their *Now and Beyond* report locally "because they didn't like two lines in it." But managers are also responsible for writing some of the content, and some exercised their editorial hand to "tell our side of the story," at times even introducing a defensive tone as they responded to their critics and perceived slights. Early reports on Newmont's Indonesian operations, for example, delegitimized and trivialized critics, dismissing Sulawesi residents who alleged that Minahasa Raya mine tailings were poisoning their waters as a "small group" whose claims had been conclusively disproven by scientists. A report on Batu Hijau depicted labor disputes at Batu Hijau as "politically influenced" and described the Indonesian government's decision to lower the mine's environment rating (Program for Pollution Control, Evaluation and Rating) from green (very good) to blue (compliance) as "political" (Newmont Mining Corporation 2005b:9).

I am generally sympathetic to scholarly and activist concerns that voluntary stakeholder reporting fails to inform—and potentially manipulates public perceptions—of social and environmental impacts. A quick example of such failure in the case of Newmont is the large data set included on environmental emissions, water usage, wildlife mortalities, fines paid, cyanide consumption, and so forth. Presented thus in aggregate form, it is of little use to critics, obscuring, for example, Newmont's position as one of the top sulfur oxide polluters in Australia and the second-largest consumer of electricity in Nevada (the largest at that time supposedly being the Mirage Hotel and Casino). Because such critiques closely resemble one another and seem destined to become increasingly redundant, however, it might be fruitful to shift ethnographic attention to corporate awareness of this skepticism. Rather than seeing stakeholder reports (or any other form of public corporate speech) either as a reflection of the inner life and beliefs of "the corporation" or as necessarily successful attempts to hoodwink the public, we might pay closer attention to public reactions and the anxieties these produce.

An executive in Denver complained to me that though Newmont was always careful to send *Now and Beyond* reports to Friends of the Earth, the activists on the receiving end were equally careful to return them unopened, thereby communicating their rejection of this form of corporate speech. Another form of activist response to CSR reports is parody: sustainability reports are easy to spoof and excellent fodder for the culture-jamming work or countercultural carnival (Foster 2008:185) that Boyer and Yurchak (2010) identify as a hallmark of late liberalism.

The weight accorded these reports by some mine managers, then, seems disproportionate to that accorded by a wider audience. Newmont's

CSR and communications executives in Denver seemed cognizant of this disjuncture. At one meeting, a communications executive raised the *Social Balance* report produced and widely distributed by the Minera Yanacocha mine in Peru. He made a face and said the reports were far too rosy, giving him a "sugar rush." Discussing shortcomings of the *Now and Beyond* reports, which the CSR and communications executives admitted "contained precious little data" and were geographically "imbalanced," the executives agreed that future reports needed to "have more meat on them" and a "more uniform authorial voice." After the CSR executive mused that such reports are probably of little value to local communities, the communications executive responded that Newmont ought simply to produce a corporate-wide report that "would be more honest in addressing our real audience: NGOs, journalists, and such, not local stakeholders." Debates will undoubtedly continue to unfold in Newmont and other companies over who actually consumes stakeholder reports, the most appropriate modes of disseminating them, how to make them "living" documents that foster interaction with stakeholders, how to balance qualitative and quantitative data, and so forth.[22] Newmont and other companies will also continue to devise new measures, such as hiring external sustainability-assurance agencies (e.g., Bureau Veritas, World Monitors) to examine its reports and provide assurance letters[23]—although, as Fonseca (2010:359) notes, such attempts to address the "credibility gap" of voluntary sustainability reporting still lack popular "credibility as a tool to increase credibility." I suspect that, despite such efforts, stakeholder reporting will remain a stigmatized speech genre.[24]

CONCLUSION

The auditors had made many a compromise as they carried out their "idealistic" labor: accepting in-house translators, conceding an extra half star they felt was undeserved, and framing social issues in terms of the "crude business case" and corporate risk. Yet being blocked, waylaid, and compromised can reinforce the sense of what remains to be done, of the scope of ongoing improvement needed. The auditors also had occasion to feel they scored small victories, recorded improvements, connected with audit skeptics, and found opportunities to speak more forcefully than the system of stars or language of standards allowed. It is this sense of social progress within capitalism that refreshes the auditors' commitment to their project, that of reforming corporations by reworking corporate boundaries and responsibilities.

After the auditors left Batu Hijau for Australia, the mine's managers continued struggling to contain the crises I described in the beginning of the chapter. They negotiated with workers, "socialized" tailings among local residents concerned about the potential health impact of mine waste, and kept close tabs on events unfolding in Sumatra and Sulawesi. To my knowledge, nothing ever came of the search for the Bali-bombing terrorist supposedly lurking in the mine's vicinity. In 2006, however, an alleged Jemaah Islamiyah member from Singapore who had fled the country in December 2001 was arrested at the religious school (*pondok pesantren*) in Tongo, where, it turned out, he had been "quietly teaching" English for several years, in classrooms built with Newmont support (ICG 2007:12).

Conclusion

"Soft Is Hard"

In chapter 1, I recounted how engineers at Newmont's headquarters had asked the land manager to promise to expedite a small land purchase for a construction camp in Ghana, only to be refused. Observing that one hasty land deal could imperil the whole lot, the manager warned the engineers: "Soft issues are hard issues." Newmont's CSR experts often used variations of this "soft is hard" formulation in everyday discourse, and it featured prominently in a PowerPoint presentation that the Denver CSR executives put together to train colleagues in "community outrage" management.

Soft and *hard* invoke a welter of meanings, prominent among them an assumed opposition between the "soft" terrain of uncertain and intersubjective human relations in mining and the "hard," "technical" engineering aspects (Edwards 1990; Røyrvik 2011:116, 119–21). CSR experts stake a claim for the status of their work by insisting that human relations are hard in two senses: they are difficult, even intractable at times, and they generate "hard" costs. Familiar Newmont examples of such "hard" soft issues include long and expensive criminal lawsuits against PT Newmont Pacific Nusantara's president Rick Ness over submarine tailings disposal on the Indonesian island of Sulawesi, and Newmont's inability to mine the Cerro Quilish or Conga deposits in Peru as a result of staunch local opposition. Soft and hard also have obvious gender and sexual connotations; elevating CSR issues from the former to the latter relies on the valorization of a stereotypically masculine quality.

The "soft is hard" meme challenges not only the ascendancy of technical over social knowledge but also the separability of the two in the first place. An operations executive I spoke to in Denver expressed both appreciation for what he construed as soft issues and desire to keep them at a distance; he believed, moreover, that this stance was reasonable, maintainable. He preferred an engineering problem any day to a farmer blaming a Newmont mine for the death of his livestock. Describing himself as a "linear chap," he explained that "if you can pick where you put a mine," the best is "an arid environment with no people. . . . The worst is lots of rain and lots of people." CSR's ideal role, from his perspective, would be that of forming a protective bubble around the technological sphere of mining so that engineering crews could get on with their work without being distracted by social issues. CSR executive Helen Macdonald commented that this unreconstructed engineer's "bubble theory" was "a good bubble to burst." A mine cannot be separated from issues of permitting and property law. Technical skills cannot be separated from finding, hiring, housing, feeding, and caring for people with those skills. And the use of explosives, electric shovels, haul trucks, giant crushers, and tailings pipelines cannot be separated from safety requirements, environmental concerns, and aesthetic beliefs.

I was reminded of the gendered dichotomy between soft and hard issues in mining by Elizabeth Krause's contribution to a 2013 debate on developing noncapitalist economies, published in the pages of *Anthropology News*. Discussing her unresolved intellectual conflict between "strong theory" and "weak theory" approaches to capitalism, Krause writes, "I take comfort in the confidence and materiality of strong theory. A good example is the work of political economy legend Eric Wolf. A capitalist system dominates. It exploits. It creates inequality. It needs to be undone. The task feels concrete." Krause finds that the "weak theory" approach, by contrast, is attractive and intriguing but leaves her "uneasy." She identifies it with the antiessentialist work of joint scholar J.K. Gibson-Graham (1996, 2006), who seeks to challenge "capitalocentric" perspectives that treat capitalism as a unitary and coherent system, with all economic activity analyzed in relation to it. Krause finds this approach—with its stress that meanings and identities are open, incomplete, and indeterminate—lacking in coherence, difficult "to square with a strong materialist method," and ultimately lacking analytical purchase on the "stable and taken-for-granted 'there' of a capitalist system."

This strong theory/weak theory dichotomy could be mapped onto analysis of corporations as well. In the eyes of some, those who see and condemn corporations as profit-maximizing institutions adhere to "strong" theory and call it like it is, while those with antiessentialist views of the firm (as multiple, indeterminate, and socially constituted) are weak, "wishy-washy and willy-nilly" (Krause 2013). It may be more useful to subvert this dichotomy, beginning by appreciating how essentialist positions are constructed and what they can accomplish. Feminist theorist Diana Fuss insists we consider essentialisms in the plural, interrogating but not dismissing them. Fuss (1989:20) also stresses that we classify essentializing acts in ways that embed normative assumptions about speaking subjects—with some framed as deliberately "deploying" and "activating" strategic essentialisms, others as passively "falling" or "lapsing" into them.

Conservative and critical-progressive scholars and activists both produce—in their different ways—the essentializing view of the corporation as *Homo economicus*. Conservative enactments tend to offer normative accounts of what corporations should do, at worst licensing the abandonment of social and environmental values, stakeholders, and anything else purported to stand in the way of profit. The assumptions of conservative and critical-progressive scholars can be strikingly similar, even as they are used to reach sharply contrasting conclusions.

Does the notion that the corporation is multiple constitute a betrayal of critical-progressive forms of contestation and critique invested in enactments of the corporation as *Homo economicus?* Only, I would argue, if we assume that critical-progressive practice hinges on the truth of a singular form of enactment. Maria Puig de la Bellacasa (2011:91) implies that activism sometimes hinges on attachments to particular visions and nonnegotiable positions. Debunking these essentialisms and labeling their adherents as fundamentalists and conspiracy theorists may express a mistrust of radical ways of politicizing things, and a readiness to moderate the critical standpoints that produce oppositional knowledges.[1] Yet activist practices for bringing about change themselves often rest on multiplicity, and on the possibilities that reside in multiplicity, even when they assert singularity. Pragmatic activism involves negotiating complex interdependencies, complicated acts of translation, and misunderstandings (Kirksey 2012; Tsing 2005). If activists use the *Homo economicus* view of a mining company to bolster accusations of social and environmental harm, they may improve its worker compensation or stop toxic dumping, even as they fall short of a bigger goal such as nationalizing a mine or closing it down. The corporation has budged, becoming something other than what it was. Defining advocacy "as a performance of ethics in anticipation of the future[,] . . . where there is never only one way to do things," Kim Fortun (2001:16) calls for an uncoupling of advocacy from the modernist ideals of the rational and unwavering individual armed with absolute, "hard" (rigid and inflexible) truths. Advocacy work would be severely constrained if it could not tolerate the contradictions necessarily raised by its multiple tools (law, poetry, science, protest, parodies) and essentialist modes of apprehending corporations, communities, and states.[2]

Annemarie Mol (2002:165) asserts that "we live in an underdetermined world, where doubt can always be raised," making it all the more important to consider just how, "given this possibility, we can still act." She proposes that, rather than seeking assurance that our knowledge is true to its objects, we instead ask whether various practices are good for the human and nonhuman subjects who are involved in it. What is considered good and is sought after, what is considered bad and fought against, is also multiple and political (165–66, 176–77).

If the corporation is multiple, then our analytics must be multiple as well. Locating the research for this book at Newmont's corporate headquarters in Denver and near a mine site in Indonesia enabled me to witness firsthand efforts to unify the corporation, as well as the temporal, geographic, and epistemological divides that pull it apart into distinct relations and practices. Disputes over sustainable development and patronage enactments of the corporation are settled, I show, not by a single, metaphysical, profit-maximizing corporate actor but by numerous actors who—through struggles that take place in paddy fields, in mosques, in air-conditioned offices, and on public roads—give shape to community-development infrastructure, religious philanthropy, local hiring, and other expressions of corporate responsibility.

This perspective enables us to understand more clearly why early attempts by activists to unite residents of southwest Sumbawa in opposition to the socially and environmentally destructive "Newmonster" in their backyard foundered on competing enactments of Newmont as responsible miner and vital patron. At the same time, the Newmonster enactment has been successful in preventing mining in other settings and may become more salient for southwest Sumbawans too as the end of the mine nears. Approaching the corporation as multiple demands that we trace out the palpable, material processes through which such enactments are constituted over time in situated geographies.

Notes

INTRODUCTION

1. Weber (1947:102) insisted that social collectivities such as the "state," "nation," "corporation," or "family" might be regarded as individual persons for legal or practical purposes, but "for sociological purposes there is no such thing as a collective personality which 'acts.'" Sociologists nonetheless had to study how ideas about collective actors "have a meaning in the minds of individual persons, partly as of something actually existing, partly as something with normative authority. . . . Actors thus in part orient their action to them, and in this role such ideas have a powerful, often a decisive, causal influence on the course of action of real individuals" (102).

2. Oinas (2006) argues that firm boundaries are multidimensional rather than blurred or fuzzy, and that an adequate theory of the firm boundary should be able to account for this. My approach instead is to examine how understandings of agency and responsibility are intertwined in shifting understandings of corporations.

3. Legally, corporations are independent entities that own themselves (Stout 2012). The popular perception that shareholders legally own corporations is, albeit mistaken, widespread and influential (e.g. Reich 2010).

4. Mitchell's discussion of government sovereignty, which focuses on more negative, repressive, and exclusionary technologies, contrasts with Jessica Cattelino's discussion (2008, especially chap. 4) of how Florida Seminoles, who were once federal welfare recipients, today exercise political and economic sovereignty through casino wealth. Cattelino explores more positive forms of the materialization of Seminole sovereignty in, for example, housing and kitchen appliances, medically insured bodies, government buildings and thatched chickees, and nutritionally balanced hot meals delivered to the homes of senior citizens.

5. Mol extends her conceptual apparatus to the corporation in a brief remark about the McDonald's corporation as "a fascinating multiple object, with endless similarities and differences between its various outlets, worldwide" (2002:180). Similarly, Callon and Latour (1981:294) depict state Leviathans as "imbricated," incapable of being stabilized by any one metaphor (e.g., machine, market, code, body, war), "not just *one* Leviathan but many, interlocked one into another like chimera, each one claiming to represent the reality of all, the programme of the whole. Sometimes some of them manage to distort the others so horribly that for a while they seem the only soul in this artificial body."

6. Village residents responded to the fogging operations in divergent ways: some threw doors and windows open when they heard the noisy rumble and hiss of the trucks approaching, in the hope that the white gas would clear mosquitoes out of their homes; others quickly shut their houses down to keep out the fumes. On occasion I heard residents who were more sensitive to the larvicidal fog retching helplessly.

7. Coumans's general point touches on a broader ongoing debate over the ethical dilemmas raised by anthropologists conducting research for military or business organizations (see, e.g., Rohde 2007; and the Network of Concerned Anthropologists, https://sites.google.com/site/concernedanthropologists/).

8. Karl Polanyi (2001) characterized economic exchange in premarket societies as "embedded"—that is, governed by social and kinship obligations—in contrast to "disembedded" market societies, where individuals are atomized, rationally calculating, and pursuing maximum gain.

9. In its emphasis on the corporeal investment of the researcher, Ortner's discussion of ethnography and fieldwork resembles Erving Goffman's vivid and ethically troubling description (1989:125–26) of participant observation as a technique "of getting data . . . by subjecting yourself, your own body and your own personality, and your own social situation, to the set of contingencies that play upon a set of individuals, so that you can physically and ecologically penetrate their circle of response to their social situation, or their work situation, or their ethnic situation, or whatever. So that you feel close to them while they are responding to what life does to them. I feel that the way this is done is to not, of course, just listen to what they talk about, but to pick up on their minor grunts and groans as they respond to their situation. When you do that, it seems to me, the standard technique is to try to subject yourself, hopefully, to their life circumstances, which means that although, in fact, you can leave at any time, you act as if you can't and you try to accept all of the desirable and undesirable things that are a feature of their life. That 'tunes your body up[,]' and with your 'tuned-up' body and with the ecological right to be close to them (which you've obtained by one sneaky means or another), you are in a position to note their gestural, visual, bodily response to what's going on around them and you've been pathetic enough—because you've been taking the same crap they've been taking—to sense what it is that they're responding to."

10. Patty Keller, in her remarks at the Risk@Humanities Conference, Society for the Humanities, Cornell University, October 27, 2012, called these etymological roots to my attention.

11. The persistence of ideals of independence and objectivity for ethno-graphic research on corporations or the military is striking because postmodern critiques in the 1980s have given these ideals an almost quaint ring in today's discipline (e.g., Clifford and Marcus 1986). Indeed, where anthropologists can align their own political perspectives with those of their research subjects, they often call for more overtly political, collaborative, and action-oriented forms of research (e.g., Razsa and Kurnik 2012; Scheper-Hughes 1995). In anthropol-ogy, according to Urban and Koh (2013:152), research uncovering adverse external effects of corporations is ethically uncontroversial, in contrast to "engaging with the corporation's inner workings: the perspective of the manag-ers and of the corporation as agent" (see also Golub 2013).

12. CSR is related to, and in various ways overlaps with, a host of cognate movements such as organics, fair trade, base-of-the-pyramid initiatives, and socially responsible investing (Besky 2013; Browne and Milgram 2009; Carrier and Luetchford 2012; De Neve, Luetchford, and Pratt 2008; Guthman 2004; Dietrich 2013; Jaffee 2007; Reichman 2011, ch. 5; Schwittay 2011; Welker and Wood 2011). Some proponents of these cognate movements distinguish their work from "conventional" CSR with arguments that they are more radical, transformative, grassroots, and authentic (Hart 2010).

13. In legal theory, the nature of the corporation remains indeterminate. Various scholars have shown that the legal trope of corporate personhood is politically polyvalent, potentially open to being adopted for conservative or progressive purposes. Although corporate personhood has been used to extend constitutional protections, including Fourteenth Amendment rights, to corpora-tions, conservative legal scholars (who identify with the law-and-economics school of thought or as contractarians) have questioned corporate boundaries and reification and argued for disaggregating the corporation.

Noting that "conservative academics have been doing a good job of practical theorizing in recent years," Millon (1990:251) calls for critical scholars to do more "to apply their theoretical insights to important practical problems." Without an explicit call for more progressive legal theory, Davis (2009:67) makes a similar point about the legal indeterminacy of corporations, pointing out that "pragmatic legal thinkers do not seek to resolve what a corporation 'really' is, but to apply a theory of the corporation that best serves society's interests, or that best predicts how judges might rule." Dewey (1926:655–56) argues that "'person' signifies what law makes it signify," and could "be used simply as a synonym for a right-and-duty bearing unit." For Dewey (661, 663), then, corporations should be understood in terms of their mutual relations with others rather than in their inner essence and nature; "will" and "interests" are emergent functions rather than intrinsic force or structure. Gold (2012) explores how judges actively maintain uncertainty with regard to the theory of the firm.

14. Benson (2011), however, has shown that Philip Morris has strategically supported legal regulation in domains that would deflect attention from corpo-rate agency and responsibility (by, e.g., focusing public attention on the identity-card-checking practices of tobacco retailers at the point of purchase) or afford a competitive advantage to the firm (e.g., Philip Morris' support of FDA regulation of tobacco).

15. Some scholars, however, have explored newer mine labor issues under the rubric of CSR, such as HIV/AIDS in the South African mine workforce (Rajak 2011a), and the negative safety implications of rampant outsourcing of various parts of the production process to subcontractors (Rolston 2010).

16. As a result of broader trends in the mining industry, the anthropology of mining has expanded from a focus on labor dynamics—including cultural practices, capitalist critiques, labor recruitment and migration, ethnic relations, and the political agency of mine workers and their families (Godoy 1985; Nash 1979; Powdermaker 1962; Taussig 1980; Wilson 1941)—to the study of mine closures and layoffs, privatization, labor subcontracting and restructuring, and capital-intensive mine demands for a small, stable, and trained workforce (Donham 2011; Ferguson 1999; Ferry 2005; Finn 1998; Gill 2000; Godoy 1985; Rajak 2010; Ribeiro 1995; Robinson 1986; Smith 2008; Smith and Helfgott 2010). Recent anthropological work has also focused on the social and environmental consequences of mining megaprojects and the ethical dilemmas faced by anthropologists engaged with states, corporations, communities, and activists in supporting or opposing mining (Ballard and Banks 2003; Biersack 1999; Harper 2005; Jacka 2005; Kirsch 2006).

17. Although corporate critics have argued that publicly traded corporations in the United States are legally obligated to maximize profits for shareholders (Achbar and Abbott 2003; Fortun 2001:104), legal scholar Lynn Stout (2012) maintains that this view lacks a proper legal foundation. Indeed, examples abound of courts shielding corporate directors from any legal obligation to maximize shareholder wealth, and of courts upholding stakeholder interests over shareholder profits (Davis 2009; Paine 2003; Stout 2008).

18. In the documentary *The Corporation* (Achbar and Abbott 2003), shareholder activist Robert Monks argues, from a critical standpoint, that "whether you obey the law or not is a matter of whether its cost effective. If the chance of getting caught and the penalty are less than it costs to comply, people think of it as being just a business decision." This naturalizes law-breaking behavior by business in a way that goes beyond what Friedman's doctrine countenances.

19. OED defines *greenwashing* as the "creation or propagation of an unfounded or misleading environmentalist image." *Pinkwashing* refers to the participation of businesses that make carcinogenic products in "pink ribbon" campaigns against breast cancer (the Breast Cancer Action organization has developed this critique in multiple campaigns, see http://bcaction.org/; see also Jain 2007). *Bluewashing* refers to businesses that abuse human rights and adopt and use the UN logo through membership in the UN's Global Compact.

20. In my approach to corporate "responsibility," I take inspiration from Ahmed's call (2012:1, 5–6, 179) for asking as an open question what institutional "diversity" does by proceeding with a sense of uncertainty rather than from "the presumption of our own criticality," which, she argues, "can be a way of protecting ourselves from complicity."

21. In his critique of the globalization concept, Frederick Cooper (2001) shows that its political valence is unclear, since globalization has been the subject of promarket celebration ("the Banker's Boast"), liberal mourning ("the Social Democrat's Lament"), and more politically ambiguous analysis (the

postmodern "Dance of the Flows and Fragments"). He also criticizes its lack of historical specificity and agency. In his critical account of neoliberalism, David Harvey (2005) points to structural adjustment policies and specific actors and policies (e.g., the IMF, World Trade Organization, large corporations) and offers a particular geographic and historical genesis (e.g., the Chicago school, Chile as a lab experiment). Harvey and other economic geographers (Peck 2010; Peck and Tickell 1994) emphasize neoliberalism's uneven quality (e.g., countries in the global South are forced to dismantle agricultural subsidies that are maintained intact in the global North, and in the United States austerity for social programs is embraced alongside rampant overspending for military weapons and a prison-industrial complex housing millions). Bishnupriya Ghosh and Bhaskar Sarkar discussed how critique can "pulverize granularity" in a talk ("Speculations on Affirmative Speculation," given at the Risk@Humanities Conference, Society for the Humanities, Cornell University, October 27, 2012).

22. The challenge is to try to understand how capitalism works in practice without lending to it a "logic, energy, and coherence" that it lacks, without attributing "an internal rationality, an element of sameness, or an inherent power that is then given credit for what happened" (Mitchell 2002:14). Yanagisako (2002:6) makes the related point that capitalism is not structured by a single logic and is not a single historical process (see also Shever 2012).

23. Accounting scholar Michael Power (2007:4, 22) similarly argues for extending to formal organizations social theorists' insights on cultivating risk reflexivity and entrepreneurial risk-taking for individuals (Beck 1992; Giddens 1990).

24. In southwest Sumbawa, I found the term *fanatic (fanatik)* had very positive connotations and was used by village residents in ways similar to its use by Christians in Sulawesi as described by Aragon (2000:27). Peter Just (2001), by contrast, heard the term used in a negative description of Bimanese Sumbawans. Dutch colonial official and scholar Snouk Hurgronje (1931:285–86) remarked on the religiosity of Sumbawans after encountering two important teachers from West Sumbawa during his 1884–85 stay in Mecca. Zeinuddin Sumbawa and Omar Sumbawa apparently settled permanently in the city and established a following of Sumbawan and Malay-speaking students.

25. See Strassler (2010:181–84) for a discussion of similar pregnancy rituals in Java and how photographic documentation practices have altered them.

26. For accounts of similar ritual meals elsewhere in Indonesia, see Geertz (1960:11–15) on *slametan* or *kenduren* in Java, and Bowen (1993) on *kenduri* among Gayo people of Sumatra.

27. When McDonald's opens up franchises around the globe, James Watson (2006:7) notes, the company goes through a localizing process in which "McDonald's does not always call the shots." In Indonesia, localizing meant Islamizing, particularly in the wake of the 2001 U.S. invasion of Afghanistan, when McDonald's restaurants became a target of protest. Restaurant managers and employees were trained to respond to protests by unfurling green banners stating, "This store is owned by a Muslim, Bambang Rachmadi," and by presenting photos of Rachmadi, the owner of the national franchise, and his wife in full Muslim dress (Shubert 2001). A CNN reporter (Shubert 2001) noted the "Muslim makeover"

of McDonald's restaurants each Friday (signaled by Arabic music, workers' dress, and mosque attendance), the posting of signs in Arabic declaring the food as halal, and Golden Arches pointing the way to prayer rooms.

28. Local residents did reserve criticism for the mechanisms through which these flows were organized. A member of the village governing apparatus in the transmigrant village SP2, for example, said that a bull that Comrel was supposed to deliver for the Day of Sacrifice arrived only after he called the Comrel manager to ask after its whereabouts. When it arrived, moreover, it proved to be the right age but underweight. He felt Comrel should have bought a bull from SP2 residents themselves rather than from a contractor (and deposed village head) from Sekongkang.

29. Laidlaw (2010) adopts these terms from Latour (2005) but calls greater attention to the ethical and political stakes attached to agentive shifts.

30. One pastor told me his work was hampered by a regency law stipulating that a church could be established only after gathering a minimum congregation of three thousand Christians.

31. Because of Paddy's Pub's exclusionary policy of charging Indonesians, but not foreigners, an entrance fee, the group had not ended up entering the club. The planners of the attack probably deliberately targeted nightclubs with such policies to maximize foreign casualties and minimize national casualties.

32. Newmont officials believed the bombing, which occurred at night and did not injure anyone, was actually the work of members of the Indonesian police force who were trying to shake down the company and discredit 911, the private security firm Newmont had contracted. Conboy (2006:176) claims that the police later linked the bombing to Jemaah Islamiyah, and that PT NNT was later considered as a potential target for a much larger bombing before Jemaah Islamiyah leaders settled on Paddy's Pub and the Sari Club, the targets of the 2002 Bali bombing.

33. Economic geographer Joshua Barkan (2012, 2013) has more recently explored the corporation through a disciplinary lens influenced by Foucault and Agamben.

34. Newmont's founder also founded the Boyce Thompson Institute for Plant Research, now at Cornell University, and named it after his parents (http://bti.cornell.edu/about-bti/history/).

35. These New Deal measures included the growth of new federal agencies with jurisdiction over business; the National Recovery Administration's "Blue Eagle" campaign, which abolished child labor and established minimum wages and a maximum work week for various industries; the Wagner act protecting workers' rights to unionize; and the establishment of the Securities and Exchange Commission to regulate stock trading (see Ramsey 1973:92).

36. Stearns and Allan (1996) argue that, whereas merger movements around 1900, in the 1920s, and in the 1980s were sparked by lax government enforcement of antitrust legislation, the 1960s were an exception. Antitrust legislation was equipped to handle vertical and horizontal integrations but not the formation of conglomerates.

37. The board's decision was reviewed by the Supreme Court of Delaware, the state in which Newmont, like the majority of publicly traded U.S. corpora-

tions, became incorporated owing to its lax provisions (through which Delaware won the "race to the bottom" between states; Cary 1974) and to subsequent elaboration of legal precedent. While the board's dividend distribution was a "scorched earth" strategy that might have destroyed the company, Newmont's 1987 annual report relates that the Supreme Court approved the defensive measures as "reasonable" given Pickens's "secret acquisition of shares, the 'bear hug' letter, the coercive partial tender offer and inadequate price" (Newmont 1988:4). The bear hug letter is a "hostile tender offer, usually with considerable muscle behind it" (Hirsch 1986:830). For a discussion of the warfare and courtship terminology that evolved along with the shareholder value movement, see Hirsch (1986).

38. Employees might be better versed today, since Newmont's website now offers a timeline and video on company history (http://newmont.com/about /history), and a more up-to-date account of corporate history is also available (Morris 2010). In his research on managerial life, Jackall (1988:93) encountered a similar dearth of historical documentation, noting that a chemical company he studied had generated only one document offering details about corporate history over a twenty-nine-year period.

39. Newmont had a significant stake in several mines in apartheid-era South Africa until 1988. Newmont's annual reports suggest that the company's mining operations modestly resisted apartheid (e.g., the 1979 annual report recounts that white workers went on strike to protest the desegregation of job positions historically reserved for whites only), and in the mid-1980s endorsed the Sullivan Principles (Newmont 1980:9; Newmont 1986:4). For a critical analysis of the Sullivan Principles, see Seidman (2003); for a discussion of the role of mining in creating and supporting apartheid, see Packard (1989) and Mangaliso (1997). For a discussion of the postapartheid defense of the industry before the Truth and Reconciliation Commission, see Rajak (2011a).

1. "WE NEED TO NEWMONTIZE FOLK"

1. Newmont's reign as the world's largest gold producer ended in 2006, when Barrick acquired Placer Dome.

2. For convenience and consistency, I will use *CSR* to refer to Anderson and Macdonald's department as well as that department's counterparts at mine sites, although in fact Newmont's mine sites have managers assigned in Public Affairs, Social Affairs, Community Development, and Community and External Relations Departments who are undertaking CSR-related work.

3. Written in the wake of global financial failures, Hirokazu Miyazaki's study (2013:139, 141) of Japanese arbitrageurs notes that producing standard critiques of capitalism is an "infinitely renewable endeavor." Miyazaki asks if the contemporary moment might represent "an occasion for critics of capitalism to stop and withhold their impulse to see history repeating itself."

4. Newmont opened the Malozemoff Technical Facility in 1997. Mozingo's 2011 study of "pastoral capitalism" traces how such corporate campuses, corporate estates, and office parks were invented and popularized, and how they have transformed corporations as well as reshaped the urban and suburban geography.

5. Only Utes and a portion of a Navajo reservation have official recognition in the southwest corner of the state. My thanks to Sean Teuton for calling my attention to this fact.

6. The school today brands its identity and mission as "Earth, Energy, Environment," with a triangle logo. See Colorado School of Mines, www.mines .edu/ and http://ccit.mines.edu/UserFiles/Mines_IDGuide_080309edit.pdf.

7. For example, the National Mining Hall of Fame and Museum in Leadville, Colorado. See www.mininghalloffame.org/.

8. See Denver Mining Club, www.denverminingclub.org/.

9. See "MTF Hosts Kids' Science Day," Newmont, November 30, 2010, www.newmont.com/features/our-people-features/MTF-Hosts-Kids-Science-Day. The 2010 Science Day event included learning how cyanide is used to dissolve gold, gold panning, and making ice cream with liquid nitrogen.

10. For example, *Colorado Biz* magazine selected Newmont as a winner in its Energy/Natural Resources category in 2010 (see Lisa Marshall, "Top Company 2010: Newmont Mining," *Colorado Biz,* November 1, 2010, www.cobizmag. com/articles/top-company-2010-newmont-mining). Colorado State University's Business College Council invited CEO Wayne Murdy to give the keynote address at its annual Business Day (Gordon 2003), and the University of Denver conferred its International Bridge Builders Award upon Murdy in recognition of his accomplishments in promoting corporate ethics and humanitarianism at Newmont (Lewis 2007).

11. Similarly, Jackall (1988:37) argues that although managerial work is interdependent, "the necessarily fragmented functions performed day-to-day by managers in one area often put them at cross purposes with managers in another. Nor do competitiveness and conflict result only from the broad segmentation of functions. Sustained work in a product or service area not only shapes crucial social affiliations but also symbolic identifications, say, with particular products or technical services that mark managers in their corporate arenas." In his ethnography of a high-tech corporation, Kunda ([1992] 2006:171), by contrast, found engineers identifying with the firm as a whole. This may reflect the fact that he was predominantly studying engineers rather than executives with more diverse training. It may also reflect a practice in that firm of frequently shifting individuals between different work groups, so that allegiances did not sediment over long stretches of time. Jacoby (2005) portrays rotations of managers in Japan as tending to support loyalty and identification to a firm (rather than to a discipline), in contrast to the U.S. executive whose disciplinary identification is portable.

12. In another meeting Alan complained that people incorrectly assume that his work is easy, asking, "What's so hard about buying land?"

13. Adding "Loss Prevention" to "Health and Safety" builds the business case for the discipline right into its name, calling attention to the potential losses (e.g., trained workers, machinery and equipment damage, production shutdowns) that may be incurred by not attending to health and safety.

14. On a seemingly obsessive (but still highly fallible) corporate focus on safety, see Coll (2012), who describes how Exxon's safety practices became standardized and spread to other corporations, and Røyrvik (2011:80, 89–90).

15. There is a parallel here with human resources in the United States, which, Jacoby (2005) notes, tends to flourish during times of external challenge (e.g., during mass unionism in the 1930s and 1940s, in the period of fresh government regulations in the 1970s, and during a tight labor market) but has more difficulty in developing positive internal justifications for itself as a discipline at other times.

16. Similarly, Kunda ([1992] 2006:70) shows that proponents of the corporate culture ideology at a high-tech company insisted that their philosophy represented the "operating fabric" of the company and should not be dismissed as "motherhood statements."

17. Fortun (2001:329) describes how a promoter of "envirocomm" (environmental communication) is "part messiah, part therapist" for the corporation under attack.

18. For further perspectives on women's experiences of and responses to gender stereotypes in corporate and office environments, see also Fisher 2012 on early senior women on Wall Street; Inoue 2006 on gender and linguistic ideologies in Japanese office settings; and Yano 2011 on the "Nisei" (second-generation Japanese American) flight attendants recruited by Pan Am. On the labor of emotional management more broadly, see Hochschild (1983) 2012.

19. For a historical discussion of the low prestige and power of human resources departments in the United States, and a comparison with Japan, where HR has occupied a prominent position in firms, see Jacoby (2005).

20. This is consistent with the caricatured representation of lawyers that Jackall (1988:206) says populates managers' cognitive maps: "legal eagles or legal beagles in wool pinstripes who, if they had their way, would tie managers' hands completely."

21. The gold mining industry is a heavy user of cyanide, using leach pads to separate the metal from the ore.

22. See the discussion of reserve replacement, and Exxon Mobil's creative calculations of reserves, in Coll (2012).

23. See *Choropampa: The Price of Gold,* Guarango, www.guarango.org /choropampa/en/awardandscreenings.html for a list of awards and screenings, accessed on July 3, 2012.

24. Like other PR firms, APCO carries out semiclandestine work, including the "cultural production of ignorance" (Proctor and Schiebinger 2008)—for example, its role (for client Philip Morris) in creating the Advancement for Sound Science Coalition to discredit the EPA's finding that secondhand smoke is a Group A human carcinogen (Ong and Glantz 2001).

25. Marcello Veiga, a mercury expert and professor in mining engineering at the University of British Columbia, suggested the likelihood that Newmont's mercury buyer was supplying small-scale miners (personal communication, April 2003). When I asked Newmont officials who worked in Peru about the mercury's final destination, they claimed uncertainty. After the spill, Newmont gave the matter more oversight and began shipping Minera Yanacocha's mercury off to Spain. In 2011, Newmont halted the sale of mercury from Peru to Europe and began contracting with a German company "to stabilize and retire the mercury from commerce," so that it would be stored underground in a

legacy salt mine and "not end up in the hands of artisanal and small-scale gold miners." (See Newmont's statement "Retirement of Elemental Mercury," Newmont, 2012, www.beyondthemine.com/2012/environmental_stewardship/mercury_management/retirement_of_elemental_mercury.)

26. According to my calculations, only about 120 of the 330 pounds of mercury spilled would fit in two large coke bottles (assuming each could hold two liters).

27. Newmont's first CSR collegiate in 2002 was held at Minera Yanacocha, suggesting that senior executives decided that learning from that mine site was worth the extra time and expense it would take to bring the managers there rather than to corporate headquarters.

28. After watching the film, one Newmont manager recalled that a senior executive from Buenaventura, Newmont's Peruvian partner company, had proposed suing the campesinos for "stealing" Newmont's mercury.

29. Remedial and compensatory measures cost Newmont some $15 million in the short-term alone, and the CEO estimated that costs would reach $50 million in the long-term.

30. In a variety of company settings, Jackall (1988:24) observed an "intense interest in everything the CEO does and says," and endless speculation about the CEO's "plans, intentions, strategies, actions, style, public image, and ideological leanings of the moment." In Murdy's case, this extended to an attentiveness to the interests and beliefs of his close family members.

31. In a larger analysis of managerial beleaguerment under social and environmental criticism, Jackall (1988:164) notes that his interviews "are filled with managers who claim to have been verbally assaulted not only by strangers at cocktail parties, but by their children's teachers when they visit schools, and even by their children themselves at the breakfast table for being supposedly callous and insensitive to the social consequences of business activity." The relationship between a tobacco lobbyist and his son is a prominent theme in the film *Thank You for Smoking* (Reitman 2006), based on Christopher Buckley's 1994 novel.

32. For a critical discussion of the management consulting industry and the literature produced by business gurus and sages, see Jackall (1988:147–51).

33. The new identity and values were transmitted to all employees in internal memoranda dated June 28, July 12, and August 21 2002. The values, which have subsequently undergone some minor revisions, included: "Act with integrity, trust, and respect./Reward an entrepreneurial spirit, a determination to excel, and a commitment to action./Demand leadership in safety, stewardship of the environment, and social responsibility./Develop the best people in pursuit of excellence./Insist on teamwork and honest communication./Demand positive change by continually seeking out and applying best practices."

34. Collins (2001:215) explains that Philip Morris's success taught him "that it is not the *content* of a company's values that correlates with performance, but the *strength of conviction* with which it holds those values, whatever they might be. This is one of those findings that I find difficult to swallow, but that are completely supported by the data." This emphasis on "values" is similar to the 1980s discovery of, and emphasis on, corporate culture, which emerged partially in response to a sense that culture was the secret to Japanese business success (Deal

and Kennedy 1982; Marcus 1998; Ouchi 1981). Kunda ([1992] 2006:15) situated the 1980s concern in a longer history of "normative control" in organizations, which proponents and supporters such as Elton Mayo, the architect of the human relations department, saw as a benign attempt to make work fulfilling and overcome conflicts and divisions between organizations and individuals by aligning the two. Critics (Mills 1951; Whyte 1956) instead saw in successful normative control the organizational annexation of the realm of meaning and the emergence of the "organization man," whose thoughts, feelings, experiences, and desires were under bureaucratic control. Rather than assuming that normative control actually works—for better or worse—as it is supposed to, Kunda's approach ([1992] 2006:15) explored the actual practices through which the ideology of a high-tech company is imparted, invoked, and contested. Kunda found engineers engaged in both role embracement and distancing, and the affirmation and transgression of ritual frames and ideologies. Engineers variously described company ideology as "happy horseshit," "the old song and dance," "Big Brother shit," and "fluff" (52, 98, 112). For another analysis of company ideology, see Rohlen (1974, especially chapt. 2).

35. Røyrvik's discussion (2011) of the Norwegian corporation Hydro's adoption of the Capital Value Process decision-support model makes an interesting comparison (the model was originally developed by Amoco, and subsequently developed by BP after the company took over Amoco). Røyrvik shows that managers evaluated the model positively in terms of its adaptability to any scale (scalability), and it served to spread the financialization of the corporation by propagating the notion that all employees are stewards of capital value. By contrast, Newmont's attempted transformation is meant to turn all employees into stewards of the social license, although this too can be justified by invoking long-term financial objectives.

36. The dominance of risk discourse in CSR at Newmont is evident elsewhere. In 2007, for example, a shareholder resolution was passed with close to 92 percent support for a global review of Newmont's "polices and practices relating to existing and potential opposition from local communities and to [Newmont] operations and the steps taken to reduce such opposition." The study directors framed the review as a "forward-looking initiative" in which they were charged with identifying "risks and opportunities."

37. Thanks to Karl Palmås for calling my attention to the applicability of Callon's discussion of internalizing externalities to CSR.

38. Macdonald said Newmont had "paid a lot for" the Business for Social Responsibility guidebook, noting that in order for it to appear neutral and legitimate not all the examples used in the guide could be drawn from the company. The authors of the guidebook (BSR 2003:2) thanked Newmont Mining Corporation for its "generous support" for the project.

39. Universal ethics are in this regard similar to the making of scientific facts, which are supposed to lose their trace of authorship and be freed from the local circumstances of their production in order to achieve the status of fact rather than artifact (MacKenzie 2009:9).

40. One University of Mataram researcher who took part in the assessment told me he had unsuccessfully applied for jobs at Newmont on multiple occasions,

but still hoped to get one in the future. This may have influenced him to overemphasize the positive and neglect the negative aspects of Batu Hijau's social performance.

41. In *The Social Production of Indifference,* Michael Herzfeld (1992:1, 33) depicts bureaucrats' indifference as a lack of care for "human needs and suffering," part of a "rejection of those who are different" that "permits and even tacitly encourages genocide and intracommunal killings." If we can treat care as "official business," then Stevenson's understanding of indifference is compatible with Weber's discussion (1946a:215–16) of how bureaucracy's "specific nature, which is welcomed by capitalism, develops the more perfectly the more the bureaucracy is 'dehumanized,' the more completely it succeeds in eliminating from official business love, hatred, and all purely personal, irrational, and emotional elements which escape calculation."

42. Jackall (1988:132–33) points to a similar tendency, with respect to workers, among the executives he studied, who "find the sometimes coarse characterizations of workers made by plant managers to be 'insensitive.' . . . Social insulation permits and encourages a lofty viewpoint that, on its face, 'respects the dignity of the workers,' but seems devoid of the feel of the texture of workers' lives and of the gut-level empathy that such knowledge can bring. . . . At the highest levels . . . workers become wholly abstract categories." Similarly, in an interaction I observed between the president of Newmont Nusa Tenggara and the manager of Community Relations, the latter assured the former that Tongo villagers would never demonstrate. "Why is that?" the president asked. "Because they lack the human resources," the manager responded, turning the president's expectant smile (he was ready to hear something positive about Tongo villagers and their relations with the mine, rather than a remark about their backwardness) into a crestfallen expression.

43. Through conversations with another senior Australian executive who had come from Normandy, Macdonald came to understand that the resistance to the Integrated Management System she experienced at Newmont derived from contradictory management approaches. Managers in Newmont were driven by government regulations, whereas the Australian mining industry was driven more by managing risk, which led to a greater emphasis on internal forms of control. From this perspective, attention to risk can be progressive, setting higher standards than required by government.

44. Executive compensation, for example, is a social-responsibility issue that neither executive took up. According to the AFL-CIO website, in 2012 Newmont's CEO Richard O'Brien received $10,525,876 in total compensation, roughly 304 times the average worker's pay of $34,645 (www.aflcio.org /Corporate-Watch/CEO-Pay-and-You).

2. "PAK COMREL IS OUR REGENT WHOM WE RESPECT"

1. On other occasions the ustadz criticized the mine's social and moral impacts, as well as Newmont for paying insufficient attention to religious development.

2. This conveniently large and round number is in fact rather complex. It is based on lost revenue for one day of shutdown. Actual losses would in fact vary depending on the ore grade being processed and current commodity prices. But unprocessed ore does not evaporate; the mine could simply add an additional day to operations for each day of shutdown. There are, however, other costs, including paying workers who are not actually on the job, costs associated with temporarily shutting down and restarting parts of the mine, and resources devoted to dealing with whatever may have caused shutdown in the first place (e.g., for negotiating with demonstrators or fixing some technological breakdown), reputational damage, and the risk of not meeting targets for debt repayments.

3. Mining companies, including Newmont, routinely adopt this definition as their own, although a senior Environment executive in Denver complained that it had grown "stale." See, for example, Rio Tinto (2002:2); Newmont Mining Corporation (www.newmont.com/en/social/sustainable/ourdefinition /index.asp); the International Council on Mining and Metals (www.icmm.com /html/icmm_principles.php). See Kottak (1999) for a critique of sustainable development.

4. The Indonesian state continued to grant vast concessions to extractive industries in the post-Soeharto period (Saraswati and Musthofid 2002).

5. In the rest of this book, I often use "Newmont" rather than "PT NNT" where it is evident that I am discussing the operator of the mine in Sumbawa. My primary motive is simply to reduce my use of acronyms to make the book more readable. PT NNT seems more precise on the surface but is also complex given that operational control resides with the American company while owner- ship is more widely distributed. The ambiguities in these terms reflect the very ambiguity of my object of research, the corporation. In Sumbawan villages, people alternately referred to "Newmont," "NNT," "PT," and sometimes *dalam* or "inside," invoking the gated and enclosed spaces of Townsite (*dalam* was also used in the past to speak of courtly authority or the palace).

6. Merukh passed away in 2011. For more on his involvement in other min- ing projects, which included a stake in the Bre-X mining scandal, analyzed by Tsing (2005), see Kemp (2008).

7. Similarly, when BP sued contractors involved in the Deepwater Horizon disaster, BP was not only seeking to recover money for damages but also perfor- matively separating itself from its contractors, looking to the court system to pronounce them as external parties who shared culpability for the disaster.

8. Natural disasters and government demands shaped village settlement pat- terns over the course of the twentieth century. During the Dutch colonial and wartime Japanese occupations, as well as in the postcolonial era, state authori- ties pressured upland populations to resettle in the lowlands. Most resettled in Tongo and Benete villages. Others resettled as a result of two natural disasters in the 1970s: a flood that destroyed the hamlet of Sekongkang Tengah, and a tsunami in 1977 that destroyed a coastal hamlet that was itself a recent resettle- ment from the uplands. Maluk village also became a transmigration site in the 1980s. For more on this local settlement history, see chapter 2 in Welker (2006); for more on upland/lowland dynamics in Indonesia, see Li (1999a).

9. Residents plant paddy in irrigated fields (*sawah*) and rain-dependent, or dry, fields (*ladang*). In dry fields and gardens, farmers plant various vegetables and legumes, including tomatoes, green beans, corn, mung beans, soybeans, sweet potatoes, and chili peppers. Many residents have fruit trees by their homes and in their gardens, and they plant larger stands or orchards with mango, guava, papaya, oranges, sawo, and jackfruit. Others planted coconut trees, candlenut, cashews, and teak for commercial harvest. Sumbawans also consume wild plant leaves as vegetables, herbs (e.g., *aru* and *ruku* leaves are used in the signature Sumbawan fish dish called *sepat*), and medical treatments (e.g., bitter leaves are consumed to protect against malaria). Many residents keep chickens and goats near their homes and some maintain herds of water buffalo, cows, and horses, making additional use of mountain forests for hunting, wild honey, firewood, bamboo, timber, and various plants, animals, and objects used by shamans. Residents also catch fish from local rivers but generally prefer fish from the sea, with men using cast nets to catch the fish at low tide and women, men, and children combing the intertidal reef platforms to collect edible seaweed, abalone, mussels, sea urchins, mollusks, octopus, and fish.

10. I heard this from village residents. One survey in the mine's environmental impact assessment found that fifty-five workers came from Tongo-Sejorong, twenty-three from Sekongkang Atas, thirteen from Sekongkang Bawah, and twenty from Beru and Belo (PT NNT 1996:D-145).

11. During this time, Newmont also had to rely on local infrastructure, such as it was, including local roads, airports in Mataram and Sumbawa Besar, and the port, Poto Tano, to the north.

12. Pay figures quoted to me by former workers varied. One man told me he earned 3,000 rupiah a day. Another said he started at 4,000 rupiah a day in 1991 for being a porter and was earning 7,750 rupiah a day for chainsaw work when he stopped working years later. There was also a standard pay rate for carrying a sack of sand or a rock sample two kilometers. During exploration, the exchange rate was approximately 2,000 rupiah to 1 U.S. dollar.

13. Landowners received 10 million rupiah per hectare for prime agricultural land, 7 million rupiah per hectare for more marginal garden or swidden land. After the project ends, the land will be ceded to the government. In total, according to NNT land section data from 2003, Newmont purchased 805 hectares from 424 documented landowners, of which 18 were women and 406 were men.

14. The impossibility of anticipating the actual impacts of a megaproject render problematic the notion of "free, prior informed consent" that some activists argue should be obtained from local or indigenous communities before an extractive industry project moves forward. Consent is necessarily generated through relations of power. Joel Robbins (2004:180) analyzes a poignant and dramatic case of consent, in which, during a government-sponsored meeting between Urapmin people of Papua New Guinea and the Kennecott Mining Company, Urapmin entreated Kennecott to "destroy our ground" despite social disruption already unleashed by the company's early exploration work (Robbins 2004, see prologue; 2006). In the end, the company failed to uncover mineral deposits worth pursuing further.

15. See Schrauwers (1999) for a useful analysis of the dynamics of such petty trade ventures in highland Sulawesi.

16. A few, however, were newcomers from the town of Taliwang and elsewhere in the region.

17. According to Goethals (1961), additional important characteristics for secular and religious leaders included being native to the village, having family members in the preceding generation who held leadership status, possessing considerable inherited wealth, being of the parental or grandparental generation in age status, having shamanic skills and scriptural competence, and having wives with special competence.

18. According to an early survey prepared for Newmont (Adisoewignyo, Sayuti, Ardana, and Yasin 1998:24–25), only 10 percent of residents in the villages near the mine had a middle school education, and a mere 1 percent had completed high school.

19. Hierarchies of mine employment were also reflected in recreation activities and organizations. The American leader of Batu Hijau's Craft Room, a feminized space where quilting was popular, told me that she had to argue against other women who wanted to keep out Newmont's female workers and domestic servants. The leadership structure of the NNT wives' organization, Ikanura, paralleled the hierarchy of the women's husbands' offices and positions. In organizing themselves along these lines, the women replicated the "State Ibuism" structure of Dharma Wanita (Women's Duty), a mandatory Soeharto-era organization for female government employees and the wives of government employees (Sunindyo 1996; Suryakusuma 1996). On how company hierarchy is reflected in company housing for a Japanese bank, see Rohlen (1974:225–33); on company housing for employees of a petroleum firm in Equatorial Guinea, see Appel (2012b).

20. The standoff was resolved after the protesters, Newmont officials, and the MPs agreed that the MPs would get out of their large luxury buses, which Newmont officials feared would not be able to navigate the local roads, and dispersed in Toyota SUVs (the popular and relatively cheap Kijangs) to travel via the public road.

21. Other Newmont employees, village residents, and activists accused particular individuals, both Indonesian and expatriate, of obtaining positions in Newmont by threatening the company or of accepting bribes from large contractors. Rumors also circulated that Newmont might be lying about the actual quality of its concentrate or the amount the company shipped out. One American manager told me some Indonesians initially believed that the tailings disposal pipeline was actually carrying ore concentrate out to sea to be picked up by waiting submarines, which would smuggle the concentrate out of Indonesian waters, allowing the firm to avoid tax and royalty payments. At pains to dispel such rumors, Newmont officials created brochures that were meant to frame low-grade-ore mining in terms comprehensible to local residents. These illustrated that the amount of unprocessed ore that could be placed in a fifty-kilogram sack of the kind used to store rice would yield only the equivalent of a few rice grains in copper and gold. From a different perspective, such rumors of illegal behavior may provide a critical commentary on behavior that is made

legal and legitimate through various mechanisms (e.g., the Contract of Work allowing foreign corporations to profit from Indonesia's natural resources, or payments to government officials and other parties being sanctioned as long as receipts can be produced).

22. Serikat Buruh Sejahtera Indonesia, which is more radical in its demands and organizing tactics than is Serikat Pekerja Seluruh Indonesia, a government-sanctioned union.

23. In keeping with its Contract of Work with the Indonesian government, the company pays dead rent on the mining concession, as well as mineral royalties, personal and corporate income taxes, withholding taxes, a value-added tax on purchase and sale of goods, stamp duties, import duties, land and building taxes, fees for construction permits, underground water fees, forestry permit fees and rents, state land compensation, general administrative fees, a surface water lease, a vehicle tax, and a tax on vehicle ownership transfers.

24. Regional Administration Law 22/1999 devolved political authority, and the Intergovernmental Balance Law 25/1999 set out the fiscal arrangements. The laws gave regencies new responsibilities for education, culture, health, environment, labor, transportation, public works, trade and industry, and natural resource management. Local parliaments were empowered to elect the regents and determine their budgets and bureaucratic structures. Under the new laws, provinces would retain 80 percent of mining, forestry, and fisheries revenues (areas of special autonomy such as Aceh and West Papua retain higher levels). Of the 80 percent, the province retains 16 percent, paying 32 percent of the balance (around a quarter of the total) to the regency where extraction takes place (*kabupaten penghasil*) and splitting the remainder between other regencies based on a calculation of population and needs. In the first quarter of 2004, Newmont paid approximately $40 million to the central government, of which Sumbawa regency was supposed to receive roughly $10 million.

25. In the early 1950s, many development theorists predicted that decolonizing nations with abundant oil and minerals to exploit would prosper (structuralists Hirschman [1958] and Prebisch [1950] disagreed). Reviewing the resource-curse literature and debates, Ross (1999) concludes that we still lack empirically robust accounts that would specify the political and economic causal mechanisms linking resource wealth to poor economic performance, corruption, and violence (see also Rosser 2006; Watts 2004; Weszkalnys 2011). Scholarly doubt notwithstanding, the resource-curse thesis has captured the imagination of mining reformers, who routinely embed their transparency recommendations in some version of it (e.g., Goldwyn 2004; Humphreys, Sachs, and Stiglitz 2007; Shultz 2005:14).

Requirements that American oil and mining companies disclose taxes and other fees paid to foreign governments were part of the Dodd-Frank financial reform law and have faced stiff industry opposition. In the context of SEC debates over the disclosure requirements, the Brookings Institution submitted a research note identifying Newmont and the Norwegian company Statoil as two companies that voluntarily disclosed payments (Krauss 2012).

Although it has not been universally embraced by extractive industries, revenue transparency has been criticized as yet another neoliberal technology for blaming and disciplining states in the global South for their underdevelopment (Abrahamsen 2000; Doornbos 2003; Marcus and Powell 2003:330). Critics have noted that corruption is often framed as a pathology of the global South, which must be tutored by mature Northern countries to live by modern norms (Brown and Cloke 2004; Kahn and Formosa 2002). Some contest this view by noting that countries in the global North are as ridden with corruption as those in the South (Brown and Cloke 2004; Haller and Shore 2005; Kahn and Formosa 2002; Pardo 2004). Some have also noted that structural adjustment policies have exacerbated corruption (Brown and Cloke 2004; Elyachar 2005a; Hasty 2005; Smith 2003). Indeed, the anticorruption narratives of some revenue transparency proponents note with paternalistic dismay that although many resource-rich states in the global South have plenty of wealth, they fail to use it in a prudent fashion (Goldwyn 2004; STC 2003, 2005).

Other critics note that the resource-curse literature often positions extractive companies themselves as politically innocent actors (Barry 2006; Visser 2012; Watts 2004), overlooking the role of these corporations in promoting corruption, not to mention environmental degradation, loss of land and livelihood, and various forms of violence. Little evidence has emerged thus far that revenue transparency promotes good governance or prevents corruption (Visser 2012). For a discussion of the World Bank's partnership with Exxon Mobil in Chad and the failure of its revenue transparency and management plans, see Coll (2012, especially chaps. 7 and 16, and chap. 24 on Equatorial Guinea) and Visser (2012). For the perspective of an anthropologist working as part of an advisory group to the World Bank and the Chad and Cameroon governments as the pipeline project took shape, see Guyer (2011). More broadly, Visser (2012) argues that the Extractive Industry Transparency Initiative has legitimated the ongoing expansion of extractive industry operations in partnership with the World Bank by falsely claiming to address the resource curse. Critiquing the treatment of ongoing resource extraction as inevitable and suggesting that countries would often be better off leaving their resources in the ground, Visser notes that the World Bank has played an important role in mitigating political risk for extractive industry companies and in pushing countries to adopt reform policies that loosen social and environmental regulations and increase the profits and security of foreign resource investors.

Keefe (2013) presents a more complex picture of the efforts of revenue transparency proponents to target bribe-givers from the global North.

26. An American consultant told me that on another occasion, when CEO Wayne Murdy was visiting and taking part in a graduation event for Newmont employees, the regent demanded that the company dispatch its helicopter to pick him up.

27. Some of the issues that arise in cases of divestment include financing, the divestment of shares still under pledge agreements to international lenders, and the implications of ownership for operational control.

28. On one occasion when various NGO guests were touring the mine, Ibu Comdev told an expatriate consultant to transport one group in his more modest vehicle rather than using that of the senior manager of External Relations. The consultant's car ended up needing water, causing his group to be left

behind. Furious, he complained that all of this occurred because Ibu Comdev was trying as always to cultivate "an image of simplicity and small budgets" that was "patently false and implausible to villagers anyway."

29. With Newmont, there were more economic opportunities for civil servants in the region, but also greater economic pressure given the high cost of living near the mine. Contractors in Maluk joked about teachers standing at the blackboard taking business calls on their mobile phones; according to these contractors, if you asked those teachers' students what two times two is they would not know, but they could probably tell you what an "invoice" or "PO" (purchase order) is. They then acknowledged that teachers did not really earn enough in the region and were forced to engage in side business.

30. The senior manager of External Relations asserted that he was the one who insisted on government involvement in various community development projects over Ibu Comdev's objections. These conflicting accounts may suggest that one of them was misrepresenting the other, or they may apply to different occasions. They are consistent, however, in taking government involvement in development projects as a virtue.

31. After a different trip to Sumbawa Besar, a senior member of the Community Development department, Pak Sukri, appearing demoralized, described meetings he had held with the education and agriculture agencies as "useless." The head of the agriculture agency was nice and acted concerned, but claimed he could not afford to send any staff support. The education meeting was more frustrating because the agency head kept repeating that programs were up to Pak Sukri (terserah), seeming indifferent and unwilling to contribute support, and also claiming he did not have the budget to do anything.

3. "MY JOB WOULD BE FAR EASIER IF LOCALS WERE ALREADY CAPITALISTS"

1. For an account of a similar scene in response to Exxon Mobil's "Father Christmas mode" of thoughtless giving in the conflict zone of Aceh, see Coll (2012:399).

2. The actual lifespan of a mine depends on a number of factors. On an average day, the Batu Hijau mine extracts six hundred thousand tons of ore. The higher-grade ore is processed first while the low- and medium-grade ore is stockpiled. How long the mine operates will depend in part on prevailing metal prices, which determine the economic feasibility of recovery at lower ore grades. Further, after the mine began operating, exploration continued in order to assess whether the lifespan of the mine could be extended through underground mining. Rumors circulated even in Batu Hijau's early years of operation claiming that the mine might close sooner than expected.

3. From 1985 on, Indonesian social, religious, and political organizations were required to formally adopt Pancasila as their sole ideological foundation. Pancasila was inculcated through ideological education courses and exams from primary school to the university level, and through television, songs, and marching. "The most important attribute of an Indonesian citizen," writes Antlöv (1995:41) in his study of Javanese village-state relations, "is loyalty to

Pancasila." To the extent that Sumbawans participate in official activities, they participate too as the audience and articulators of Pancasila discourse. Newmont's Environmental Impact Assessment found in a survey with one hundred respondents that, despite low levels of formal education, 32 percent had participated in some kind of training, and that 25.8 percent of the courses taken "were related to ideological development, such as upgrading courses for the comprehension and implementation of Pancasila (the national ideology) and community development" (PT NNT 1996:D126).

4. The coercive dimensions of these discourses is evident in the way they are taken up in popular discourse (Herzfeld 2005). One woman, for example, joked about giving someone Pancasila, holding her hand up to show she meant a slap in the face (her five fingers corresponding to Pancasila's five principles). I also heard Sumbawans using the expression "menggotongroyongkan orang" to mean communally killing a person, similar to forming a lynch mob.

5. According to Honna (2001), during the 1990s prominent army leaders became concerned that economic and political liberalization—and an increasing gap between rich and poor—posed as significant a threat to Pancasila as did communism.

6. Similarly, see Dunn (2004) on how socialist ideologies provided factory workers with values and an interpretive framework they used to frame the obligations of the factory to them after its privatization.

7. For a broader discussion of movements and charismatic figures bringing together entrepreneurial values and Islam in Indonesia, see Rudnyckyj (2010) and Hoesterey (2008, 2012). Moreton (2009:106) discusses a parallel Christian popular genre on Jesus as businessman.

8. Similarly, in an annual environmental impact report researchers noted an improvement in the cultural values of villagers, citing these social indicators: "There is a more positive outlook on life, activities of working to improve status and produce new work (improvement in work ethic), the time orientation is more in the direction of the future, and relations between people are tending loosen from dependence on others (improved level of independence)." Ironically, the report then goes on to describe a range of perceived moral erosions (PPLH 2001:v).

9. It should be noted that several of the problems mentioned here are not unique to corporate-sponsored cooperatives. At a Newmont-sponsored cooperative training in May 2002, a government official said that 40 percent of the 350 cooperatives in the district were classified as "unhealthy." Popularized during the Soeharto era, cooperatives are widely viewed as bodies established to receive (and misspend) government aid.

10. Based on an abridged list of local businesses registered in the LBI, provided on July 1, 2002.

11. Keynes (1936) coined the phrase "multiplier effect" to refer to the way spending can stimulate consumption and further demand, thus stimulating a local economy.

12. Aa Gymnastiar, a very popular national religious figure, touched on this theme as well in a joke during a speech at a Newmont sponsored visit: Three men stranded on a deserted island release a genie from a bottle who grants them

three wishes in gratitude. The British man and the French man make their wishes first, and both request being transported back to their wonderful lives in London and Paris, respectively, where beautiful wives, sports cars, and jobs await them. The Indonesian, considering his mediocre prospects back home and finding himself alone, wishes for his French and British companions to be returned to the island.

13. Following Just (1991), social jealousy can be seen as a "civic emotion." Sumbawans are often stereotypically described (and describe themselves) as given to impassioned outbursts of emotion (*cepat emosi*). But as one Sumbawan man explained to me, this can be interpreted as a positive trait: it is better to wear your machete where it is easily visible, tied to the front of the waist, than to wear a small but lethal dagger (*keris*) like a Javanese, hidden at the back (see also Just 1991:295).

14. Adam Smith elaborated the concept of relative deprivation in *The Wealth of Nations* (see Cassidy 2006). Marx (2000:284) similarly remarked, "A house may be large or small; as long as the surrounding houses are equally small it satisfies all social demands for a dwelling. But let a palace arise beside the little house, and it shrinks from a little house to a hut. The little house shows now that its owner has only very slight or no demands to make; and however high it may shoot up in the course of civilization, if the neighbouring palace grows to an equal or even greater extent, the occupant of the relatively small house will feel more and more uncomfortable, dissatisfied, and cramped within its four walls. . . . The rapid growth of productive capital brings about an equally rapid growth of wealth, luxury, social wants, social enjoyments. Thus, although the enjoyments of the worker have risen, the social satisfaction that they give has fallen in comparison with the increased enjoyments of the capitalist, which are inaccessible to the worker, in comparison with the state of development of society in general. Our desires and pleasures spring from society; we measure them, therefore, by society and not by the objects which serve for their satisfaction. Because they are of a social nature, they are of a relative nature."

4. "WE IDENTIFIED FARMERS AS OUR TOP SECURITY RISK"

1. Indonesian transmigration projects have been beset by inequitable distributions of resources (owing to corruption but also to the impossibility of allocating two hectare plots of equivalent land to each family), lack of public infrastructure, rapid environmental degradation, and forced displacements of local people, which have sometimes led to ethnic and religious conflicts and violence (Aragon 2005; Li 2007).

2. SP1 was settled in 1995 with roughly one thousand settlers (217 households), while SP2 was established in June 1996 with a population of around eight hundred (162 households; Ingratubun n.d.:2). Approximately 20 percent of the settlers were Sumbawan, with some from Tongo who had been displaced from their farmland; 25 percent came from Bali; and 55 percent came from Lombok. Balinese transmigrants at times encounter discrimination over their Hindu religious traditions and pork consumption. As fellow Muslims, the

majority of transmigrants from Lombok have gained greater acceptance among Sumbawans but are nonetheless subject to discrimination.

3. The 1960 Basic Agrarian Law had limited private ownership to two hectares of land. The Indonesian Communist Party sought to implement the law, sparking land disputes that were implicated in some of the later killings of alleged communists.

4. Indonesia maintained high levels of agricultural subsidies for rural elites through oil revenues and Western support. Western donor programs, in turn, were often inspired by neo-Malthusian, Cold War fears of a Red revolution by hungry peasants (Escobar 1995; Finnemore 1997; Kearney 1996; Perkins 1997) and were designed to benefit agribusiness corporations in the global North (Mitchell 2002).

5. Other Green Revolution environmental impacts catalogued by scholars include a loss of genetic diversity and a decline in local knowledge, persistent toxic residue in the food chain, contamination of water systems, algal blooms and coral reef damage, soil exhaustion and erosion, and water shortages (Ellen 2007; Fox 1991; Gupta 1998; Hefner 1990; Lansing 1991; Winarto 2004).

6. IPM arose as a new paradigm for entomologists in the 1960s and 1970s (Winarto 2004)—ironically, at the same time that the Green Revolution was spreading uniform high-yield rice varieties and pesticides.

7. Even though Indonesia did not train 2.5 million farmers (the goal set forth in the presidential decree), the Food and Agriculture Organization considered the field schools a successful model and exported them across China, South Asia, and Southeast Asia, ultimately graduating some 2 million farmers from such trainings. In 2002, the organization terminated its Asian field school program because, according to former staff with whom I spoke, pesticide producers were putting pressure on their governments to cut funding to the UN agency after the Food and Agriculture Organization's IPM staff produced several documentaries lambasting multinational corporations such as Bayer for marketing pesticides that poisoned farmers and caused environmental damage (e.g., *Toxic Trail*, which aired on BBC in April 2001). The decision to close the program was officially represented as a result of recommendations by an independent review team (Field Alliance 2001).

8. Even in the early years of Bimas, Alexis Rieffel (1969:129) notes, the notion that the farmer "should be the 'subject' rather than the 'object' of the program" already sounded clichéd.

9. For various perspectives on and critiques of collaborations between anthropologists and the development industry, see Cernea (1991), Kottak (1990), Escobar (1991), and Ferguson (1997).

10. Hull (2010:278) complicates this genealogy and political trajectory (from radical to neoliberal) by showing that, rather than simply constituting a new orthodoxy accompanying the neoliberal retreat of the state, participatory speech genres have "roots in the ideological confrontations with authoritarianism" that accompanied World War II and its aftermath.

11. With *hybrid agronomy,* I am employing, in a rather different fashion, a term that Akhil Gupta (1998) used to capture how farmers in north India fluidly shift between discursive modes that academic literature might ascribe to

discrete epistemological systems (i.e., "indigenous" or "traditional ecological knowledge" versus rational-scientific knowledge).

12. For example, farmers recalled the rice varieties PB5, PB8, PB34, and IR36 that were precursors to IR64, which remains the dominant variety planted today. Pesticides farmers used included diazinon, Sumithion, Sevin, and dieldrin, and fertilizers included urea, TSP (triple superphosphate), KCL (potassium chloride), Sampurna B, Sampurna D, and Alami. The combinations were often shifted as agronomists created new weapons in the biological arms race against increasingly resistant pests.

13. The rice varieties the farmers listed included *padi tembaga, padi bulaing, padi numpu kunyit, padi minyak, padi gamal putih, padi gamal merah, padi roket, padi rowat,* and *padi sose.*

14. The corporations involved included the Swiss company CIBA (Chemical Industries of Basel, Switzerland), the West German companies Hoeschst and A.H.T., Japan's Mitsubishi, and an Indonesian company called Coopa, which Richard W. Franke (1974) notes became embroiled in scandal because it was apparently owned by generals and it siphoned off development monies without providing contracted services (also see Lansing 1991:112).

15. Farmers had repeatedly experienced this problem with mung beans. After harvest, they had no place to store the beans and needed cash from selling their crops, but were paid exceedingly low prices. Nestle, one of the large buyers, uses the mung beans in some of its toddler formulas.

16. Facilitators were, perhaps unwittingly, reviving a village farming laboratory model the Sukarno administration had experimented with in the 1950s (Franke 1974:16).

17. Joanna Davidson (2010) illustrates how the knowledge practices of Diola rice cultivators in Guinea-Bissau stand at odds with the assumptions of development practitioners that knowledge is an extractable resource that can and should be democratically shared.

18. One Participatory Rural Appraisal handbook features many drawings of women, illustrating their idealized participation, but very few appear among the book's photographs from actual participatory events (KPDTNT 1996).

19. Rudnyckyj (2010) explains that class-based differences in Emotional and Spiritual Quotient training uptake are not simply a matter of cultural intelligibility. Middle- and upper-class participants were, he says, more complicit in the corruption and bribery that characterized the Soeharto era than workers and foremen had been and, therefore, were more interested in the promise that Emotional and Spiritual Quotient held as a path for processing and expiating their sins.

20. Heiko Henkel and Roderick Stirrat (2001) argue that participants absorb the new responsibilities in a process tantamount to what Foucault called subjection—that is, they come to "freely" see themselves through the lens of participatory discourse. David Mosse (2001:25) writes, "This shift from an open, exploratory system towards a closed one is not to be understood as intentional. It is the side-effect of institutional factors that are unlikely to be perceived by project actors themselves, by their supporting bureaucracies, or even by external observers." Similarly, Kothari (2001:145) claims, "Participatory practitioners may interpret the actions and expressions of participants as 'local culture' when they

are also the product of these processes of normalization, but are not seen to embody power relations since they appear to be articulated and believed in by all. People absorb these cultural tropes, which are then recursively practised almost ritualistically, and it is the widespread acceptance of, and conformity to, these practices that make it difficult to interpret them as expressions of power or demonstrations of inequalities."

21. The Foucault-inspired contributors to Cooke and Kothari's volume on participatory development as tyranny, many of whom had been development practitioners and thus had considerable experience facilitating participatory development, fall into this camp. The editors (Cooke and Kothari 2001:x) extend special gratitude to "those awkward participants who have made our role as 'facilitators' uncomfortable, by asking difficult questions, by challenging the process, by refusing to go along with consensus, by questioning our legitimacy as facilitators, or just by remaining silent." While the authors thus attach a positive valence to resistance, the volume contains little substantive engagement with this resistance. Kothari (2001:151) notes, "Subversive participants can also choose to opt out of the participatory process completely, although they are often characterized as uncooperative or even social deviants." Henkel and Stirrat (2001:178) claim that those who resist participatory dogma are treated by facilitators to the "damning of the heretic."

22. James C. Scott (1985) noted that, in rural Malaysia, some of the wealthiest villagers wore old clothes and would call attention to this fact when faced with questions about their wealth.

23. The village motivator (*penggerak desa*) is also similar to the figure of the "native demonstrator," trained by missionaries in African colonial settings to follow an exemplary lifestyle and propagate it within her or his community (Burke 1996:46–52). See also Hull's discussion (2010:274) of the idea of a "natural leader" in democratic speech technologies.

5. "CORPORATE SECURITY BEGINS IN THE COMMUNITY"

1. On the intersection of environmental activism and indigenous political claims, anthropologists have explored the political possibilities that activist networks hold for historically marginalized people, as well as the theoretical, methodological, political, and ethical challenges they pose for the practice of anthropology itself (Brown 1993; Field 1999; Hodgson 2002a; Kirsch 2006, 2007; Ramos 1998; Turner 1991; Wright 1988); shifts from class to identity politics (Alvarez, Dagnino, and Escobar 1998; Warren 1998); the uses and liabilities of "ecologically noble savage" stereotypes (Conklin 1997; Conklin and Graham 1995; Nadasdy 2005); the political positioning of indigeneity claims (Li 2000, 2001; Ramos 1998); the putative universals of indigeneity (Bowen 2000; Muehlebach 2001); gains in tangible and intellectual property rights (Brown 1998; Conklin 2002); the "NGOification" and depoliticization of new social movements (Hodgson 2002b; Igoe 2003); and the local consequences of indigenous participation in transnational and interethnic settings (Oakdale 2004). On the growth of these movements in relation to mining specifically, see Ballard and Banks (2003), Gedicks (2001), and Gjording (1991).

2. By "political Others" I refer to those whose actions may strike us as repugnant or reactionary rather than politically progressive (Harding 2000; Mahmood 2005; McCarthy 2002).

3. See Voluntary Principles on Security and Human Rights, http://voluntary-principles.org/.

4. See "Introduction," Voluntary Principles on Security and Human Rights, http://voluntaryprinciples.org/principles/introduction, accessed August 15, 2012.

5. The fourth principle takes note of company impacts on local communities and advises contributing "to the welfare of the local community while mitigating any potential for conflict where possible." See ibid.

6. Project Underground closed in 2004.

7. As scholars have noted, "community" has, since the Industrial Revolution, often been nostalgically articulated as bounded by moral obligations, geography, and kinship, against an atomized individualized "society" (Amit 2002; Amit and Rapport 2002; Creed 2006).

8. Newmont managers often differed on whether improved standards could be attributed to internal commitment or to external pressure. For example, several officials told me that Tom Enos, then PT NNT's president, insisted that Newmont spare no expense on water management after seeing one river clouded with waste from construction activity. But a Denver executive told me instead that Newmont originally had comprehensive water management plans, which it had abandoned as too expensive, only to subsequently reinstitute the plans after export-import banks threatened to withdraw financing because of Newmont's failure to meet water standards.

9. Critics have disputed corporate technoscience on submarine tailings disposal and raised questions of environmental justice in relation to where the disposal practice has been used, arguing it would be unacceptable in North America (Coumans 2002a, 2002b, 2002c; Dixon 2002; Moody 2001).

10. One journalist noted that Batu Hijau representatives try to get each mine visitor to accept a "nontoxic" tailings souvenir gift (*NTB Post* 2002b).

11. For Sumbawans, as for people from the neighboring islands of Lombok and Sumba, catching and consuming nyale is an important social event (Ecklund 1977; Hoskins 1993).

12. Similarly, neo-Malthusian fears that overpopulation and poverty would invariably lead to environmental breakdown became dominant at the World Bank during the early 1990s (Goldman 2005; Peet and Watts 1993:227).

13. If this decline had indeed taken place, it could be attributed not only to villagers' enlarged economic power (and declining need to engage in subsistence activities), but to the fact that, caught up in the time discipline of wage labor regimes, many were less able to participate in social activities that depend on alternative calendars and tidal fluctuations.

14. By 2004, managers had given up hope that the regency government could be cajoled or coerced into paying for local waste disposal. Newmont bought garbage trucks for the subdistricts and offered to cover part of the costs of collection, although the shortfall in funding continued to mean that garbage disposal responsibilities were a source of ongoing dispute in villages.

15. Chris Anderson (1989) published an article debunking the myth of the ecologically noble savage, based on his observations of Australian Aborigines (see also Macintyre and Foale 2002). As Nadasdy (2005) points out, debates over the reality of the ecologically noble savage have overlooked the culturally specific nature of assumptions about what it means to be "environmental."

16. For nuanced accounts of how socioeconomic marginality and political identity are entangled in the use of bombs and cyanide in fishing, see Lowe (2006, especially ch. 5) and Walley (2004).

17. In Indonesia, powerful military and business elites are often involved in illegal logging and mining. In practice, the relationship between formal and informal mining is not simply one of competition. Corporate public statements often portray "illegal mining" as an environmental Other, but forms of cooperation and symbiosis exist. Newmont's Minahasa Raya mine in Sulawesi, for example, allowed "illegal miners" some use of company infrastructure. Many workers at the mine, moreover, invested their salary or severance pay in "illegal mining." Batu Hijau's low ore grade precludes the establishment of informal mining around the mine.

18. Although the statement that Newmont did not use mercury and arsenic to process its ore at Minahasa Raya may be technically correct, Newmont released at least thirty-three tons of mercury into the atmosphere and sea around the mine from mercury that occurred naturally in the ore (Perlez 2004).

19. *Project Green Shield* refers to the use of an environmental, or "green," strategy and appearance to shield Batu Hijau from the company's detractors.

20. The consultants' use of the term *floating mass* derives from the Soeharto regime's concept (*massa mengambang*) and 1971 policy for depoliticizing rural Indonesians, who were supposed to avoid political distractions (political parties were banned at the village level) and concern themselves solely with economic development.

21. For other critical treatments of transparency, see Hasty (2005), Marcus and Powell (2003), Morris (2004), and West and Sanders (2003). With the waning of post–Cold War euphoria over NGOs as emblems of "civil society" (Fisher 1997), some critics have argued that NGOs must address their "accountability deficit" by instituting more free market mechanisms and working with corporations (Kovach, Neligan, and Burall 2003; SustainAbility 2003). The American Enterprise Institute, a conservative Washington think tank, imposes "transparency" on select NGOs with a website monitoring their activities and displaying their tax statements and annual revenues (see www.aei.org; www .ngowatch.org; also Stecklow 2006). Conversely, activists and academics have argued that market incentives and corporate intimacy tend to compromise NGOs and precipitate dysfunctionalities in their practices (Chapin 2004; Cooley and Ron 2002).

22. Newmont disproportionately affects the forest resources of Tongo village because of the mine operation's proximity. Tongo residents rely on the forests for traditional medicines, subsistence food, and building materials, as well as primary commodities like honey, rattan, palm sugar, and the fragrant gaharu wood. They also allow livestock to graze and seek watering holes in the forests. Where the Indonesia People's Forum article describes Newmont's

appropriation of land without compensation, I infer that Bu Halimah was talking about all the *forest*land, not lowlands *agricultural* land. Bu Halimah and several other Newmont critics have petitioned Newmont and the government for formal compensation for palm sugar producers, but their efforts have been thwarted because the government insists that village residents are not really indigenous (*masyarakat adat*) and thus cannot claim special forest privileges (see Li 2000, 2001 on the indigenous category in Indonesia, and the difficulties of obtaining recognition).

23. The tailings pipeline passes close to Tongo and through village agricultural land, and it leaked several times during Batu Hijau's first year of operation. Tongo residents also carry out their marine foraging at a closer proximity to the tailings dumping ground than other villagers. Many also express concern over the mine's impact on their freshwater because of three dams located upstream of the village that treat acidic, heavy-metal-bearing water from the mine pit. Although an official from PT NNT's environment department assured Tongo residents that the mine operates a "closed" water system, during heavy rains the company has already carried out several "controlled overflow releases" of dam water into the Sejorong River, which flows through Tongo. Further, Tongo residents and some Batu Hijau managers have expressed concern over the potential impact of the mine drawing heavily from an aquifer near Tongo to meet the mine's freshwater needs.

24. On several occasions I heard Community Relations staff joking over how ignorant or stupid (*bodoh*) Tongo villagers are. When, as I mentioned earlier, the Community Relations manager assured Batu Hijau's president that Newmont had nothing to fear from the village because of Tongo's lack of "human resources" (*sumber daya manusia*), he was implying that Tongo villagers did not have the education and public relations skills to mount a serious challenge to the company.

25. Some provincial politicians and local academics also condemned the attack and called upon Newmont to take responsibility for it (*Lombok Post* 2002a; *NTB Post* 2002a). The provincial governor called for Newmont to take responsibility if the arsenic accusations proved true (*Nusa* 2002), while the regent in Sumbawa Besar charged that the NGO team was "wild" for not informing his office of the research plans and results (*Lombok Post* 2002b).

26. The Indonesian name for the Alliance of Near-Mine Communities for Justice is Aliansi Masyarakat Lingkar Tambang untuk Keadilan.

27. This analytic creeps into academic work as well. In a critique of ARCO's divide-and-rule strategies in Ecuador, for example, Sawyer (2003:85–86) describes one group of Indians accepting "trinkets" from the company that become "talismans of progress and fetishes of modernity" serving "to pry open and transform local senses of self and property" until the Indians became "docile and compliant." Sawyer (2003:89) goes on to distinguish "the warped desires of a few small hamlets" from the "larger, more powerful indigenous communities" that had "articulate, savvy spokespersons who denounced the marginalization, inequality, and exploitation that oil operations produced" and demanded from ARCO "alternative forms of development."

28. Similar moral-political hybrids are forged between activists and local people against resource extraction (e.g., Conklin and Graham 1995).

6. "WE SHOULD BE LIKE STARBUCKS"

1. Newmont managers told me the Five Star Integrated Assessment is an "assessment" rather than an "audit" because it is designed to capture breadth and range rather than the depth implied by the term *audit*. Those who conducted the assessment identified professionally as auditors, and I use this term to describe them throughout the chapter.

2. A mine worker told me that a haul truck driver would not even notice running over a human body, comparing it to squashing a bug under a motorbike tire. Some mine workers blamed the accident on the fatigue of the driver. An Australian engineer blamed the contractor himself for agreeing to work under unsafe conditions (behind a berm that was about a third the size of the tires on the haul truck), while the engineer's wife argued that Newmont was to blame since the company should have routed the trucks another way. This would have added an extra forty minutes to each journey into and out of the mine pit, reducing daily tonnage.

3. At smaller mine operations, Newmont might assign only one auditor per discipline and limit the assessment to three days.

4. Appointing more expatriates signals corporate commitment, since they generally cost more to hire and maintain than "national" workers, but there is also a conflation here between expatriates and high standards and quality.

5. Normandy initially developed the Five Star Integrated Assessment for its environmental mitigation programs. By 2000, the company had expanded it to assess the company's community development, as well as its health and safety programs.

6. Organizational sociologists have studied how related institutional practices are established and how they diffuse, becoming obligatory features for large organizations that wish to be seen as legitimate (Powell and DiMaggio 1991).

7. From executives at other mining companies, I heard similar claims: that their own auditing programs were unique and particularly well-developed, the best in the business.

8. Personal communication, 2004.

9. See http://beyondthemine.com/2010/assurance/voluntary_participation_ in_organizations_&_initiatives/. Each of these codes and frameworks has its own history, as well as membership, public reporting, and independent assurance requirements. See, for example, www.icmm.com/our-work/sustainable-development-framework, www.globalreporting.org, www.cyanidecode.org, www.accountability.org/standards/aa1000as/index.html, www.iso.org, www .ohsas-18001-occupational-health-and-safety.com/, and www.theclimateregis try.org/.

10. On the indigenous category in Indonesia, see Li (2000, 2001); on the human and ecological consequences of the Tambora eruption see Oppenheimer (2003).

11. Boele said that going through people's stuff becomes an ingrained habit, humorously recalling that once a bank manager got annoyed with him when he began sifting through her papers while sitting at her desk *after* the audit had been completed.

12. Strathern (2006:190) extends to her own work a concern about the ability of the audit to incorporate criticism "without a murmur" into its exercise.

13. Similarly, Sara Ahmed (2012:73, 75) describes diversity workers in universities switching between languages, and between business and social justice models, depending on their evaluation of what will work for their audiences in a particular context.

14. The auditors acknowledged that they were financially well-compensated for their work, but found it draining owing to its intensity and travel demands, which could also put strains upon personal lives and other family members.

15. To "trend" an issue means setting up categories to capture meaningful qualitative and quantitative changes over time. Demonstrations, for example, might be categorized by the issues or demands motivating them, or by their scale, their popular support, and the mechanisms used to resolve them.

16. The threat posed by an individual suddenly leaving a company with her or his Rolodex (a now dated technology for storing business cards) illustrates the danger posed to a company by overreliance on the personal charisma and social networks of individuals.

17. Not all managers felt they deserved more stars. A community development manager from Newmont's Minera Yanacocha mine in Peru recalled after the first assessment that one auditor told him, "If I could give you less than one star in some categories I would." Acknowledging the depth of the mine's "social challenges," this manager said, "The GM [general manager] saw our low scores and wanted us to set an objective, like an average of 3.5 stars next time around. I said, 'You're crazy! You've been at elevation for too long.'" (The Peruvian mine is at an altitude of around fifteen thousand feet.)

18. To my knowledge, at least some of those villagers who were interviewed in 2003 did receive these, but none had made any use of the document to generate change in Newmont. These documents do not tend to be useful to outside critics.

19. Of the 202 people left dead by the bombing, 88 were Australian and 38 were Indonesian.

20. Spence (2009) offers a Gramscian critique of current social accounting practices as regressive because they are rooted in the economic base, suggesting that emancipatory forms of social accounting articulated by civil society are nonetheless possible.

21. Based on its early reports, Jenkins and Yakovleva (2006) characterized Newmont as an "adolescent" reporter (more grown up than an "infant" reporter but not yet "mature"), and classified the reports themselves as "deluxe" (above "standard" or "economy" reports).

22. Two panels on these themes were held at, for example, the 2009 Net Impact Conference at Cornell University. Net Impact is an organization for business school students and professionals devoted to sustainable business, social entrepreneurship, and CSR.

23. For an example of an assurance letter, see "Report Assurance," Newmont, http://beyondthemine.com/2010/assurance/2010_assurance_letter/.

24. One could, for example, perform the kind of analytic work on a corporate stakeholder report that Hilgartner (2000), drawing upon Erving Goffman

and the sociology of science, performs on the reports of the National Academy of Sciences. But whereas the latter has widespread influence and credibility that make the staging of legitimacy or the rise of controversy publicly significant, a voluntary corporate stakeholder report is from the outset seen as a partisan document meant to persuade, reassure, and pacify people.

CONCLUSION

1. In defending "a feminist vision of care that engages with persistent forms of exclusion, power and domination," and in developing the concept of "matters of care," Puig de la Bellacasa is responding to work by Bruno Latour, including an article (2004) on "matters of concern." In the article, Latour questions conspiracy theorists alongside scholars whom he casts as recycling ready-made critiques and claiming privileged insight into the hidden "powerful causalities" structuring life.

2. Kim Fortun (2001:175–76, 249–52) claims that advocacy requires a "bifocalism" that is tricky to sustain, recounting some of the contradictions that mark her own experience, such as arguing for more, better science and questioning conventional faith in science; writing off dissent among victims and emphasizing the heterogeneity of epistemic communities; working for local remedy and demanding fundamental reform; making strident truth claims about body counts and wrestling with uncertainties; and relying on undemocratic organizational structures to accomplish activist objectives and criticizing those structures.

Bibliography

Abrahamsen, Rita. 2000. *Disciplining Democracy: Development Discourse and Good Governance in Africa*. London: Zed Books.

Abrams, Philip. 1988. "Notes on the Difficulty of Studying the State" (1977). *Journal of Historical Sociology* 1(1):58–89.

Abu-Lughod, Lila. 1991. "The Romance of Resistance: Tracing Transformations of Power through Bedouin Women." *American Ethnologist* 17(1):41–55.

Achbar, Mark, and Jennifer Abbott. 2003. *The Corporation*. Canada: Zeitgeist Films. DVD.

Adisoewignyo, H. Wargono, Rosiady H. Sayuti, I.G. Lanang Ardana, and Muaidy Yasin. 1998. "Laporan Penelitian Identifikasi Potensi dan Prospek Pengembangan Usaha Mikro di Kawasan Penambangan PT. NNT (Kecamatan Jereweh, Taliwang dan Seteluk)." Unpublished report prepared for PT NNT by Lembaga Penelitian Universitas Mataram.

Agrawal, Arun. 2005. *Environmentality: Technologies of Government and the Making of Subjects*. Durham, NC: Duke University Press.

Ahmed, Sara. 2004. *The Cultural Politics of Emotion*. New York: Routledge.

———. 2012. *On Being Included: Racism and Diversity in Institutional Life*. Durham, NC: Duke University Press.

Alatas, Syed Hussein. 1977. *The Myth of the Lazy Native*. London: Frank Cass.

Allen, William T. 1992–93. "Our Schizophrenic Conception of the Business Corporation." *Cardozo Law Review* 14:261–81.

Allison, Anne. 1994. *Nightwork: Sexuality, Pleasure, and Corporate Masculinity in a Tokyo Hostess Club*. Chicago: University of Chicago Press.

Althusser, Louis. 1971. "Ideology and Ideological State Apparatuses (Notes towards an Investigation)." In *Lenin and Philosophy, and Other Essays*. London: New Left Books.

Alvarez, Sonia E., Evelina Dagnino, and Arturo Escobar. 1998. *Cultures of Politics/Politics of Cultures: Re-Visioning Latin American Social Movements.* Boulder, CO: Westview Press.

AMEC Geomatrix. 2010. *Social Impact Assessment, Batu Hijau Project.* Prepared for PT Newmont Nusa Tenggara. Sumbawa, Indonesia: AMEC Geomatrix.

Amit, Vered. 2002. *Realizing Community: Concepts, Social Relationships and Sentiments.* London: Routledge.

Amit, Vered, and Nigel Rapport, eds. 2002. *The Trouble with Community: Anthropological Reflections on Movement, Identity and Collectivity.* London: Pluto Press.

Anderson, Christopher. 1989. "Aborigines and Conservationism: The Daintree-Bloomfield Road." *Australian Journal of Social Issues* 24(3):214–17.

Andrews, Thomas G. 2008. *Killing for Coal: America's Deadliest Labor War.* Cambridge, MA: Harvard University Press.

Anteby, Michel. 2013. "Relaxing the Taboo on Telling Our Own Stories: Upholding Professional Distance *and* Personal Involvement." *Organization Science* 24(4):1277–90.

Antlöv, Hans. 1995. *Exemplary Centre, Administrative Periphery: Rural Leadership and the New Order in Java.* Richmond, U.K.: Curzon Press.

Appel, Hannah. 2012a. "Offshore Work: Oil, Modularity, and the How of Capitalism in Equatorial Guinea." *American Ethnologist* 39(4):692–709.

———. 2012b. "Walls and White Elephants: Oil Extraction, Responsibility, and Infrastructural Violence in Equatorial Guinea." *Ethnography* 13(4):439–65.

Applbaum, Kalman. 2010. "Shadow Science: Zyprexa, Eli Lilly and the Globalization of Pharmaceutical Damage Control." *BioSocieties* 5:236–55.

Aragon, Lorraine V. 2000. *Fields of the Lord: Animism, Christian Minorities, and State Development in Indonesia.* Honolulu: University of Hawai'i Press.

———. 2005. "Mass Media Fragmentation and Narratives of Violent Action in Sulawesi's Poso Conflict." *Indonesia* 79(1–55).

Aretxaga, Begoña. 2003. "Maddening States." *Annual Review of Anthropology* 32:393–410.

Aspinall, Edward. 2013. "A Nation in Fragments: Patronage and Neoliberalism in Contemporary Indonesia." *Critical Asian Studies* 45(1):27–54.

Atwood, J. Brian. 2002. "The Development Imperative: Creating the Preconditions for Peace." *Journal of International Affairs* 55(2):333–49.

Avi-Yonah, Reuven S. 2005. "The Cyclical Transformations of the Corporate Form: A Historical Perspective on Corporate Social Responsibility." *Delaware Journal of Corporate Law* 30(3):767–818.

Bakan, Joel. 2004. *The Corporation: The Pathological Pursuit of Profit and Power.* New York: Free Press.

Bali Post. 2002a. "Barisan Rakyat Tolak Kedatangan LSM ke Tambang Newmont." June 7.

———. 2002b. "Newmont Diduga Bekingi Panghadangan LSM." June 24.

Ballard, Chris, and Glenn Banks. 2003. "Resource Wars: The Anthropology of Mining." *Annual Review of Anthropology* 32:287–313.

Barkan, Joshua. 2013. *Corporate Sovereignty: Law and Government under Capitalism*. Minneapolis: University of Minnesota Press.

———. 2012. "The Corporation as Disciplinary Institution." In *The Wiley-Blackwell Companion to Economic Geography*, ed. T. J. Barnes, J. Peck, and E. Sheppard, 472–485. Oxford: Wiley-Blackwell.

Barker, Joshua. 1999. "Surveillance and Territoriality in Bandung." In *Figures of Criminality in Indonesia, the Philippines, and Colonial Vietnam*, edited by V. L. Rafael, 95–127. Ithaca, NY: Southeast Asia Program Publications, Cornell University.

Barry, Andrew. 2006. "Technological Zones." *European Journal of Social Theory* 9(2):239–53.

Basuki, A. R. and Yuyud, I. 2002. *Laporan Evaluasi dan Analisis 2001: KSU Somil Jaya, KSU Kemuning Jaya, KSU Perdana Karya Mandiri*. Report on Local Business Development. Benete: Community Development Department, PT Newmont Nusa Tenggara.

Beck, Ulrich. 1992. *Risk Society: Towards a New Modernity*. London: Sage.

Benson, Peter. 2011. *Tobacco Capitalism: Growers, Migrant Workers, and the Changing Face of a Global Industry*. Princeton, NJ: Princeton University Press.

Benson, Peter, and Stuart Kirsch. 2010a. "Capitalism and the Politics of Resignation." *Current Anthropology* 51(4):459–86.

———. 2010b. "Corporate Oxymorons." *Dialectical Anthropology* 34:45–48.

Berle, Adolf A., and Gardiner C. Means. (1932) 1968. *The Modern Corporation and Private Property*. New York: Harcourt, Brace and World.

Besky, Sarah. 2013. *The Darjeeling Distinction: Labor and Justice on Fair-Trade Tea Plantations in India*. Berkeley: University of California Press.

Biersack, Aletta. 1999. "The Mount Kare Python and His Gold: Totemism and Ecology in the Papua New Guinea Highlands." *American Anthropologist* 101(1):68–87.

Boas, Franz. 1889. "On Alternating Sounds." *American Anthropologist* 2(1):47–54.

Boele, Richard, and Deanna Kemp. 2005. "Social Auditors: Illegitimate Offspring of the Audit Family?" *Journal of Corporate Citizenship* 17:109–19.

Boltanski, Luc. 1999. *Distant Suffering: Morality, Media, and Politics*. Cambridge: Cambridge University Press.

Boltanski, Luc, and Eve Chiapello. 2005. *The New Spirit of Capitalism*. London: Verso.

Bond, David. 2013. "Governing Disaster: The Political Life of the Environment during the BP Oil Spill." *Cultural Anthropology* 28(4):694–715.

Borneman, John, and Abdellah Hammoudi, eds. 2009. *Being There: The Fieldwork Encounter and the Making of Truth*. Berkeley: University of California Press.

Bornstein, Erica, and Peter Redfield, eds. 2011. *Forces of Compassion: Humanitarianism between Ethics and Politics*. Santa Fe: School for Advanced Research Press.

Bowen, John. 1986. "On the Political Construction of Tradition: *Gotong Royong* in Indonesia." *Journal of Asian Studies* 45(3):545–61.

————. 1993. *Muslims through Discourse: Religion and Ritual in Gayo Society*. Princeton, NJ: Princeton University Press.

————. 2000. "Should We Have a Universal Concept of 'Indigenous Peoples' Rights? Ethnicity and Essentialism in the Twenty-First Century." *Anthroplogy Today* 16(4):12–16.

Boyer, Dominic. 2006. "*Ostalgie* and the Politics of the Future in Eastern Germany." *Public Culture* 18(2):361–81.

Boyer, Dominic, and Alexei Yurchak. 2010. "American Stiob: Or, What Late-Socialist Aesthetics of Parody Reveal about Contemporary Political Culture in the West." *Cultural Anthropology* 25(2):179–221.

BPS (Badan Pusat Statistik)-Statistics Indonesia, BAPPENAS (Badan Perencanaan Pembangunan Daerah), UNDP (United Nations Development Programme). 2004. *The Economics of Democracy: Financing Human Development in Indonesia*. Indonesia Human Development Report. Jakarta: BPS-Statistics, BAPPENAS, UNDP.

Brandt, Allan M. 2007. *The Cigarette Century: The Rise, Fall, and Deadly Persistence of the Product That Defined America*. New York: Basic Books.

Brenner, Suzanne. 1996. "Reconstructing Self and Society: Javanese Muslim Women and 'the Veil.'" *American Ethnologist* 23(4):673–97.

Brown, Ed, and Jonathan Cloke. 2004. "Neoliberal Reform, Governance and Corruption in the South: Assessing the International Anti-Corruption Crusade." *Antipode* 36(2):272–94.

Brown, Michael F. 1993. "Facing the State, Facing the World: Amazonia's Native Leaders and the New Politics of Identity." *L'Homme* 33(2–4):307–26.

————. 1998. "Can Culture Be Copyrighted?" *Current Anthropology* 39(2):193–222.

Browne, Katherine E., and B. Lynne Milgram, eds. 2009. *Economics and Morality: Anthropological Approaches*. Lanham, MD: AltaMira Press.

Brubaker, Rogers, and Frederick Cooper. 2000. "Beyond 'Identity.'" *Theory and Society* 29:1–47.

BSR (Business for Social Responsibility). 2003. *The Social License to Operate*. San Francisco: BSR.

Bubandt, Nils. 2006. "Sorcery, Corruption, and the Dangers of Democracy in Indonesia." *Journal of the Royal Anthropological Institute* 12:413–31.

Buckley, Christopher. 1994. *Thank You for Smoking*. New York: Random House.

Burke, Timothy. 1996. *Lifebuoy Men, Lux Women: Commodification, Consumption, and Cleanliness in Modern Zimbabwe*. Durham, NC: Duke University Press.

Cabellos, Ernesto, and Stephanie Boyd. 2002. *Choropampa: The Price of Gold*. Brooklyn, NY: Icarus Films.

Callon, Michel. 1998. "An Essay on Framing and Overflowing: Economic Externalities Revisited by Sociology." In *The Laws of the Markets*, edited by M. Callon, 244–69. Oxford: Blackwell/Sociological Review.

————. 2009. "Civilizing Markets: Carbon Trading between *in vitro* and *in vivo* Experiments." *Accounting, Organizations and Society* 34(3–4):535–48.

Callon, Michel, and Bruno Latour. 1981. "Unscrewing the Big Leviathan: How Actors Macro-Structure Reality and How Sociologists Help Them to Do

So." In *Advances in Social Theory and Methodology: Toward an Integration of Micro- and Macro-Sociologies,* edited by K. Knorr-Cetina and A.V. Cicourel, 277–301. Boston: Routledge and Kegan Paul.

Carrier, James G., and Peter Luetchford, eds. 2012. *Ethical Consumption: Social Value and Economic Practice.* New York: Berghahn Books

Cary, William L. 1974. "Federalism and Corporate Law: Reflections upon Delaware." *Yale Law Journal* 83(4):663–705.

Cassidy, John. 2006. "Relatively Deprived." *New Yorker* (April 3).

Cattelino, Jessica R. 2008. *High Stakes: Florida Seminole Gaming and Sovereignty.* Durham, NC: Duke University Press.

———. 2011. "'One Hamburger at a Time': Revisiting the State-Society Divide with the Seminole Tribe of Florida and Hard Rock International." *Current Anthropology* 52(S3):S137–S149.

Cepek, Michael L. 2011. "Foucault in the Forest: Questioning Environmentality in Amazonia." *American Ethnologist* 38(3):501–15.

Cernea, Michael M. 1991. *Putting People First: Sociological Variables in Rural Development.* New York: Oxford University Press.

Chandler, Alfred D. 1977. *The Visible Hand: The Managerial Revolution in American Business.* Cambridge, MA: Belknap Press.

Chapin, Mac. 2004. "A Challenge to Conservationists." *World Watch Magazine* (November–December):17–31.

Clifford, James, and George E. Marcus, eds. 1986. *Writing Culture: The Poetics and Politics of Ethnography.* Berkeley: University of California Press.

Coll, Steve. 2012. *Private Empire: ExxonMobil and American Power.* New York: Penguin.

Collins, Jim. 2001. *Good to Great: Why Some Companies Make the Leap . . . and Others Don't.* New York: HarperCollins.

Collinson, David, and Jeff Hearn, eds. 1996. *Men as Managers, Managers as Men: Critical Perspectives on Men, Masculinities, and Managements.* London: Sage.

Conboy, Kenneth J. 2006. *The Second Front: Inside Asia's Most Dangerous Terrorist Network.* Jakarta: Equinox.

Conklin, Beth A. 1997. "Body Paint, Feathers, and VCRs: Aesthetics and Authenticity in Amazonian Activism." *American Ethnologist* 24(4):711–37.

———. 2002. "Shamans versus Pirates in the Amazonian Treasure Chest." *American Anthropologist* 104(4):1050–61.

Conklin, Beth A., and Laura R. Graham. 1995. "The Shifting Middle Ground: Amazonian Indians and Eco-Politics." *American Anthropologist* 97(4):695–710.

Conley, John M., and Cynthia A. Williams. 2005. "Engage, Embed, and Embellish: Theory versus Practice in the Corporate Social Responsibility Movement." *Journal of Corporation Law* 31(1):1–38.

Cooke, Bill, and Uma Kothari, eds. 2001. *Participation: The New Tyranny?* London: Zed Books.

Cooley, Alexander, and James Ron. 2002. "The NGO Scramble: Transnational Action and Organizational Survival." *International Security* 27(1):5–39.

Cooper, Frederick. 2001. "What Is the Concept of Globalization Good For? An African Historian's Perspective." *African Affairs* 100:189–213.

Cooper, Frederick, and Randall M. Packard. 1997. Introduction to *International Development and the Social Sciences: Essays on the History and Politics of Knowledge,* edited by F. Cooper and R.M. Packard, 1–41. Berkeley: University of California Press.

Cooper, Frederick, and Ann Laura Stoler, eds. 1997. *Tensions of Empire: Colonial Cultures in a Bourgeois World.* Berkeley: University of California Press.

Corrigan, Philip, and Derek Sayer. 1985. *The Great Arch: English State Formation as Cultural Revolution.* Oxford: Blackwell.

Coumans, Catherine. 2002a. "Canadian Legislation on Submarine Tailings Disposal." In *STD Toolkit,* 12. Berkeley: Project Underground and MiningWatch Canada.

———. 2002b. "The Case against Submarine Tailings Disposal." *Mining Environmental Management* 10(5):14–18.

———. 2002c. "Mining's Problem with Waste." In *STD Toolkit,* 1–4. Berkeley: Project Underground and MiningWatch Canada.

———. 2011. "Occupying Spaces Created by Conflict: Anthropologists, Development NGOs, Responsible Investment, and Mining." *Current Anthropology* 52(S3):S29–S43.

CoW (Contract of Work). 1986. *Contract of Work between the Government of the Republic of Indonesia and PT Newmont Nusa Tenggara.* Benete: PT Newmont Nusa Tenggara.

Creed, Gerald W., ed. 2006. *The Seductions of Community: Emancipations, Oppressions, Quandaries.* Santa Fe, NM: School of American Research.

Cribb, R.B. 1990. *The Indonesian Killings of 1965–1966: Studies from Java and Bali.* Clayton, Victoria, Australia: Centre of Southeast Asian Studies, Monash University.

Cross, Jamie. 2011. "Detachment as a Corporate Ethic: Materializing CSR in the Diamond Supply Chain." *Focaal* 2011(60):34–46.

Cruikshank, Barbara. 1999. *The Will to Empower: Democratic Citizens and Other Subjects.* Ithaca, NY: Cornell University Press.

Das, Veena, and Deborah Poole. 2004. "State and Its Margins: Comparative Ethnographies." In *Anthropology in the Margins of the State,* edited by V. Das and D. Poole, 3–33. Santa Fe, NM: School of American Research Press.

Davidson, Joanna. 2010. "Cultivating Knowledge: Development, Dissemblance, and Discursive Contradictions among the Diola of Guinea-Bissau." *American Ethnologist* 37(2):212–26.

Davis, Gerald F. 2009. *Managed by the Markets: How Finance Reshaped America.* Oxford: Oxford University Press.

Davis, Susan G. 1997. *Spectacular Nature: Corporate Culture and the Sea World Experience.* Berkeley: University of California Press.

De Koninck, Rodolphe. 1979. "The Integration of the Peasantry: Examples from Malaysia and Indonesia." *Pacific Affairs* 52(2):265–293.

De Neve, Geert, Peter Luetchford, and Jeffrey Pratt, eds. 2008. "Hidden Hands in the Market: Ethnographies of Fair Trade, Ethical Consumption, and Corporate Social Responsibility." *Research in Economic Anthropology* 28.

Deal, Terrence E., and Allan A. Kennedy. 1982. *Corporate Cultures: The Rites and Rituals of Corporate Life.* Reading, MA: Addison-Wesley.

Dean, Mitchell. 1999. *Governmentality: Power and Rule in Modern Society.* London: Sage.

Delcore, Henry D. 2003. "Nongovernmental Organizations and the Work of Memory in Northern Thailand." *American Ethnologist* 30(1):61–84.

Denning, Michael. 2010. "Wageless Life." *New Left Review* 66:79–97.

Dewey, John. 1926. "The Historic Background of Corporate Legal Personality." *Yale Law Review* 35(6):655–73.

Dezenhall, Eric. 1999. *Nail 'Em!: Confronting High-Profile Attacks on Celebrities and Businesses.* Amherst, NY: Prometheus Books.

Dietrich, Alexa S. 2013. *The Drug Company Next Door: Pollution, Jobs, and Community Health in Puerto Rico.* New York: NYU Press.

Dixon, Kevin. 2002. "American Legislation Pertaining to STD." In *STD Toolkit,* 11. Berkeley: Project Underground and MiningWatch Canada.

Donham, Donald. 2011. *Violence in a Time of Liberation: Murder and Ethnicity at a South African Gold Mine.* Durham, NC: Duke University Press.

Doornbos, Martin. 2003. "'Good Governance': The Metamorphosis of a Policy Metaphor." *Journal of International Affairs* 57(1):3–17.

Douglas, Mary. 1966. *Purity and Danger: An Analysis of Concepts of Pollution and Taboo.* London: Routledge.

Douglas, Mary, and Steven Ney. 1998. *Missing Persons: A Critique of the Social Sciences.* Berkeley: University of California Press.

Dudley, Kathryn Marie. 1994. *The End of the Line: Lost Jobs, New Lives in Postindustrial America.* Chicago: University of Chicago Press.

Dunn, Elizabeth C. 2004. *Privatizing Poland: Baby Food, Big Business, and the Remaking of Labor.* Ithaca, NY: Cornell University Press.

———. 2007. "*Escherichia coli,* Corporate Discipline and the Failure of the Sewer State." *Space and Polity* 11(1):35–53.

Echols, John M., and Hassan Shadily. 1989. *An Indonesian-English Dictionary.* 3rd ed., revised and edited by John U. Wolff and James T. Collins. Ithaca, NY: Cornell University Press.

Ecklund, Judith Louise. 1977. "Marriage, Seaworms, and Song: Ritualized Responses to Cultural Change in Sasak Life." PhD diss., Cornell University.

Edwards, Paul N. 1990. "The Army and the Microworld: Computers and the Politics of Gender Identity." *Signs* 16(1):102–27.

Ellen, Roy. 2007. Introduction to *Modern Crises and Traditional Strategies: Local Ecological Knowledge in Island Southeast Asia,* edited by R. Ellen, 1–45. New York: Berghahn Books.

Elyachar, Julia. 2005a. "Comment on 'How to Ignore Corruption: Reporting the Shortcomings of Development in South Africa.'" *Current Anthropology* 46(1):113.

———. 2005b. *Markets of Dispossession: NGOs, Economic Development, and the State in Cairo.* Durham, NC: Duke University Press.

Escobar, Arturo. 1991. "Anthropology and the Development Encounter: The Making and Marketing of Development Anthropology." *American Ethnologist* 18(4):658–82.

———. 1995. *Encountering Development: The Making and Unmaking of the Third World.* Princeton, NJ: Princeton University Press.

Esposito, Roberto. 2006. "The Immunization Paradigm." *diacritics* 36(2):23–49.

Farmer, Paul. 2004. "An Anthropology of Structural Violence." *Current Anthropology* 45(3):305–25.

Faubion, James D., George E. Marcus, and Michael M. J. Fischer. 2009. *Fieldwork Is Not What It Used To Be: Learning Anthropology's Method in a Time of Transition*. Ithaca, NY: Cornell University Press.

Feldman, Martha S., and James G. March. 1981. "Information in Organizations as Signal and Symbol." *Administrative Science Quarterly* 26(2):171–86.

Ferguson, James. 1997. "Anthropology and Its Evil Twin: 'Development' in the Constitution of a Discipline." In *International Development and the Social Sciences: Essays on the History and Politics of Knowledge*, edited by F. Cooper and R. M. Packard, 150–75. Berkeley: University of California Press.

———. 1999. *Expectations of Modernity: Myths and Meanings of Urban Life on the Zambian Copperbelt*. Berkeley: University of California Press.

———. 2005. "Seeing Like an Oil Company: Space, Security, and Global Capital in Neoliberal Africa." *American Anthropologist* 107(3):377–82.

———. 2006. *Global Shadows: Africa in the Neoliberal World Order*. Durham, NC: Duke University Press.

———. 2012. "Structures of Responsibility." *Ethnography* 13(4):558–62.

Ferguson, James, and Akhil Gupta. 2002. "Spatializing States: Toward an Ethnography of Neoliberal Governmentality." *American Ethnologist* 29(4):981–1002.

Ferry, Elizabeth Emma. 2005. *Not Ours Alone: Patrimony, Value, and Collectivity in Contemporary Mexico*. New York: Columbia University Press.

Field, Les. 1999. "Complicities and Collaborations: Anthropologists and the 'Unacknowledged Tribes' of California." *Current Anthropology* 40(2):193–209.

Field Alliance. 2001. "Review Team Recommends New IPM Organization." The Field Alliance, www.thefieldalliance.org.

Finn, Janet L. 1998. *Tracing the Veins: Of Copper, Culture, and Community from Butte to Chuquicamata*. Berkeley: University of California Press.

Finnemore, Martha. 1997. "Redefining Development at the World Bank." In *International Development and the Social Sciences: Essays on the History and Politics of Knowledge*, edited by F. Cooper and R. M. Packard, 203–27. Berkeley: University of California Press.

Fisher, Melissa S. 2012. *Wall Street Women*. Durham, NC: Duke University Press.

Fisher, William F. 1997. "Doing Good? The Politics and Antipolitics of NGO Practices." *Annual Review of Anthropology* 26:439–64.

Fleming, Peter, and André Spicer. 2007. *Contesting the Corporation: Struggle, Power and Resistance in Organizations*. Cambridge: Cambridge University Press.

Fligstein, Neil. 1990. *The Transformation of Corporate Control*. Cambridge, MA: Harvard University Press.

Flyvbjerg, Bent. 2001. *Making Social Science Matter: Why Social Inquiry Fails and How It Can Succeed Again*. Cambridge: Cambridge University Press.

Fogarty, Timothy J. 1996. "The Imagery and Reality of Peer Review in the US: Insights from Institutional Theory." *Accounting, Organizations and Society* 21(2–3):243–67.

Fonseca, Alberto. 2010. "How Credible Are Mining Corporations' Sustainability Reports? A Critical Analysis of External Asssurance under the Requirements of the International Council on Mining and Metals." *Corporate Social Responsibility and Environmental Management* 17:355–70.

Fortun, Kim. 2001. *Advocacy after Bhopal: Environmentalism, Disaster, New Global Orders*. Chicago: University of Chicago Press.

Foster, Robert J. 2007. "The Work of the New Economy: Consumers, Brands, and Value Creation." *Cultural Anthropology* 22(4):707–31.

———. 2008. *Coca-Globalization: Following Soft Drinks from New York to New Guinea*. New York: Palgrave Macmillan.

———. 2011. "The Uses of Use Value: Marketing, Value Creation, and the Exigencies of Consumption Work." In *Inside Marketing: Practices, Ideologies, Devices*, edited by D. Zwick and J. Cayla, 42–57. Oxford: Oxford University Press.

Foucault, Michel. 1978. *The History of Sexuality*. Vol. 1: *An Introduction*. New York: Pantheon.

———. 1979. *Discipline and Punish: The Birth of the Prison*. New York: Vintage.

———. 1991. "Governmentality." In *The Foucault Effect: Studies in Governmentality*, edited by C. G. Graham Burchell and Peter Miller. Chicago: University of Chicago Press.

———. 1997. *Ethics: Subjectivity and Truth. The Essential Works of Michel Foucault, 1954–1984*. Vol. 1. Edited by Paul Rabinow. New York: New Press.

Fox, James J. 1991. "Managing the Ecology of Rice Production in Indonesia." In *Indonesia: Resources, Ecology, and Environment*, edited by J. Hardjono, 61–84. Singapore: Oxford University Press.

Francis, Paul. 2001. "Participatory Development at the World Bank: The Primacy of Process." In *Participation: The New Tyranny?* edited by B. Cooke and U. Kothari, 72–87. London: Zed Books.

Frank, Thomas. 1997. *The Conquest of Cool: Business Culture, Counterculture, and the Rise of Hip Consumerism*. Chicago: University of Chicago Press.

Franke, Richard W. 1974. "Miracle Seeds and Shattered Dreams." *Natural History* 83(1):10–18, 84–88.

Freire, Paulo. 1970. *Pedagogy of the Oppressed*. New York: Herder and Herder.

Friedman, Milton. 1970. "A Friedman Doctrine—the Social Responsibility of Business Is to Increase Its Profits." *New York Times Magazine*, September 13.

Frontline. 2005. "Peru: The Curse of Inca Gold." PBS.org, www.pbs.org/frontlineworld/stories/peru404/.

———. 2013. "The Retirement Gamble." PBS.org, http://www.pbs.org/wgbh/pages/frontline/retirement-gamble/.

Furnivall, J. S. 1991. *The Fashioning of Leviathan: The Beginnings of British Rule in Burma*. Canberra, Australia: Department of Anthropology, Research School of Pacific Studies, Australian National University.

Fuss, Diana. 1989. *Essentially Speaking: Feminism, Nature and Difference.* New York: Routledge.

Gade, Anna M. 2004. *Perfection Makes Practice: Learning, Emotion, and the Recited Qur'an in Indonesia.* Honolulu: University of Hawai'i Press.

Galt, Ryan E. 2013. "From *Homo economicus* to Complex Subjectivities: Reconceptualizing Farmers as Pesticide Users." *Antipode* 45(2):336–56.

Gardner, Katy. 2012. *Discordant Development: Global Capitalism and the Struggle for Connection in Bangladesh.* London: Pluto Press.

Gedicks, Al. 2001. *Resource Rebels: Native Challenges to Mining and Oil Corporations.* Cambridge, MA: South End Press.

Geertz, Clifford. 1960. *The Religion of Java.* Chicago: University of Chicago Press.

———. 1963. *Agricultural Involution.* Berkeley: University of California Press.

———. 1973. *The Interpretation of Cultures.* New York: Basic Books.

George, Kenneth M. 1998. "Designs on Indonesia's Muslim Communities." *Journal of Asian Studies* 57(3):693–713.

———. 2010. *Picturing Islam: Art and Ethics in a Muslim Lifeworld.* Chichester, U.K.: Wiley-Blackwell.

———. 2014. "Putting the Quirks and Murk to Work: Disciplinary Reflections on the State of Indonesian Studies." In *Producing Indonesia: The State of the Field of Indonesian Studies,* edited by E. Tagliacozzo, 33–45. Ithaca, NY: Southeast Asia Publications, Cornell University.

Gibson-Graham, J.K. 1996. *The End of Capitalism (as We Knew It): A Feminist Critique of Political Economy.* Cambridge, MA: Blackwell.

———. 2006. A *Postcapitalist Politics.* Minneapolis: University of Minnesota Press.

Giddens, Anthony. 1990. *The Consequences of Modernity.* Stanford, CA: Stanford University Press.

Gilbert, Margaret. 1989. *On Social Facts.* Princeton, NJ: Princeton University Press.

Gill, Lesley. 2000. *Teetering on the Rim: Global Restructuring, Daily Life, and the Armed Retreat of the Bolivian State.* New York: Columbia University Press.

Gjording, Chris N. 1991. *Conditions Not of Their Choosing: The Guaymí Indians and Mining Multinationals in Panama.* Washington, DC: Smithsonian Institution Press.

Godelier, Maurice. 1999. *The Enigma of the Gift.* Chicago: University of Chicago Press.

Godoy, Ricardo. 1985. "Mining: Anthropological Perspectives." *Annual Review of Anthropology* 14:199–217.

Goethals, Peter R. 1961. *Aspects of Local Government in a Sumbawan Village (Eastern Indonesia).* Ithaca, NY: Southeast Asia Program, Cornell University.

Goffman, Erving. 1959. *The Presentation of Self in Everyday Life.* New York: Doubleday.

———. 1989. "On Fieldwork." *Journal of Contemporary Ethnography* 18(2):123–32.

Gold, Andrew S. 2012. "Theories of the Firm and Judicial Uncertainty." *Seattle University Law Review* 35(4):1087–108.

Goldman, Michael. 2005. *Imperial Nature: The World Bank and Struggles for Social Justice in the Age of Globalization*. New Haven, CT: Yale University Press.

Goldwyn, David L. 2004. "Extracting Transparency." *Georgetown Journal of International Affairs* 5(1):5–16.

Golub, Alex. 2014. *Leviathans at the Gold Mine: Creating Indigenous and Corporate Actors in Papua New Guinea*. Durham, NC: Duke University Press.

Golub, Alex, and Mooweon Rhee. 2013. "Traction: The Role of Executives in Localising Global Mining and Petroleum Industries in Papua New Guinea." *Paideuma* 59:215–36.

Gordon, Julie. 2003. "Mining Chief Brings Ethics Message." *Coloradoan*, February 7.

Graeber, David. 2001. *Toward an Anthropological Theory of Value: The False Coin of Our Own Dreams*. New York: Palgrave.

———. 2006. "Beyond Power/Knowledge: An Exploration of the Relation of Power, Ignorance and Stupidity." Malinowski Memorial Lecture presented at the London School of Economics, May 25.

———. 2009. *Direct Action: An Ethnography*. Edinburgh: AK Press.

Gramsci, Antonio. 1971. *Selections from the Prison Notebooks of Antonio Gramsci*. Translated by Q. Hoare and G. Nowell-Smith. New York: International Publishers.

———. (1926) 1994. "Some Aspects of the Southern Question." In *Gramsci: Pre-Prison Writings,* edited by R. Bellamy, 313–36. Cambridge: Cambridge University Press.

Granovetter, Mark. 1985. "Economic Action and Social Structure: The Problem of Embeddedness." *American Journal of Sociology* 91:481–510.

Gupta, Akhil. 1998. *Postcolonial Developments: Agriculture in the Making of Modern India*. Durham, NC: Duke University Press.

Guthman, Julie. 2004. *Agrarian Dreams: The Paradox of Organic Farming in California*. Berkeley: University of California Press.

———. 2011. *Weighing In: Obesity, Food Justice, and the Limits of Capitalism*. Berkeley: University of California Press.

Guyer, Jane I. 2011. "Blueprints, Judgment, and Perseverance in a Corporate Context." *Current Anthropology* 52(S3):S17–S27.

Hacking, Ian. 1990. *The Taming of Chance*. Cambridge: Cambridge University Press.

Hadiz, Vedi R. 2010. *Localising Power in Post-Authoritarian Indonesia: A Southeast Asia Perspective*. Stanford, CA: Stanford University Press.

Hailey, John. 2001. "Beyond the Formulaic: Process and Practice in South Asian NGOs." In *Participation: The New Tyranny?* edited by B. Cooke and U. Kothari, 88–101. London: Zed Books.

Haller, Dieter, and Cris Shore, eds. 2005. *Corruption: Anthropological Perspectives*. London: Pluto.

Hansen, Gary. 1971. "Episodes in Rural Modernization: Problems in the Bimas Program." *Indonesia* 11:63–81.

Hansen, Thomas Blom, and Finn Stepputat. 2001. Introduction to *States of Imagination: Ethnographic Explorations of the Postcolonial State*, edited by T.B. Hansen and F. Stepputat, 1–38. Durham, NC: Duke University Press.

Harding, Susan Friend. 2000. *The Book of Jerry Falwell: Fundamentalist Language and Politics*. Princeton, NJ: Princeton University Press.

Harper, Krista. 2005. "'Wild Capitalism' and 'Ecocolonialism': A Tale of Two Rivers." *American Anthropologist* 107(2):221–33.

Hart, Gillian. 2001. "Development Critiques in the 1990s: *Culs de sac* and Promising Paths." *Progress in Human Geography* 25(4):649–58.

———. 2004. "Geography and Development: Critical Ethnographies." *Progress in Human Geography* 28(1):91–100.

Hart, Gillian Patricia, Andrew Turton, and Benjamin White, eds. 1989. *Agrarian Transformations: Local Processes and the State in Southeast Asia*. Berkeley: University of California Press.

Hart, Stuart L. 2010. *Capitalism at the Crossroads: Next Generation Business Strategies for a Post-Crisis World*. Upper Saddle River, NJ: Wharton School Publishing.

Harvey, David. 2005. *A Brief History of Neoliberalism*. Oxford: Oxford University Press.

Hasty, Jennifer. 2005. "The Pleasures of Corruption: Desire and Discipline in Ghanaian Political Culture." *Cultural Anthropology* 20(2):271–301.

Hecht, Gabrielle. 2002. "Rupture-Talk in the Nuclear Age: Conjugating Colonial Power in Africa." *Social Studies of Science* 32(5–6):691–727.

Hefner, Robert W. 1990. *The Political Economy of Mountain Java: An Interpretive History*. Berkeley: University of California Press.

———. 2000. *Civil Islam: Muslims and Democratization in Indonesia*. Princeton, NJ: Princeton University Press.

Helmreich, Stefan. 2009. *Alien Ocean: Anthropological Voyages in Microbial Seas*. Berkeley: University of California Press.

Henkel, Heiko, and Roderick Stirrat. 2001. "Participation as Spiritual Duty; Empowerment as Secular Subjection." In *Participation: The New Tyranny?* edited by B. Cooke and U. Kothari, 168–84. London: Zed Books.

Heryanto, Ariel. 1988. "The Development of 'Development.'" *Indonesia* 46(October):1–24.

———. 1995. *Language of Development and Development of Language: The Case of Indonesia*. Canberra, Australia: Department of Linguistics, Research School of Pacific and Asian Studies.

———. 2006. *State Terrorism and Political Identity in Indonesia: Fatally Belonging*. New York: Routledge.

Heryanto, Ariel, and Vedi R. Hadiz. 2005. "Post-Authoritarian Indonesia: A Comparative Southeast Asian Perspective." *Critical Asian Studies* 37(2):251–75.

Herzfeld, Michael. 1992. *The Social Production of Indifference: Exploring the Symbolic Roots of Western Bureaucracy*. New York: Berg.

———. 2005. *Cultural Intimacy: Social Poetics in the Nation-State*. New York: Routledge.

Hetherington, Kregg. 2011. *Guerrilla Auditors: The Politics of Transparency in Neoliberal Paraguay.* Durham, NC: Duke University Press.

High, Holly. 2009. "The Road to Nowhere? Poverty and Policy in the South of Laos." *Focaal* 53(2009):75–88.

Hildebrand, Vanessa. 2009. "Sumbawan Obstetrics: The Social Construction of Obstetrical Practice in Rural Indonesia." Phd diss., Washington University, Saint Louis.

Hilgartner, Stephen. 1992. "The Social Construction of Risk Objects: Or, How to Pry Open Networks of Risk." In *Organizations, Uncertainties, and Risk,* edited by J. F. Short and L. B. Clarke, 39–53. Boulder, CO: Westview Press.

———. 2000. *Science on Stage: Expert Advice as Public Drama.* Stanford, CA: Stanford University Press.

Hill, Jane H., and Judith T. Irvine. 1993. Introduction to *Responsibility and Evidence in Oral Discourse,* edited by J. H. Hill and J. T. Irvine, 1–23. Cambridge: Cambridge University Press.

Hirsch, Paul M. 1986. "From Ambushes to Golden Parachutes: Corporate Takeovers as an Instance of Cultural Framing and Institutional Integration." *American Journal of Sociology* 91(4):800–37.

Hirschman, Albert O. 1958. *The Strategy of Economic Development.* New Haven, CT: Yale University Press.

———. (1977) 1997. *The Passions and the Interests: Political Arguments for Capitalism before Its Triumph.* Princeton, NJ: Princeton University Press.

Hobbes, Thomas. 1886. *Leviathan, or, The Matter, Form, and Power of a Commonwealth, Ecclesiastical and Civil.* London: George Routledge and Sons.

Hochschild, Arlie Russell. (1983) 2012. *The Managed Heart: Commercialization of Human Feeling.* Berkeley, CA: University of California Press.

Hodgson, Dorothy L. 2002a. "Introduction: Comparative Perspectives on the Indigenous Rights Movement in Africa and the Americas." *American Anthropologist* 104(4):1037–49.

———. 2002b. "Precarious Alliances: The Cultural Politics and Structural Predicaments of the Indigenous Rights Movement in Tanzania." *American Anthropologist* 104(4):1086–97.

Hoesterey, James. 2008. "Marketing Morality: The Rise, Fall and Rebranding of Aa Gym." In *Expressing Islam: Religious Life and Politics in Indonesia,* edited by G. Fealy and S. White, 95–112. Singapore: Institute of Southeast Asian Studies.

———. 2012. "Prophetic Cosmopolitanism: Islam, Pop Psychology, and Civic Virtue in Indonesia." *City and Society* 24(1):38–61.

Holmes, Douglas R. 1989. *Cultural Disenchantments: Worker Peasantries in Northeast Italy.* Princeton, NJ: Princeton University Press.

Honna, Jun. 2001. "Military Ideology in Response to Democratic Pressure during the Late Suharto Era: Political and Institutional Contexts." In *Violence and the State in Suharto's Indonesia,* edited by B. R. O'G. Anderson, 54–89. Ithaca, NY: Southeast Asia Program Publications, Cornell University.

Horwitz, Morton J. 1985. "*Santa Clara* Revisited: The Development of Corporate Theory." *West Virginia Law Review* 88(2):173–224.

Hoskin, Keith, and Richard Macve. 1994. "Writing, Examining, Disciplining: The Genesis of Accounting's Modern Power." In *Accounting as Social and Institutional Practice,* edited by A. G. Hopwood and P. Miller, 67–97. Cambridge: Cambridge University Press.

Hoskins, Janet. 1993. *The Play of Time: Kodi Perspectives on Calendars, History, and Exchange.* Berkeley: University of California Press.

Hull, Matthew S. 2010. "Democratic Technologies of Speech: From WWII America to Postcolonial Delhi." *Journal of Linguistic Anthropology* 20(2):257–82.

———. 2012. *Government of Paper: The Materiality of Bureaucracy in Urban Pakistan.* Berkeley: University of California Press.

Humphreys, Macartan, Jeffrey Sachs, and Joseph E. Stiglitz. 2007. *Escaping the Resource Curse.* New York: Columbia University Press.

Hurgronje, C. Snouck. 1931. *Mekka in the Latter Part of the 19th Century.* Leiden, Netherlands: Brill.

Hutter, Bridget M., and Michael Power. 2005. "Organizational Encounters with Risk: An Introduction." In *Organizational Encounters with Risk,* edited by B. M. Hutter and M. Power. Cambridge: Cambridge University Press.

ICG (International Crisis Group). 2007. *Indonesia: Jemaah Islamiyah's Current Status.* Asia Briefing No. 63. Jakarta: International Crisis Group.

Igoe, James. 2003. "Scaling Up Civil Society: Donor Money, NGOs, and the Pastoralist Land Rights Movement in Tanzania." *Development and Change* 34(5):863–85.

IIED (International Institute for Environment and Development) and WBCSD (World Business Council for Sustainable Development. 2002. *Meeting Report on Corruption Issues in the Mining and Minerals Sector.* Berlin: International Institute for Environment and Development and World Business Council for Sustainable Development.

Illich, Ivan. 1971. *Deschooling Society.* New York: Harper and Row.

Inda, Jonathan Xavier. 2005. "Analytics of the Modern: An Introduction." In *Anthropologies of Modernity: Foucault, Governmentality, and Life Politics,* edited by J. X. Inda, 1–22. Malden, MA: Blackwell.

Ingold, Tim. 2000. *The Perception of the Environment: Essays on Livelihood, Dwelling and Skill.* London: Routledge.

Ingratubun, Gudrun Fenna. N.d. "Participatory Situation and Problem Analysis in Two Transmigration Villages in West-Sumbawa, Indonesia." Unpublished report archived in PT NNT's Community Development files.

Inoue, Miyako. 2006. *Vicarious Language: Gender and Linguistic Modernity in Japan.* Berkeley: University of California Press.

IPPHTI (Ikatan Petani Pengendalian Hama Terpadu Indonesia). N.d. *IPPHTI: Apa dan Siapa.* Jakarta: IPPHTI.

Jacka, Jerry K. 2005. "Emplacement and Millennial Expectations in an Era of Development and Globalization: Heaven and the Appeal of Christianity for the Ipili." *American Anthropologist* 107(4):643–53.

Jackall, Robert. 1988. *Moral Mazes: The World of Corporate Managers.* New York: Oxford University Press.

Jacoby, Karl. 2003. *Crimes against Nature: Squatters, Poachers, Thieves, and the Hidden History of American Conservation*. Berkeley: University of California Press.

Jacoby, Sanford M. 2005. *The Embedded Corporation: Corporate Governance and Employment Relations in Japan and the United States*. Princeton, NJ: Princeton University Press.

Jaffee, Daniel. 2007. *Brewing Justice: Fair Trade Coffee, Sustainability, and Survival*. Berkeley: University of California Press.

Jain, S. Lochlann. 2007. "Cancer Butch." *Cultural Anthropology* 22(4): 501–38.

Jenkins, Heledd, and Natalia Yakovleva. 2006. "Corporate Social Responsibilty in the Mining Industry: Exploring Trends in Social and Environmental Disclosure." *Journal of Cleaner Production* 14:271–84.

Jones, Carla. 2010a. "Better Women: The Cultural Politics of Gendered Expertise in Indonesia." *American Anthropologist* 112(2):270–82.

———. 2010b. "Materializing Piety: Gendered Anxieties about Faithful Consumption in Contemporary Urban Indonesia." *American Ethnologist* 37(4):617–37.

Juris, Jeffrey S. 2008. *Networking Futures: The Movements against Corporate Globalization*. Durham, NC: Duke University Press.

Just, Peter. 2001. *Dou Donggo Justice: Conflict and Morality in an Indonesian Society*. Lanham, MD: Rowman and Littlefield.

Kahn, Joel S., and Francesco Formosa. 2002. "The Problem of 'Crony Capitalism': Modernity and the Encounter with the Perverse." *Thesis Eleven* 69:47–66.

Kanter, Rosabeth Moss. 1977. *Men and Women of the Corporation*. New York: Basic Books.

Kantorowicz, Ernst Hartwig. 1997. *The King's Two Bodies: A Study in Mediaeval Political Theology*. Princeton, NJ: Princeton University Press.

Keane, Webb. 2005. "Comment on 'Engineers and Political Dreams: Indonesia in the Satellite Age.'" *Current Anthropology* 46(5):720–21.

———. 2010. "Minds, Surfaces, and Reasons in the Anthropology of Ethics." In *Ordinary Ethics: Anthropology, Language, and Action*, edited by M. Lambek, 64–83. New York: Fordham University Press.

Kearney, Michael. 1996. *Reconceptualizing the Peasantry: Anthropology in Global Perspective*. Boulder, CO: Westview Press.

Keck, Margaret E., and Kathryn Sikkink. 1998. *Activists beyond Borders: Advocacy Networks in International Politics*. Ithaca, NY: Cornell University Press.

Keefe, Patrick Radden. 2013. "Buried Secrets." *New Yorker* (July 8 and 15):50–63.

Kemp, Deanna, John R. Owen, and Shashi van de Graaff. 2012. "Corporate Social Responsibility, Mining, and 'Audit Culture.'" *Journal of Cleaner Production* 24:1–10.

Kemp, Melody. 2008. "Fools' Gold in Indonesia." *Asia Times*, December 19.

Keynes, John Maynard. 1936. *The General Theory of Employment, Interest and Money*. New York: Harcourt and Brace.

Khurana, Rakesh. 2002. *Searching for a Corporate Savior: The Irrational Quest for Charismatic CEOs.* Princeton, NJ: Princeton University Press.

King, Brayden G., Teppo Felin, and David A. Whetten. 2010. "Finding the Organization in Organizational Theory: A Meta-Theory of the Organization as a Social Actor." *Organization Science* 21(1):290–305.

Kipnis, Andrew B. 2008. "Audit Cultures: Neoliberal Governmentality, Socialist Legacy, or Technologies of Governing?" *American Ethnologist* 35(2):275–89.

Kirksey, Eben. 2012. *Freedom in Entangled Worlds: West Papua and the Architecture of Global Power.* Durham, NC: Duke University Press.

Kirsch, Stuart. 2006. *Reverse Anthropology: Indigenous Analysis of Social and Environmental Relations in New Guinea.* Stanford, CA: Stanford University Press.

———. 2007. "Indigenous Movements and the Risks of Counterglobalization: Tracking the Campaign against Papua New Guinea's Ok Tedi Mine." *American Anthropologist* 34(2):303–21.

———. 2010a. "Sustainability and the BP Oil Spill." *Dialectical Anthropology* 34:295–300.

———. 2010b. "Sustainable Mining." *Dialectical Anthropology* 34(1):87–93.

Knobe, Joshua. 2005. "Theory of Mind and Moral Cognition: Exploring the Connections." *Trends in Cognitive Sciences* 9(8):357–59.

Kondo, Dorinne K. 1990. *Crafting Selves: Power, Gender, and Discourses of Identity in a Japanese Workplace.* Chicago: University of Chicago Press.

Kothari, Uma. 2001. "Power, Knowledge and Social Control in Participatory Development." In *Participation: The New Tyranny?* edited by B. Cooke and U. Kothari, 139–52. London: Zed Books.

Kottak, Conrad P. 1990. "Culture and 'Economic Development.'" *American Anthropologist* 92(3):723–31.

———. 1999. "The New Ecological Anthropology." *American Anthropologist* 101(1):23–35.

Kovach, Hetty, Caroline Neligan, and Simon Burall. 2003. *Power without Accountability?* Global Accountability Report 1. London: One World Trust.

KPDTNT (Konsorsium Pengembangan Dataran Tinggi Nusa Tenggara). 1996. *Berbuat Bersama Berperan Setara: Acuan Penerapan Participatory Rural Appraisal.* Bandung, Indonesia: Driya Media.

Krause, Elizabeth L. 2013. "My Trouble with the Anti-Essentialist Struggle." *Anthropology News* 54(1–2):18.

Krauss, Clifford. 2012. "U.S. Oil and Mining Companies Must Disclose Payments to Foreign Governments." *New York Times,* August 23.

KSU Somil Jaya. 2002. *Laporan Kegiatan SKU Somil Jaya, Periode 1 Januari–31 Maret.* Monthly cooperative reports filed in PT Newmont Nusa Tenggara's Community Development Department.

———. 2003. *Laporan Pertanggung Jawaban Pengurus Koperasi Serba Usaha Somil Jaya, Rapat Anggota Tahunan, Tahun Buku 2002.* Report prepared for cooperative annual members' meeting, Tongo-Sejorong 2002.

Kunda, Gideon. (1992) 2006. *Engineering Culture: Control and Commitment in a High-Tech Corporation.* Philadelphia: Temple University Press.

Kusno, Abidin. 2010. *The Appearances of Memory: Mnemonic Practices of Architecture and Urban Form in Indonesia*. Durham, NC: Duke University Press.

Laidlaw, James. 2010. "Agency and Responsibility: Perhaps You Can Have Too Much of a Good Thing." In *Ordinary Ethics: Anthropology, Language, and Action*, edited by M. Lambek, 143–64. New York: Fordham University Press.

Lampland, Martha, and Susan Leigh Star. 2009. *Standards and Their Stories: How Quantifying, Classifying, and Formalizing Practices Shape Everyday Life*. Ithaca, NY: Cornell University Press.

Lansing, John Stephen. 1991. *Priests and Programmers: Technologies of Power in the Engineered Landscape of Bali*. Princeton, NJ: Princeton University Press.

Latour, Bruno. 1987. *Science in Action: How to Follow Scientists and Engineers through Society*. Cambridge, MA: Harvard University Press.

———. 2004. "Why Has Critique Run out of Steam? From Matters of Fact to Matters of Concern." *Critical Inquiry* 30(2):225–48.

———. 2005. *Reassembling the Social: An Introduction to Actor-Network-Theory*. Oxford: Oxford University Press.

———. 2012. "'What's the Story?' Organizing as a Mode of Existence." In *Agency without Actors?: New Approaches to Collective Action*, edited by J.-H. Passoth, B.M. Peuker, and M.W.J. Schillmeier, 163–77. London: Routledge.

Leal, Pablo Alejandro. 2007. "Participation: The Ascendancy of a Buzzword in the Neoliberal Era." *Development in Practice* 17(4–5):539–48.

LeCain, Timothy J. 2009. *Mass Destruction: The Men and Giant Mines That Wired America and Scarred the Planet*. New Brunswick, NJ: Rutgers University Press.

Leith, Denise. 2003. *The Politics of Power: Freeport in Suharto's Indonesia*. Honolulu: University of Hawaii Press.

Lemke, Thomas. 2001. "'The Birth of Bio-Politics': Michel Foucault's Lecture at the Collège de France on Neo-Liberal Governmentality." *Economy and Society* 30(2):190–207.

Leve, Lauren G. 2001. "Between Jesse Helms and Ram Bahadur: Participation and Empowerment in Women's Literacy Programming in Nepal." *PoLAR* 24(1):108–28.

Lévi-Strauss, Claude. 1992. *Tristes Tropiques*. New York: Penguin.

Lewis, Al. 2007. "Not All That Glitters Is Good." *Denver Post*, August 5.

Li, Fabiana. 2009. "Documenting Accountability: Environmental Impact Assessment in a Peruvian Mining Project." *PoLAR* 32(2):218–36.

Li, Tania Murray. 1999a. "Compromising Power: Development, Culture, and Rule in Indonesia." *Cultural Anthropology* 14(3):295–322.

———. 1999b, ed. *Transforming the Indonesian Uplands: Marginality, Power, and Production*. Amsterdam: Harwood Academic Publishers.

———. 2000. "Articulating Indigenous Identity in Indonesia: Resource Politics and the Tribal Slot." *Comparative Studies in Society and History* 42(1): 149–79.

———. 2001. "Masyarakat Adat, Difference, and the Limits of Recognition in Indonesia's Forest Zone." *Modern Asian Studies* 35(3):645–76.

———. 2007. *The Will to Improve: Governmentality, Development, and the Practice of Politics.* Durham, NC: Duke University Press.

List, Christian, and Philip Pettit. 2011. *Group Agency: The Possibility, Design, and Status of Corporate Agents.* Oxford: Oxford University Press.

Litvin, Daniel. 2003. *Empires of Profit: Commerce, Conquest and Corporate Responsibility.* New York: Texere.

Livesey, Sharon M., and Kate Kearins. 2002. "Transparent and Caring Corporations? A Study of Sustainability Reports by the Body Shop and Royal Dutch/Shell." *Organization and Environment* 5(3):233–58.

Locke, John. (1690) 2001. *An Essay Concerning Human Understanding.* Kitchener, Ontario, Canada: Batoche Books.

Lombok Post. 2002a. "LSM dan Korban Tambang Diintimidasi?" June 14.

———. 2002b. "Tim Studi Banding Dituding Liar." June 18.

Lowe, Celia. 2006. *Wild Profusion: Biodiversity Conservation in an Indonesian Archipelago.* Princeton, NJ: Princeton University Press.

MacDougall, John M. 2003. "Self-Reliant Militias: Homegrown Security Forces Wield Great Power in Lombok." *Inside Indonesia* 73, www.insideindonesia.org/feature-editions/self-reliant-militias.

Macintyre, Martha, and Simon Foale. 2002. *Politicised Ecology: Local Responses to Mining in Papua New Guinea.* Working Paper No. 33. Canberra, Australia: Resource Management in Asia-Pacific Program Seminar Series, Australian National University.

Macintyre, Martha, Wendy Mee, and Fiona Solomon. 2008. "Evaluating Social Performance in the Context of an 'Audit Culture': A Pilot Social Review of a Gold Mine in Papua New Guinea." *Corporate Social Responsibility and Environmental Management* 15(2):100–110.

MacKenzie, Donald A. 2009. *Material Markets: How Economic Agents Are Constructed.* Oxford: Oxford University Press.

Maha Adi, I.G.G., and Soepriyanto Khafid. 2002. "Yang Merana Karena Arsen." *Tempo*, June 30.

Mahmood, Saba. 2005. *Politics of Piety: The Islamic Revival and the Feminist Subject.* Princeton, NJ: Princeton University Press.

Mahsun, Idrus Abdullah, H.L. Said Ruhpina, Mumbrita Sulaimi, Mohammed Saleh Rahmandayani, and Amir Hamzah. 1998. "Laporan Penelitian Perubahan Perilaku Sosial Budaya dan Pengembangan Masyarakat di Kecamatan Jereweh, Taliwang, dan Seteluk, Kabupaten Sumbawa." Unpublished report prepared for PT NNT by Lembaga Penelitian Universitas Mataram.

Mamdani, Mahmood. 2004. *Good Muslim, Bad Muslim: America, the Cold War, and the Roots of Terror.* New York: Pantheon.

Mangaliso, Mzamo P. 1997. "South Africa: Corporate Social Responsibility and the Sullivan Principles." *Journal of Black Studies* 28(2):219–38.

Marcus, George E. 1995. "Ethnography in/of the World System: The Emergence of Multi-Sited Ethnography." *Annual Review of Anthropology* 24: 95–117.

————. 1997. "The Uses of Complicity in the Changing Mise-en-Scène of Anthropological Fieldwork." *Representations* 59(Summer):85–108.

————. 1998. *Corporate Futures: The Diffusion of the Culturally Sensitive Corporate Form.* Chicago: University of Chicago Press.

Marcus, George E., and Michael G. Powell. 2003. "From Conspiracy Theories in the Incipient New World Order of the 1990s to Regimes of Transparency Now." *Anthropological Quarterly* 76(2):323–34.

Mark, Gregory A. 1987. "The Personification of the Business Corporation in American Law." *University of Chicago Law Review* 54(4):1441–83.

Marquand, David. 1992. "The Enterprise Culture: Old Wine in New Bottles?" In *The Values of the Enterprise Culture: The Moral Debate,* edited by P. Heelas and P. Morris, 61–72. London: Routledge.

Marriott, McKim. 1976. "Hindu Transactions: Diversity without Dualism." In *Transaction and Meaning,* edited by B. Kapferer, 109–37. Philadelphia: Institute for the Study of Human Issues.

Martin, Emily. 1994. *Flexible Bodies: Tracking Immunity in American Culture from the Days of Polio to the Age of AIDS.* Boston: Beacon Press.

Marx, Karl. 1964. *The Eighteenth Brumaire of Louis Bonaparte.* New York: International Publishers.

————. 1992. *Capital: A Critique of Political Economy.* Vol. 1. London: Penguin.

————. 2000. *Karl Marx: Selected Writings.* Edited by David McLellan. Oxford: Oxford University Press.

Masco, Joseph. 2006. *The Nuclear Borderlands: The Manhattan Project in Post-Cold War New Mexico.* Princeton, NJ: Princeton University Press.

Mathews, Andrew S. 2005. "Power/Knowledge, Power/Ignorance: Forest Fires and the State in Mexico." *Human Ecology* 33(6):795–820.

Mauss, Marcel. 1985. "A Category of the Human Mind: The Notion of the Person, The Notion of Self." In *The Category of the Person: Anthropology, Philosophy, History,* edited by M. Carrithers, S. Collins, and S. Lukes, 1–25. Cambridge: Cambridge University Press.

————. 1990. *The Gift: The Form and Reason for Exchange in Archaic Societies.* New York: W.W. Norton.

Mazzarella, William. 2003. *Shoveling Smoke: Advertising and Globalization in Contemporary India.* Durham, NC: Duke University Press.

McCarthy, James. 2002. "First World Political Ecology: Lessons from the Wise Use Movement." *Environment and Planning A* 34(1281–302).

McCarthy, John F. 2011. "The Limits of Legality: State, Governance and Resource Control in Indonesia." In *The State and Illegality in Indonesia,* edited by E. Aspinall and G. van Klinken, 89–106. Leiden, Netherlands: KITLV Press.

McLeod, Ross H. 2011. "Institutionalized Public Sector Corruption: A Legacy of the Suharto Franchise." In *The State and Illegality in Indonesia,* edited by E. Aspinall and G. van Klinken. Leiden, Netherlands: KITLV Press.

McVey, Ruth. 1990. "Teaching Modernity: The PKI as an Educational Institution." *Indonesia* 50(2):5–28.

Merry, Sally Engle. 2011. "Measuring the World: Indicators, Human Rights, and Global Governance." *Current Anthropology* 52(S3):S83–S95.

Metzl, Jonathan, and Anna Rutherford Kirkland, eds. 2010. *Against Health: How Health Became the New Morality*. New York: New York University Press.

Meyer, John W. 2010. "World Society, Institutional Theories, and the Actor." *Annual Review of Sociology* 36:1–20.

Meyer, John W., and Ronald L. Jepperson. 2000. "The 'Actors' of Modern Society: The Cultural Construction of Social Agency." *Sociological Theory* 18(1):100–120.

Meyerson, Debra. 2001. *Tempered Radicals: How People Use Difference to Inspire Change at Work*. Boston: Harvard Business School Press.

Migdal, Joel S. 2001. *State in Society: Studying How States and Societies Transform and Constitute One Another*. Cambridge: Cambridge University Press.

Miller, Daniel. 2003. "The Virtual Moment." *Journal of the Royal Anthropological Institute* 9(1):57–75.

Miller, Peter. 1992. "Accounting and Objectivity: The Invention of Calculating Selves and Calculable Spaces." *Annals of Scholarship* 9(1–2):61–86.

———. 1994. "Accounting as Social and Institutional Practice: An Introduction." In *Accounting as Social and Institutional Practice*, edited by A. G. Hopwood and P. Miller, 1–39. Cambridge: Cambridge Univeristy Press.

Miller, Peter, Trevor Hopper, and Richard Laughlin. 1991. "The New Accounting History: An Introduction." *Accounting, Organizations and Society* 16(5–6):395–403.

Miller, Peter, and Ted O'Leary. 1987. "Accounting and the Construction of the Governable Person." *Accounting, Organizations and Society* 12(3):235–65.

Millon, David. 1990. "Theories of the Corporation." *Duke Law Journal* 1990(2):201–62.

Mills, C. Wright. 1951. *White Collar: The American Middle Classes*. New York: Oxford University Press.

Milne, Markus J., Kate Kearins, and Sara Walton. 2006. "Creating Adventures in Wonderland: The Journey Metaphor and Environmental Sustainability." *Organization* 13(6):801–39.

MinergyNews. 2002a. "Aksi Penghadangan Murni Datang dari Warga." June 18.

———. 2002b. "ComRel PT NNT Hadang Peserta Studi Banding Korban Tambang." June 15.

———. 2002c. "FPPMM-NTB Siap Bertanggung Jawab Atas Aksi Penghadangan." June 18.

———. 2003. "Diduga, Kombat Dipecah Belah." February 14.

Mitchell, Timothy. 1999. "Society, Economy, and the State Effect." In *State/Culture: State-Formation after the Cultural Turn*, edited by G. Steinmetz, 76–97. Ithaca, NY: Cornell University Press.

———. 2002. *Rule of Experts: Egypt, Techno-politics, Modernity*. Berkeley: University of California Press.

Miyazaki, Hirokazu. 2013. *Arbitraging Japan: Dreams of Capitalism at the End of Finance*. Berkeley: University of California Press.

Mol, Annemarie. 2002. *The Body Multiple: Ontology in Medical Practice*. Durham, NC: Duke University Press.

Monk, Kathryn A., Yance De Fretes, and Gayatri Reksodiharjo-Lilley. 1997. *The Ecology of Nusa Tenggara and Maluku*. Hong Kong: Periplus Editions.

Moody, Roger. 2001. *Into the Unknown Regions: The Hazards of STD.* London: SSC and International Books.

Moore, Donald S. 1999. "The Crucible of Cultural Politics: Reworking 'Development' in Zimbabwe's Eastern Highlands." *American Ethnologist* 26(3):654–89.

Moreton, Bethany. 2009. *To Serve God and Wal-Mart: The Making of Christian Free Enterprise.* Cambridge, MA: Harvard University Press.

Morris, Jack H. 2010. *Going for Gold: The History of Newmont Mining Corporation.* Tuscaloosa: University of Alabama Press.

Morris, Rosalind. 2004. "Intimacy and Corruption in Thailand's Age of Transparency." In *Off Stage, On Display: Intimacy and Ethnography in the Age of Public Culture,* edited by A. Shryock, 225–43. Stanford, CA: Stanford University Press.

Mosse, David. 2001. "'People's Knowledge,' Participation and Patronage: Operations and Representations in Rural Development." In *Participation: The New Tyranny?* edited by B. Cooke and U. Kothari, 16–35. London: Zed Books.

———. 2005. *Cultivating Development: An Ethnography of Aid Policy and Practice.* London: Pluto Press.

Mozingo, Louise A. 2011. *Pastoral Capitalism: A History of Suburban Corporate Landscapes.* Cambridge, MA: MIT Press.

Muehlebach, Andrea. 2001. "'Making Place' at the United Nations: Indigenous Cultural Politics at the UN Working Group on Indigenous Populations." *Cultural Anthropology* 16(3):415–48.

Murdy, Wayne. N.d. "Social License to Operate." Internal memo, Newmont Mining Corporation. Denver.

Myers, Fred R. 1994. "Culture-Making: Performing Aboriginality at the Asia Society Gallery." *American Ethnologist* 21(4):679–99.

Nadasdy, Paul. 2005. "Transcending the Debate over the Ecologically Noble Indian: Indigenous Peoples and Environmentalism." *Ethnohistory* 52(2): 291–331.

Nash, June C. (1979) 1993. *We Eat the Mines and the Mines Eat Us: Dependency and Exploitation in Bolivian Tin Mines.* New York: Columbia University Press.

Newmont Mining Corporation. 1980. *Newmont Mining Corporation Annual Report 1979.*

———. 1986. *Newmont Mining Corporation Annual Report 1985.*

———. 1988. *Newmont Mining Corporation Annual Report 1987.*

———. 1989. *Newmont Mining Corporation Annual Report 1988.*

———. 2005a. *Now and Beyond 2004: Corporate Responsibility Report.* Denver: Newmont Mining Corporation.

———. 2005b. *Now and Beyond 2004: Batu Hijau, Indonesia.* Public report.

———. 2012. *Community Relationships Review Annual Report.* Denver: Newmont Mining Corporation.

Nichols, Nick. 2001. *Rules for Corporate Warriors: How to Fight and Survive Attack Group Shakedowns.* Bellevue, WA: Merril Press.

Nilhuhdian and Wawi. 2002. "Local People Swept Away by the Newmont Dam." *Indonesia People's Forum Bulletin*, no. 6:8.

NTB Post *(Nusa Tenggara Barat Post)*. 2002a. "Akan Lahir, Generasi Idiot di NTB." June 24.

———. 2002b. "Kita Perlu Penerapkan Sikap Kehati-hatian." May 28.

———. 2002c. "Pernyataan Sikap Badan Eksekutif Unsa dan Mapala Unsa." June 14.

Nusa. 2002. "Gubernur NTB Minta Newmont Bertanggungjawab." June 17.

Oakdale, Suzanne. 2004. "The Culture-Conscious Brazilian Indian: Representing and Reworking Brazilian Indianness in Kayabi Political Discourse." *American Ethnologist* 31(1):60–75.

Oinas, Päivi. 2006. "The Many Boundaries of the Firm." In *Understanding the Firm: Spatial and Organizational Dimensions,* edited by M. Taylor and P. Oinas, 35–60. Oxford: Oxford University Press.

O'Malley, Pat, Lorna Weir, and Clifford Shearing. 1997. "Governmentality, Criticism, Politics." *Economy and Society* 26(4):501–17.

O'Neill, Phillip, and J.K. Gibson-Graham. 1999. "Enterprise Discourse and Executive Talk: Stories That Destabilize the Company." *Transactions of the Institute of British Geographers* 24(1):11–22.

Ong, Aihwa. 1987. *Spirits of Resistance and Capitalist Discipline: Factory Women in Malaysia.* Albany: State University of New York Press.

Ong, Elisa K., and Stanton A. Glantz. 2001. "Constructing 'Sound Science' and 'Good Epidemiology': Tobacco, Lawyers, and Public Relations Firms." *American Journal of Public Health* 91(11):1749–57.

Oppenheimer, Clive. 2003. "Climatic, Environmental and Human Consequences of the Largest Known Historic Eruption: Tambora Volcano (Indonesia) 1815." *Progress in Physical Geography* 27(2):230–59.

Ortner, Sherry B. 1995. *Resistance and the Problem of Ethnographic Refusal.* Comparative Studies in Society and History 37(1):173–93.

Osborne, Thomas. 1994. "Bureaucracy as a Vocation: Governmentality and Administration in Nineteenth-Century Britain." *Journal of Historical Sociology* 7(3):289–313.

Ouchi, William G. 1981. *Theory Z: How American Business Can Meet the Japanese Challenge.* Reading, MA: Addison-Wesley.

Packard, Randall M. 1989. *White Plague, Black Labor: Tuberculosis and the Political Economy of Health and Disease in South Africa.* Berkeley: University of California Press.

Paine, Lynn Sharp. 2003. *Value Shift: Why Companies Must Merge Social and Financial Imperatives to Achieve Superior Performance.* New York: McGraw-Hill.

Paley, Julia. 2001. "The Paradox of Participation." *PoLAR* 24(1):1–12.

Pardo, Italo, ed. 2004. *Between Morality and the Law: Corruption, Anthropology and Comparative Society.* Burlington, VT: Ashgate.

Paxton, Robert O. 1997. *French Peasant Fascism: Henry Dorgère's Greenshirts and the Crises of French Agriculture, 1929–1939.* New York: Oxford University Press.

Peck, Jamie. 2010. *Constructions of Neoliberal Reason*. Oxford: Oxford University Press.

Peck, Jamie, and Adam Tickell. 1994. "Jungle Law Breaks Out: Neoliberalism and Global-Local Disorder." *Area* 26(4):317–26.

Peet, Richard, and Michael Watts. 1993. "Introduction: Development Theory and Environment in an Age of Market Triumphalism." *Economic Geography* 69(3):227–53.

Peluso, Nancy Lee. 1992. *Rich Forests, Poor People: Resource Control and Resistance in Java*. Berkeley: University of California Press.

Peluso, Nancy Lee, and Peter Vandergeest. 2001. "Genealogies of the Political Forest and Customary Rights in Indonesia, Malaysia, and Thailand." *Journal of Asian Studies* 60(3):761–812.

Perkins, John H. 1997. *Geopolitics and the Green Revolution: Wheat, Genes, and the Cold War*. New York: Oxford University Press.

Perlez, Jane. 2004. "Mining Giant Told It Put Toxic Vapors into Indonesia's Air." *New York Times*, December 22.

Polanyi, Karl. 2001. *The Great Transformation: The Political and Economic Origins of Our Time*. Boston: Beacon Press.

Popkin, Samuel L. 1979. *The Rational Peasant: The Political Economy of Rural Society in Vietnam*. Berkeley: University of California Press.

Porter, Michael E., and Mark R. Kramer. 2002. "The Competitive Advantage of Corporate Philanthropy." *Harvard Business Review* 80(12):57–68.

Porter, Theodore M. 1995. *Trust in Numbers: The Pursuit of Objectivity in Science and Public Life*. Princeton, NJ: Princeton University Press.

Powdermaker, Hortense. 1962. *Copper Town: Changing Africa—the Human Situation on the Rhodesian Copperbelt*. New York: Harper and Row.

Powell, Walter W., and Paul DiMaggio, eds. 1991. *The New Institutionalism in Organizational Analysis*. Chicago: University of Chicago Press.

Power, Michael. 1997. *The Audit Society: Rituals of Verification*. Oxford: Oxford University Press.

———. 2003a. "Auditing and the Production of Legitimacy." *Accounting, Organizations and Society* 28(4):379–94.

———. 2003b. "Corporate Responsibility and Risk Management." In *Risk and Morality*, edited by R. V. Ericson and A. Doyle, 145–64. Toronto: University of Toronto Press.

———. 2007. *Organized Uncertainty: Designing a World of Risk Management*. Oxford: Oxford University Press.

PPLH (Pusat Penelitian Lingkungan Hidup Universitas Mataram). 2001. *Studi Dampak Sosial Ekonomi dan Sosial Budaya Kegiatan Penambangan PT. Newmont Nusa Tenggara. Laporan Akhir*. Report prepared by PPLH for PT NNT. Mataram: PPLH.

Prebisch, Raúl. 1950. *The Economic Development of Latin America and Its Principal Problems*. New York: United Nations.

Prentice, Rachel. N.d. "Control and Ethics among Operating Teams" (working title). Manuscript in progress.

Pressman, Edward. 2001. "Newmont and Pollution." Letter to the editor. *Jakarta Post*, May 4.

Proctor, Robert, and Londa L. Schiebinger, eds. 2008. *Agnotology: The Making and Unmaking of Ignorance*. Stanford, CA: Stanford University Press.

PT NNT (PT Newmont Nusa Tenggara). 1996. *Multisector/Integrated Environmental Impact Assessment*. Main Report, Batu Hijau Copper-Gold Project, Jereweh District, Sumbawa Regency, Nusa Tenggara Province, Indonesia. PT Newmont Nusa Tenggara.

———. 2000. *External and Internal Demonstrations against PT. NNT or Sub-Contractors*. Benete, Sumbawa: Community Relations, PT NNT.

———. 2001. *External and Internal Demonstrations against PT. NNT or Sub-Contractors*. Benete, Sumbawa: Community Relations, PT NNT.

———. 2002. *Community Development Strategy and Project Clarification*. Benete: PT Newmont Nusa Tenggara.

———. 2003. *Andal Annual Reporting 2002, Com Dev Input*. Report prepared by Community Development, PT Newmont Nusa Tenggara, in fulfillment of the Government of Indonesia's Environmental Impact Assessment requirements. Benete: PT Newmont Nusa Tenggara.

PU (Project Underground). N.d. *Newmonster: The Story of One Gold Mining Company and the Struggle to Stop It*. Berkeley, CA: Project Underground.

Puig de la Bellacasa, Maria. 2011. "Matters of Care in Technoscience: Assembling Neglected Things." *Social Studies of Science* 41(1):85–106.

Rajak, Dinah. 2010. "'HIV Is Our Business': The Moral Economy of Treatment in a Multinational Mining Company." *Journal of the Royal Anthropological Institute* 16(3):551–71.

———. 2011a. *In Good Company: An Anatomy of Corporate Social Responsibility*. Stanford, CA: Stanford University Press.

———. 2011b. "Theatres of Virtue: Collaboration, Consensus, and the Social Life of Corporate Social Responsibility." *Focaal* 60(Summer):9–20.

Ramage, Douglas E. 1995. *Politics in Indonesia: Democracy, Islam, and the Ideology of Tolerance*. New York: Routledge.

Ramos, Alcida Rita. 1998. *Indigenism: Ethnic Politics in Brazil*. Madison: University of Wisconsin Press.

Ramsey, Robert Henderson. 1973. *Men and Mines of Newmont: A Fifty-Year History*. New York: Octagon Books.

Rankin, Katharine. 2001. "Governing Development: Neoliberalism, Microcredit and Rational Economic Woman." *Economy and Society* 30(1):18–37.

Razsa, Maple, and Andrej Kurnik. 2012. "The Occupy Movement in Žižek's Hometown: Direct Democracy and a Politics of Becoming." *American Ethnologist* 39(2):238–58.

Redfield, Peter. 2012. "The Unbearable Lightness of Ex-Pats." *Cultural Anthropology* 27(2):358–82.

Reich, Robert. 2010. "BP Strawmen Won't Fix the Gulf." *Huffington Post*, June 14, www.huffingtonpost.com/robert-reich/bp-strawmen-wont-fix-the_b_612001.html.

Reichman, Daniel R. 2011. *The Broken Village: Coffee, Migration, and Globalization in Honduras*. Ithaca, NY: Cornell University Press.

Reitman, Jason. 2006. *Thank You for Smoking*. United States: Fox Searchlight Pictures. DVD.

Resnick, Stephen A., and Richard D. Wolff. 1987. *Knowledge and Class: A Marxian Critique of Political Economy.* Chicago: University of Chicago Press.

Ribeiro, Gustavo Lins. 1995. "Ethnic Segmentation of the Labor Market and the 'Work Site Animal': Fragmentation and the Reconstruction of Identities within the World System." In *Articulating Hidden Histories: Exploring the Influence of Eric R. Wolf,* edited by J. Schneider and R. Rapp, 336–50. Berkeley: University of California Press.

Rieffel, Alexis. 1969. "The BIMAS Program for Self-Sufficiency in Rice Production." *Indonesia* 8:103–33.

Riles, Annelise. 2000. *The Network Inside Out.* Ann Arbor: University of Michigan Press.

———. 2006. "Introduction: In Response." In *Documents: Artifacts of Modern Knowledge,* edited by A. Riles, 1–38. Ann Arbor: University of Michigan Press.

Rio Tinto. 2001. *Global Business, Local Neighbour: Community Relations.* London: Rio Tinto.

———. 2002. *Sustainable Development: Rio Tinto's Contribution in the Rio Decade.* Corporate brochure. London: Rio Tinto.

Ripken, Susanna K. 2009. "Corporations Are People Too: A Multi-Dimensional Approach to the Corporate Personhood Puzzle." *Fordham Journal of Corporate and Financial Law* 15:97–177.

Robbins, Joel. 2004. *Becoming Sinners: Christianity and Moral Torment in a Papua New Guinea Society.* Berkeley: University of California Press.

———. 2006. "On Giving Ground: Globalization, Religion, and Territorial Detachment in a Papua New Guinea Society." In *Territoriality and Conflict in an Era of Globalization,* edited by M. Kahler and B.F. Walter. Cambridge: Cambridge University Press.

Robinson, Kathryn May. 1986. *Stepchildren of Progress: The Political Economy of Development in an Indonesian Mining Town.* Albany: State University of New York Press.

Robison, Richard. 1986. *Indonesia: The Rise of Capital.* Sydney: Allen and Unwin.

Rogers, Douglas. 2012. "The Materiality of the Corporation: Oil, Gas, and Corporate Social Techologies in the Remaking of a Russian Region." *American Ethnologist* 39(2):284–96.

Rohde, David. 2007. "Army Enlists Anthropology in War Zones." *New York Times,* October 5.

Rohlen, Thomas P. 1974. *For Harmony and Strength: Japanese White-Collar Organization in Anthropological Perspective.* Berkeley: University of California Press.

Rolston, Jessica Smith. 2010. "Risky Business: Neoliberalism and Workplace Safety in Wyoming Coal Mines." *Human Organization* 69(4):331–42.

Roper, Michael. 1994. *Masculinity and the British Organization Man since 1945.* Oxford: Oxford University Press.

Rose, Nikolas S. 1999. *Powers of Freedom: Reframing Political Thought.* Cambridge: Cambridge University Press.

Ross, Michael L. 1999. "The Political Economy of the Resource Curse." *World Politics* 51:297–322.

Rosser, Andrew. 2006. *The Political Economy of the Resource Curse: A Literature Survey*. Sussex: Institute of Development Studies.

Røyrvik, Emil A. 2011. *The Allure of Capitalism: An Ethnography of Management and the Global Economy in Crisis*. New York: Berghahn Books.

Rudnyckyj, Daromir. 2009a. "Market Islam in Indonesia." *Journal of the Royal Anthropological Institute* 15:S183–S201.

———. 2009b. "Spiritual Economies: Islam and Neoliberalism in Contemporary Indonesia." *Cultural Anthropology* 24(1):104–41.

———. 2010. *Spiritual Economies: Islam, Globalization, and the Afterlife of Development*. Ithaca, NY: Cornell University Press.

Ryter, Loren. 2001. "Pemuda Pancasila: The Last Loyalist Free Men of Suharto's Order?" In *Violence and the State in Suharto's Indonesia*, edited by B.R. O'G. Anderson, 124–55. Ithaca, NY: Southeast Asia Program Publications, Cornell University.

Sahlins, Marshall David. 1972. *Stone Age Economics*. Chicago: Aldine-Atherton.

Sai, Siew Min. 2006. "'Eventing' the May 1998 Affair: Problematic Representations of Violence in Contemporary Indonesia." In *Violent Conflicts in Indonesia: Analysis, Representation, Resolution*, edited by C.A. Coppel, 39–57. London: Routledge.

———. 2010. "Pugilists from the Mountains: History, Memory, and the Making of the Chinese-Educated Generation in Post-1998 Indonesia." *Indonesia* 89:149–78.

Sandman, Peter M. 1993. *Responding to Community Outrage: Strategies for Effective Risk Communication*. Fairfax, VA: American Industrial Hygiene Association.

Saraswati, Muninggar Sri, and Musthofid. 2002. "Indonesia's Concession Areas Exceed the Country's Total Area." *Jakarta Post*, September 28.

Sawyer, Suzana. 2003. "Subterranean Techniques: Corporate Environmentalism, Oil Operations, and Social Injustice in the Ecuadorian Rain Forest." In *In Search of the Rain Forest*, edited by C. Slater, 69–100. Durham, NC: Duke University Press.

———. 2006. "Disabling Corporate Sovereignty in a Transnational Lawsuit." *PoLAR* 29(1):23–43.

Scheper-Hughes, Nancy. 1995. "The Primacy of the Ethical: Propositions for a Militant Anthropology." *Current Anthropology* 36(3):409–20.

Schneider, Jane, and Peter T. Schneider. 2003. *Reversible Destiny: Mafia, Antimafia, and the Struggle for Palermo*. Berkeley: University of California Press.

Schoenberger, Erica. 2001. "Corporate Autobiographies: The Narrative Strategies of Corporate Strategists." *Journal of Economic Geography* 1:277–98.

Schrauwers, Albert. 1999. "'It's Not Economical': The Market Roots of a Moral Economy in Highland Sulawesi." In *Transforming the Indonesian Uplands: Marginality, Power, and Production*, edited by T. Li, 105–29. Amsterdam: Harwood Academic Publishers.

Schüll, Natasha Dow. 2012. *Addiction by Design: Machine Gambling in Las Vegas*. Princeton, NJ: Princeton University Press.

Schuman, Michael. 2001. "Stolen Treasure: How Big Mining Lost a Fortune in Indonesia." *Wall Street Journal*, May 16.

Schwittay, Anke. 2011. "The Marketization of Poverty." *Current Anthropology* 52(S3):S71–S82.

Scott, James C. 1976. *The Moral Economy of the Peasant: Rebellion and Subsistence in Southeast Asia*. New Haven, CT: Yale University Press.

———. 1985. *Weapons of the Weak: Everyday Forms of Peasant Resistance*. New Haven, CT: Yale University Press.

Seidman, Gay W. 2003. "Monitoring Multinationals: Lessons from the Anti-Apartheid Era." *Politics and Society* 31(3):381–406.

Shamir, Ronen. 2008. "The Age of Responsibilization: On Market-Embedded Morality." *Economy and Society* 37(1):1–19.

———. 2010. "Capitalism, Governance, and Authority: The Case of Corporate Social Responsibility." *Annual Review of Law and Social Science* 6:531–53.

Sharma, Aradhana. 2008. *Logics of Empowerment: Development, Gender, and Governance in Neoliberal India*. Minneapolis: University of Minnesota Press.

Sharma, Aradhana, and Akhil Gupta. 2006. "Introduction: Rethinking Theories of the State in an Age of Globalization." In *The Anthropology of the State: A Reader*, edited by A. Sharma and A. Gupta. Malden, MA: Blackwell.

Shearman, Phil. 2002. "A Look at the Industry." In *STD Toolkit*, 13. Berkeley: Project Underground and MiningWatch Canada.

Shever, Elana. 2008. "Neoliberal Associations: Property, Company, and Family in the Argentine Oil Fields." *American Ethnologist* 35(4):701–16.

———. 2010. "Engendering the Company: Corporate Personhood and the 'Face' of an Oil Company in Metropolitan Buenos Aires." *PoLAR* 33(1):26–46.

———. 2012. *Resources for Reform: Oil and Neoliberalism in Argentina*. Stanford, CA: Stanford University Press.

Shiraishi, Saya S. 1997. *Young Heroes: The Indonesian Family in Politics*. Ithaca, NY: Southeast Asia Program Publications, Cornell University.

Shore, Cris, and Susan Wright. 2000. "Coercive Accountability: The Rise of Audit Culture in Higher Education." In *Audit Cultures: Anthropological Studies in Accountability, Ethics, and the Academy*, edited by M. Strathern, 57–89. London: Routledge.

Shubert, Atika. 2001. "McDonald's Adapts to Anti-U.S. Protests in Indonesia." *CNN*, October 23, http://edition.cnn.com/2001/WORLD/asiapcf/southeast/10/23/ret.indonesia.mcdonalds/index.html.

Shultz, Jim. 2005. *Follow the Money: A Guide to Monitoring Budgets and Oil and Gas Revenues*. New York: Open Society Institute.

Sidel, John Thayer. 2004. "Bossism and Democracy in the Philippines, Thailand, and Indonesia: Towards an Alternative Framework for the Study of 'Local Strongmen.'" In *Politicising Democracy: The New Local Politics and Democratisation*, edited by J. Harriss, K. Stokke, and O. Törnquist. Houdmills, UK: Palgrave Macmillan.

Skillen, Tony. 1992. "Enterprise: Towards the Emancipation of a Concept." In *The Values of the Enterprise Culture: The Moral Debate,* edited by P. Heelas and P. Morris, 73–82. London: Routledge.

Smith, Adam. (1776) 1937. *The Wealth of Nations.* New York: Modern Library.

Smith, Benjamin. 2003. "'If I Do These Things, They Will Throw Me Out': Economic Reform and the Collapse of Indonesia's Political Order." *Journal of International Affairs* 57(1):113–28.

Smith, Jessica M. 2008. "Crafting Kinship at Home and Work: Women Miners in Wyoming." *WorkingUSA* 11:439–58.

Smith, Jessica M., and Frederico Helfgott. 2010. "Flexibility or Exploitation? Corporate Social Responsibility and the Perils of Universalization." *Anthropology Today* 26(3):20–23.

Sontag, Susan. 2003. *Regarding the Pain of Others.* New York: Farrar, Straus and Giroux.

Soule, Sarah Anne. 2009. *Contention and Corporate Social Responsibility.* New York: Cambridge University Press.

Spence, Crawford. 2009. "Social Accounting's Emancipatory Potential: A Gramscian Critique." *Critical Perspectives on Accounting* 20(2):205–27.

STC (Save the Children). 2003. *Lifting the Resource Curse: Extractive Industry, Children and Governance.* London: Save the Children.

———. 2005. *Beyond the Rhetoric: Measuring Revenue Transparency in the Oil and Gas Industries.* London: Save the Children.

Stearns, Linda Brewster, and Kenneth D. Allan. 1996. "Economic Behavior in Institutional Environments: The Corporate Merger Wave of the 1980s." *American Sociological Review* 61(4):699–718.

Stecklow, Steve. 2006. "Did a Group Financed by Exxon Prompt IRS to Audit Greenpeace?" *Wall Street Journal,* March 22.

Steedly, Mary Margaret. 1999. "The State of Culture Theory in the Anthropology of Southeast Asia." *Annual Review of Anthropology* 28:431–54.

Steinberger, Michael. 2004. "Psychopathic C.E.O.'s." *New York Times Magazine,* December 12.

Stern, Philip J. 2011. *The Company-State: Corporate Sovereignty and the Early Modern Foundation of the British Empire in India.* New York: Oxford University Press.

Stevenson, Lisa. 2012. "The Psychic Life of Biopolitics: Survival, Cooperation, and Inuit Community." *American Ethnologist* 39(3):592–613.

Stoler, Ann Laura. 1977. "Rice Harvesting in Kali Loro: A Study of Class and Labor Relations in Rural Java." *American Ethnologist* 4(4):678–98.

Stout, Lynn A. 2008. "Why We Should Stop Teaching *Dodge v. Ford.*" *Virginia Law and Business Review* 3(1):163–76.

———. 2012. *The Shareholder Value Myth: How Putting Shareholders First Harms Investors, Corporations, and the Public.* San Francisco: Berrett-Koehler.

Strassler, Karen. 2010. *Refracted Visions: Popular Photography and National Modernity in Java.* Durham, NC: Duke University Press.

Strathern, Marilyn. 1988. *The Gender of the Gift: Problems with Women and Problems with Society in Melanesia.* Berkeley: University of California Press.

————, ed. 2000. *Audit Cultures: Anthropological Studies in Accountability, Ethics, and the Academy.* London: Routledge.

————. 2006. "Bullet-Proofing: A Tale from the United Kingdom." In *Documents: Artifacts of Modern Knowledge,* edited by A. Riles. Ann Arbor: University of Michigan.

Striffler, Steve. 2002. *In the Shadows of State and Capital: The United Fruit Company, Popular Struggle, and Agrarian Restructuring in Ecuador, 1900–1995.* Durham, NC: Duke University Press.

Subramanian, Ajantha. 2010. "Comment on 'Capitalism and the Politics of Resignation.'" *Current Anthropology* 51(4):479–80.

Suchman, Lucy. 2007. *Human-Machine Reconfigurations: Plans and Situated Actions.* Cambridge: Cambridge University Press.

Sumbawa Ekspres. 2000. "PT. NNT Setor Royalti US$2,5 Juta Lebih." May 1.

————. 2002. "Tokoh Masyarakat Sekongkang Bantah Adanya Tindakan Kekerasan." June 14.

Sunindyo, Saraswati. 1996. "Murder, Gender, and the Media: Sexualizing Politics and Violence." In *Fantasizing the Feminine in Indonesia,* edited by L.J. Sears, 120–39. Durham, NC: Duke University Press.

Suryakusuma, Julia I. 1996. "The State and Sexuality in New Order Indonesia." In *Fantasizing the Feminine in Indonesia,* edited by L.J. Sears, 92–119. Durham, NC: Duke University Press.

SustainAbility. 2003. *The 21st Century NGO: In the Market for Change.* London: SustainAbility.

Tan, Andrea. 2011. "Newmont Sues Indonesia's Merukh over $300 Million Loan." Bloomberg.com, January 26, www.bloomberg.com/news/2011-01-26/newmont-sues-indonesia-s-merukh-for-breaching-terms-of-300-million-loan.html.

Tapscott, Don, and David Ticoll. 2003. *The Naked Corporation: How the Age of Transparency Will Revolutionize Business.* New York: Free Press.

Taussig, Michael T. 1980. *The Devil and Commodity Fetishism in South America.* Chapel Hill: University of North Carolina Press.

Thedvall, Renita. 2012. "Negotiating Impartial Indicators: Putting Transparency into Practice in the EU." *Journal of the Royal Anthropological Institute* 18:311–29.

Thrift, Nigel, and Kris Olds. 1996. "Refiguring the Economic in Economic Geography." *Progress in Human Geography* 20(3):311–37.

Tidey, Sylvia. 2013. "Corruption and Adherence to Rules in the Construction Sector: Reading the 'Bidding Books.'" *American Anthropologist* 115(2):188–202.

Tsing, Anna Lowenhaupt. 1993. *In the Realm of the Diamond Queen: Marginality in an Out-of-the-Way Place.* Princeton, NJ: Princeton University Press.

————. 2003. "The News in the Provinces." In *Cultural Citizenship in Island Southeast Asia: Nation and Belonging in the Hinterlands,* edited by R. Rosaldo, 192–222. Berkeley: University of California Press.

————. 2005. *Friction: An Ethnography of Global Connection.* Princeton, NJ: Princeton University Press.

Tuchman, Gaye. 2009. *Wannabe U: Inside the Corporate University*. Chicago: University of Chicago Press.

Turner, Terence. 1991. "Representing, Resisting, Rethinking: Historical Transformations of Kayapo Culture and Anthropological Consciousness." In *Colonial Situations*, edited by G. W. Stocking, 285–313. Madison: University of Wisconsin Press.

———. 1995. "An Indigenous People's Struggle for Socially Equitable and Ecologically Sustainable Production: The Kayapo Revolt against Extractivism." *Journal of Latin American Anthropology* 1(1):98–121.

Tyson, Adam. 2013. "Vigilantism and Violence in Decentralized Indonesia: The Case of Lombok." *Critical Asian Studies* 45(2):201–30.

Urban, Greg, and Kyung-Nan Koh. 2013. "Ethnographic Research on Modern Business Corporations." *Annual Review of Anthropology* 42: 139–58.

van Klinken, Gerry, and Edward Aspinall. 2011. "Building Relations: Corruption, Competition and Cooperation in the Construction Industry." In *The State and Illegality in Indonesia*, edited by E. Aspinall and G. van Klinken, 139–63. Leiden, Netherlands: KITLV Press.

van Klinken, Gerry, and Joshua Barker. 2009. *State of Authority: The State in Society in Indonesia*. Ithaca, NY: Southeast Asia Program Publications, Cornell University.

Visser, Kees. 2012. *Lessons of Transparency from EITI*. Bangkok: Focus on the Global South.

Wade, Terry, and Marco Aquino. 2012. "Left, Right Criticize Humala over Deadly Peru Clashes." Reuters, July 5, www.reuters.com/article/2012/07/05 /us-peru-newmont-idUSBRE86416X20120705.

Walley, Christine J. 2004. *Rough Waters: Nature and Development in an East African Marine Park*. Princeton, NJ: Princeton University Press.

Ward, Kerry. 2009. *Networks of Empire: Forced Migration in the Dutch East India Company*. Cambridge: Cambridge University Press.

Warren, Kay B. 1998. *Indigenous Movements and Their Critics: Pan-Maya Activism in Guatemala*. Princeton, NJ: Princeton University Press.

Watson, James L. 2006. "Introduction: Transnationalism, Localization, and Fast Foods in East Asia." In *Golden Arches East: McDonald's in East Asia*, edited by J. L. Watson, 1–38. Stanford, CA: Stanford University Press.

Watts, Michael. 2004. "Resource Curse? Governmentality, Oil and Power in the Niger Delta, Nigeria." *Geopolitics* 9(1):50–80.

Weber, Max. 1946a. "Bureaucracy." In *From Max Weber: Essays in Sociology*, edited by H. H. Gerth and C. W. Mills, 196–244. New York: Oxford University Press.

———. 1946b. "The Sociology of Charismatic Authority." In *From Max Weber: Essays in Sociology*, edited by H. H. Gerth and C. W. Mills, 245–52. New York: Oxford University Press.

———. 1947. *The Theory of Social and Economic Organization*. Translated by A. M. Henderson and T. Parsons. New York: Free Press.

———. 1978. *Economy and Society: An Outline of Interpretive Sociology*. Berkeley: University of California Press.

————. 1992. *The Protestant Ethic and the Spirit of Capitalism*. London: Routledge.

Welker, Marina. 2006. "Global Capitalism and the 'Caring Corporation': Mining and the Corporate Social Responsibility Movement in Indonesia and Denver." PhD diss., University of Michigan.

————. 2009. "'Corporate Security Begins in the Community': Mining, the Corporate Social Responsibility Industry, and Environmental Advocacy in Indonesia." *Cultural Anthropology* 24(1):142–79.

————. 2012. "The Green Revolution's Ghost: Unruly Subjects of Participatory Development in Rural Indonesia." *American Ethnologist* 39(2):389–406.

Welker, Marina, and David Wood. 2011. "Shareholder Activism and Alienation." *Current Anthropology* 52(S3):S57–S69.

West, Harry G., and Todd Sanders, eds. 2003. *Transparency and Conspiracy: Ethnographies of Suspicion in the New World Order*. Durham, NC: Duke University Press.

Weszkalnys, Gisa. 2011. "Cursed Resources, or Articulations of Economic Theory in the Gulf of Guinea." *Economy and Society* 40(3):345–72.

White, Richard. 1991. *The Middle Ground: Indians, Empires, and Republics in the Great Lakes Region, 1650–1815*. Cambridge: Cambridge University Press.

Whyte, William Hollingsworth. 1956. *The Organization Man*. New York: Simon and Schuster.

Williams, Raymond. 1973. *The Country and the City*. New York: Oxford University Press.

Willis, Paul E. 1977. *Learning to Labour: How Working Class Kids Get Working Class Jobs*. Farnborough, U.K.: Saxon House.

Wilson, Godfrey. 1941. *An Essay on the Economics of Detribalization in Northern Rhodesia*. Livingstone, Northern Rhodesia: Rhodes-Livingstone Institute.

Winarto, Yunita T. 2004. *Seeds of Knowledge: The Beginning of Integrated Pest Management in Java*. New Haven, CT: Yale University Southeast Asia Studies.

Wright, Robin M. 1988. "Anthropological Presuppositions of Indigenous Advocacy." *Annual Review of Anthropology* 17:365–90.

Yanagisako, Sylvia Junko. 2002. *Producing Culture and Capital: Family Firms in Italy*. Princeton, NJ: Princeton University Press.

Yano, Christine R. 2011. *Airborne Dreams: "Nisei" Stewardesses and Pan American World Airways*. Durham, NC: Duke University Press.

Young, Iris Marion. 2006. "Katrina: Too Much Blame, Not Enough Responsibility." *Dissent* 53(1):41–46.

Žižek, Slavoj. 2006. "Nobody Has to Be Vile." *London Review of Books* 28(7):10.

Index

Abrams, Philip, 4

AccountAbility, 188

agriculture, 129–56; integrated pest management, 134–35, 137, 145, 154, 239nn6,7; and Islam, 21; and land disposession, 131; and local hiring, 132; and transmigration program, 131–32, 238–39nn1,2. *See also* farmer trainings; Green Revolution

Ahmed, Sara, 43, 57, 203, 222n20, 246n13

Aidarus, 178

Allen, Kenneth D., 224n36

Alliance of Near-Mine Communities for Justice, 179, 244n26

ameliorative discipines, 41–42. *See also* Corporate Social Responsibility

Amphibi, 20

Anderson, Chris: background of, 33–34; and charismatic vs. rationalizing tactics, 44–46, 47; and Choropampa mercury spill, 51–52, 54, 228n26; and Colorado mining culture, 37; and contested nature of Corporate Social Responsibility, 42, 44; and disciplinary identification, 39; and geologist roles, 48–49; and Newmont corporate transformation, 55, 58, 60–61; on noble savage myth, 243n15; transfer of, 64–65

Annan, Kofi, 15

Antlöv, Hans, 236–37n3

APCO, 50, 227n24

Appel, Hannah, 79–80

Aragon, Lorraine V., 223n24

Aspirasi, 163

auditing practices, 185, 187–89, 245nn6,7. *See also* Five Star Integrated Assessment

bad apples approach, 52–53, 159–60

Bakan, Joel, 160

Bakrie, Aburizal, 92

Bali bombing (2002), 25–26, 207, 224nn31,32, 246n19

Ballard, Chris, 71

Banks, Glenn, 71

Basic Agrarian Law, 239n3

Batu Hijau mine: expatriate employees, 24–25, 245n4; exploration phase, 73–74, 120, 232nn10–12; preconstruction/construction phases, 74–79, 232nn13,14. *See also* local hiring; Newmont relations with local community

Benson, Peter, 15, 221n14

Bergman, Lowell, 53

Berle, Adolf A., 28

Bimas program, 133, 239n8

Blair, Tony, 89

bluewashing, 14, 222n19

Boele, Richard, 61, 191–93, 192, 194, 245n11

bottom line. *See* corporate-interests perspective

Macdonald, Helen *(continued)*
44–45, 46–47; and Choropampa
mercury spill, 54; and disciplinary
identification, 39, 40, 41; and geologist
roles, 48; on Newmont as patron, 59,
69; and Newmont corporate transformation, 57, 58, 60, 61–62, 63–64,
229n38, 230n43; on soft vs. hard issues,
216; transfer of, 64–65
Malozemoff Technical Facility, 225n4
Mamdani, Mahmood, 22
managerial roles. *See* executive/managerial
roles
maps: Indonesia, 8; Southwest Sumbawa, 9;
West Sumbawa regency, 90
Marx, Karl, 238n14
Mauss, Marcel, 4
Mayo, Elton, 229n34
McDonald's, 223–24n27
Means, Gardiner C., 28
Médecins Sans Frontières (Doctors Without
Borders), 63
mercury contamination, 50–55, 186,
227–28nn25–29, 243n18
Merukh, Jusuf, 72–73, 92, 231n6
Meyerson, Debra, 93
Millon, David, 221n13
Mineral Information Institute, 37–39
mining industry, anthropology of,
222n16
Mitchell, Timothy, 3–4, 223n22
Miyazaki, Hirokazu, 225n3
Mol, Annemarie, 5, 16, 218, 220n5
Monks, Robert, 222n18
Montesinos, Vladimiro, 53
moral corporation: bad apples approach,
159–60; and Choropampa mercury spill,
52–53, 54; and Corporate Social
Responsibility, 17, 34–35; and
Newmont as patron, 12, 86–87; and
Newmont corporate transformation,
58–59; and Newmont relations with
Indonesian state, 73, 231n7; and profit
maximization imperative, 160; and risk
management, 58–59; and Western
virtue/Indonesian corruption narrative,
73, 86–87. *See also* Newmont as
environmentally responsible
Morris, Jack, 42
Mosse, David, 240n20
Muhammadiyah, 21
Multi Daerah Bersaing, 92
Multicapital, 92–93
multiplier effect, 121, 237n11

Murdy, Wayne, 39, 51, 55, 56, 59–60,
226n10, 228n30
Myers, Fred, 34

Nadasdy, Paul, 243n15
neoliberalism: and auditing practices, 188;
and Corporate Social Responsibility,
14–15, 16–17; farmer trainings on,
140–41, 240n15; Foucault on, 130; vs.
globalization, 17, 222–23n21; and local
enterprise, 118; and Pancasila, 237n5;
and participatory development, 239n10;
questioning stance on, 17, 18, 223n22;
and revenue transparency, 234–35n25;
and sustainable development model, 17,
71, 102, 105, 154–55
Net Impact, 246n22
New Deal, 29, 224n35
New Order regime. *See* Soeharto regime
Newmonster narrative, 160–61, 242n7
Newmont: Ghana mine operation, 30, 35,
39, 49, 65; history of, 28–30, 224–
25nn1,3,5,37,38; legal team, 46,
227n20; public relations firms, 50,
170–74, 227n24; Uzbekistan venture,
27–28, 50; visibility of, 33, 187
Newmont as environmentally responsible,
161–74; and attacks on NGOs, 169–74,
243n20; and Corporate Social
Responsibility, 161; and illegal mining,
169, 243n17; internal vs. external
motivation, 242n8; Project Green
Shield, 172–74, 243n19; and tailings
disposal, 10, 162–64, 242nn9,10; and
Western virtue/Indonesian corruption
narrative, 164–68, 242nn11,13,14; and
Women's Empowerment Workshop
incident, 179
Newmont as patron, 30–31, 127–28; and
agriculture, 134; community coproduc-
tion of, 69; community criticisms, 74,
76, 224n28, 230n1, 233–34n21;
community demands, 32, 82, 83, 84–86,
103–4, 180; and cooperatives, 115; and
corporate-interests perspective, 106; and
corporate security, 159; and embedded
research, 11, 12; and entrepreneurial
values training, 110–12; and exploration
phase, 74, 232nn10–12; and farmer
trainings, 131; financial implications of,
69, 70, 231n2; and Islamization policy,
21, 22–23, 224n28; and local elites, 78,
87–88; and local enterprise, 82, 102,
110–12; and moral corporation, 12,

subject-formation, 129–31, 148, 240–41n20
Sukarno, 19, 124, 133, 140
Sumbawa: Islam in, 20–21, 223n24; maps, 9, 90; marine foraging, 10, 165–67, 242n11; natural resources, 73, 104, 108, 232n9; and Pancasila, 237n3; poverty, 73–74; village settlement patterns, 231n8. *See also* Batu Hijau mine; local elites; local enterprise; local hiring; Newmont relations with local community
Sumitomo Corporation, 72, 92
sustainable development model, 30, 69, 127–28; and civil servant opportunities, 95, 236n29; and Corporate Social Responsibility, 16–17, 102; definitions of, 70, 231n3; and entrepreneurial values training, 108–14, 237n8; and farmer trainings, 154–55; and gender, 104, 105; and modesty, 93, 235–36n28; moral limitations of, 125–26; and neoliberalism, 17, 71, 102, 105, 154–55; Newmont adoption of, 93–94, 103–4; and Newmont corporate transformation, 64; as oxymoron, 70–71; reform agenda, 114–20; rivalry with patronage model, 106–7; and state responsibilities, 93–98, 236nn30,31. *See also* farmer trainings

tailings disposal: and environmental impacts of mining, 7, 32, 183, 233n21, 244n23; and Newmont as environmentally responsible, 10, 162–64, 242nn9,10
Tapscott, Don, 210
"Taste of Colorado" festival (Denver), 37–39
terrorism fears: and Bali bombing (2002), 25–26, 207, 224nn31,32, 246n19; and Five Star Integrated Assessment, 207, 209; and Islamization policy, 25–26, 224nn31,32; and Jemaah Islamiyah rumor, 184, 213
Thompson, William Boyce, 28
Thrift, Nigel, 26
Ticoll, David, 210
Tidey, Sylvia, 118
Tongo, 176, 243–44nn22–24. *See also* local elites; local enterprise; local hiring;

Newmont relations with local community
transmigration program, 19, 20, 131–32, 231n8, 238–39nn1,2
Tutut (Siti Hardiyanti Rukmana), 75

UN Conference on Environment and Development (1992), 70
UN Global Compact, 15, 222n19
Urban, Greg, 221n11
U.S. foreign policy, 21–22, 24, 223–24n27

van de Graaf, Shashi, 205
Visser, Kees, 235n25
voluntary corporate responsibility codes, 13, 14–15, 47, 56, 158–59, 188, 242n5, 245n9
Voluntary Principles on Security and Human Rights, 158–59, 242n5

Watson, James, 223n27
Weber, Max, 44, 198–99, 219n1, 230n41
Western virtue/Indonesian corruption narrative: and expatriate employees, 245n4; and Islamization policy, 24; and lightness vs. heaviness, 230n42; and local enterprise, 101, 108, 110, 126; and moral corporation, 73, 86–87; and Newmont as environmentally responsible, 164–68, 242nn11,13,14
Willis, Paul, 131, 155
Winarto, Yunita T., 150
Women's Empowerment Workshop incident (2002), 157, 177–82
World Bank, 235n25
Wright, Susan, 192

Yakovleva, Natalia, 246n21
Yanagisako, Sylvia Junko, 108, 223n22
Yayasan Olat Parigi, 103, 121, 134, 139, 154, 176
Young, Iris Marion, 2
Yurchak, Alexei, 211

Žižek, Slavoj, 66
Zulkifli, KH. Muhadli, 90, 91, 106